Socialization and Communication in Primary Groups

World Anthropology

General Editor

SOL TAX

Patrons

CLAUDE LÉVI-STRAUSS
MARGARET MEAD
LAILA SHUKRY EL HAMAMSY
M. N. SRINIVAS

MOUTON PUBLISHERS · THE HAGUE · PARIS
DISTRIBUTED IN THE USA AND CANADA BY ALDINE, CHICAGO

Socialization and Communication in Primary Groups

Editor

THOMAS R. WILLIAMS

MOUTON PUBLISHERS · THE HAGUE · PARIS
DISTRIBUTED IN THE USA AND CANADA BY ALDINE, CHICAGO

ISBN 90-279-7730-5 (Mouton)
0-202-01156-9 (Aldine)
Jacket photo by Thomas R. Williams
Cover and jacket design by Jurriaan Schrofer
Indexes by John Jennings
Printed in the Netherlands

General Editor's Preface

In every human society, relating to people must always have been a subject of thought. Relations in primary groups — whether with kin or neighbors, whether within or across generations — present problems universally. However old, these are always also new, and subjects of study that never die. In the behavioral sciences, new insights develop in respect to the oldest subjects (e.g. Freud on the family) or to newer situations (e.g. morale on the assembly line) and make all older subjects new. This book thus illustrates how anthropological concepts (older and newer) are clarified and enriched when applied not to culture or even to cultures or communities, but to any constellations of "persons together." This and a companion volume, *Psychological anthropology*, are creations of an organizer-editor inspired by an unusual international Congress.

Like most contemporary sciences, anthropology is a product of the European tradition. Some argue that it is a product of colonialism, with one small and self-interested part of the species dominating the study of the whole. If we are to understand the species, our science needs substantial input from scholars who represent a variety of the world's cultures. It was a deliberate purpose of the IXth International Congress of Anthropological and Ethnological Sciences to provide impetus in this direction. The *World Anthropology* volumes, therefore, offer a first glimpse of a human science in which members from all societies have played an active role. Each of the books is designed to be self-contained; each is an attempt to update its particular sector of scientific knowledge and is written by specialists from all parts of the world. Each volume should be read and reviewed individually as a separate volume on its own given subject. The set as a whole will indicate what changes are in store for anthropology as scholars from the developing countries join in studying the species of which we are all a part.

The IXth Congress was planned from the beginning not only to include as many of the scholars from every part of the world as possible, but also with a view toward the eventual publication of the papers in high-quality volumes. At previous Congresses scholars were invited to bring papers which were then read out loud. They were necessarily limited in length; many were only summarized; there was little time for discussion; and the sparse discussion could only be in one language. The IXth Congress was an experiment aimed at changing this. Papers were written with the intention of exchanging them before the Congress, particularly in extensive pre-Congress sessions; they were not intended to be read aloud at the Congress, that time being devoted to discussions — discussions which were simultaneously and professionally translated into five languages. The method for eliciting the papers was structured to make as representative a sample as was allowable when scholarly creativity — hence self-selection — was critically important. Scholars were asked both to propose papers of their own and to suggest topics for sessions of the Congress which they might edit into volumes. All were then informed of the suggestions and encouraged to re-think their own papers and the topics. The process, therefore, was a continuous one of feedback and exchange and it has continued to be so even after the Congress. The some two thousand papers comprising *World Anthropology* certainly then offer a substantial sample of world anthropology. It has been said that anthropology is at a turning point; if this is so, these volumes will be the historical direction-markers.

As might have been foreseen in the first post-colonial generation, the large majority of the Congress papers (82 percent) are the work of scholars identified with the industrialized world which fathered our traditional discipline and the institution of the Congress itself: Eastern Europe (15 percent); Western Europe (16 percent); North America (47 percent); Japan, South Africa, Australia, and New Zealand (4 percent). Only 18 percent of the papers are from developing areas: Africa (4 percent); Asia-Oceania (9 percent); Latin America (5 percent). Aside from the substantial representation from the U.S.S.R. and the nations of Eastern Europe, a significant difference between this corpus of written material and that of other Congresses is the addition of the large proportion of contributions from Africa, Asia, and Latin America. "Only 18 percent" is two to four times as great a proportion as that of other Congresses; moreover, 18 percent of 2,000 papers is 360 papers, 10 times the number of "Third World" papers presented at previous Congresses. In fact, these 360 papers are more than the total of ALL papers published after the last International Congress of Anthropological and Ethnological Sciences which was held in the United States (Philadelphia, 1956).

The significance of the increase is not simply quantitative. The input of scholars from areas which have until recently been no more than subject matter for anthropology represents both feedback and also long-awaited theoretical contributions from the perspectives of very different cultural, social, and historical traditions. Many who attended the IXth Congress were convinced that anthropology would not be the same in the future. The fact that the next Congress (India, 1978) will be our first in the "Third World" may be symbolic of the change. Meanwhile, sober consideration of the present set of books will show how much, and just where and how, our discipline is being revolutionized.

Readers of this book (and its companion volume) will also be interested in those others in the series that deal with communications and language; adolescence and the religions of the sexes; education; mental health; and cultures, ethnic relations, and social change as described for many areas of the world.

Chicago, Illinois SOL TAX
September 3, 1975

Table of Contents

Introduction

THOMAS R. WILLIAMS

The papers in this volume are derived from two distinct areas of contemporary anthropological research. These areas commonly are termed "socialization" (the intergenerational transmission of culture), and "communication" (the interpersonal sharing of cultural and social information). Scholars concerned with these areas of research understand that both socialization and communication occur in the context of PRIMARY GROUPS, or social groups characterized by intimate, face-to-face associations and a high degree of cooperation.

Primary groups are basic to the forming of the cultural and social components of the individual self. Thus, the essential result of life in primary groups is not only the development of a self structure that contains a biologically derived "I" and a reflectively based "me" (cf. G. Mead 1934), but also a primary group, "we." A substantial part of the human self is derived from learning the common attitudes, outlooks and ways of behaving that are typical of the primary groups in which humans mature. In primary groups individuals also acquire the kinds of broad mutual identifications that make possible the interaction of large numbers of humans.

In their early years, human individuals live in just a few types of primary groups; the family, the playgroup, and a neighborhood or local community. These groups are marked by their relative permanence, the intensity and frequency of contacts between members, and the cultivation of deep emotional ties. For the most part, participation in such primary groups is not optional for an infant or child. These groups place restraints upon an individual's behavior; he is compelled by a variety of physical and verbal techniques to act in ways deemed acceptable by primary group members. It should be noted, however, that because of the development of deep emotional ties between members of these primary groups most children come to readily accept restraints upon their activities as both reasonable and "good." In time, most children regularly act alone with reference to such primary group restraints in a "self-socialization" fashion (Williams 1972a, 1975), that is, children come to apply to themselves, through use of their capacities for reflection, cognition, etc., the rules and limits set by their primary groups and thus shape, or operantly condition, their own behavior in ways that would be approved by members of their primary groups. In other words, through primary groups, children come to act regularly in ways that, if they were adults, they would approve of.

Socialization research has developed quite rapidly in the past three decades.[1] Similarly, basic studies of the nature of human communication in primary groups have expanded significantly in the past two decades.[2] The papers in this volume illustrate some of the kinds of basic research being conducted in socialization and communication. These papers also indicate a growing trend toward the development of a new theoretical outlook in which socialization and communication in primary groups are treated as related and interdependent processes, that is, as contributing equally to the development of the individual self and behavior. Another way to state this would be to note that the process of socialization in primary groups is dependent upon effective communication, while the process of communication between members of primary groups depends upon effective socialization.

These papers on socialization and communication also contribute to a resolution of an apparent theoretical paradox in the definition of the nature of culture. In a review of Geertz's (1973) conception of culture, Goodenough (1974) has succinctly stated the essence of this paradox; while culture is directly observable in "significant symbols" (Geertz 1973)

[1]   For discussions of socialization research see Brim (1968); Burton (1968); Child (1954); Clausen (1968); Cohen (1971); Danziger (1970); Elkin (1960); Elkin and Handel (1972); Gearing (i.p.); Goslin (1969); Greenberg (1970); Greenstein (1968); Henry (1960); Kluckhohn (1939); LeVine (1969, 1973); Mayer (1970); McNeil (1969); Mead (1963, 1972); Middleton (1970); Scribner and Cole (1973); Shimhara (1970); Whiting (1968); Williams (1972a, 1972b, 1975); and Williams, ed. (1975).
[2]   For references to research concerned with the nature of human communication in primary groups see Bateson (1971); Birdwhistell (1970); Blurton-Jones (1972); Brown (1974); Caudill (1969); Forston and Larson (1968); Gerbner, Rittolsti, Krippendorff, Paisley, and Stone (1969); Gesell (1940); Hall (1963, 1966); Hymes (1967); Jaffe and Feldstein (1970); Kendon (1967, 1970, 1972); Liberman (1967); Lind (1965); Little (1965); McGrew (1972); Rheingold, Gewirtz, and Ross (1959); Scheflen (1964, 1965); Trager (1958); and Watson and Graves (1966).

and their associated meanings, created and maintained by groups of humans in the course of social behavior, such symbols and their meanings demonstrably are acquired by individuals through use of particular features of human biology (e.g. reflexes, drives, capacities) and so become internalized within the biological structure of individuals. Thus the apparent theoretical paradox for culture theorists: culture is a system of directly observable symbols/meanings acquired and used by individuals in ways that largely are incapable of being directly observed. In other words, the phenomenon of culture is to be located conceptually both "outside" as well as "inside" the human individual. Goodenough (1974: 435) has termed a resolution of this theoretical paradox as "the crux of the problem of cultural theory."

There have been two contrasting theoretical approaches to studies of culture. One approach, based on the 19th century traditions of naturalism, positivism, and biological evolution, depicts culture as existing entirely OUTSIDE human individuals, that is, as an autonomous, superpsychical, and superorganic phenomenon, subject to its own laws, internal dynamics, and phases of development. This theoretical view has been often expressed through use of a common-sense example: in the course of time, individuals are born into, live out their lives, and die as members of a culture, but the culture continues in an existence independent of the life of any individual.

A contrasting view of the nature of culture has depicted this phenomenon as located INSIDE human beings, that is, as a product of individual learning and intellectual activities, fully subject to human understanding, control and direction. This approach to culture is derived from the general humanistic tradition of the European Renaissance and the rationalism of the 18th century philosophers of the Age of Enlightenment. The common-sense example used to illustrate this view of culture notes simply that in each generation individuals have contributed, through invention and other intellectual activities, to the accumulated store of ideas that comprise the culture learned by infants and children who in turn will contribute their ideas to the body of culture possessed by a human group.

The impact and influence of these markedly different theoretical approaches are well illustrated in the various definitions of culture noted by Kroeber and Kluckhohn (1952), as well as in the works of culture theorists (cf. Kaplan and Manners 1972; Harris 1968). One can see clearly the various problems arising from considering culture to be located either "outside" or "inside" the human individual. And from study of such definitions and theoretical accounts, one can understand that Geertz (1973) has adopted an essentially superorganic theoretical viewpoint, while to a lesser degree, Goodenough (1974) has assumed the correctness of the humanistically based theoretical view of the nature of culture.

The papers in this IXth ICAES volume provide further evidence in support of a general conclusion derived from a substantial body of empirical evidence, based upon systematic studies of socialization and communication in human primary groups, indicating that culture is not to be located theoretically in either the EXTRA-SOMATIC (i.e. "outside," superorganic) or INTRA-SOMATIC (i.e. "inside") dimension of human existence. To the contrary, evidence from studies of socialization and communication indicate that culture exists in both human dimensions, or locations, as one of two key factors in an ongoing cybernetic interaction process expressed in the equation: CULTURE ↔ HUMAN BIOLOGY (cf. Bajema 1972, i.p.; LeVine 1969, 1973; Williams 1972a, 1972b).

It is useful to note in brief explanation of this point that since the appearance of the hominids, sometime between fifteen and ten million years before the present (Pilbeam 1972:125), natural selection has promoted the production of genotypes which enhance individual educability. Dobzhansky (1972:372) has estimated that natural selection for individual human educability has operated in *Homo sapiens* and his hominid precursors for at least 100,000 generations, or some two million years. Recent fossil hominid evidence suggests, however, that natural selection for human educability probably has operated for a much longer time, possibly for three to five million years, or for some 250,000 human generations (cf. Leakey 1972; Howell 1969).

Through natural selection for educability in the course of ongoing biological evolution, hominids became genetically adapted to life in a CULTURAL rather than a NATURAL environment, that is, hominids no longer were adapting solely to specific features of local physical settings. And so humans came to be possessed of an evolutionary heritage in which a new natural phenomenon, CULTURE, began to interact with a continuing natural phenomenon, HUMAN BIOLOGY, in a mutually dependent or cybernetic process. As changes occurred in human biology through the action of natural selection, culture was directly affected, while as changes occurred in a developing culture system, human biology was directly affected. Thus, beginning three to five million years before the present the human evolutionary heritage came to contain culture as a powerful directive force for human biology, while at the same time culture itself was directed and shaped by human biology. I have suggested (Williams 1972b) some ways in which this mutually dependent interaction process might have commenced and proceeded in considering the nature of the

contemporary socialization process. Hockett (1973) also has noted some
ways that such a cybernetic process might have proceeded in the origin of
human communication. In essence the equation CULTURE $\leftrightarrow$ HUMAN
BIOLOGY recognizes that for a very long period of time humans have
been born possessed of a biological structure shaped by natural selection
for life in a cultural system.

As a phenomenon, then, culture is not located "outside" or "inside"
human individuals. Rather, culture must be viewed as one of two key
factors in a cybernetic equation, with each factor dependent upon and at
the same time acting as a directive force for the other factor. In thinking
about these ideas concerning the nature of culture it is helpful to note that
the chimpanzee, man's closest contemporary primate relative, does not
possess such an evolutionary heritage. Although structurally similar to
man, chimpanzees do not behave like men since they lack the evolutionary
heritage derived from millions of years of complex interactions between
an evolving chimpanzee biology and a system of culture.

Mead (1972:xi) has expressed the hope that the days have now passed
when it was necessary to waste time on sterile discussions concerning the
respective importance of culture and human biology (or "nature vs.
nurture"). Mead notes too that although her students used to rebel and
accuse her of trying to have the argument both ways when she would
lecture one day concerning the importance of innate human capacities
and then the next concerning the different ways personal character is
formed in different cultures, we now in fact can have both culture and
human biology in our theoretical formulations, since inborn capacities
become human capabilities only when cultural and human social
experience makes it possible for them to manifest themselves. In other
words, a cybernetic view of the interdependence of culture and human
biology allows us to dispense with theoretically unproductive arguments
concerning the primacy of culture or human biology that have hindered
anthropology as well as other human sciences.

In another context, Wallace (1970) has noted that it is the primary
business of anthropology and anthropologists to develop a scientific
theory of culture. It seems clear, in light of contemporary knowledge
concerning the processes of socialization and communication in human
primary groups, as well as new data of human evolution, that a continuation, as for instance in the discussions by Geertz (1973) and
Goodenough (1974) pitting "culture" against "human biology," simply
extends the intellectual life-span of outdated ideas concerning man. There
are new and more efficient ways of viewing human life derived from
studies of the processes of socialization and communication in human

primary groups and the introduction into anthropology of cybernetic concepts. These ways will contribute to a considerably revised scientific theory of culture as basic questions concerning the cybernetic inter-relationships between culture and human biology (i.e. CULTURE ↔ HUMAN BIOLOGY) are systematically investigated (cf. Byers 1972; Chapple 1970). It appears now that the most important questions in conducting the business of modern anthropology, and for anthropologists, are those that involve such systematic investigation of the interdependence of culture and human biology.

The papers included in this volume of the ICAES *World Anthropology* series contribute to resolution of the apparent theoretical paradox in defining the nature of culture. These papers do not, with some exceptions, touch upon data of systematic investigations of the interrelationships between culture and human biology. Rather, they are concerned essentially with reporting data of socialization and communication in human primary groups, or in presentation of theory regarding these processes. The papers in this volume are important contributions to the business of modern anthropology because authors do not waste time on sterile arguments regarding the primacy of culture or human biology. The main direction of papers in this volume is unmistakably clear; a significant theoretical watershed has been passed — at least in these two areas of anthropological research (i.e. socialization and communication) — in the search for ways to understand man.

The papers selected for inclusion in this volume were chosen after a lengthy editorial process. I have described the ways I proceeded with my editorial tasks in another volume of the *World Anthropology* series (Williams, ed. 1975). However, it is appropriate to note briefly that editorial decisions were based upon the specific charge given by Dr. Sol Tax, as President of the IXth ICAES, to session organizers and editors. In essence this charge was that to be published, papers must be professionally competent and complete, that is, in a form capable of being published. A number of papers that might have been included in this volume were submitted in a form that did not meet the specification that papers be ready for publication. Other papers were too lengthy — more than 200 pages in some instances — for inclusion in this volume. Too, some papers were not included in this volume because authors believed data in-completely analyzed or insufficient for publication.

I have selected papers for this volume without requiring that each one be rewritten to meet a common format or writing style. Thus, ways of presenting data and conclusions vary between papers. This does not significantly impede the flow of ideas and data in succeeding papers.

The papers in this volume are grouped into three parts. The first part contains papers concerned with various features of the socialization process. The next part of the volume contains papers discussing selected aspects of the process of communication. The third part of the volume presents a paper providing a theoretical statement concerning the human individual as a locus of culture.

The limitations of space in this volume preclude the inclusion of extensive editorial discussion and citations placing each paper in the specific context of particular traditions in contemporary socialization and communication research. However, readers unfamiliar with the literature of specialized research topics will find that it is possible to build a reading bibliography from citations included in most papers. In addition, the socialization and communication studies cited in the references section will provide a bibliography for reading on selected topics. Readers should not view these papers as summary expressions of research topics, that is, as "handbook" or "review" articles.

It usually is difficult to say whether a volume of papers written for one international anthropological meeting will have any significant impact on the kinds of future research conducted in a discipline. However, I believe that, in the instance of the papers in this volume, it is clear that these works collectively mark a turning point in the development of research on socialization and communication in primary groups. These papers demonstrate an advancing level of competency in such research, illustrate a continuing search for conceptual precision and clarity of expression and exhibit the intense concern of a large and increasing number of able scholars seeking to comprehend processes fundamental to human life. This work should not be viewed as the end, but rather as an early stage in the course of development of two viable traditions of contemporary anthropological research.

REFERENCES

BAJEMA, C.
  1972   Transmission of information about the environment in the human species: a cybernetic view of genetic and cultural evolution. *Social Biology* 19:224–226.
  i.p.   "Differential transmission of genetic and cultural (non-genetic) information about the environment: a cybernetic view of genetic and cultural evolution in animal species," in *Evolutionary models and studies in human diversity*. Edited by R. J. Meier, C. Otten, and F. Abdel-Hameed. World Anthropology. The Hague: Mouton.

BATESON, M. C.
1971   "The interpersonal context of infant vocalization." *Quarterly Progress Report 100*, Research Laboratory of Electronics, M.I.T. January 15: 170–176.

BIRDWHISTELL, R.
1970   *Kinesics and context: essays on body motion communication*. Philadelphia: University of Pennsylvania Press.

BLURTON-JONES, N., *editor*
1972   *Ethological studies of child behavior*. Cambridge: Cambridge University Press.

BRIM, O.
1968   "Socialization: adult socialization," in *International encyclopedia of the social sciences* 14. Edited by D. S. Sills, 555–562. New York: Macmillan and Free Press.

BROWN, R.
1974   *A first language*. Cambridge, Massachusetts: Harvard University Press.

BURTON, R.
1968   "Socialization: psychological aspects," in *International encyclopedia of the social sciences* 14. Edited by D. S. Sills, 534–545. New York: Macmillan and Free Press.

BYERS, P.
1972   "From biological rhythm to cultural pattern: a study of minimum units." Unpublished Phd. dissertation, Columbia University.

CAUDILL, W.
1969   "Tiny dramas: vocal communication between mother and infant in Japanese and American families," in *Proceedings of the Second Conference on Culture and Mental Health*. Edited by W. Lebra. Honolulu: Social Science Research Institute, University of Hawaii.

CHAPPLE, E.
1970   *Culture and biological man: explorations in behavioral anthropology*. New York: Holt, Rinehart and Winston.

CHILD, I.
1954   "Socialization," in *Handbook of social psychology*, volume two. Edited by G. Lindzey, 655–692. Cambridge, Massachusetts: Addison-Wesley.

CLAUSEN, J., *editor*
1968   *Socialization and society*. Boston: Little, Brown.

COHEN, Y.
1971   "The shaping of men's minds: adaptations to the imperatives of culture," in *Anthropological perspectives on education*. Edited by M. Wax, S. Diamond, and F. Gearing, 19–50. New York: Basic Books.

DANZIGER, K., *editor*
1970   *Readings in child socialization*. Oxford: Pergamon Press.

DOBZHANSKY, T.
1972   The ascent of man. *Social Biology* 19:367–378.

ELKIN, F.
1960   *The child and society: the process of socialization*. New York: Random.

ELKIN, F., G. HANDEL
1972   *The child and society*. New York: Random House.
FORSTON, R., C. LARSON
1968   The dynamics of space: an experimental study in proxemic behavior among Latin Americans and North Americans. *Journal of Communication* 18:109–116.
GEARING, F., L. SANGREE, *editors*
i.p.   *Toward a general cultural theory of education*. World Anthropology. The Hague: Mouton.
GEERTZ, C.
1973   *The interpretation of cultures*. New York: Basic Books.
GERBNER, G., O. RITTOLSTI, K. KRIPPENDORFF, W. PAISLEY, P. STONE, *editors*
1969   *The analysis of communication content*. New York: Wiley.
GESELL, A.
1940   *The first five years of life: a guide to the study of the pre-school child*. New York: Harper.
GOODENOUGH, W.
1974   Review of *The interpretation of cultures* by C. Geertz. *Science* 186: 435–436.
GOSLIN, D., *editor*
1969   *Handbook of socialization theory and research*. Chicago: Rand McNally.
GREENBERG, E.
1970   *Political socialization*. New York: Atherton.
GREENSTEIN, F.
1968   "Socialization; political socialization," in *International encyclopedia of the social sciences* 14. Edited by D. S. Sills, 551–555. New York: Macmillan and Free Press.
HALL, E.
1963   A system for the notation of proxemic behavior. *American Anthropologist* 65:1003–1026.
1966   *The hidden dimension*. Garden City, New York: Doubleday.
HARRIS, M.
1968   *The rise of anthropological theory*. New York: Crowell.
HENRY, J.
1960   A cross-cultural outline of education. *Current Anthropology* 1:267–305.
HOCKETT, C.
1973   *Man's place in nature*. New York: McGraw-Hill.
HOWELL, F.
1969   Remains of *Hominidae* from Plio-Pleistocene formations in the lower Omo Basin, Ethiopia. *Nature* 223:1234.
HYMES, D.
1967   "The anthropology of communication," in *Human communication theory*. Edited by F. E. X. Dance. New York: Holt, Rinehart and Winston.
JAFFE, J., S. FELDSTEIN
1970   *Rhythms of dialogue*. New York: Academic Press.
KAPLAN, D., R. MANNERS
1972   *Culture theory*. Englewood Cliffs, New Jersey: Prentice-Hall.

KENDON, A.
    1967 Some functions of gaze-direction in social interaction. *Acta Psychologica* 26:22–63.
    1970 Movement coordination in social interaction: some examples described. *Acta Psychologica* 32:100–125.
    1972 "Some relationships between body motion and speech," in *Studies in dyadic communication.* Edited by M. Seigman and L. Pope, 177–210. Elmsford, New York: Pergamon Press.
KLUCKHOHN, C.
    1939 Theoretical bases for an empirical method of studying the acquisition of culture by individuals. *Man* 39:98–103.
KROEBER A., C. KLUCKHOHN
    1952 *Culture: a critical review of concepts and definitions* (XLVII, number one). Papers of the Peabody Museum of American Archaeology and Ethnology, Harvard University.
LEAKEY, R.
    1972 New fossil evidence for the evolution of man. *Social Biology* 19:99–114.
LE VINE, R.
    1969 "Culture, personality and socialization; an evolutionary point of view," in *Handbook of socialization theory and research.* Edited by D. Goslin, 509–541. Chicago: Rand McNally.
    1973 *Culture, behavior and personality.* Chicago: Aldine.
LIBERMAN, P.
    1967 *Intonation, perception and language.* Cambridge, Massachusetts: M.I.T. Press.
LIND, J., editor
    1965 *Newborn infant cry.* Uppsala: Almqvist and Wiksells.
LITTLE, K.
    1965 Personal space. *Journal of Experimental Psychology* 1:237–247.
MAYER, P.
    1970 *Socialization: the approach from social anthropology.* London: Tavistock.
MC GREW, W.
    1972 *An ethological study of children's behavior.* London: Academic Press.
MC NEIL, E.
    1969 *Human socialization.* Belmont, California: Brooks/Cole.
MEAD, G. H.
    1934 *Mind, self and society.* Chicago: University of Chicago Press.
MEAD, M.
    1963 Socialization and enculturation. *Current Anthropology* 4:184–188.
    1972 "Foreword," in *Introduction to socialization: human culture transmitted.* By T. R. Williams. St. Louis: C. V. Mosby.
MIDDLETON, J., editor
    1970 *From child to adult.* Garden City, New York: Natural History Press.
PILBEAM, D.
    1972 Adaptive response of hominids to their environment as ascertained by fossil evidence. *Social Biology* 19:367–478.

RHEINGOLD, H., J. GEWIRTZ, H. ROSS
  1959   Social conditioning of vocalizing in the infant. *Journal of Comparative and Physiological Psychology* 52:68–73.
SCHEFLEN, A.
  1964   The significance of posture in communication systems. *Psychiatry* 27:316–331.
  1965   *Stream and structure of communicational behavior.* Behavioral Studies Monograph Number 1, Eastern Psychiatric Institute. Philadelphia: Commonweatlh of Pennsylvania.
SCRIBNER, S., M. COLE
  1973   Cognitive consequences of formal and informal education. *Science* 182:553–559.
SHIMHARA, N.
  1970   Enculturation – a reconsideration. *Current Anthropology* 11:143–154.
TRAGER, G.
  1958   Paralanguage: a first approximation. *Studies in Linguistics* 13:1–12.
WALLACE, A.
  1970   *Culture and personality* (first revised edition). New York: Random House.
WATSON, O., T. GRAVES
  1966   Quantitative research in proxemic behavior. *American Anthropologist* 68:971–985.
WHITING, J.
  1968   "Socialization: anthropological aspects," in *International encyclopedia of the social sciences* 14. Edited by D.S. Sills, 545–551. New York: Macmillan and Free Press.
WILLIAMS, T.
  1972a *Introduction to socialization: human culture transmitted.* St. Louis: C. V. Mosby.
  1972b "The socialization process: a theoretical perspective," in *Primate socialization.* Edited by F. Poirier, 207–260. New York: Random House.
  i.p.   "Commentary on 'A general cultural theory of education' by Frederick Gearing, et al.," in *Toward a general cultural theory of education.* Edited by Frederick Gearing and Lucinda Sangree. World Anthropology. The Hague: Mouton.
WILLIAMS, T., *editor*
  1975   *Psychological anthropology.* World Anthropology. The Hague: Mouton.

PART ONE

Socialization: A Brief Review of Directions of Research

JUDITH K. BROWN

The purpose of this introduction is not to provide a comprehensive overview of the past twenty years of socialization research. Rather it is to identify three directions this research has been taking. First, it has exhibited responsiveness to the social problems of our day. Second, the study of socialization has become relevant for all the subdisciplines of anthropology. Finally, socialization research has reflected the changing theoretical concerns of the discipline.

Yet the study of socialization has not neglected its traditional focus on the child-rearing practices of non-Western peoples. The collection of data on enculturation is now informed by new research trends. For example, Draper (1971a, 1971b, n.d.) has explored the cultural ecology of !Kung childhood[1] and Konner (1972) has provided an ethological study of !Kung infancy. Both research efforts serve to augment the previously scant record of child rearing among hunter-gatherers, societies which have been of particular interest to anthropologists in recent years.

Yet the collection of data has also moved into areas largely unanticipated twenty years ago, areas suggested by social concerns of our times. The desirability of group care for young children has been a matter of dispute arising both from a reconsideration of the role of women and from attempts to cope with the problems of poverty. The group rearing of children and the concomitant reduced socializing responsibility of the immediate family have been examined among the Hutterites, for whom such child rearing has a long tradition (Hostetler and Huntington 1967, 1968), and in the

---

[1] Cultural ecology has also informed the work of Munroe and Munroe and their co-workers (R. L. Munroe and R. H. Munroe 1967, n.d.; R. H. Munroe and R. L. Munroe 1971).

planned, innovative subculture of the kibbutz (Spiro 1958). In the future, child rearing in mainland China will provide yet another example. The material available so far is only fragmentary, but promising (see, for example, Green 1963: 49–56; Lazure 1962).

Yet another new area for research, the classroom, is presently of interest to anthropologists concerned about the quality of education available to American minorities and to children of the westernizing world. The importance of this trend is evident from the publication of entire series of books devoted to such research efforts: Anthropology and Education, Case Studies in Education and Culture.[2] One recent example, in which a research tool developed by anthropologists is applied to the educational problems of minority school children, analyzes the filmed classroom behavior of Eskimo children and their teachers in a variety of Alaskan schools (Collier 1973). In yet another innovative study, three Africans present their recollections of village childhood and early schooling in accounts informed by a college course in human development (Fox 1967). The political socialization of the urban poor has come under scrutiny (Harrington 1972) and the schooling of American Indians has been re-examined (see, for example, M. Wax, R. Wax, and Dumont 1964; R. Wax 1967; Wolcott 1967; Berry 1969; Cazden and John 1971; Miller 1971; Thomas and Wahrhaftig 1971; Chadwick 1972).

The study of socialization has always shared its domain with developmental psychology. Twenty years ago psychoanalytic theory and social learning theory strongly influenced both fields. More recently, interest in infant development produced a body of research on African infancy (Ainsworth 1967; also see R. L. Munroe, R. H. Munroe, and LeVine 1972: 74–81). Today, the cognitive-developmental approach and the work of Piaget[3] have opened new areas for socialization research. Psychologists such as Jahoda, Kohlberg, and Bruner and his co-workers have brought a cross-cultural perspective to their formulations. This intermingling of the disciplines is not without its problems (Richards 1970; Edgerton 1970). Yet it has led to the experimental investigation of cultural influences on intellectual processes (e.g. Cole, Gay, Glick, and Sharp 1971) and to concrete suggestions (based on an examination of traditional Kpelle culture) for the improved teaching of mathematical concepts to Kpelle children (Gay and Cole 1967).[4]

[2]   See also, for example, Lindquist (1970) and M. Wax, Diamond, and Gearing (1971).
[3]   That a recent review article in *American Anthropologist* (T. Turner 1973) should be devoted to Piaget's formulations indicates the extensiveness of his recent influence in anthropology.
[4]   For a meticulous review of this extensive literature for Africa, see Evans (1970) and Price-Williams (1969).

A second major trend removes socialization research from the confines of cultural anthropology and gives it relevance for the other subfields of anthropology. It is perhaps indicative of this trend that a recent book of readings, *Anthropological perspectives on education* (M. Wax, Diamond, and Gearing 1971), contains an entire section dealing with linguistics and culture, as well as a paper on primate behavior (Washburn 1971). The new text on socialization by Williams (1972a), which includes chapters on archaeology, physical anthropology and anthropological linguistics, could as easily serve to introduce the entire discipline of anthropology as to introduce socialization. In two more recent papers, Williams (1972b, 1973) explores the significance of socialization for human evolution.[5] Field studies of the rearing of young, particularly among non-human primates, have provided a widened perspective from which to view all human child rearing (see, e.g., Bowlby 1969; Poirier 1972; Blurton-Jones 1972). Even British social anthropology, long aloof from the study of socialization (Richards 1970) has provided an entire volume devoted to the subject (Mayer 1970).[6] And Whiting and his co-workers have embarked on cross-cultural research related to physical anthropology (Gunders and J. Whiting 1964; Landauer and J. Whiting 1964; J. Whiting 1965) and archaeology (J. Whiting and Ayres 1968).

Recent socialization research has also reflected developments within cultural anthropology: a concern with adaptation and ecology and a concern with societal complexity and evolution. To illustrate the first, I will present examples from the growing body of cross-cultural research. To illustrate the second, I will cite the Six Cultures Project.

There has been a prolonged association between cross-cultural research and the study of socialization. Over the years, the former has been the subject of frequent reappraisals and refinements.[7] This has resulted in greater methodological rigor. In addition, a number of coded variables relevant to socialization research have become available for an increased number of societies (Murdock 1967; Barry, Bacon, and Child 1967; Barry and Paxson 1971), making possible large-scale correlational studies (Textor 1967). But cross-cultural research on socialization has also

[5]   Also see LeVine (1969) and Mourant (1973) for further explorations of the relationship of socialization and human evolution.
[6]   In this volume Richards suggests that "the study of ritual and myth from the socialization point of view" would constitute an exciting new direction for field work (Richards 1970:12). Her own study (Richards 1956) and the numerous works by V. Turner (e.g. 1964, 1967) concerned with initiation rituals are perhaps the major contributions to such socialization research (see also Grindal 1973).
[7]   Among the telling criticisms are those by Mead (1963). The recent literature devoted to the cross-cultural method is too extensive to be cited here. Several examples may be found in Naroll and Cohen (1970).

experienced modifications in the underlying basic model (Harrington and J. Whiting 1972). Many earlier cross-cultural studies were concerned with the relationship of child rearing to adult personality or to projective systems which gave indirect evidence of adult personality.[8] In recent years, the emphasis has shifted to a greater concern with the antecedents of child rearing:[9] household structure and residence patterns, subsistence activities, the nutritional quality of staple crops, climactic and environmental conditions, and even historical factors.[10]

This change in emphasis can be traced in a series of studies of male initiation rites.[11] The earliest of these (J. Whiting, Kluckhohn, and Anthony 1958) suggested that the ceremonies were a response to certain child-rearing conditions which exacerbated oedipal rivalry. A subsequent paper (Burton and J. Whiting 1961) still emphasized child-rearing antecedents, but these were traced to residence patterns and household composition and the rites were seen as a response to sex identity conflict. The psychological nature of these explanations was sharply criticized (Cohen 1964; Young 1962). Partly in response to these objections, Whiting published yet another paper (J. Whiting 1964) in which "extra-systematic" antecedents were suggested. The humid, tropical setting of societies which practice male initiation was seen to provide staple crops low in protein which in turn necessitated long nursing, which in turn was related to a long post-partum sex taboo, polygyny, and partilocal residence, all previously identified as among the antecedent conditions for the celebration of male initiation rites.[12]

The decline of the influence of psychoanalytic theory, with its strong emphasis on the primacy of early childhood experiences, can be inferred: the subject of these studies was adolescent initiation.[13] The first study does identify early childhood experiences as antecedents. The second paper

[8] For a review of this literature, see Harrington and Whiting (1972).
[9] The complicated relationship between antecedent and consequent variables in this form of research has been suggested by LeVine (among others): "Thus child training may be CAUSE with respect to the behavior of individuals, but is EFFECT with respect to the traditional values which aid in the maintenance of social structures" (1960:57).
[10] J. Whiting, Chasdi, Antonovsky, and Ayres (1966) indicate that historical events served to shape the basic values which in turn influenced the child-rearing methods of three societies which shared a similar geographic and climactic setting.
[11] The findings and methods of these studies will not be reviewed here. For a summary, see Brown (i.p.).
[12] Female initiation rites have been studied cross-culturally by Brown (1963). Residence patterns were suggested as antecedents as well as a major subsistence contribution by women. The latter was subsequently found to be related to the nature of the subsistence base (Brown 1970).
[13] Similarly in the research of Barry, Bacon, and Child (1957, 1967; Barry, Child, and Bacon 1959) the major focus was on middle childhood.

shifts its emphasis to antecedent variables of greater interest to anthropologists: household compositions and residence patterns. The final paper reflects the recent concern of anthropology with cultural adaptation and ecology.

Perhaps the most ambitious of all research projects in socialization, the Six Cultures Project was designed to study "child rearing and its causes and consequences in six different cultures" (J. Whiting, et al. 1966). The origins of this study reach back to the 1930's and 1940's and the interdisciplinary research approach of the Yale Institute of Human Relations. Three immediate predecessors of the project are identified by its authors: the cross-cultural study, *Child training and personality* (J. Whiting and Child 1953); the intracultural study, *Patterns of child rearing* (Sears, Maccoby, and Levin 1957) and the replicative study, "The learning of values" (J. Whiting, Chasdi, Antonovsky, and Ayres 1966). Viewed by its authors as the culmination of preceding studies, the Six Cultures Project combined all three research strategies.

Innovative not only in design but also in method, the study involved "pre-planned field work." Before the research teams went into the field, their members and the senior investigators drew up a detailed field guide (J. Whiting, et al. 1966). In addition to general advice on field methods, it suggested parameters for the social units to be studied in order to insure their comparability. Further, it detailed the major hypotheses of the study, identified the data relevant for these and offered concrete suggestions for the collection of such data. The value of the field guide has been demonstrated also through use in subsequent studies (e.g. Williams 1969).

Five field teams undertook research in 1954–1955 and a sixth went into the field in 1955.[14] The resulting ethnographies offered extensive information on the lives of infants and children (B. Whiting 1963). A subsequent volume, *Mothers of six cultures: antecedents of child rearing* (Minturn and Lambert 1964), analyzed interviews which were administered to a sample of mothers in each of the societies. These interviews were broadly similar in content and attempted to focus on concrete action.

The final volume, still in press (J. Whiting and B. Whiting i.p.), will analyze data based on observations of child behavior. It is significant that

---

[14] The Rājpūts of Khalapur, India, were studied by Leigh Minturn and John T. Hitchcock. The Mixtecans of Juxtlahuaca, Mexico, were studied by Kimball and Romaine Romney. The New Englanders of Orchard Town, U.S.A., were studied by John and Ann Fischer. Tarong, an Ilocos barrio in the Philippines, was studied by William and Corinne Nydegger. Taira, an Okinawan village, was studied by Thomas and Hatsumi Maretzki. And Nyansongo, a Gusii community in Kenya, was studied by Robert and Barbara LeVine. First published in a collected volume (B. Whiting 1963), each study was subsequently also published separately.

the Six Cultures Project concentrated on observation in favor of the projective tests typical of earlier studies. In part a reflection of the general decline of cross-cultural projective testing, this decision resulted in a promising new source of cross-cultural data (B. Whiting and J. Whiting 1970). A sample of children, stratified by age and sex, was chosen for each of the six societies. The children were repeatedly observed, interacting with others, in settings which sampled their typical activities. These five minute observations were recorded in narrative style and subsequently coded (not by the field workers) for certain types of behavior relevant to the hypotheses of the study. Barnouw offers a brief preview of the results of the analysis:

Children of the three groups which make up Type A [societies] ... OFFER SUPPORT significantly more, and SEEK HELP and SEEK DOMINANCE significantly less than the children in Type B [societies]. Children of Type A also OFFER HELP and SUGGEST RESPONSIBILITY more than do the children of Type B. It was hypothesized that the Type A cultures stress the importance of the group, while the Type B cultures are more individualistic.[15]
... a more significant factor in differentiating the two types [of societies] is degree of cultural complexity.
... There seems to be an evolutionary progression from Type A to Type B cultures ... (1973:209–210).

The Six Cultures Project has provided not only new data but also innovative methods for gathering and analyzing information on socialization. Furthermore, the theoretical model, which informed the original research design and its hypotheses, has proved sufficiently flexible to accommodate the elaboration of alternative hypotheses which have come to light, and which "will explain the observed relations and so insure the continuing growth of the discipline" (Strodtbeck 1964: 229). The relationship between child behavior and societal complexity and the significance of socialization for social evolution were probably not anticipated by the planners of the Six Cultures Project twenty years ago. But at that time, these were not the concerns of anthropology. Socialization research has been alert in responding to the trends within the discipline.

Any number of introductory texts, as well as the unguarded comments of some of our colleagues, would suggest that the study of socialization is not within the mainstream of present-day anthropology. To counter this misconception, I have tried to demonstrate that research in socialization has been responsive to the social problems of our day. Furthermore, the study of socialization has become relevant for all the subfields of anthropology and has reflected the recent concerns of the larger discipline. The

---

[15] Greenfield and Bruner (1969) also speak of "individualistic self-consciousness" and of a "collective orientation" in identifying cultural influences on cognitive growth.

reader is invited to find evidence for these trends in the papers which follow.

REFERENCES

AINSWORTH, MARY D. SALTER
  1967 *Infancy in Uganda.* Baltimore: Johns Hopkins Press.
BARNOUW, VICTOR
  1973 *Culture and personality* (revised edition). Homewood, Illinois: Dorsey Press.
BARRY, HERBERT, M. K. BACON, IRVIN CHILD
  1957 A cross-cultural survey of some sex differences in socialization. *Journal of Abnormal and Social Psychology* 55:327–332.
  1967 "Definitions, ratings and bibliographic sources for child training practices of 110 cultures," in *Cross-cultural approaches.* Edited by Clellan S. Ford, 293–331. New Haven: Human Relations Area Files Press.
BARRY, HERBERT, IRVIN CHILD, M. K. BACON
  1959 Relation of child training to subsistence economy. *American Anthropologist* 61:51–63.
BARRY, HERBERT, LEONORA PAXSON
  1971 Infancy and early childhood: cross cultural codes 2. *Ethnology* 10:466–508.
BERRY, BREWTON
  1969 *The education of American Indians: a review of the literature.* U.S. Department of Health, Education, and Welfare, Office of Education. Washington, D.C.: Government Printing Office.
BLURTON-JONES, N.
  1972 "Comparative aspects of mother-child contact," in *Ethological studies of child behavior.* Edited by N. Blurton-Jones, 305–328. New York: Cambridge University Press.
BOWLBY, JOHN
  1969 *Attachment and loss,* volume one. New York: Basic Books.
BROWN, JUDITH K.
  1963 A cross-cultural study of female initiation rites. *American Anthropologist* 65:837–853.
  1970 A note on the division of labor by sex. *American Anthropologist* 72:1073–1078.
  i.p. "Recent trends in the study of initiation rites," in *Studies in adolescence: a book of readings in adolescent development,* third edition. Edited by Robert E. Grinder. New York: Macmillan.
BURTON, ROGER, JOHN W. M. WHITING
  1961 The absent father and cross-sex identity. *Merrill-Palmer Quarterly* 7:85–95.
CAZDEN, COURTNEY B., VERA P. JOHN
  1971 "Learning in American Indian children," in *Anthropological perspectives on education.* Edited by Murray L. Wax, Stanley Diamond, and Fred O. Gearing, 252–272. New York: Basic Books.

CHADWICK, BRUCE A.
1972   "The inedible feast," in *Native Americans today: sociological perspectives*. Edited by Howard Bahr, Bruce A. Chadwick, and Robert C. Day, 131–145. New York: Harper and Row.

COHEN, YEHUDI
1964   *The transition from childhood to adolescence*. Chicago: Aldine.

COLE, MICHAEL, JOHN GAY, JOSEPH GLICK, DONALD SHARP
1971   *The cultural context of learning and thinking: an exploration in experimental anthropology*. New York: Basic Books.

COLLIER, JOHN, JR.
1973   *Alaskan Eskimo education: a film analysis of cultural confrontation in the schools*. New York: Holt, Rinehart and Winston.

DRAPER, PAT
1971a   "!Kung Bushman childhood: some aspects of social and physical space and the relation of these factors to the socialization of aggression." Paper read at the Northeastern Anthropological Association Meetings, Albany, New York.
1971b   "!Kung childhood: a review of the Barry, Child and Bacon Hypothesis regarding the relation of child rearing practices to subsistence economy." Paper read at the American Anthropological Association Meetings, New York.
n.d.   "The cultural ecology of Bushman childhood." Typescript.

EDGERTON, ROBERT B.
1970   "Method in psychological anthropology," in *A handbook of method in cultural anthropology*. Edited by Raoul Naroll and Ronald Cohen, 338–352. Garden City: Natural History Press.

EVANS, JUDITH L.
1970   *Children in Africa: a review of psychological research*. New York: Teachers College Press.

FOX, LORENE, *editor*
1967   *East African childhood: three versions*. New York: Oxford University Press.

GAY, JOHN, MICHAEL COLE
1967   *The new mathematics and an old culture*. New York: Holt, Rinehart and Winston.

GREEN, FELIX
1963   *China* (second printing). New York: Ballantine Books.

GREENFIELD, PATRICIA MARKS, JEROME S. BRUNER
1969   "Culture and cognitive growth," in *Handbook of socialization theory and research*. Edited by David Goslin, 633–657. Chicago: Rand McNally.

GRINDAL, BRUCE
1973   " 'Washing away the hand': a later life rite of passage among the Sisala of Northern Ghana." Paper read at the Central States Anthropological Society Meetings. St. Louis.

GUNDERS, S. M., JOHN W. M. WHITING
1964   "The effects of periodic separation from the mother during infancy upon growth and development." Paper read at the International Congress of Anthropological and Ethnological Sciences, Moscow.

HARRINGTON, CHARLES
1972 "Pupils, peers and politics." Paper read at the Council on Anthropology and Education Meetings, Montreal.
HARRINGTON, CHARLES, JOHN W. M. WHITING
1972 "Socialization process and personality," in *Psychological anthropology* (new edition). Edited by Francis L. K. Hsu, 469–507. Cambridge: Schenkman.
HOSTETLER, JOHN A., GERTRUDE E. HUNTINGTON
1967 *The Hutterites in North America.* New York: Holt, Rinehart and Winston.
1968 Communal socialization patterns in Hutterite society. *Ethnology* 7:331–355.
KONNER, M. J.
1972 "Aspects of the developmental ethnology of a foraging people," in *Ethological studies of child behavior.* Edited by N. Blurton-Jones, 285–304. New York: Cambridge University Press.
LANDAUER, T. K., JOHN W. M. WHITING
1964 Infantile stimulation and adult stature of human males. *American Anthropologist* 66:1007–1028.
LAZURE, DENIS
1962 The family and youth in new China: psychoanalytic observations. *Journal of the Canadian Medical Association* 86:179–183.
LE VINE, ROBERT A.
1960 The internalization of political values in stateless societies. *Human Organization* 19:51–58.
1969 "Culture, personality, and socialization: an evolutionary view," in *Handbook of socialization theory and research.* Edited by David Goslin, 503–541. Chicago: Rand McNally.
LINDQUIST, HARRY M., *editor*
1970 *Education: readings in the processes of cultural transmission.* New York: Houghton Mifflin.
MAYER, PHILIP
1970 *Socialization: the approach from social anthropology.* Association of Social Anthropology Monograph 8. London: Tavistock.
MEAD, MARGARET
1963 Socialization and enculturation. *Current Anthropology* 4:184–188.
MILLER, FRANK C.
1971 "Involvement in an urban university," in *The American Indian in urban society.* Edited by Jack O. Waddell and O. Michael Watson, 312–340. Boston: Little, Brown.
MINTURN, LEIGH, WILLIAM W. LAMBERT
1964 *Mothers of six cultures: antecedents of child rearing.* New York: John Wiley.
MOURANT, A. E.
1973 The evolution of brain size, speech, and psychosexual development. *Current Anthropology* 14:30–32.
MUNROE, ROBERT L., RUTH H. MUNROE
1967 "Maintenance-system determinants of child development among the

Logoli of Kenya." Paper read at the American Anthropological Association Meetings, Washington, D.C..

n.d.   "Report on research activities, child development research unit, 1966–67 and 1970–71." Typescript.

MUNROE, ROBERT L., RUTH H. MUNROE, ROBERT LE VINE

1972   "Africa," in *Psychological anthropology* (new edition). Edited by Francis L. K. Hsu, 71–120. Cambridge: Schenkman.

MUNROE, RUTH H., ROBERT L. MUNROE

1971   Household density and infant care in an East African society. *Journal of Social Psychology* 83:3–13.

MURDOCK, G. P.

1967   *Ethnographic atlas*. Pittsburgh: University of Pittsburgh Press.

NAROLL, RAOUL, RONALD COHEN, *editors*

1970   *A handbook of method in cultural anthropology*. Garden City: Natural History Press.

POIRIER, FRANK E., *editor*

1972   *Primate socialization*. New York: Random House.

PRICE-WILLIAMS, D. R.

1969   *Cross-cultural studies*. Baltimore: Penguin Books.

RICHARDS, AUDREY I.

1956   *Chisungu: a girls' initiation ceremony among the Bemba of Northern Rhodesia*. New York: Grove Press.

1970   "Socialization and contemporary British anthropology," in *Socialization: the approach from social anthropology*. Edited by Philip Mayer, 1–32. Association of Social Anthropology Monograph 8. London: Tavistock.

SEARS, R., ELEANOR E. MACCOBY, HARRY LEVIN

1957   *Patterns of child rearing*. Evanston: Row, Peterson.

SPIRO, MELFORD

1958   *Children of the kibbutz*. Cambridge: Harvard University Press.

STRODTBECK, F.

1964   "Considerations of meta-method in cross-cultural studies," in *Transcultural studies in cognition*. Edited by A. K. Romney and Roy G. D'Andrade, 223–229. *American Anthropologist* 66, Part 2.

TEXTOR, ROBERT

1967   *A cross-cultural summary*. New Haven: Human Relations Area Files Press.

THOMAS, ROBERT K., ALBERT L. WAHRHAFTIG

1971   "Indians, hillbillies, and the 'education problem,'" in *Anthropological perspectives on education*. Edited by Murray L. Wax, Stanley Diamond and Fred O. Gearing, 230–251. New York: Basic Books.

TURNER, TERENCE

1973   Piaget's structuralism. *American Anthropologist* 75:351–373.

TURNER, VICTOR

1964   "Betwixt and between: the liminal period in *rites de passage*," in *Symposium on new approaches to the study of religion: proceedings of the 1964 Annual Spring Meeting of the American Ethnological Society*. Edited by June Helm, 4–20. Seattle: University of Washington Press.

1967 "Mukanda: the rite of circumcision," in *The forest of symbols*. Edited by Victor Turner, 151–279. Ithaca: Cornell University Press.

WASHBURN, SHERWOOD L.

1971 "On the importance of the study of primate behavior for anthropologists," in *Anthropological perspectives on education*. Edited by Murray L. Wax, Stanley Diamond, and Fred O. Gearing, 91–97. New York: Basic Books.

WAX, MURRAY L., ROSALIE H. WAX, ROBERT V. DUMONT, *editors*

1971 *Anthropological perspectives on education*. New York: Basic Books.

WAX, MURRAY L., ROSALIE H. WAX, ROBERT V. DUMONT

1964 *Formal education in an American Indian community*. Society for the Study of Social Problems, Monograph 1.

WAX, ROSALIE H.

1967 The warrior dropouts. *Trans-Action* 4:40–46.

WHITING, BEATRICE B., *editor*

1963 *Six cultures: studies of child rearing*. New York: John Wiley.

WHITING, BEATRICE B., JOHN W. M. WHITING

1970 "Methods for observing and recording behavior," in *A handbook of method in cultural anthropology*. Edited by Raoul Naroll and Ronald Cohen, 282–315. Garden City: Natural History Press.

WHITING, JOHN W. M.

1964 "Effects of climate on certain cultural practices," in *Explorations in cultural anthropology*. Edited by Ward H. Goodenough, 511–544. New York: McGraw-Hill.

1965 "Menarcheal age and infant stress in humans," in *Sex and behavior*. Edited by Frank A. Beach, 221–233. New York: John Wiley.

WHITING JOHN W. M., BARBARA AYRES

1968 "Inferences from the shape of dwellings," in *Settlement archaeology*. Edited by K. C. Chang, 117–133. Palo Alto: National Press Books.

WHITING, JOHN W. M., ELEANOR CHASDI, HELEN ANTONOVSKY, BARBARA AYRES

1966 "The learning of values," in *The peoples of Rimrock: a comparative study of values*. Edited by E. Z. Vogt and Ethel Albert, 83–125. Cambridge: Harvard University Press.

WHITING, JOHN W. M., IRVING L. CHILD

1953 *Child training and personality*. New Haven: Yale University Press.

WHITING, JOHN W. M., RICHARD KLUCKHOHN, ALBERT ANTHONY

1958 "The function of male initiation ceremonies at puberty," in *Readings in social psychology*. Edited by Eleanor E. Maccoby, T. Newcomb, and E. Hartley, 359–270. New York: Henry Holt.

WHITING, JOHN W. M., BEATRICE B. WHITING

i.p. *Children of six cultures*.

WHITING, JOHN W. M., *et al.*

1966 *Field guide for the study of socialization*. New York: John Wiley.

WILLIAMS, THOMAS R.

1969 *A Borneo childhood: enculturation in Dusun society*. New York: Holt, Rinehart and Winston.

1972a *Introduction to socialization: human culture transmitted*. St. Louis: C. V. Mosby.

1972b "The socialization process: a theoretical perspective," in *Primate socialization.* Edited by Frank E. Poirier, 207–260. New York: Random House.

1973 "Origins of the socialization process." Paper read at the Central States Anthropological Society Meetings, St. Louis.

WOLCOTT, HARRY F.

1967 *A Kwakiutl village and school.* New York: Holt, Rinehart and Winston.

YOUNG, FRANK

1962 The function of male initiation ceremonies: a cross-cultural test of an alternative hypothesis. *American Journal of Sociology* 67:379–391.

The Nonsocial Behavior of Young Liberian Kpelle Children and Its Social Context

GERALD M. ERCHAK

The study presented here is an outgrowth of two bodies of research, that of Michael Cole and John Gay and their associates (e.g. Gay and Cole 1967;Cole 1971; Cole, et al. 1971) and that of John and Beatrice Whiting and their associates (e.g. B. Whiting 1963; Minturn, et al. 1964; Whiting and Whiting i.p.). Cole and his fellow researchers have been studying cognition and learning among the Kpelle of Liberia for some time in order to determine the factors that prevent tribal children from performing successfully in Liberia's Western-style government schools (Cole and Gay 1972: 1068). Their results, while impressive and provocative, are largely the product of psychological experiments; they lack solid ethnographic data on the learning environment of the Kpelle child and refer to this lack as a "major gap in our research" (Cole, et al. 1971:219). My own research, a small part of which is presented here, is an attempt to at least partially fill that gap. The Whitings have been developing a data bank of cross-culturally comparable materials on child behavior and child rearing based on behavior observations carried out by their students and research associates who used similar methods of data collection and analysis. My data are additional input to this project.

This study is based on field research in a town in Nyafokwele Chiefdom, lower Bong County, Liberia carried out in 1970–1971. The research was made possible by a Fulbright Research/Lecture Grant to me, OE Grant #OEG-0-71-1695 to Michael Cole, and a grant from the Department of Social Relations, Harvard University. I am indebted to Michael Cole and John and Beatrice Whiting for their assistance, both financial and advisory, in carrying out this project.

THE PEOPLE

The subjects of this study are the Kpelle, a group of swidden rice horti-
culturalists numbering between four and five hundred thousand people in
Liberia and Guinea. They are the largest ethnic group in Liberia, and
make up about 20 percent of the population of that country. Because the
main highway in Liberia bisects Kpelleland, they have been exposed to a
great deal of Westernizing influence in the last twenty-five years but,
except for some superficial changes, they have remained quite resistant
to it. A prominent factor in the retention of much of their traditional
culture is, no doubt, the profoundly conservative influence of the men's
and women's secret societies, the Poro and Sande; these institutions are
universal among the Kpelle, who also share them with many neighboring
groups (see Fulton 1972). Politically, the Kpelle are a loose network of
chiefdoms, a system Gibbs labels a "polycephalous associational state"
(Gibbs 1965: 216).

METHOD

This research was conducted in Kien-taa, a town of about 200 people in
the Nyafokwele Chiefdom.[1] Because the earliest years are the most critical
in affecting intellectual development, a sample of twenty children of "pre-
school" age was selected. Half were boys and half girls; half were
approximately one to three years old and half were four to six.[2] The
typical Kpelle working day can be divided into six distinct periods of
activity; each child was observed equally during each of these time units.
Children were observed for fifteen minutes twice in each of these time
units during the rainy season and twice more in each unit during the dry
season (see Whiting and Whiting 1970). This schedule was thought useful
because Kpelle activities vary with the season. This time sampling provided a total of 24 fifteen-minute observations for each of the twenty children
in the sample, or 480 in all. Thus, each subject was observed for a total of
six hours, which constituted a representative composite day for each
child. These behavior observations were supplemented by observations of
a less systematic sort as well as by parent interviews and standard ethnographic methods (see Hilger 1966; J. Whiting, et al. 1966; Slobin 1967).
    The observations were coded according to a system which has been

---

[1]   "Kien-taa" is a fictitious name.
[2]   Children under about ten months of age were omitted from the study because I do
not feel professionally qualified to study the special problems of early infancy.

devised and successfully used by the Whitings (Whiting and Whiting n.d.a). This code was modified somewhat to include individual behavior as well as social interaction. It is the child's individual, self-initiated, non-social behavior that is the subject of this analysis. The behavior need not be solitary, although in the case of older children in the sample it may well be performed in solitude. A discrete, codable unit of behavior is defined as NONSOCIAL if it is: (a) individual, i.e. it is performed by only one child; (b) self-initiated, i.e. it is carried out by the child in response to his own concerns, rather than in response to another individual; and (c) egocentric in aim, i.e. the action is not meant to alter another's behavior (engage in social interaction).

The categories of nonsocial behavior that occurred often enough to demand coding are:[3]

MANL (Manual)   The child practices skills which involve the use of his hands, e.g. constructs an object, practices a handiwork skill such as plaiting a straw mat, etc. The child explores with his hands, e.g. pokes something with a stick or other object, manipulates an object, etc.

IMIT (Imitative)   The child does something he sees or saw someone else do, pretends to be something he cannot be, role-plays, etc. The child is learning by observation.

PHSK (Physical skill)   The child practices a physical skill such as walking, crawling, jumping, etc.

ATNT (Attention)   The child watches someone or something for two minutes or more; occasionally, the child listens to a radio or phonograph.

TOYS (Toys)   The child plays with a toy.

HSOB (Household objects)   The child plays with a household object such as a pot or broom.

BTAN (Beats an animal)   The child beats an animal, throws an object at it, attempts to beat it or throw something at it, or chases an animal with obvious intent to harm it.

[3]   The categories listed here are those that emerged after collapsing previous categories subsequent to cross-tabulation by computer. The original code was a finer breakdown of nonsocial behavior. More inclusive categories lent themselves more readily to analysis and increased intercoder reliability, since certain categories, e.g. "satisfies own needs" and "acts responsibly," were not easily distinguished and so were collapsed into one category.

ANGR (Anger)   The child vents anger, frustration, or annoyance, has a temper tantrum, cries, screams, etc.

XNTR (Explores nature)   The child explores the natural environment, plays with an animal, examines a leaf, etc.

INTL (Intellectual)   The child practices an intellectual skill such as writing, counting, or reading.

SRSP (Self-reliant/responsible)   The child acts responsibly through his own motivation or satisfies his own needs without requesting or receiving help.

MSIN (Miscellaneous individual)   All other self-initiated, nonsocial behavior (from Whiting and Whiting n.d.b).

After coding and punching, the data were subjected to cross-tabulation and analysis of variance.

ANALYSIS: CHILDREN'S NONSOCIAL BEHAVIOR

Before proceeding with the analysis of the individual behavior of the children, I would like to point out that, although children under ten months of age were not subjected to the same scrutiny as their slightly older siblings and peers, they were indeed observed. The rather superficial data obtained on them indicate that their first few months of life are like those in most other African societies described elsewhere. The child is always with the mother, often on her back. The mother is extremely indulgent during this period: the breast is offered on demand and the infant is held and caressed at the slightest whimper. Fathers, too, tickle, fondle, and entertain the infants.

Toward the end of the first year the child becomes quite mobile. He can crawl away from his mother and explore his surroundings. He is often carried about on the back of someone other than his mother, generally an older sister's. In short, the child, his environment, and the relationship of the one to the other, are undergoing critical changes. How these changes are managed can have a lasting effect on the child's course of development. It is these critical years that are under investigation here.

The residual, "miscellaneous, individual" (MSIN) category of behavior will be ignored. "Attentive" (ATNT) behavior will be dealt with separately after the discussion of the other categories because it is really qualitatively different from the others and was more difficult to observe. For the other categories, analyses of variance were carried out on both the frequencies of the behavior (total n for each child) and the proportion of the behavior in relation to all other discrete acts, including social interaction, for a particular child (the percentage of all a child's acts that the total n of a particular child represents).[4] The independent variables were SEX and AGE. The latter was treated dichotomously: one through three years and four through six years.

Nonsocial behavior involves roughly 45.4 percent of the discrete acts of Kpelle boys one to three years of age and 44.4 percent of the acts of girls of the same age group; there is no sex difference at all. For the four to six year age group, the figures are 33.6 percent for boys and 35.7 percent for girls. Again, there is no sex difference but an age difference has emerged. As the child grows older, proportionately more of his behavior is directed to social interaction and less to individual activities. The child is becoming more a member of a social group and less a self-concerned ego. The proportion score means and frequency score means for each of the four age-sex groups are listed in Tables 1a and 1b for each behavior category; these give a very crude breakdown of the nonsocial behavior. The indices are extremely rough since in some categories the scores of one or two children are quite deviant from the others in the group. Of course the

Table 1a. Mean proportion scores for sex-age groups (in percent)

Sex-age groups	Boys 1–3	Girls 1–3	Boys 4–6	Girls 4–6
Beh. categ.				
MANL	12.3	9.8	8.4	8.9
IMIT	1.8	2.3	.9	.7
PHSK	3.5	4.7	2.1	2.5
ATNT	5.5	6.4	6.4	6.4
TOYS	2.4	.4	1.2	.8
HSOB	3.5	5.6	2.1	1.6
BTAN	.9	.4	1.2	.4
ANGR	1.3	1.9	.2	.6
XNTR	6.7	5.0	3.8	4.2
INTL	0.0	.1	.9	.3
SRSP	2.4	3.9	2.2	6.4
MSIN	5.1	3.9	4.2	2.9
Total	45.4	44.4	33.6	35.7

Table 1b. Mean frequency scores for sex-age groups

Sex-age groups	Boys 1–3	Girls 1–3	Boys 4–6	Girls 4–6
Beh. categ.				
MANL	18.4	14.2	14.0	15.0
IMIT	2.8	3.4	1.8	1.6
PHSK	4.8	6.6	4.0	4.4
ATNT	7.8	9.2	10.6	10.8
TOYS	3.4	0.6	2.4	1.6
HSOB	5.4	7.6	3.4	2.8
BTAN	1.4	.6	2.0	0.8
ANGR	1.6	2.8	0.4	1.0
XNTR	9.4	7.0	6.6	7.4
INTL	0.0	0.2	1.6	0.6
SRSP	3.8	6.0	4.0	11.0
MSIN	7.4	5.6	7.8	4.8

[4] The proportion score does not represent percentages of TIME, only percentages of total acts.

Table 2a.   Mean proportion scores for sex and age groups (in percent)

Group	Boys	Girls	1–3	4–6
Beh. categ.				
MANL	10.3	9.3	11.0	8.7
IMIT	1.4	1.5	2.1	.8
PHSK	2.8	3.6	4.1	2.3
ATNT	5.9	6.4	5.9	6.4
TOYS	1.8	.6	1.4	1.0
HSOB	2.8	3.6	4.6	1.9
BTAN	1.1	.4	.7	1.6
ANGR	.8	1.3	1.6	.4
XNTR	5.2	4.6	5.8	4.0
INTL	.4	.2	.1	.6
SRSP	2.3	5.1	3.2	4.3
MSIN	4.6	3.4	4.5	3.5
Total	39.4	40.0	45.0	35.5

Table 2b.   Mean frequency scores for sex and age groups

Group	Boys	Girls	1–3	4–6
Beh. categ.				
MANL	16.2	14.6	16.3	14.5
IMIT	2.2	2.5	3.1	1.7
PHSK	4.4	5.5	5.7	4.2
ATNT	9.2	10.0	8.5	10.7
TOYS	2.9	1.1	2.0	2.0
HSOB	4.4	5.2	6.5	3.1
BTAN	1.7	0.7	1.0	1.4
ANGR	1.0	1.9	2.2	0.7
XNTR	8.0	7.2	8.2	7.0
INTL	0.8	0.4	0.1	1.1
SRSP	3.9	8.5	4.9	7.5
MSIN	7.6	5.2	6.5	6.3

analysis of variance remedies this problem. Tables 2a and 2b present the same data for sex and age groups rather than for combined sex-age groups.

The first result, perhaps not surprisingly to child psychologists, is a negative one. There are no significant sex or age differences in either the frequencies or proportion scores of the following categories of nonsocial acts: "manual" (MANL), "imitative" (IMIT), "physical skill" (PHSK), or "explores nature" (XNTR). It seems that boys and girls engage in these four behaviors about equally and, furthermore, that the behaviors occur at a more or less constant rate throughout the first few years. However, there are trends which, while not significant at the .05 level, are nearly so; a more precise study might, in fact, find them to be significant. In brief, "imitative" behavior seems to decrease with age. This decrease probably does not apply to observational learning but only to other forms of imitation, e.g. imitating a car or a dog. There is also some evidence that the proportion of a child's acts that concern the exploration of nature drops off somewhat with age. If this trend is a valid one, it perhaps suggests that the older child is more selective about the subjects of his curiosity.

Analysis did yield significant SEX differences for the categories of "toys" (TOYS), "beats animal" (BTAN), and "self-reliant/responsible" (SRSP). Boys play with toys relatively (proportion scores) more than girls (see Table 3). The sex difference in frequencies was almost significant. Kpelle toys for the most part consist of little "cars" made of sardine cans with pieces of wood for wheels, a large wheel with long sticks attached to it that a child can "drive," and a sort of a wheelbarrow that a child can ride while

Table 3. Analysis of variance: TOYS (proportion scores)

	SS	MS	d.f.	F
Sex	7.08	7.08	1	5.36*
Age	.92	.92	1	.70
Interaction	3.13	3.13	1	2.37
Error	21.12	1.32	16	

*Significant at the .05 level.

Table 4. Analysis of variance: BTAN (frequencies)

	SS	MS	d.f.	F
Sex	5.00	5.00	1	4.65*
Age	.80	.80	1	.74
Interaction	.20	.20	1	.19
Error	17.20	1.08	16	

*Significant at the .05 level

another child pushes. These three toys are manufactured by older boys either for their own use (in which case their younger brothers and peers can get a turn) or for the younger boys. Boys one to six learn how to make them by watching their older brothers. Girls are largely excluded. It is significant that all three toys are "cars" of some sort; Kpelle women do not drive cars under any circumstances and neither, it seems, do little Kpelle girls.

The data for absolute frequencies further indicate that Kpelle boys abuse or attempt to abuse animals significantly more than the girls (see Table 4). The proportion score difference is also almost significant. However, the *n*'s are so small in this category that this writer will not draw any conclusions, but will only suggest that this may indicate an early sex difference in aggression. The boys rush after dogs, chickens, goats, snakes, etc. while girls are more timid.

Girls act both relatively (proportion scores) and absolutely (frequencies) more responsibly and self-reliantly than boys (see Tables 5a and 5b). Kpelle girls begin to care for infants, sweep the house, and fetch water at about age six; the data indicate that while still much younger, the girls, subtly encouraged by their mothers and older sisters, are "practicing"

Table 5a. Analysis of variance: SRSP (frequencies)

	SS	MS	d.f.	F
Sex	105.8	105.8	1	5.94*
Age	33.8	33.8	1	1.90
Interaction	28.8	28.8	1	1.62
Error	284.8	17.8	16	

*Significant at the .05 level

Table 5b. Analysis of variance: SRSP (proportion scores)

	SS	MS	d.f.	F
Sex	40.33	40.33	1	6.19*
Age	6.50	6.50	1	1.00
Interaction	8.98	8.98	1	1.38
Error	104.21	6.51	16	

*Significant at the .025 level

these and other tasks and are also learning how to manage for themselves. Aside from driving weaver birds from the rice farm, Kpelle boys do very little practical work until about ten or eleven; there is very little reason for them to act responsibly from one to six years of age.

There are significant AGE differences in the categories of "household objects" (HSOB), "anger" (ANGR), and "intellectual" (INTL). The children between the ages of one and three play with household objects significantly more than their older siblings (see Tables 6a and 6b). This difference is consistent with the fact that virtually every time a child's mother or other adult catches a child playing with a household object, she stops him immediately. By the time the child is four, he has learned what not to play with; there are a few objects he is allowed to play with and these become the focus of his interest. At age four to six, the child is still reprimanded when he is discovered playing with a forbidden household object, but his infractions are less frequent than when he was younger.

Table 6a.   Analysis of variance: HSOB (frequencies)

	SS	MS	d.f.	F
Sex	3.2	3.2	1	.37
Age	57.8	57.8	1	6.59*
Interaction	9.8	9.8	1	1.12
Error	140.4	8.8	16	

*Significant at the .025 level

Table 6b.   Analysis of variance: HSOB (proportion scores)

	SS	MS	d.f.	F
Sex	3.70	3.70	1	.65
Age	36.45	36.45	1	6.42*
Interaction	8.45	8.45	1	1.49
Error	90.78	5.67	16	

*Significant at the .025 level

Younger children vent their anger, frustration, or annoyance more readily and more frequently than older children (see Tables 7a and 7b). This observation, of course, merely confirms the common-sense notion that younger children cry more, have temper tantrums more easily, vent their anger more readily and frequently, etc. than older children.

Table 7a.   Analysis of variance: ANGR (frequencies)

	SS	MS	d.f.	F
Sex	3.2	3.2	1	1.78
Age	12.8	12.8	1	7.11*
Interaction	.2	.2	1	.11
Error	28.8	1.8	16	

*Significant at the .025 level

Table 7b.   Analysis of variance: ANGR (proportion scores)

	SS	MS	d.f.	F
Sex	1.20	1.20	1	1.07
Age	7.32	7.32	1	6.55*
Interaction	0.4	.04	1	0.4
Error	17.88	1.12	16	

*Significant at the .025 level

Finally, the data indicate that older children practice intellectual skills more than younger children (see Tables 8a and 8b). This age difference is significant; but because the n's are particularly small in this category, this researcher regards the conclusion only as a possibility rather than a fact. However, this possibility is not a surprising one. A very small number of children in Kien-taa sporadically attended classes held by a private, self-appointed tutor nearby. The children in the age range from four to six would sometimes imitate the older children's writing, counting, and so

Table 8a. Analysis of variance: INTL (frequencies)

	SS	MS	d.f.	F
Sex	.8	.8	1	.92
Age	5.0	5.0	1	6.08*
Interaction	1.8	1.8	1	2.18
Error	13.2	.8	16	

*Significant at the .05 level

Table 8b. Analysis of variance: INTL (proportion scores)

	SS	MS	d.f.	F
Sex	.24	.24	1	1.03
Age	1.46	1.46	1	6.20*
Interaction	.58	.58	1	2.46
Error	3.76	.24	16	

*Significant at the .025 level

forth. Occasionally, they would even receive a "lesson" in return for a small favor. Children in the lower age group were less likely to understand and/or imitate the schoolchildren's intellectual activities.

One category of nonsocial behavior remains to be analyzed, that of "attention" (ATNT), specifically "watching" because listening to a radio or phonograph is extremely rare. Between 5.5 percent and 6.5 percent of a Kpelle child's total acts, irrespective of sex or age, is "watching" behavior. Since the average time a child spent watching, if it were recorded as such, was about two minutes, it was calculated that a Kpelle child spends something like 5 percent of his time during his waking hours intently watching things. It must be emphasized that this is a crude measurement and is only mentioned in the hope that it might be suggestive to other researchers. The data are firmer, however, in the area of WHAT the child watches and confirm the experimental psychological notion that children watch people rather than things and moderately novel events rather than ordinary ones. Children aged one to three watch people almost exclusively; only twice were children observed watching something other than people. Of course, novelty for these young children encompasses a wider range of people and activities than it does for children four to six. Accordingly, the young children will watch everyday activities such as someone threshing rice, cooking, eating, bathing, diapering a baby, children fighting, or children playing, as well as more novel events such as strange people walking by, or someone weaving, re-thatching a roof, picking a thorn out of his foot, scaling a fish, picking coconuts, or sewing at a sewing machine.

Older children still mainly watch people; only eight out of over sixty instances involved something other than people. But these children rarely intently watched mundane activities, such as threshing rice, as did their younger siblings. Activities had to be quite novel to hold these children's attention, and what they considered novelty covered, of course, a narrower range of things. The Kpelle children between the ages of four and six watched such activities as a woman weaving a fishnet, a medicine woman administering an ordeal test for virginity to some girls, the town chief debating with some men, a man weaving homespun cloth, the blacksmith making a knife, a cooperative work group making mud for house walls, a man writing Arabic, a man tuning a radio, people daubing a new house, a man dressing a baby's sore, or an insane woman shouting in the market-place. More precise measurement of watching behavior is necessary in order to make these data more than merely suggestive of hypotheses. But they are consistent with what we know of child development.

ANALYSIS: THE SOCIAL CONTEXT (THE RESPONSE OF OTHERS)

Excluding the category of "attention" (ATNT), approximately 25 percent of the sample children's nonsocial acts are part of a SEQUENCE of inter-dependent acts involving the response or reaction of another individual to the child's act.[5] For boys between the ages of one and three, this figure is about 27 percent; for girls one to three, about 34 percent; for boys four to six, about 22 percent; and for girls four to six, about 17 percent. These figures, then, represent the proportion of nonsocial acts that actually instigate social interaction. The assumption is that a great amount of basic learning is occurring while a child is behaving individually and that the nature of the response of others, particularly mothers and other adults, to these acts, when and if they do notice them, may be crucial in shaping a child's orientation to learning and to exploring his environment and may affect intellectual development in general. In this section we shall briefly examine social interaction, i.e. the social context of a child's non-social behavior, when it occurs in direct response to a specific nonsocial act in a sequence. Thos occurrences in which a child responds to him-self in a sequence will not be discussed.

Responses of others will be labeled POSITIVE, NEGATIVE, or NEUTRAL, depending on whether it seems likely that they would encourage the child to continue his behavior or to repeat it, or would discourage him or prevent him from carrying out a particular act. A "neutral" label indicates that the effect on the child is ambiguous. Following the Whitings, we refer to the responses of others as MANDS, which are all the "ways in which an individual attempts to change the behavior of another" (B. Whiting n.d.: 4).[6] A lengthy discussion of each of the many categories of mands are well outside of the focus of this paper; instead, only those which actually

[5]   See Whiting and Whiting (n.d.a: 9) for a discussion of behavioral sequences.
[6]   "All social interaction is seen as a transaction between two individuals in which one individual seeks to change the behavior of another" (B. Whiting n.d.: 3).

occurred as responses to nonsocial behavior will be listed according to whether they are positive, negative, or neutral in effect.

Positive mands include offering material goods, food (including the breast), help, information, comfort, approval, attention, or praise, seeking or offering sociability, seeking competition, and teaching. Negative mands include telling the child to stop what he is doing or to move away, theatening, shaming, or annoying the child, taking things from him, and

Table 9. Responses of others to child's nonsocial behavior

Category Response	MANL	IMIT	PHSK	TOYS	HSOB	BTAN	ANGR	XNTR	INTL	SRSP	MSIN	Totals
Boys 1–3												
Peer-positive	3	0	2	0	0	0	2	0	0	0	2	9
Peer-negative	1	0	0	1	2	0	0	2	0	1	1	8
Peer-neutral	0	0	0	0	0	0	0	0	0	0	1	1
Adult-positive	1	0	0	1	0	0	2	2	0	0	3	9
Adult-negative	9	0	10	0	4	1	0	9	0	2	12	47
Adult-neutral	0	0	0	0	0	0	0	0	0	1	1	2
Total responses	14	0	12	2	6	1	4	13	0	4	20	76
Girls 1–3												
Peer-positive	2	0	0	1	2	0	0	2	0	0	0	7
Peer-negative	0	0	0	0	0	0	0	0	0	0	0	0
Peer-neutral	0	0	0	0	0	0	0	0	0	0	0	0
Adult-positive	3	0	4	1	3	0	4	0	0	1	3	19
Adult-negative	7	1	15	0	8	0	4	2	0	6	12	55
Adult-neutral	0	1	0	1	3	0	2	1	0	2	1	11
Total responses	12	2	19	3	16	0	10	5	0	9	16	92
Boys 4–6												
Peer-positive	3	1	0	0	0	0	1	0	2	0	0	7
Peer-negative	0	2	2	0	0	1	0	2	0	2	1	10
Peer-neutral	0	0	0	0	0	0	0	1	0	0	1	2
Adult-positive	2	0	0	0	0	0	0	0	0	0	1	3
Adult-negative	5	0	2	1	7	2	1	2	0	0	6	26
Adult-neutral	0	0	0	0	0	0	0	1	0	0	3	4
Total responses	10	3	4	1	7	3	2	6	2	2	12	52
Girls 4–6												
Peer-positive	1	0	0	0	0	0	0	2	0	0	0	3
Peer-negative	0	0	0	0	1	0	0	0	0	0	0	1
Peer-neutral	0	0	0	0	0	0	0	0	0	0	0	0
Adult-positive	1	0	0	0	0	0	0	0	0	3	0	4
Adult-negative	6	2	6	0	4	1	2	3	1	3	4	32
Adult-neutral	0	0	0	0	0	0	0	0	0	2	2	4
Total responses	8	2	6	0	5	1	2	5	1	8	6	44

seeking submission. Neutral mands include most prosocial mands, e.g. mands concerning social behavior or etiquette.

The data on the responses of others to children's nonsocial behavior are presented in Table 9. One statistic is immediately striking: while peer responses are positive at least as often as they are negative, adult responses are overwhelmingly negative for every sex-age group. While it is understood that the *n*'s are too small to permit generalization, it should be noticed that adult responses are most consistently negative to the forms of behavior that, perhaps, are the most crucial to intellectual development: "manual," "plays with household objects," and "explores nature," as well as "practices physical skill," and the uncoded "miscellaneous individual" category. The figures suggest the hypothesis that Kpelle mothers respond in a largely negative fashion to a child's individual efforts to learn when they happen to notice the child's behavior. The child is thus discouraged from learning on his own and channeled into the narrower traditional channels of learning. This hypothesis could be tested with a considerably larger sample.

REFERENCES

COLE, MICHAEL
  1971   "Culture and cognitive processes," in *Introductory psychology*. Edited by B. Maher. New York: J. Wiley.
COLE, MICHAEL, *et al.*
  1971   *The cultural context of learning and thinking*. New York: Basic Books.
COLE, MICHAEL, JOHN GAY
  1972   Culture and memory. *American Anthropologist* 74(5):1066–1084.
FULTON, RICHARD M.
  1972   The political structures and functions of Poro in Kpelle society. *American Anthropologist* 74(5):1218–1233.
GAY, JOHN, MICHAEL COLE
  1967   *The new mathematics and an old culture*. New York: Holt, Rinehart and Winston.
GIBBS, JAMES L., JR.
  1965   "The Kpelle of Liberia," in *Peoples of Africa*. Edited by J. L. Gibbs, Jr. New York: Holt, Rinehart and Winston.
HILGER, SISTER M. INEZ
  1966   *Field guide to the ethnological study of child life*. New Haven: Human Relations Area Files Press.
MINTURN, LEIGH, *et al.*
  1964   *Mothers of six cultures: antecedents of child rearing*. New York: J. Wiley.

SLOBIN, DAN, *editor*
 1967   *Field manual for cross-cultural study of the acquisition of communicative competence* (second draft). Berkeley: University of California.
WHITING, BEATRICE
 n.d.   "General introduction to the observation of social behavior." Mimeographed manuscript. Department of Social Relations, Harvard University.
WHITING, BEATRICE, *editor*
 1963   *Six cultures: studies of child rearing.* New York: J. Wiley.
WHITING, BEATRICE, JOHN W. M. WHITING
 1970   "Methods for observing and recording behavior," in *Handbook of methods in cultural anthropology.* Edited by R. Naroll and R. Cohen. New York: Natural History Press.
 n.d.a "Instructions for coding." Mimeographed manuscript, Harvard University.
 n.d.b "Code sheet for activities, categories of mands, style and compliance." Mimeographed manuscript, Harvard University.
WHITING, JOHN W. M., BEATRICE WHITING
 i.p.   *Children of six cultures.*
WHITING, JOHN, *et al.*
 1966   *Field guide for the study of socialization.* New York: J. Wiley.

Child Rearing in India:
A Case Study in Change and
Modernization

SUSAN SEYMOUR

Within the field of psychological anthropology it has generally been assumed that child-rearing practices are critical to personality development and hence a worthy topic of study. The model used for the Six Culture Study (B. Whiting 1963) probably expresses many of the assumptions underlying such research, i.e. different patterns of child rearing will lead to differences in the personality of children and thus to differences in adult personality. The model also suggests that ecology, economic, political, and social organization of a society will "set the parameters for the behavior of the agents of child rearing" (1963: 5). Thus, a set of causal relationships are implied which suggest that extensive changes in the structure of a society should lead to changes in child-rearing practices and, in turn, to changes in modal personality.

The preponderance of child-rearing studies, however, have tended to focus on sociocultural continuity rather than on change by trying to demonstrate how certain child-rearing practices effectively socialize a child to fit a given social system. Fewer investigations have been concerned with the dynamic interrelationship of the factors of social structure and child rearing. The purpose of this paper is, therefore, to try to spell out some of those interrelationships for a town in India that has been experiencing rapid socioeconomic change.

Research in India was conducted from October 1965 to August 1967 and was supported by an NIMH research grant, M.H. 11480, in conjunction with an NIMH predoctoral fellowship, 5-Fl-MH-21,057.

THE PROBLEM AND ITS SETTING

Bhubaneswar, Orissa, India, offered an ideal location for the investigation of the dynamic interrelationship of certain socioeconomic and child-rearing variables due to the rapid change and growth it had experienced since 1947 when it was selected as the capital of the new state of Orissa. Previous to 1947 Bhubaneswar had been a traditional temple town and pilgrimage center with an agricultural base. Rice was the staple crop and members of the Brahmin caste were dominant. By 1965 the population had jumped from some 10,000 to over 50,000, and two different ways of life had been brought into confrontation.

On the west side of Bhubaneswar lies the "Old Town" with a population structured along caste lines, having little or no formal education and engaging in such traditional pursuits as agriculture and priestly services. People live in tightly-knit groups based on caste and kinship and their houses, which have no modern conveniences such as electricity and running water, are densely clustered around medieval Hindu temples. By contrast, on the east side of Bhubaneswar is the "New Capital" with a modern, educated elite and other civil servants brought in to run the state government. It is a planned city of administration with broad, intersecting avenues forming blocks where houses are built in neat rows with Western-style gardens, electricity, and running water. The houses are of different sizes, or "types," and are assigned to members of the civil service according to their status, i.e. the higher a man's status in the government hierarchy, the larger the house he will have. Thus, people live in dispersed homes in non-kin neighborhoods. In addition, by contrast to the Old Town where the traditional system of stratification based on caste still prevails, in the New Capital a class system based on education, occupation, and income is emerging due to the emphasis placed on these factors by the state civil service.

Bhubaneswar is, therefore, a locus of modernization, using the term in this case to mean the introduction of a cash economy, formal schooling, new occupations such as civil service jobs, a system of stratification based on achieved rather than ascribed status, the growth of urbanism, and movement away from large, extended households to smaller, nuclear ones. However, in 1965 it offered the unusual opportunity of catching a population at two different stages of development, the one at the more traditional end of the continuum and the other at the more modern end. Thus, it was possible to use a cross-sectional strategy to investigate how changes in these areas might affect the child-rearing process and hence the child's developing personality. It was hypothesized, using the Whiting model, that differences in the socioeconomic organization of the Old Town and the New Capital should affect how parents reared their children and that different patterns of parent-child behavior should be evident.

More specifically, the concern of this paper will be to try to demonstrate how certain socioeconomic factors affect interpersonal relations in Indian households, which in turn affect how children are reared. The behavioral focus will be on the handling of dependence and independence in the child. This behavioral syndrome was selected for investigation because the Indian social system has frequently been described as emphasizing such dependent qualitites as submission, passivity, obedience, and duty in the child and de-emphasizing such independent qualities as initiative and individualism (Taylor 1944, 1948; Nimkoff 1960; Carstairs 1958; Murphy 1953). It was hypothesized that if such a characterization were at all accurate, these behavioral tendencies should be displayed more in the Old Town than in the New Capital where changed socioeconomic conditions allowing for greater achievement and mobility should lead to a greater concern with independent qualities.

METHODOLOGY

Twenty-four households were selected, twelve from the Old Town and twelve from the New Capital, for systematic observation of parent-child behavior. In addition to the sample representing the more traditional and the more modern sides of town, it was also stratified for each area in order to discover if there were significant differences in household organization and child-rearing practices among different socioeconomic groups. The findings for class and caste have been described elsewhere (Seymour 1971), and the focus of this paper will be on Old Town-New Capital differences. Briefly, the sample included only native Oriya-speakers, all of whom were Hindu. The ones from the Old Town had been born and reared there, while those from the New Capital were new arrivals who either had been attracted by the job opportunities there or had been assigned a post there in the state civil service. In the Old Town caste was used as the diagnostic criterion of socioeconomic status, while in the New Capital the household head's education, income, and position in the civil service hierarchy were used.

A modification of the techniques developed for the Six Culture Study (J. Whiting, et al. 1966) were used for recording, coding, and analyzing parent-child behavior. Each of the twenty-four households was visited regularly over an eighteen-month period and numerous behavior proto-cols recorded, amounting to sixteen hours of systematic observation per household. By "systematic" is meant that each household was visited the same total amount of time during selected periods of the day, and all parent-child interactions were recorded for a given time period. These time periods varied from fifteen to sixty minutes each depending upon the on-going activities of a household.

In order to enhance comparability from household to household, four periods of the day were selected that focused on activities common to all households. These four behavior settings were: (1) early morning, when women rise and prepare meals for the men and children of the household; (2) late morning, when men are generally off at work and older children off at school, and when women bathe, dress, and feed their young children and eat their meals; (3) late afternoon, when school children return home, eat light foods, play, and study, and women begin to prepare the evening meal; and (4) late evening, when children eat and go to sleep. From twenty to thirty behavior protocols were compiled for each household, which comprised four hours of observation for each of the four periods outlined. The total of sixteen hours of observation per household included only the formal periods of observation, not all the informal visiting that also occurred regularly. Oriya was the primary mode of communication as very few people, other than the most highly educated men in the New Capital, spoke much English.

Mother and mother-surrogate interactions with the child were the focus of observation. Although mothers were those who most often cared for the child in Bhubaneswar, a variety of other persons, such as grandmoth-ers, fathers, aunts, and older siblings, helped out. Thus, the way all of these persons handled the child's expressions of dependence and inde-pendence was of interest. For the purposes of the study dependent behav-ior was defined as the child's efforts to elicit responses of help, care, and nurture from others, to remain near or in physical contact with certain others, and to look to others for attention. Independence was defined as the child's efforts to undertake activities on his own, to entertain himself rather than look to others for attention, and to try to satisfy his own instrumental needs. The concern was with the early development of dependence and independence in the child, and thus the sample included only children from birth to ten years. The data to be presented in tabular form are based on 9,301 parent-child interactions and children's individ-ualistic acts coded from the behavior protocols.

HOUSEHOLD STRUCTURE AND INTERPERSONAL RELATIONS

Although it is not clear that modernization will lead to the disappearance of the joint family in India, there is evidence that important elements in family structure are changing (see Mandelbaum 1970, for a review of the literature). A comparison of Old Town and New Capital sample households in Bhubaneswar perhaps exemplifies these changes (Table 1). In the

Table 1.   Some characterizing features of Old Town and New Capital sample households

	Old Town (N=12)	New Capital (N=12)
Household structure	75 percent joint	100 percent nuclear or supplemental nuclear
Household size	58 percent large (over 10 members) Range: 6–24	83 percent small (under 10 members) Range: 5–12
Education of household head	66.3 percent under 4 years Range: 0–11 years	66.3 percent B.A. degree or better Range: 4–19 years
Education of wife of household head	75 percent none Range: 0–5 years	50 percent 10 years or more Range: 0–15 years
Occupation of household head	75 percent by caste	100 percent civil service

Old Town sample, for instance, a preponderance of households were large (58 percent having over ten members) and joint in structure (75 percent being either lineal and/or collateral joint). In the New Capital sample, most households were small (83 percent having fewer than ten members) and all were nuclear or supplemented nuclear in structure. "Supplemented nuclear" refers to a situation where a man, his wife, and children lived together with one or two other kinsmen temporarily residing with them. These contrasts in size and structure of households between the two populations of Bhubaneswar were paralleled by important differences in interpersonal relations within households.

In the Old Town households, both joint and nuclear, traditional patterns of authority and respect were observed. For example, the oldest male in a household had authority and was shown respect and deference by all other members of the household. His wife had authority over the other women of the household, especially young daughters-in-law. She essentially determined when a young wife could spend time with her husband and children. Avoidance relations between fathers-in-law and daughters-in-law were maintained. Wives showed their husbands respect by never eating with them. Rather, they prepared the food and served their husbands meals, always waiting to eat until after their husbands and children had been fed. In general, women of middle and upper socioeconomic status were relegated to the indoors, keeping their heads covered and lowered at all times and observing ritual seclusion at the time of menstruation and childbirth. Lower class women were freed from some of these restraints because they had to work as laborers outside the home.

In the Old Town, even if a household were not properly joint in structure, people lived in neighborhoods surrounded by close kin and caste members and the behavior patterns associated with joint family living tended to be reinforced. The joint household was still the ideal. This meant that a child grew up surrounded by many close kin, but in a situation where much of his behavior was highly regulated. His father took little or no care of him. His parents could not openly communicate with one another, nor with him. His mother became ritually impure each month and was supposed to be avoided, and when a younger sibling was born, he could not go near her for several weeks.

By contrast, in the New Capital where households were smaller and nuclear, interpersonal relations were quite different. In these households where husbands and wives were not surrounded by kin and not subject to the authority of elders, traditional patterns of authority and respect associated with joint family living were disappearing. For example, many husbands and wives took their meals together rather than separately. Many entertained and went out visiting together, something unheard of in the Old Town. Two couples even slept together separate from their children, whereas the general pattern throughout Bhubaneswar was for a woman to sleep with her children apart from her husband. In addition, most husbands shared in the rearing of their children, a task relegated to women in the Old Town. In general, a more informal, conjugal type relationship between husband and wife seemed to be emerging which was symbolized by women not wearing their sarees over their heads, not observing menstrual and post-partum seclusion, and not avoiding their fathers-in-law when they visited. The extent to which old patterns were discarded and new ones adopted appeared to be a function of the age and level of education of the women, i.e. the younger and more educated the wife, the closer and more equalitarian the husband-wife relationship.

There were, therefore, striking differences in the organization and behavior patterns of these two sets of households which can be related to different socioeconomic conditions which prevailed in each area. In the Old Town people lived in extended kin groups, occupations were largely determined by caste, and most adults had little or no formal education (Table 1). As of 1967 the new educational and occupational opportunities available in the New Capital had had little impact on the more traditional patterns of living in the Old Town. By contrast, residence in the New Capital involved a decreased emphasis on kinship, resulting in smaller, nuclear households who had greater autonomy. Most people had left their extended kin behind in other towns and villages when they moved to the New Capital. Caste was also of less importance due to the emphasis placed on education by the state civil service which dominated the town. Thus, neighborhoods were not organized along caste lines, but rather by status in the government hierarchy. Only Sweepers were relegated to a separate neighborhood.

Because of the emphasis on formal education in state civil service jobs, there had been a selection for educated persons in the New Capital. In contrast with the Old Town, 66.3 percent of the New Capital sample household heads had at least a B.A., and many had more advanced degrees (Table 1). Most of their wives also had some formal schooling, half of them having had at least ten years as compared with 75 percent of the Old Town wives having had none. All New Capital parents, whether educated or not, were concerned that their children receive an education and have a chance to improve their socioeconomic status. In the New Capital there were schools ranging from the nursery level to college, and many young men and women were going on to college. Consequently, marriage in the New Capital tended to be later than in the Old Town where girls married at thirteen and fourteen years and boys married when they graduated from high school. Thus, there were many socioeconomic factors affecting interpersonal relations within Old Town and New Capital households, especially the husband-wife one, which in turn affected the rearing of children.

PATTERNS OF CHILD REARING

In general, the care of children in Bhubaneswar was strikingly casual and impersonal. Children were taken for granted and their basic needs attended to, but they received little other special attention or stimulation. The situation was similar to that described for Khalapur, India, by Minturn and Hitchcock (1966). In response to such passive care children learned at an early age that, if they were to receive attention, they must make their need known. Thus, they tended to become actively demanding. However, mothers and their surrogates responded positively to their children's demands only 50 percent or less of the time, thereby creating an intermittent reinforcement situation which resulted in children making even more demands. Bhubaneswar children tended, therefore, to be actively dependent, although there were discernable differences between the Old Town and the New Capital both in their behavior and that of their parents.

In the Old Town a child was born into a large, communal setting where he was just one among many household members and where group coop- eration and interdependence, not individuality, were emphasized. Here a young child was even less a focus of attention than in the New Capital. For example, Old Town mothers and their surrogates initiated many fewer nurturing and stimulating acts with their children than New Capital mothers and their surrogates (see Tables 2 and 3 for a comparison of rates). In addition, much of the care extended Old Town children was of

Table 2.   Maternal nurture of Old Town and New Capital children[1]

	Old Town (N=100)			New Capital (N=55)		
Offers	Nr of acts	Percent	Rate[2]	Nr of acts	Percent	Rate[2]
Comfort	292	34.8	4.6	203	28.2	5.1
Help	36	4.3	.6	39	5.4	.9
Food	194	23.1	3.1	152	21.1	3.8
Hand feeds	71	8.5	1.1	56	7.8	1.4
Hygienic care	184	21.9	2.9	217	30.2	5.5
Carries	63	7.5	1.0	52	7.2	1.3
Total	840	100.0	13.3	719	100.0	17.9

[1]   With d. f. = 5, X^2 of 17.47 is associated with $p < .005$.
[2]   Rate refers to the number of acts performed per child for a standardized period of time.

Table 3.   Maternal stimulation of Old Town and New Capital children[1]

	Old Town (N=100)			New Capital (N=55)		
	Nr of acts	Percent	Rate[2]	Nr of acts	Percent	Rate[2]
Smiles at	2	2.1	.03	1	0.6	.03
Plays with	26	26.8	.4	37	23.6	.9
Offers object	22	22.7	.3	12	7.6	.3
Offers information	4	4.1	.06	4	2.5	.06
Teaches words	17	17.5	.3	44	28.0	1.1
Teaches motor skill	4	4.1	.06	26	16.6	.7
Teaches handiwork	1	1.0	.01	2	1.3	.03
Tutors	14	14.4	.2	16	10.2	.4
Encourages	7	7.2	.1	15	9.6	.4
Total	97	100.0	1.5	157	100.0	3.9

[1]   With d. f. = 8, X^2 of 23.81 is associated with $p < .005$.
[2]   Rate refers to the number of acts performed per child for a standardized period of time.

a passive and unfocused variety. For example, mothers would hold, comfort, and nurse their young while tending to other activities. Consequently, as soon as a child learned to crawl or walk, he would approach his mother, take her breast and nurse while she continued to chop vegetables or attend to other chores.

In the New Capital maternal nurture consisted less of an unfocused comforting of the child and more of helping him to do things and keeping him bathed and dressed ("Hygienic Care" in Table 2). The greater concern with cleanliness and dress is perhaps a response to modernization. In addition, maternal stimulation of the child in the New Capital consisted more of instructing him in some way (68.2 percent of the acts recorded) and less of simply entertaining him (31.8 percent of the acts recorded). By contrast, the figures for the Old Town were 51.6 percent and 48.3 percent respectively (Table 3). There was more of an emphasis on learning how to do things in the New Capital, although for both areas rates of overt stimulation were low. However, in the New Capital it was the more educated mothers who actively instructed their children in various activities.

In the Old Town households child care was dispersed among more persons than in New Capital households, a child's mother and father performing a smaller proportion of nurture acts recorded than in the New Capital (Table 4). In large Old Town households there were usually

Table 4. Proportion of nurtural acts performed by mothers versus mother-surrogates

Mother/mother surrogate	Old Town ($N=100$)	New Capital ($N=55$)
Mother	53	58
Father	5	11
Grandmother	10	12
Older sibling, female	17	5
Older sibling, male	4	3
Mother's sister	1	2
Father's sister	4	0
Father's brother's wife	2	0
Neighbor or servant	4	9
Total	100	100

more persons to help out, with older female siblings playing a particularly active role in the care of younger siblings. By contrast, in New Capital households where a child grew up in a relatively small family not surrounded by numerous kin, he not only received attention from fewer persons, but he tended to receive more individualized attention. It was only in these households that mothers were observed actively playing with and instructing their children. They were also somewhat more responsive to their children's demands, responding positively 51.2 percent of the time as compared with 42.8 percent for Old Town mothers and their surrogates.

The contrast in Old Town and New Capital parent-child behavior appears to be a function of several different variables, e.g. household size, household structure and level of parental education, which are in turn related to the factors of change and modernization already outlined. The smaller size of New Capital households resulted in increased mother-child and father-child interaction, given that there were fewer persons in these households for children to interact with than in Old Town households. Consequently, in the New Capital 69 percent of all nurture acts recorded were performed by mothers and fathers in comparison with a figure of 58 percent for the Old Town (Table 4). The nuclear structure of New Capital households was also an important factor in that there were fewer restraints on interpersonal relations, allowing husbands and wives to interact more freely with one another and with their children. Thus, New Capital fathers took a more active role in the rearing of their children, performing more than two times the number of nurture acts than Old Town fathers (Table 4). In the New Capital where a more conjugal husband-wife relationship was emerging, there was also developing a more intense set of ties between parents and children as evidenced by many more instances of sibling rivalry and temper tantrums on the part of children.

Education has already been mentioned as a factor affecting the husband-wife relationship and the consequent handling of children and as a factor affecting the amount of stimulation children received. It was only the more educated New Capital parents who, for example, taught their children words for things and provided them with toys. In the Old Town children had no toys other than occasional flimsy balloons or plastic dolls purchased during some religious festival. By contrast, in the New Capital children had manufactured toys and board games from such places as New Delhi and Calcutta and were encouraged to play with them. The critical factor was probably that their parents took an interest in how they occupied their time and what they learned, whereas Old Town parents were generally unconcerned. Another factor which is probably also related to education was that New Capital parents used a higher proportion of verbal techniques relative to physical ones in controlling children than did Old Town parents (Table 5).

Table 5. Maternal use of verbal versus non-verbal control of Old Town and New Capital children[1]

	Old Town ($N=100$)			New Capital ($N=55$)		
	Nr of acts	Percent	Rate[2]	Nr of acts	Percent	Rate[2]
Verbal	696	63.3	11.1	862	73.6	21.6
Non-verbal	403	36.7	6.4	309	26.4	7.7
Total	1099	100.0	17.4	1171	100.0	29.3

[1] With d. f. $=1$, X^2 of 27.37 is associated with $p < .001$.
[2] Rate refers to the number of acts performed per child for a standardized period of time.

CHILDREN'S BEHAVIOR:
EXPRESSIONS OF DEPENDENCE AND INDEPENDENCE

Just as there were some significant differences between the Old Town and the New Capital in the handling of children, so too were there differences in children's behavior. Although children expressed high rates of dependent behavior in both parts of Bhubaneswar, New Capital children showed much higher rates of seeking nurture from others than did Old Town children (Table 6). They were more actively seeking both in terms of rates

Table 6. Old Town and New Capital children (birth-10 years) seek nurture[1]

	Old Town ($N=63$)			New Capital ($N=40$)		
Seeks	Nr of acts	Percent	Rate[2]	Nr of acts	Percent	Rate[2]
Comfort	188	30.5	2.9	186	27.9	4.7
Physical contact	92	14.9	1.5	145	21.7	3.6
Proximity	136	22.1	2.2	95	14.2	2.4
Help	40	6.5	.6	35	5.2	.9
Food	144	23.4	2.3	179	26.8	4.5
Objects	15	2.4	.2	19	2.8	.5
Direction	1	.2	.01	8	1.2	.2
Total	616	100.0	9.8	667	100.0	16.7

[1] With d. f. $=7$, X^2 of 28.59 is associated with $p < .001$.
[2] Rate refers to the number of acts per child for a standardized period of time.

of such acts and in terms of the kinds of acts they performed. For example, although both sets of children expressed some desire to be near certain other persons, New Capital children engaged more frequently in seeking physical contact (actually maintaining contact with another person), while Old Town children engaged in more passive proximity seeking (simply trying to remain near some other person). Similarly, New Capital children performed a higher proportion of acts seeking food, objects, and directions, while Old Town children performed a higher proportion of acts seeking comfort (crying or otherwise complaining and awaiting the assistance of some other person). The former might be characterized as more active forms of dependence and the latter more passive.

These differences in the expressions of dependence by Old Town and New Capital children might be related to differences in maternal responsiveness. Since New Capital mothers were somewhat more responsive to their children's dependent demands, it might be argued that their children received more reinforcement for such behavior and, hence, were more actively dependent. However, neither set of mothers and mother-surrogates was highly responsive, given that they responded positively to their children's requests no more than half the time. A more adequate explanation, therefore, would make reference to the general attitudes and expectations for children which prevailed in each part of town.

In the Old Town, for example, where adult roles and occupations were largely predetermined, there was little feeling that children required much guidance. In fact, there was little concept of "child rearing" *per se*. People assumed that, given time, children would grow up and absorb the norms and values of those around them. Thus, children were left largely on their own to entertain themselves and gradually learn adult behavior. The situation conformed to what Williams (1972) has called "self-enculturation" in that children learned primarily through their own efforts of observation and imitation rather than from explicit instruction by adults. The system was adapted to a relatively unchanging society where there were few alternatives for growing children. Thus, the somewhat more passive nurture-seeking by Old Town children might be viewed as a response to the rather passive, laissez-faire atmosphere in which they grew up.

In the New Capital, on the other hand, where parents were more aware of changing conditions and the opportunities for social mobility and economic achievement, there was somewhat more active and explicit child-care. Children were given more individualized attention, especially with regard to school, for which they were tutored daily. The more active nurture-seeking by New Capital children may, then, be a response to more active child rearing by New Capital parents. The fact that New Capital children were also more actively self-reliant would tend to confirm this interpretation.

When children tried to perform some instrumental act for themselves, such as bathing, dressing, or feeding themselves, rather than looking to someone else to do these things for them, it was coded as self-reliance. Similarly, when they entertained themselves by finding some object to play with, building things, or roughhousing with others, rather than demanding their parents' attention, it was also coded as self-reliance. Table 7 presents the figures for these two forms of self-reliance, "self-

Table 7.   Old Town and New Capital children (birth-10 years) perform self-reliant acts[1]

	Old Town (N=63)			New Capital (N=40)		
	Nr of acts	Percent	Rate[2]	Nr of acts	Percent	Rate[2]
Self-care	273	34.2	4.3	429	39.0	10.7
Self-entertainment	525	65.8	8.3	671	61.0	16.8
Total	798	100.0	12.7	1100	100.0	27.5

[1]   With d. f. =1, X^2 of 4.35 is associated with $p < .05$.
[2]   Rate refers to the number of acts per child for a standardized period of time.

care" and "self-entertainment," for Old Town and New Capital children. New Capital children performed both more self-reliant acts than Old Town children and a higher proportion of "self-care" acts relative to "self-entertainment" ones.

The higher rate of self-reliance acts for New Capital children fits the more active model for parent-child behavior already described for the New Capital. It is also congruent with the greater emphasis placed there on teaching the child. Although there was not a great deal of conscious emphasis put on the child's developing competence and capacities for self-reliance in either part of Bhubaneswar, there was more of this in the New Capital than in the laissez-faire atmosphere of the Old Town. In the New Capital children were allowed and even sometimes encouraged to bathe, dress, and feed themselves, for example, whereas in the Old Town mothers frequently interfered with these efforts on the part of children. Many Old Town mothers, for instance, forcibly fed their children up to the age of seven or eight. In addition, infantile dependence was less extended in the New Capital where babies were weaned by two years or sooner, while in the Old Town nursing might continue for four or five years.

The emphasis put on self-enculturation in the Old Town encouraged children to entertain themselves, although they were frequently observed just sitting and watching others. On the other hand, the ability to perform instrumental acts at an early age was not particularly encouraged in households where interdependence, not self-reliance, was valued. The greater proportion of "self-entertainment" to "self-care" acts in the Old Town by comparison to the New Capital is, therefore, consistent with these facts. In the New Capital, on the other hand, where children were expected to achieve both educationally and professionally, one might expect the development of a greater concern with self-care as well as self-entertainment.

SOME CONCLUSIONS

These findings for Bhubaneswar regarding the impact of socioeconomic change and modernization on child-rearing patterns are similar to those for several other studies conducted both within and outside India. Two studies (Kennedy 1954; Mencher 1963) comparing more and less modern households in India found that in smaller, more modern households with more educated parents, the husband-wife relationship was more open and equalitarian. Fathers also took a greater role in child-care, and socialization was concerned less with teaching the child obedience, respect, and passivity and more with encouraging self-reliance, individual initiative, and educational and professional goals.

Prothro (1961) and LeVine, et al. (1967) have made similar observations for Lebanon and Nigeria respectively. The LeVine study compared father-child relationships in more and less modern households in Ibadan and discovered that there were two different ideologies operating which affected how fathers treated their children. In the more traditional households the child was not viewed as having a will of his own, and fathers tended to emphasize respect for authority, obedience, and submission. By contrast, in the more modern, elite households the child was viewed more as a small adult whose individual tendencies required expression and encouragement even if parental authority were occasionally threatened. Thus, elite fathers were more open and affectionate with their children, seeking to amuse them and paying them more attention than the traditional fathers. They took a more active role in child-care, tolerated more expressions of aggression against themselves, and allowed their children to choose their own occupations. The study concludes that there has been a shift from an ideology of authoritarian constraint to an egalitarian fostering of self-direction in the child.

This shift in ideology is similar to that identified for two more developed nations, Russia (Inkeles 1963) and the U.S.A. (Bronfenbrenner 1963). Thus, the changing patterns of parent-child behavior in Bhubaneswar seem to fit a more general, cross-cultural set of trends. There is a change toward greater egalitarianism in husband-wife relations which is associated with fathers participating more in the child-rearing process. Children are treated more as individuals, and hence their spontaneous desires are treated more permissively, specifically including expressions of dependence. Children are less subject to social constraints and freer to make independent choices regarding occupations, etc. And parent-child relations are more openly warm and affectionate, a topic to be discussed below.

The Bhubaneswar data (1965) suggest that household size and structure are important variables affecting the child-rearing process. Murdock and Whiting (1951) once hypothesized that infants would be more indulged in large, extended households where there were many hands to care for them than in smaller, nuclear households. In Bhubaneswar, however, just the reverse was the case. There was more mother-child interaction in smaller, nuclear New Capital households, and New Capital mothers were also more responsive to their children's demands. These findings correspond with a study of household density and infant care by the Munroes (1971) who found that among the Logoli of Kenya increased household density was related to decreased mother-child interaction. In larger, more dense households mothers were absorbed into other activities and older siblings did a large share of taking care of the children. Although there was less exclusive care by mothers in these households, the Munroes did find that infants were held more frequently and responded to more quickly. However, they mention that high amounts of care did not seem to be paralleled by equally high amounts of overt affectionate responses. Rather, in the larger, more dense households there seemed to be a diffuseness of emotional bonds.

The reduction of mother-child interaction in extended households has also been noted by Minturn and Lambert (1964) in their analysis of the Six Culture data. They also found that mothers in the large, joint households of Khalapur, India, rated lowest on their measure of affect. LeVine, et al. (1967) have suggested that the key variable affecting parent-child interaction and the expression of affect is not simply household size, but rather the functions a household must perform. They theorize that when the household is the principal unit charged with carrying out most societal functions, there will be a formalization of roles by age and sex to ensure these functions are met and a certain measure of interpersonal distance will be maintained to protect the solidarity of the group from the vagaries of personal intimacy. According to this theory, then, the Old Town joint households in Bhubaneswar are adapted to a more traditional society where there are few specialized institutions and where they must fulfill most societal functions; hence, the formalization of interpersonal relations and the control of affect. In the New Capital, on the other hand, where there are specialized economic, political, and educational institutions outside the family, household organization can afford to be more informal and interpersonal relations more intimate. In this more modern setting the function of the family is reduced to producing children, providing them with emotional security, and socializing them only in part given that schools also provide this function. However, it would seem that the sheer decrease in size of households would simultaneously reduce the need for rigid mechanisms to maintain order.

The Bhubaneswar data also point to one other shift in child-rearing practices which appears to be related to socioeconomic change and modernization. That is a shift from a more passive to a more active concern with rearing children on the part of parents. In the Old Town there was no term used for child rearing and people were unable to verbalize about the process, whereas in the New Capital parents expressed a concern about their children's development. An increased consciousness of the child-rearing process is undoubtedly related to increased levels of education. It is also probably an adjustment to a changing society where educational and occupational alternatives are open to children. Under these circumstances parents cannot rely on children simply to absorb in due time appropriate patterns of behavior. Rather, children require some guidance and direction, especially if they are to achieve in certain areas. Thus, there seems to be a shift away from a situation of self-enculturation which characterized the Old Town to a more active and explicit concern with child rearing which characterized the New Capital.

Research in Bhubaneswar, therefore, has illustrated some of the ways in which socioeconomic factors, household organization, and child-rearing practices are dynamically interrelated. There is some indication that the patterns of change identified in Bhubaneswar are congruent with those occurring elsewhere in India. However, more research is required to determine this. On the other hand, many of the changes identified in Bhubaneswar do seem to fit a more general set of cross-cultural trends.

REFERENCES

BRONFENBRENNER, URIE
1963   "The changing American child: a speculative analysis," in *Personality and social systems*. Edited by N. J. Smelser and W. J. Smelser. New York: John Wiley.

CARSTAIRS, MORRIS
1958   *The twice-born: a study of a community of high caste Hindus*. Bloomington: Indiana University Press.

INKELES, ALEX
1963   "Social change and social character: the role of parental mediation," in *Personality and social systems*. Edited by N. J. Smelser and W. J. Smelser. New York: John Wiley.

KENNEDY, BETH C
1954   Rural-urban contrasts in parent-child relations in India. *Indian Journal of Social Work* 15:162–174.

LE VINE, ROBERT A., NANCY H. KLEIN, CONSTANCE R. OWEN
1967   "Father-child relationships and changing life-styles in Ibadan, Nigeria," in *The city in modern Africa*. Edited by Horace Miner. New York: Praeger.

MANDELBAUM, DAVID G.
1970   *Society in India*, volume one: *Continuity and change*, volume two: *Change and continuity*. Berkeley: University of California Press.

MENCHER, JOAN
1963   Growing up in South Malabar. *Human Organization* 22:54–65.

MINTURN, LEIGH, JOHN T. HITCHCOCK
1966   *The Rājpūts of Khalapur, India*. Six Cultures Series, Volume 3. New York: John Wiley.

MINTURN, LEIGH, WILLIAM W. LAMBERT
1964   *Mothers of six cultures*. New York: John Wiley.

MUNROE, RUTH H., ROBERT L. MUNROE
1971   Household density and infant care in an East African society. *Journal of Social Psychology* 83:3–13.

MURDOCK, GEORGE P., JOHN W. M. WHITING
1951   "Cultural determination of parental attitudes: the relationship between the social structure, particular family structure and parental behavior," in *Problems of infancy and childhood*. Edited by Milton J. E. Senn. New York: Josiah Macy, Jr., Foundation.

MURPHY, LOIS
1953   "Roots of tolerance and tensions in Indian child development," in *In the minds of men*. New York: Basic Books.

NIMKOFF, M. F.
1960   Is the joint family an obstacle to industrialization? *International Journal of Comparative Sociology*, 1:109–118.

PROTHRO, EDWIN T.
1961   *Child rearing in Lebanon*. Cambridge: Harvard University Press.

SEYMOUR, SUSAN
1971   "Caste/class and child-rearing in a changing Indian town." Paper

presented at the seventieth annual meeting of the American Anthropological Association, New York.

TAYLOR, W. S.
    1944   Behavior disorders and the breakdown of the orthodox Hindu family system. *Indian Journal of Social Work* 4:163–170.
    1948   Basic personality in orthodox Hindu culture patterns. *Journal of Abnormal Social Psychology* 43:3–12.

WHITING, BEATRICE B., *editor*
    1963   *Six cultures: studies of child rearing.* New York: John Wiley.

WHITING, JOHN W. M., IRVIN L. CHILD, WILLIAM W. LAMBERT, *et al.*
    1966   *Field guide for a study of socialization.* Six Cultures Series, Volume 1. New York: John Wiley.

WILLIAMS, THOMAS RHYS
    1972   *Introduction to socialization: human culture transmitted.* Saint Louis: C. V. Mosby.

Structural Changes in the Family in Kerala, India

GEORGE KURIAN

INTRODUCTION

A number of sociologists have argued that the nuclear family is going to be the dominant type of family structure in the modern world because it is more suitable to the modern, urban, industrial society (Goode 1963; Parsons 1961). However, there is another point of view one should take into consideration, which takes into account variable types of change depending on the needs of a particular society, the social utility of a particular society, and the social utility of a particular type of family system. From a residential point of view, the physical size of the extended family shows a definite decrease though the close kin and social network are maintained. The observations are made by Kolenda (1968: 340–341):

First, a large number of variables placeable under the rubrics of industrialization, urbanization, and westernization do seem to relate to, or at least to correlate with, a trend toward increasing proportions of nuclear families and decreasing proportions of joint families. In India, factors that appear to be related to this trend are western secular education, modern salaried occupations, development of market cash economies displacing agrarian subsistence economies. ... Second, industrialization, modernization, and westernization in their various manifestations may serve to strengthen the joint family because an economic base has been provided to support a joint family or because more hands are needed in a new family enterprise or because kin can help one another in the striving for upward mobility.

The author wishes to express his grateful thanks to the generous grant of The Canada Council in 1971–1972 for field work in Kerala, India.

In Kerala, according to evidence the author gathered from a study made in 1972 among 250 families representing all the major religious and caste groups and all regions of Kerala State, the kinship ties are still fairly strong. The study was made among middle and upper middle class families. The majority of the families, or a total of 53 percent, still hold their properties undivided; 64 percent live in nuclear families composed only of husband, wife, and unmarried children.

The purpose of this study is to comment on some of the changes in families in Kerala, which are following a progressive trend while retaining many of the basic traditions.

Kerala lies at the southernmost extremity of the Indian peninsula. It is a narrow strip of land 360 miles long; its broadest point is only seventy-five miles and its total area is 14,908 square miles. Kerala is the only typically tropical region of India comparable to Ceylon, Malaysia, and Indonesia. The state is separated from the rest of India by mountains, the Western Ghats, stretching from north to south. The mountains contribute to the heavy rainfall, which provides year-round lush green vegetation, rivers, and lagoons.

The caste system, as in the rest of India, is very much part of the social system in Kerala. Probably, it is more rigid than in the rest of India (Alexander 1971). According to the caste hierarchy, the Nambudhiri (Malayalam Brahmin) is at the top. Other Brahmins, like the Embrandhiri (Tulu Brahmins) and Pattars (Tamil Brahmins) occupy the next group. The fourth group consists of "Antarala Jatis." Intermediate castes are the traditional *ambalavasis* [temple servants].

The next important caste is the Nayars, who are themselves divided into high and low caste Sudras. Occupational and geographical factors have made the Nayar subcastes varied and complicated in their precedence, but the emphasis on the internal divisions is now lessening.

The remaining groups, which can be termed low castes, are graded according to the degree of touch and approach which is associated with each caste. The Ezhavas belong to this group. Last on the caste list are the untouchables, e.g. "Pulayas" and "Parayas." The lowest caste rung is formed by the "Nayadis" [a kind of gypsy].

Even today, Kerala is socially heterodox in Indian terms. Its caste system, though it developed an extraordinary complexity, lacked elements which were present in most other parts of India (for example, there were hardly any chiefly Kshathriyas and no merchant Vysiyas at all), but at the same time it introduced refinements of caste pollution unknown elsewhere such as the extraordinary rule by which the beggar Nayadis were not merely untouchable but unseeable, and had to earn their livings by calling for alms out of the concealment of roadside bushes (Woodcock 1967: 30).

In addition to these Hindu castes there are Christians, who claim their origin from the time of St. Thomas the Apostle, and Muslims, who were coverted by Arab traders long before the Muslim conquest of North India. In a sense, they form separate castes by themselves (Kurian 1961: 29). There are a few hundred Jews in Cochin in Kerala claiming their origin from the first century A.D.

Kerala is the most densely populated state of India; this factor reduces the standard of living in spite of the lush tropical vegetation and the very high returns per acre of land. The estimate of the population according to the 1971 census was 21,347,375. In spite of the high density and low standard of living, one comes across less visible poverty in Kerala than in other states of India.

Keralan villages bear little resemblance to the tight, squalid settlements of northern India which huddle along a single street or in a knot of houses for mutual protection. The simplicity of Keralan life tends to mask its poverty, for it goes with a sense of order. A Malayali house may be no more than a hut of sticks and dried leaves raised on a clay stoop in the midst of a dirt-floored compound; but the house and the stoop and compound will be swept clean, every one of the family's scanty possessions will have its place. There will be no rubbish festering for the flies; indeed, there will probably be no flies (Woodcock 1967: 44–47).

RESIDENTIAL PATTERN AND ITS RELATIONSHIP TO TRADITIONS

The dwellings of the Malayali are set in their own separate compounds. Houses in Kerala are almost never in tightly packed villages, as in other parts of India, but form rather a widely spread settlement.

It is in fact, difficult, if not impossible, to know when one has left one village and entered another; there is no more open ground between villages than there is between the houses within a village. The village in Malabar is thus rather an administrative idea than a physical fact (Mayer 1952: 49).

Their villages are the most open in the world, with the possible exception of Malayan Kampongs; the dwellings are scattered wherever there are trees to give them shade, and with so little sense of the need to concentrate around a focal point that the stranger is at a loss to known where one community ends and the next begins in the broad ribbon of settlement that runs, broken only by a few stretches of stony wasteland, almost all the three hundred miles from Cannanore to Trivandrum (Woodcock 1967: 45).

There is some evidence to show that independent households were found in Kerala from early times. In Travancore there has been from time immemorial a clan of large landed proprietors called Jenmies, whose lands were absolutely exempted from taxation as long as they were not alienated (Aiya 1906: 116). The rulers themselves recognized the rights of these owners. Logan in his study of Malabar has produced metal plates showing transfers of ownership as proof that such practices were prevalent (Logan 1951 [1887]). In an early Madras government report one also finds evidence of mortgaging land. The report reads, "they [Jenmies] here enjoyed landed rent, that they have pledged it for large sums, which they have borrowed on the security of the land" (Powell 1892: 159). Therefore, there is evidence of private ownership of land existing in Kerala.

While there is some evidence from tradition and history that independent households were found from early times, there is no clear-cut explanation for the preference for this as the normal type of habitation. Probably it was a national characteristic developed in Kerala through centuries. The fertile land made it possible for a family to exist on even a small plot of land of five acres with a minimum of dependence on others.

The protection from incursions from the rest of India provided by the Western Ghats also enabled people to live in relative security. The tropical climate of Kerala, suitable for growing spices like pepper, ginger, and cardamom, attracted foreign traders from the Middle East who came by sea. The constant communication with the outside world probably also helped the development of tolerance.

A tenth century poem "Suka Sannesam" [Message to a Bird] by Kalinjapallil Namboothiripadu describes the journey of the bird. The poet tells the bird that after passing through the turbulent people, Marvars of Tamil Nadu, it can cross the mountains to Kerala where it can live in peace.

Kerala has rarely experienced invasions like those that have been a recurring feature of life in North India; even Tippu Sultan was halted on the borders of Travancore. Malayalis, among whom dacoits or bandits are unknown, fear neither strangers nor neighbours, and feel no need to cling together in close communities (Woodcock 1967: 44).

The formation of Kerala culture, which was a fusion of the Sanskritic tradition of Mamboodiri Brahmins and those of the pre-Aryan culture of the Nairs, enabled the people of Kerala to resist the cultural inroads and destruction by foreign elements. Because the sense of tolerance was already established, it was possible for a religion like Christianity to find roots in Kerala as long as the new converts observed the social requisites of a caste-dominated society.

While violent religious conflicts are common in north India, Kerala has hardly any such conflicts. Traditionally, kings and chieftains practiced tolerance of diverse faiths. One of the reasons for the survival of Christianity, Islam, and Judaism was the tolerant attitude of the rulers. There are even a few instances in which churches were built with the help of Hindus at times when Christians were poor.

The relative stability, peace, and freedom from foreign invasions enabled people to live in secluded homesteads safely. Only recently has the wisdom of living in isolated homes in the middle of a few acres of land, usually far away from neighbors, been doubted; this resulted from the activities of an extreme left-wing communist group, the Naxalites, who tried to terrorize the countryside by murdering wealthy people. Fortunately, the terrorists were subdued.

The high density of population and the shortage of housing for individual families will in the future make it necessary for people to abandon the tradition of living in separate households and accept new housing schemes. However, the experience of the recent past is not very encouraging with regard to the acceptance of such housing colonies. Here is an interesting observation made by Woodcock:

A few months before we reached Trivandrum, the city council had tried to move them to blocks of workers' tenements which had been built especially to accommodate them. Everyone of the supposed beneficiaries had refused obstinately to move; the Mayor of Trivandrum drew the appropriate conclusion when he wryly remarked to me: "In Kerala every man likes enough land to give him room to swing his arms!" (Woodcock 1967: 48).

TRADITIONAL STRUCTURE OF THE FAMILY

Of the over twenty-one million people in Kerala, Ezhavas make up approximately 25 percent of the population; Christians 24 percent; Muslims 20 percent; Nayars 17 percent; scheduled caste Hindus and others 14 percent.

There are two systems of kinship, namely patrilineal and matrilineal. Generally speaking, the Nambudhiri Brahmins, Christians, and to some extent the Ezhavas and Muslims all follow the patrilineal patterns. The most important caste which follows the matrilineal tradition is the Nayars. In North Kerala Ezhavas, mostly known as Tiyyars in the North, and Muslims, known as Mapillas in the North, have been influenced by matrilineal inheritance patterns.

For the Nambudhiri the mode of kinship was essentially patrilineal. The *illam* [family] was an agnatic group consisting of all members through the side of the father. All the members had common interest in the *illam* property, which was indivisible (Rao 1955: 127). This indivisibility of property and common residence was correlated with the form of marriage practiced; marriage was allowed only for the eldest son of each *illam* (Mayer 1952: 45).

Though only the eldest son could marry, he was permitted more than one wife. Traditionally he could have up to three wives at any time, but if one should die he could then take another to replace her (Mencher 1967: 89).

As a convention, only the eldest son married and his brothers were expected to be *nitya-brahma charis* [life-long bachelors] (Nambudiri 1972: 10).

In actual practice (as far back as current records indicate) they normally formed permanent or semi-permanent liaisons, *Sambadham*, with females belonging to matrilineal castes (Mencher 1967: 89).

However, many changes have taken place as a result of the introduction of education. At present 95 percent of the boys and girls are going to school. In the age group of twenty to thirty-five, about 65 percent are English-educated (85 percent of the men and 15 percent of the women). About 20 percent of the educated men and 5 percent of the women are employed. Most of them are teachers, but there are a number of lawyers, doctors, engineers, and officials. The young Nambudhiris also decided in their new reform movement to marry girls only from their own community (Nambudiri 1972: 10).

The kinship unit among the matrilineal Nayars, corresponding to the *illam*, was the *tarawad*. The inheritance was along *marumakkathayam* [matrilineal] lines; the children belonged to their mother's *tarawad* and inherited, not from their father, but rather from their mother's brother. The eldest male member known as *karanavar* [mother's brother or brother] managed the property and, because Nayars were matrilineal, a *tarawad* might consist of: a woman; her children; children of her daughters, her brothers, and sisters; and the descendents through the sister's lines. Bilateral cross-cousin marriage was freely permitted with some preference for marriage to the mother's brother's daughter or step-daughter. There is also some evidence that polyandry was practiced among Nayars, but this is no longer found. Cross-cousin marriages, however, are still practiced to some extent (Gough 1962).

Marriage was matrilocal inasmuch as the man was the one who went to visit his wife. As an appendage of *Marumakkathayam* and the joint families system, the *Sambandam* system of marriage was prevalent among the Nayar community of Kerala. Under this system the wife used to live in her own joint family and the husband only occasionally visited her. There was no community of life between husband and wife. With the break-up of the joint family system, the *Sambandam* is giving place to the modern system of marriage and married life.

There were some exceptions to the general pattern of patriliny and matriliny because some castes have mixed these up in certain areas. However, there were no separate zones of patriliny and matriliny. But there was an intensification of the matrilineal system in North Malabar, where many of the people, including Mapillas, were matrilineal, and around Payyannur, where even a few Nambudhiri families were matrilineal, it reached the maximum. The Thiya or *Illavas*[1] [toddy-toppers], who formed the major portion of the Hindus, followed *marumakkathayam* [a matrilineal system of inheritance] in North Malabar, some parts of Cochin, and many parts of Travancore. The Nayars (traditional warriors) followed *marumakkathayam* throughout the region. The Nayars of North Malabar practiced patrilocality, but usually they followed matrilocality in other places. The Kshathriyas uniformly practiced matrilocality and were matrilineal. Among the Ambalasis there was a great variation in their affiliation to matrilineal and patrilineal systems of inheritance (Rao 1955: 126).

The study done by the author of 250 families in 1972, representing all major religious and caste groups, shows evidence of significant changes in the structure of the family.

INHERITANCE AND RESIDENTIAL PATTERN

Family properties are jointly held by 53 percent of the families and 47 percent were divided. While this is not of striking significance, the complete eclipse of the matrilineal inheritance right among the Nayars is reflected in the assumption of complete dominance by the father as the head of the family. Even among those families whose property was undivided, only one family recognized the mother's brother as its head. In all the rest the father was the head of the family. As far as the few wealthy joint families are concerned, the land ownership ceiling act, passed by the communist government of Kerala, limited ownership to only fifteen acres per family of five and weakened the joint family's ties, which were traditionally strengthened by joint property ownership. Now the right of ownership of family properties is enjoyed by all members.

However, in the study only 25 percent of the Christians claimed that all members have equal rights, and the rest of the Christians claimed that only males have property inheritance rights. The custom of dowry payments in lieu of properties is still so dominant that the question of property is not easily recognized. However, the investigator has seen instances of

---

[1] *Illavas* and *Ezhavas* are the same people.

families of Christians in which women have caused trouble by claiming property rights.

DECISION-MAKING IN THE FAMILY

While the traditional ties are weakened in the absence of joint property interests, there is still some sentiment about consulting close relatives in decision-making. Almost all the respondents have commented that for one or more major decisions other family members influence their decisions. But while other family members exert some influence over the actual decisions, only the immediate family — wife, father, mother, and brother, in that order — seem to be primarily involved in the decision-making process. Fifty-three percent of the respondents felt that the involvement of relatives in decision-making was helpful.

Among the reasons given for involvement of relatives in decision-making, the most dominant were affection, tradition of the family, and sense of obligation; affection is the most important reason, having been cited by 45.4 percent of the respondents.

MATE SELECTION AND MARRIAGE

Among the respondents, 54.5 percent married by arrangement made by their parents with the consent of the respondents. Interestingly enough, 20.4 percent of them claimed that they married by self-choice with the consent of their parents. While this is most significant in a traditional society, in which arranged marriage is still the norm, the self-choice in Kerala does not have the same meaning as in Western society. Freedom of choice does not include dating in the Western sense. It only means that the couple met each other informally through family friendships, contacts in school, college, and places of work. In large cities like Bombay, New Delhi, Bangalore, and Madras, for all but a few daring individuals, it is almost impossible to date without being frowned on by traditionalists. Exactly nine respondents said that they married by free choice without consent of parents. Parents withhold their consent when they feel quite annoyed at the idea that their youngsters are ignoring the parents traditional prerogative of choosing future spouses for their children. Even these self-choices are within the same caste. Eighty-three percent of the respondents who had arranged marriages had met their spouses before marriage. Less than half (40.5 percent) of the respondents felt that meeting informally before marriage does not contribute to happiness. The reasons were "takes excitement out of marriage" and "informal meetings lead to abuse." It seems there is a strong feeling that informal contacts are not to be encouraged, especially because the predominant majority of the respondents did not marry according to self-choice.

In the families made up of close relatives almost all respondents claim to have used free choice, but the definition of free choice has only very limited value. It is significant to note that there are fifty-two different cases of close relatives married by self-choice without parents' consent. This surely is a trend which may point to the future. However, one has to be cautious about reading too much into this because the investigator is not in a position to judge the extent to which the rate of self-choice has increased.

Good character, obedience, and ability to manage the home were listed as the qualities that are most important in a wife. The other qualities were not considered significant; on the average not more than 15 percent agreed they were important. Very few were willing to consider the subtle difference between the two factors, beauty and fair complexion. The only plausible explanation is that people are not willing to admit their color prejudices. This is definitely against the actual practice in Kerala and in other regions of India, where a premium is placed on girls with light complexions. One respondent who is a college lecturer was willing to admit the following: "Tastes differ. I am not particular whether a wife is fair in complexion or not; but it so happens that my wife has a fair complexion."

EXOGAMOUS MARRIAGES

Interreligious or intercaste or interdenominational marriages are not yet a significant issue for investigation. This was shown from the general disinterest in this question by the respondents. In a society where local community ties are still based on traditional religious and caste homogeneity, exogamous marriages are still very rare. The following comment by a respondent indicates a possible future trend.

In the present circumstances of social life in Kerala it is better to marry within the same religion. But my personal view is that marriage should be between two proper and suitable persons without looking into caste or religious differences.

CHOICE OF SPOUSES FOR CHILDREN

Only 12.37 percent were interested in arranging marriages for children according to their own ideas. Among the respondents, 65.56 percent do want to arrange marriage with the consent of their sons and daughters. This is actually what happens in most of the marriages in Kerala. In fact, sons and daughters are free to say no to a proposed arrangement if they don't like the person, and it is unlikely that the parents will push the matter. They are realistic enough not to strain their own influence on their children. Of the parents 18.7 percent were willing to allow free choice for children with parents' approval. This is probably an increasing trend. However, only 3.4 percent are willing to allow free choice without interference from the parents. This again is due to the concern of the parents to maintain religious and class exogamy.

With regard to the degree of freedom of choice 70 percent are willing to give equal freedom to both children. The rest are only willing to give freedom to sons and not to daughters. The question of giving freedom to daughters and no freedom to sons was too unorthodox for the respondents to give answers.

THE ROLE OF DOWRY PAYMENTS

When discussing the significance of arranged marriage in India, it is most important to consider the role of dowry payments. A dowry is usually paid by the girl's father and has become almost an obligation even for the poorest father. There are some variations to the custom.

Among Sanskritized castes there are certain further rules requiring payment of a dowry by the bride's father and prohibiting divorce and widow remarriage. Among the lower castes (generally the less Sanskritized groups), dowry was not uncommonly replaced by a system of bride-price and there was no taboo against either divorce or remarriage (Gore 1965: 219).

According to a law passed by the Parliament of India on May 9, 1961, to give, take, or demand a dowry is an offence, but the penalty is relatively mild — only six months in jail and fines up to 5,000 rupees ($700). However, it is difficult to eradicate an age-old custom by legislation because dowries play a definite role in the average Indian family. A dowry is paid in lieu of inheritance rights of daughters. The amount varies depending on the financial status of the family and also on the qualifications of the prospective bridegroom. In case a girl is not particularly attractive, a larger amount in dowry can be a compensating factor in clinching a marriage decision.

The custom of dowry payments has become so rigid that families with a number of daughters with only modest financial resources have extreme problems. In some cases, if the girl has a high school or university education she takes up a profession like nursing or teaching until she is able to save sufficient money to pay for the dowry. An interesting example is in Kerala State in south India, where literacy is about sixty percent, the highest in India. The predominant majority of nurses in India are from Kerala State; this may be a good testimony to the problem faced by educated girls whose parents cannot afford a substantial dowry (Kurian 1971: 305–306).

The majority of the Christians, namely 76 percent, had accepted dowries whereas 82.8 percent of the Nairs had not accepted them. This is clear evidence of the different traditions in these communities. The matrilineal rights prevalent among the Nairs until recently make the question of dowry payments unnecessary whereas dowry payments are very much a part of the lives of Christians. Legislation and social criticism have not weakened the custom. Unless the law of equality of inheritance is accepted by Christians, the practice of paying a dowry will always be a substitute to equal inheritance. Muslims and Ezhavas have also reported only a very few accepting dowries; this is a reflection of the matrilineal traditions that influence them.

Those who are in favor of dowry payments explained that they regarded them as social security for their daughters. A few claimed that prestige demands dowry payments and they can expect better matches for their daughters if a dowry is paid. The majority of those who are against dowry payments felt that there was too much commercial bargaining involved. Others mentioned that it is a financial burden and a survival of feudal social custom.

Some of the comments of the respondents are worth mentioning here:

Dowry payments may be justified amongst castes where female issues have no legal right to paternal properties. Among others money payments have become a matter of necessity for selection of proper couples, and this practice will continue even if law prohibits it.

It is a social evil ruining many families and it is not compatible with a classless society.

If a dowry is not demanded, the girl will have more affection for the husband's family.

The crux of the problem is to ensure a decent standard of living for the newlyweds either by way of employment or otherwise by the state before a legislation for the abolition of dowry is enforced.

A predominant majority were aware of the central government's legislation prohibiting dowry payments. Among them 56.4 percent felt that such legislation was progressive and good; 27.3 percent felt that without social awareness of a need for change, social legislation is not very effective.

Notwithstanding all the arguments expressed against dowry payments, it would be worthwhile to keep other advantages of the system in mind. The remark made by one respondent from the rural area is true to a great extent: "If the system of dowry is completely abolished, parents may find it difficult to get a suitable match even for their talented and able daughters if they were not blessed with beauty." One can actually go a step in a different direction. If the daughters are not well-educated and if they are below average in their physical appearance, it is rather hard for the parents to find a suitable husband without payment of a good sum as dowry. All this presupposes that nearly all marriages are arranged. In spite of the high literacy of Kerala people there is a lack of an urban culture assuring the independence of the individual, and this prevents free mixing of the sexes in most parts of the country. When an average Indian casually looks at the society in the developed countries, particularly in Europe and North America, he feels sorry for some of the girls who find it hard to get a husband because they lack the initiative and smartness which are essential qualities in such a competitive atmosphere. Although there are only a few who are left out in this effort to get a partner, even they are a blemish on the practice of extreme liberalism in the choice of partners. If there was someone in the family interested in finding a partner for such a person, her fate would not be so bad, provided the Western society would be prepared to accept such an interference. People in the West are rather sceptical about the arranged marriage in India and dismiss it as an antiquated custom. But we may ask whether it is not better that some kind of arrangement exists rather than the creation of nervous and frustrated spinsters. This is where dowry payments have a role to play. After all, every man and woman gets a chance to obtain a partner, and this system helps to provide one (Kurian 1961: 80–81).

FAMILY PLANNING

Among the respondents 97.8 percent favor family planning. The few who are against family planning cite children as security for old age as the main reason. A few, namely six Muslims and two Christians, have religious objections to family planning. Of the Christians only Roman Catholics have such objections. Of those who support family planning, the vast majority wanted better care for their children; others considered a large family a financial burden.

The majority of the respondents used artificial methods of birth control. More than half (56 percent) felt there is a need for liberalizing the present laws on abortion. The question of the superiority of abortion as a method of birth control was a difficult question to answer for the average respondent. Many (63.6 percent) felt that the government-sponsored plans are effective. Of the rest of them, all but thirteen felt that without social awareness family planning legislation is ineffective.

Some of the comments with regard to family planning were:

This is the only way to reduce poverty as there is no immediate prospect of a spectacular rise in per capita income.
There should be a tax on large families.
Government schemes are a failure in view of the large sums and number of years spent.
Misuse of public funds.
Muslim respondent: Family planning is like murdering the family.
If the majority of people practice it, then it will be good. In these days of adult franchise, the community which practices it will be politically handicapped.
Tried birth control but wife is pregnant.

MARITAL STABILITY

Divorce is so rare that it is not yet statistically significant in Kerala; this is generally true for the rest of India. Therefore, many respondents said that they had no frequent disagreements with wives. When disputes did take place, 54.54 percent of the respondents wanted to settle them by mutual talk; 40.9 percent wanted to settle them by keeping silent for some time. Only three were willing to consider separation and two divorce; this is a confirmation of the prevailing tradition of marriage stability in Kerala. Unhappiness of the children was considered by 60.4 percent to be the main problem in divorce. Others considered objections by close relatives and social disapproval to be equally serious problems. A predominant majority, namely 85.4 percent, felt that parents should stay together for the sake of their children. Most (50.9 percent) felt that divorce legislation would not affect marital stability in Kerala. The largest single group responding to this point (46.3 percent) felt that traditions are strong enough to withstand marriage break-ups.

A question that is often asked by people who have accepted self-choice as the normal manner of mate selection is how it is possible for a couple in India to adjust themselves after an arranged marriage, because they are, in a sense, strangers. The assumption is that if a young man and woman know each other in a dating situation for at least one year, the adjustment is easy. However, in actual practice in mate selection, when the two meet each other for several hours a day, they are primarily concerned with close emotional ties. Once they get married and live in the same house, life becomes different from the romantic situation. One has to face the numerous responsibilities of married life which include, among other things, reasonable efficiency of household management and planning of the limited financial resources, especially in the first years of marriage.

TOO GREAT EXPECTATIONS

The difference between self-choice marriages and arranged marriages is the relative emphasis on expectations in marriage. In a self-choice marriage a couple falls in love and gets married. However much one might claim that love that precedes marriage in modern urban industrial society is not abstract love, but is also influenced by practical considerations of compatibility, the young men and women do tend to idealize each other to a great extent. This is very important for maintaining their emotional ties. Therefore, when they get married, they have very high expectations of each other. But when they start living together and facing the many issues of daily life in a family, problems might arise. These problems can precipitate some amount of disillusionment in each other. This experience of disillusionment is inevitable because both have the maximum of expectations of each other, expectations unlikely to be realized in daily life. The majority of the couples are able to overcome this transition from the ideal to the practical without much strain because they have adequate, mature personalities enabling them to make adjustments in the early stages of married life. On the other hand, there are many who are not able to make proper adjustments. This is the beginning of serious strain in their relationships. At times the strain builds up and reaches a point at which it is impossible to make adequate adjustments.

PROBLEMS OF ADJUSTMENT

During these periods of strain, the young couple is primarily responsible for making adjustments without seeking advice from parents, kin, and friends. By the very nature of self-choice, which implies a high value on individuality and in which the relationship between parents, siblings, and friends is one of mutual respect for each other's individuality, it is not easy to accept advice at the first sign of trouble, and also it is difficult for others to initiate help without being accused of some kind of interference. In addition to these problems, the survival of self-choice marriages depends to a most significant degree on the continuation of love and common interests. Once these conditions are weakened, the couple will seriously consider the possibility of separation or divorce.

The problems of adjustment in marriage in modern urban families are emphasized in the following comments:

Consistent with the structural and geographical isolation of the conjugal family unit, parents are not expected to play a significant role in mate selection. In societies having large family systems, parents do typically participate in the selection of mates of their offspring because the new spouse will become a member of another household and kinship units; the parents and other family members have a large stake in the person selected. In our case, however, adjustment between the spouses is paramount, and relationships with other kin are largely irrelevant (Leslie 1967: 242).

In the same vein, the fact that the conjugal unit is both structurally and geographically isolated from other kin groups encourages an emphasis on romantic love as the basis for marriage and as the primary reason for staying married. Large kin groups typically discourage the flowering of romantic love because the development of intense attraction between spouses would threaten the priority of their loyalties to parents and the group. Where the large kin group is absent, however, romantic love serves as a kind of substitute for a network of detailed role prescriptions (Leslie 1967: 243).

In modern urban industrial society, in which marriage is more a civil contract than a sacrament, divorce is accepted as an alternative to unhappy marriages; therefore the social stigma against divorce is less and less relevant, especially in view of the tendency toward liberalizing divorce laws in most countries. Religion in Western society is fighting a losing battle against the liberalization of divorce laws. The most notable example is the struggle between the Italian government and the Roman Catholic church.

In arranged marriages, the young man and woman are married only after the parents and close relatives have made adequate inquiries about their compatibility with each other and in relation to the two families. In the absence of emotional commitments, it is possible for the older people to make an objective appraisal of the qualities of the young man and woman. In all the cultures in the world where marriages are arranged, these appraisals are made, and the young man and woman are informed of each other's qualities; they then expect only the minimum, but it is no exaggeration to claim that in arranged marriages most of the couples get much more than the minimum from the marriage. One also has to consider the fact that these young people do not meet a number of people before getting married; they, therefore, become less critical of each other. In modern self-choice marriages the fact that young people have had the opportunity to meet many of the opposite sex has not necessarily made these marriages more successful.

In modern Western urban families,

Often, marriage dissolution starts with the early disenchantment that results when a partner first discovers that his mate is incapable of meeting his expectations. [Peter Pineo has pointed that out.] Men often suffer disenchantment earlier in marriage than women, perhaps because their expectations are more unrealistic in the first place. But which is the first to be disillusioned is unimportant. Sooner or later one partner's disillusionment will affect the other, and the entire relationship will suffer (Klemer 1970: 32–33).

On the other hand, even in Western society, the average girl seems to be realistic about expectations in marriage while the more glamorous girls are more prone to disillusionment. Some years ago, Sidonie Gruenberg and Hilda Kretch suggested that, as far as the reality of expectations was concerned, the less advantaged girls were often luckier than those brought up in luxury. Having had less pampered childhoods, the less advantaged were likely to be much more aware of the realities of the modern relationship, including the long hours of routine involved in actual homemaking and the limitations on one's social life when small children must be cared for (Klemer 1970: 331).

A further comment with regard to expectation and adjustment in marriage by Klemer is most significant:

In this general vein, I recall that while I was walking through the waiting room of a large marriage counselling clinic, I was struck with the overrepresentation of beautiful women waiting for help with marriage problems. In later discussion with other colleagues, the hypothesis was developed that the plain or average-looking women might have possessed more realistic expectations of what the marriage relationships would provide them in terms of attention from one husband, because before marriage they had not been accustomed to a great deal of attention from large numbers of males (Klemer 1970: 33).

The saying that in self-choice marriages you fall in love and then get married while in arranged marriages you get married and then fall in love, seems most significant. In arranged marriages the strengthening of the relationships between the couples with love, in addition to the objective criteria of compatibility, contributes to maximum possible adjustments (Kurian 1971: 306–309).

In addition, the sacramental nature of marriage is still dominant in cultures in which the arranged marriage continues to exist. This means that marriage is viewed as a permanent tie, and very little consideration is given to the possibility of separation. Therefore the couple develops a greater sense of tolerance with give-and-take. After all, no two people can be ideally compatible and, therefore, the greater one's willingness to see the other person's point of view, the more chance there will be of continued success of such a marriage. If there are serious problems in a marriage, other family members will do all they can to help solve them. This is not considered interference because the good relationship between the two families is most important, and, therefore, those people who have taken an interest in arranging the marriage are willing to help the couple in their emotional and financial difficulties. This discussion about the adjustment in arranged marriages is not an attempt to claim that all such marriages are successful. In the past, when family interests were more important than those of the individuals who were getting married, it was difficult to assess the success of such marriages. However in modern arranged marriages the increasing possibility of expressing individual wishes has weakened the extreme authoritarianism of the families. On the other hand, the role of the family members in providing advice and help continues to be highly valued. This type of modified arranged marriage definitely contributes a lot to marital happiness and stability (Kurian 1974).

STATUS OF WOMEN

Among the respondents 36.36 percent felt that women should work only when their work does not result in neglect of the family. Some (28 percent), while considering the question of privileges accorded to women, indicated that they wanted women to stay at home. A number of them were willing to give women equality in social activities. However, 68 percent of the respondents were willing to accord equal privileges to women. Only 12.2 percent considered limiting equality; 55.4 percent wanted women to have equality in inheritance and 29 percent were willing to give women some share in family property. Together they definitely show significant progressive views. The question of widow remarriage is not of importance in Kerala because it was never a serious problem in that area. Curiously enough hardly any of the respondents had widows of marriageable age in their families and there were no objections to widows getting married.

PARENT-CHILD INTERACTIONS

Discipline

Only 19 percent of the respondents expect their children to obey them without question. There is a predominance of people fifty-five years and older who wanted strict obedience. Most of the parents (73.6 percent) expect obedience, but want to encourage initiative. This is a very significant progressive view.

With regard to children up to twelve years of age, 76 percent are willing to allow children to play with all classes and castes; this is really a great stride from about thirty years ago when such free contacts were not encouraged. However only 34 percent are willing to allow children of the opposite sex to play together even at that early age; this is apparently still too progressive for some people. Only 37.7 percent are willing to allow children to speak freely before adults; the traditional respect for age is still fairly strong (Mencher 1963).

There is definitely a change in the area of correcting children now, compared to the experiences of the respondents. While 15.9 percent of the respondents received spankings when young, only 9.5 percent of their own children are given such treatment. While only 43.6 percent of the respondents were corrected through persuasion, 61.36 percent of the respondents use this method for their own children. Generally there is a less strict disciplining of children. Benefits of the progressive attitude can be noted in children who show much more initiative than did the children of a generation ago, who received stricter discipline. Most of the respondents (73 percent) claimed that they have noted significant changes in the general behavior of children, compared to their own childhoods. Of them, 55 percent said that the youngsters demand more freedom. Only 28.3 percent felt that children react badly to stern authority. The majority (51.3 percent) said that their children appreciate friendly persuasion. In general the respondents' negative points of view about their children are not significant.

Children between twelve and sixteen years of age were expected to be put under some control according to respondents, among whom 29.6 percent said the children should not be allowed to meet or associate with members of the opposite sex. This is a conservative attitude, which indicates there are still people who feel freedom for teenagers means disaster. However, 65.8 percent were willing to give freedom under supervision. Only 4.6 percent were willing to give unrestricted freedom. Some (25 percent) wanted their boys and girls to study in separate educational institutions; 40.9 percent were willing to allow them to study in the same educational institution. For the rest of the questions, there was less support. It seems the parents are not all that certain about the desirability of heterosexual contacts in educational institutions. Only 27.2 percent were willing to allow children to mix freely at all levels. Many (61.8 percent) felt that sex education is the responsibility of parents and schools. One should consider this as very progressive in a society in which sex is still not discussed in public. In the last year, the investigator has noted articles appearing in newspapers and popular magazines about sex problems; this is a great step forward. It makes it less difficult to answer the question on the basis of the declining level of orthodoxy.

Most respondents, when questioned about the purpose of education, supported the view that knowledge is satisfying; this was followed by the comment that it leads to the best jobs and the country needs good leaders. The majority of the respondents (53 percent) expressed the opinion that it is better to allow children to make up their own minds with regard to their future career plans. There was much less response to other questions. By and large the answers show the awareness of the parents of the changing times, in which youth should be allowed sufficient freedom to develop on their own.

Some opinions expressed by respondents about youth are interesting:

Too much social contact leads to trouble.

Between nine and eleven years of age girls should be instructed about the problems of dealing with the opposite sex. My wife has given such instruction to a number of girls with good effects.

With the collapse of the joint family system (in which I started) children are better cared for individually and they know their responsibilities better.

The present education only gives some superficial ideas and not all are related to the realities of life.

Before completion of study in educational institutions, children should not be allowed to entangle themselves in politics. Similarly political parties should not use students to achieve their selfish ends.

I am too sensitive to instruct my children on sex matters. But I would prefer my children not to be instructed on sex matters by the present slogan-shouting teachers.

In a poor country like India people should not imitate affluent Western society and youth should avoid becoming hippies.

OLD AGE

When asked about problems concerning the elderly, 68.6 percent of the respondents expressed the opinion that parents in old age should stay with one of the children. The main reason given is affection. The minority, who preferred separate living arrangements, gave as the main reason the desire to be independent. The strong sentiment for having elderly parents in one's own home is still dominant. However, one should note that in Kerala, where single separate houses are the norm, it is still possible to find room for parents. However, in the congested city conditions which are found outside Kerala, having large families including parents under one roof is not easy. Fortunately Kerala is not so overcrowded in urban areas. A typical comment like "it is my duty to see my parents are happy" sums up the feelings of many about their parents.

CONCLUSION

The findings of the study show consistently that the so-called process of modernization is taking root in Kerala. It is important to note that there is a lot of liberal thinking with regard to marriage, family planning, the status of women, the enculturation of children, and the understanding of youth. While these findings are limited to educated people, who are occupationally well placed by Kerala standards, the fact is that the impact of education and rising standards of living among all classes results in their being affected by modernization. Although Kerala cannot boast the highest living standards in India because of the great density of population and inadequate industrialization, there is less disparity between the rich and the poor compared to most states in India, except Punjab. The radical political parties with strong trade union movements have helped to awaken the working class about their rights. However, their demands for rights, even after they are granted, are not always accompanied by greater productivity. Protection and encouragement are given to the scheduled castes and to the less privileged people to democratize the society. All this has contributed to the acceptance of change in the family and to less rigidity in social interaction.

REFERENCES

AIYA, NAGAM A.
    1906   The Tranvancore state manual, volume one. Trivandrum: Tranvancore
            Government Press.
ALEXANDER, K. C.
    1971   Caste and Christianity in Kerala. Social Compasse 17:551–560.

GOODE, WILLIAM
1963 *World revolutions and family patterns.* London: Free Press of Glencoe, Collier-Macmillan.
GORE, M. S.
1965 "The traditional Indian family," in *Comparative family systems.* Edited by M. F. Nimkoff. Boston: Houghton Mifflin.
GOUGH, KATHLEEN
1962 "Nayars of Central Kerala," in *Matrilineal kinship.* Edited by D. Schneider and K. Gough. Berkeley: University of California Press.
KLEMER, RICHARD H.
1970 *Marriage and family relationship.* New York: Harper and Row.
KOLENDA, PAULINE
1968 "Region, caste and family structure: a comparative study of the Indian 'joint' family," in *Structure and change in Indian society.* Edited by Milton Singer and Bernard S. Cohn, 340–341. Chicago: Aldine.
KURIAN, GEORGE
1961 *The Indian family in transition: a case study of Kerala Syrian Christians.* The Hague: Mouton.
1971 "Marriage and adjustment in a traditional society: a case study of India," in *The sociology of family.* Edited by Malfoor A. Kanwar. Hamden, Connecticut: Linnet Books.
1974 "Mate-selection and adjustment in marriage with special reference to Kerala," in *Family in India: a regional view.* Edited by George Kurian. The Hague: Mouton.
LESLIE, GERALD
1967 *Family in social context.* New York: Oxford University Press.
LOGAN, W.
1951 [1887] *Malabar* (Reprint of 1887 edition). Madras: Government Press.
MAYER, ADRIAN C.
1952 *Land and society in Malabar.* Bombay.
MENCHER, JOAN P.
1963 Growing up in South Malabar. *Human Organization* (Winter): 56–65.
MENCHER, JOAN P., HELEN GOLDBERG
1967 Kinship and marriage regulations among the Namboodiri Brahmans of Kerala. *Man, Journal of the Royal Anthropological Institute* 2 (September): 89.
NAMBUDIRI, KATTUMADAN NARRAYANAN
1972 *Illustrated Weekly of India* 43 (March 16):10.
PARSONS, TALCOTT
1961 "Introduction to Part Two: Differentiation and variation in social structures," in *Theories of society.* Edited by Talcott Parsons, Edward Shils, Kasper D. Neagle, and Jesse R. Pitts. New York: Free Press of Glencoe.
POWELL, BADEN
1892 *Land system of British India.* Oxford: Clarendon Press.
RAO, M. S. A.
1955 Social change in Kerala. *Sociological Bulletin* 11(2):126.
WOODCOCK, GEORGE
1967 *Kerala: a portrait of the Malabar coast.* London: Faber and Faber.

Psychological Correlates of Family Socialization in the United States and Korea

BELA C. MADAY and LORAND B. SZALAY

R. Pinot once said that "Every day society is submitted to a terrible invasion: within it a multitude of small barbarians are born. They would quickly overthrow the whole social order and all institutions of the society, if they were not disciplined and educated." In other words, it is socialization, and mainly that received in the family setting, that saves existing societies from destruction each time a new generation grows up.

In the process of socialization, the family appears to be still the most important agent, provider of a mold for the development of the social self. The family has an overwhelming influence in simple societies, and retains considerable influence in complex cultures as well. Bruner (1961), quoting Hauser (1957), said that "we find in many Asian cities that society does not become secularized, the person does not become isolated, kinship organizations do not break down, nor do social relationships in the urban environment become impersonal, superficial, and utilitarian."

The perpetuation of family organization seems to argue for per- petuation of the individual's concept of self and his relationship to the social environment as determined by family socialization. Of course, a degree of adjustment can and does take place during the adult lifespan, but this adjustment is highly preconditioned by the socialization ex- perience of early years. A signal finding of Bloom (1964: 214–215) was that "there is a negatively accelerated curve of [cognitive] development which reaches its midpoint before age five."

Characteristics of cognitive development and intelligence seem to be universal in appearance. What differs is the content and intensity of the family socialization process from one culture to another. The process is universally supposed to enable members of a society to function properly during their adult life within the space and time perimeters of their culture and age. Once removed outside these perimeters and into a culture in which the self concept is differently conceived, where the rules of the game are different, difficulties of adjustment or even of survival may arise.

Francis Hsu (1970) said that social structure is one form of expressing a value system pertinent to the self. He argues vigorously that the self concept is not only acquired through the social structure into which a person is socialized, but also is maintained throughout life by this structure — in other words, that variation in social structure results in varying patterns of self concepts. Thus, in the Chinese, Japanese, and Korean conceptualization the self is always a part of a larger kinship network, while in the American or European concept of self the person stands alone; his place in the family is weakened if not altogether denied after reaching maturation.

In this paper we try to match Hsu's hypothesis against empirical data derived from the application of the Associative Group Analysis (AGA) method to groups of Koreans and Americans (Szalay and Brent 1967). Each culture group (the sample, $N = 150$) consisted of male students (S), workers (W), and farmers (F).

The Associative Group Analysis method can be used to draw inferences on cultural meanings, attitude, cognitive organization, and subjective culture from the distributions of verbal associations (Szalay and Brent 1967; Szalay, Windle, and Lysne 1970; Szalay and D'Andrade 1972; Szalay and Maday 1973). Members of representative samples ($N = 50$–100) produce verbal associations in continued association tasks; they give to selected themes as many responses as they can think of in one minute. The responses are then weighted, based on the rank order of their emission. The weights, beginning with the first response, are $6, 5, 4, 3, 3, 3, 3, 2, 2, 1, 1, 1, \ldots$ In this study, the responses were categorized by United States and Korean coders. The total response scores obtained for the categories, or meaning components, are presented in visual form in the "semantograph." To keep the presentation as short as possible, only two of the components are discussed for each of the themes; the semantographs are followed by tables giving the responses in tabular form.

In analyzing the results, we make use only of associations given to four stimulus words: SELF, FAMILY, RELATIVES, and ANCESTORS, of the sixty words administered to the groups. We first present data relevant to the Korean and American view of self in the context of the family, and then examine a few selected family-related concepts that bear responsibility historically for having shaped family relations and structure.

Semantograph 1.   United States and Korean meanings

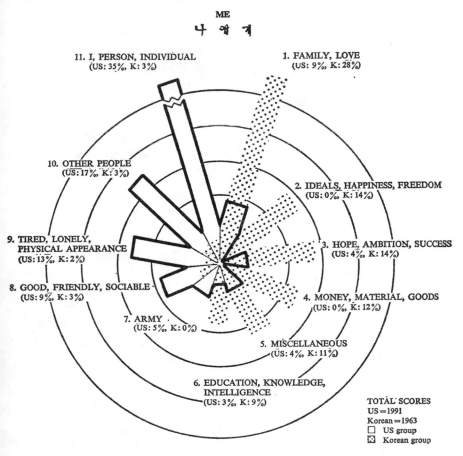

ME

나 애 기

11. I, PERSON, INDIVIDUAL
(US: 35%, K: 3%)

1. FAMILY, LOVE
(US: 9%, K: 28%)

10. OTHER PEOPLE
(US: 17%, K: 3%)

2. IDEALS, HAPPINESS, FREEDOM
(US: 0%, K: 14%)

9. TIRED, LONELY,
PHYSICAL APPEARANCE
(US: 13%, K: 2%)

3. HOPE, AMBITION, SUCCESS
(US: 4%, K: 14%)

8. GOOD, FRIENDLY, SOCIABLE
(US: 9%, K: 3%)

4. MONEY, MATERIAL, GOODS
(US: 0%, K: 12%)

7. ARMY
(US: 5%, K: 0%)

5. MISCELLANEOUS
(US: 4%, K: 11%)

6. EDUCATION, KNOWLEDGE,
INTELLIGENCE
(US: 3%, K: 9%)

TOTAL SCORES
US = 1991
Korean = 1963
☐ US group
⊡ Korean group

Even a cursory view of Semantograph 1, which summarizes associations expressed in response to the stimulus word ME, clearly shows cultural differences of diametrically-opposed character. Korean (K) responses cluster around family, love, ideals, success, and material goods, while American (US) responses show a convergence around the individual and his physical and emotional conditions, and around people other than relatives.

The responses indicate that the Korean respondents view themselves as inseparable from their family group, of which they express a clear concept. It is the family that matters when the self is examined. In association with ME, 28 percent of the Korean responses referred to family and love, compared to only 9 percent of the American responses. Only 3 percent of the Korean responses referred to the self as an individual, in contrast to 35 percent of the American responses.

The American responses stress the first person singular, an individual detached from kin affiliation, standing alone in the crowd of unrelated persons. He feels surrounded by "other people" to whom he has to relate without the assistance of his family. This effort is accompanied by loneliness, concern with physical appearance, and with positive attitudes toward others with whom he may have to team up to assure success.

Both the Korean and the American have to prove themselves in life, but to two different audiences. The American has to "sell" his worth to strangers, hence the emphasis on appearance, friendliness, and sociable behavior; the Korean has to prove himself to his family, to his kin group, hence the emphasis on ambition, ideals, and material goods in the course of striving to achieve success.

The contrast between the American "me in the world," as against the Korean "me in the family" view becomes more explicit when one compares the details of responses to two main components, "family, love" (Table 1) and "person, individual" (Table 2). Immediate family members (father, brother, mother, sister, parent) were emphasized almost exclusively by the Koreans (K $18+29+59+51+6=163$, US 6). Emphasis on emotional ties (especially love: K 154, US 44; and sweetheart, girl, and woman: K $92+52=144$, US $11+6=17$) reflect Korean concern with intimacy in personal relationships. The American concern with self (myself: US 286, K 0; I: US 167, K 46) reflects strong individualistic orientation.

What differences in the family concept are expressed by the responses of the Korean and American groups? Semantograph 2 gives us some indications. Here associations are much more overlapping than those expressed in the responses to the word ME. First-degree relatives received almost the same attention from both groups (K 1577, US 1544), but within this category significant differences exist. The American cluster is somewhat narrower, emphasizing mother and father, while the Korean cluster is broader and includes child, brother, sister. Mother and wife have relatively greater salience for the American respondents, while father has more for the Koreans. These shades of difference seem to underline the differences between the Korean and American social structures, differences in the role of the male and in the father-son relationship, as described by Hsu for the traditional Chinese family (1963).

The broader Korean concept of the family includes members of the

Table 1. Theme: ME; meaning component: FAMILY, LOVE

	US groups			Korean groups			Totals	
Responses	S	W	F	S	W	F	US	K
father	–	–	–	6	–	12	–	18
brother	–	–	–	6	7	16	–	29
mother	–	–	–	11	29	19	–	59
parent	–	6	–	11	12	28	6	51
brother and sister	–	–	–	–	6	–	–	6
family	5	–	13	–	–	–	18	–
home, house	–	12	12	11	8	7	24	26
marry, married	7	–	9	–	–	–	16	–
wife	–	10	–	–	–	–	10	–
husband	7	–	–	–	–	–	7	–
sweetheart	–	–	–	33	29	30	–	92
girl	–	11	–	–	–	–	11	–
woman	6	–	–	22	17	13	6	52
love, lover, lovely, loving, love affair	14	24	6	71	52	31	44	154
life, live	8	–	8	–	4	–	16	4
health	6	–	–	11	–	9	6	20
friend	–	11	9	14	–	20	20	34
Total	53	74	57	196	164	185	184	545
(percent)	(29)	(40)	(3)	(36)	(30)	(34)	(9)	(28)

Table 2. Theme ME; meaning component: I, PERSON, INDIVIDUAL

	US groups			Korean groups			Totals	
Responses	S	W	F	S	W	F	US	K
I	69	40	58	7	12	27	167	46
self	27	–	–	–	–	–	27	–
myself	95	92	99	–	–	–	286	–
mine	11	–	–	–	–	–	11	–
me	5	6	–	–	–	–	11	–
individual	30	–	14	–	–	–	44	–
person	23	21	16	–	15	–	60	15
man	24	14	27	–	–	–	65	–
other[1]	21	–	–	–	–	–	21	–
Total	305	173	214	7	27	27	692	61
(percent)	(44)	(25)	(31)	(11)	(44)	(44)	(35)	(3)

[1] United States: ego, being, one.

extended family, hence, the "relatives" component of the semantograph is twice as large for the Koreans as for the Americans. It is also interesting to observe the greater Korean concern with the older generation, as

Semantograph 2.   United States and Korean meanings

FAMILY

가 족

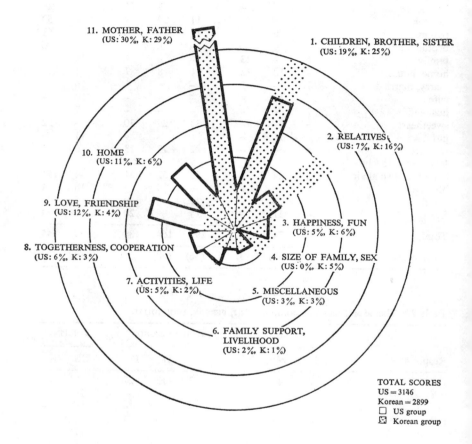

TOTAL SCORES
US = 3146
Korean = 2899
☐ US group
⊡ Korean group

shown in Table 3 (grandparents: K 61 + 74 + 15 = 150, US 13 + 8 + 6 = 27) in contrast to the American concern with children as shown in Table 4 (US 133 + 7 = 140, K 19 + 7 = 26).

Another aspect of the comparison shows that the Korean concept of family lies strictly in the dimension of people (relatives), while the American concept places heavy emphasis on the place (nest) of the family and on the intimate relationships that the family provides.

Another theme for which associations were elicited was RELATIVES (Semantograph 3). Both the Korean and the American respondents identified siblings of their parents and the children of these siblings as

Table 3. Theme: FAMILY; meaning component: RELATIVES

Responses	US groups			Korean groups			Totals	
	S	W	F	S	W	F	US	K
grandmother	3	5	5	24	32	5	13	61
grandfather	–	4	4	21	43	10	8	74
grandparents	–	3	3	3	6	6	6	15
uncle	6	11	11	–	6	7	28	13
aunt	–	12	14	–	–	–	26	–
cousin	–	7	6	–	–	–	13	–
nephew	–	2	–	10	10	10	2	30
niece	–	6	–	–	–	–	6	–
relatives, relation (blood)	47	15	21	34	28	42	83	104
brother-in-law	–	6	–	–	–	–	6	–
family member	–	–	–	30	48	90	–	168
family tree	14	8	5	–	–	–	27	–
Total	70	79	69	122	173	170	218	465
(percent)	(32)	(36)	(32)	(26)	(37)	(37)	(7)	(16)

Table 4. Theme: FAMILY; meaning component: CHILDREN, BROTHER, SISTER

Responses	US groups			Korean groups			Totals	
	S	W	F	S	W	F	US	K
sister	55	61	90	25	49	31	206	105
brother	55	87	84	67	12	81	226	270
sibling	–	–	–	68	98	85	–	251
child, children, kids	54	29	50	7	12	–	133	19
son	–	–	7	–	–	7	7	7
me, mine, myself	–	17	–	31	21	21	17	73
other[1]	–	–	4	5	–	7	4	12
Total	164	194	235	203	302	232	593	737
(percent)	(28)	(33)	(40)	(28)	(41)	(31)	(19)	(25)

[1] United States: baby; Korean: son and daughter, daughter.

the principal group constituting relatives. But here the similarity ends.
While both groups emphasize the family in association with relatives,
we know from previous data that the two groups conceive the family
in quite different terms. This difference is illustrated by the 175 Korean
responses emphasizing "one family" (Table 5), as contrasted with none
for the Americans. The Korean emphasis on family is stronger, and unity
and cohesion of relatives with the family are stressed. The United States
references to family are fewer and do not emphasize unity or cohesion.

The focus and scope of the American concept of relatives is also shown
by the stress given to mother, father, and child. In contrast, the Korean

Table 5.   Theme: RELATIVES; meaning component: FAMILY, KINSHIP

	US groups			Korean groups			Totals	
Responses	S	W	F	S	W	F	US	K
family	84	62	32	33	43	65	178	141
kin, kinship	18	9	32	–	–	27	59	27
related, relation (blood)	48	12	63	–	–	–	123	–
sister-in-law	37	20	11	–	–	–	68	–
clan	–	–	–	–	11	8	–	19
flesh and blood	–	–	–	–	8	14	–	22
genealogical, -table	–	–	–	6	7	–	–	13
family system	–	–	–	9	–	–	–	9
family name	–	–	–	12	28	17	–	57
mother's family	–	–	–	20	49	23	–	92
one family	–	–	–	24	60	91	–	175
Total	187	103	138	104	206	245	428	555
(percent)	(44)	(24)	(32)	(19)	(37)	(44)	(14)	(25)

Table 6.   Theme: RELATIVES; meaning component: MOTHER, FATHER, CHILDREN

	US groups			Korean groups			Totals	
Responses	S	W	F	S	W	F	US	K
father	41	39	68	10	7	6	148	23
mother	47	60	85	7	3	5	192	15
parent	46	18	7	–	–	–	71	–
brother	38	40	44	–	6	8	122	14
sister	38	37	56	–	9	–	131	9
brother and sister	–	–	–	16	33	46	–	95
wife	44	41	18	–	–	–	103	–
child	18	–	–	–	–	–	18	–
son	5	–	–	–	–	–	5	–
daughter	4	–	–	–	–	–	4	–
home, house	16	25	6	–	–	–	47	–
Total	297	260	284	33	58	65	841	156
(percent)	(35)	(31)	(34)	(21)	(37)	(42)	(28)	(7)

concept of relatives does not include parents and children, nor does it include grandparents. All these are too close to the individual to be thought of as just relatives; they belong to the innermost circle of the individual. Especially clear is the contrast in the case of the wife, who is considered a relative by Americans but who is not mentioned by Koreans at all (US 103, K 0) (Table 6). Though summation of a complex range of responses carries some danger, it is interesting to observe the overall difference in emphasis on first-degree relatives: Americans 841, Koreans 156.

Semantograph 3.   United States and Korean meanings

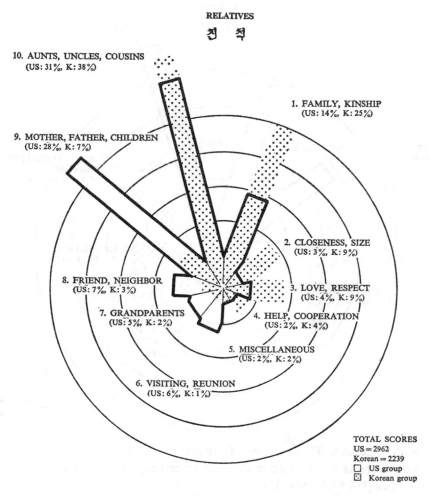

RELATIVES

친 척

10. AUNTS, UNCLES, COUSINS
(US: 31%, K: 38%)

1. FAMILY, KINSHIP
(US: 14%, K: 25%)

9. MOTHER, FATHER, CHILDREN
(US: 28%, K: 7%)

2. CLOSENESS, SIZE
(US: 3%, K: 9%)

8. FRIEND, NEIGHBOR
(US: 7%, K: 3%)

3. LOVE, RESPECT
(US: 4%, K: 9%)

7. GRANDPARENTS
(US: 5%, K: 2%)

4. HELP, COOPERATION
(US: 2%, K: 4%)

5. MISCELLANEOUS
(US: 2%, K: 2%)

6. VISITING, REUNION
(US: 6%, K: 1%)

TOTAL SCORES
US = 2962
Korean = 2239
☐ US group
⊠ Korean group

Associations with the stimulus word ANCESTORS (Semantograph 4)
seem to follow the same pattern as those for RELATIVES: one strong overlapping category, and a number of divergent associations. When analyzed'
the overlapping category also shows significant internal divergence.
Both the Korean and the United States respondents named grandfather
as the single most important ancestor, but the weight of this association
for the Koreans (420) is more than three times that for the Americans
(126), emphasizing also the importance of a male-dominated social
structure, as expressed by the patriarchal family system (Table 7).
The Korean emphasis on male progenitors becomes further apparent
from the fact that they did not associate grandmother or grandparents

Semantograph 4.   United States and Korean meanings

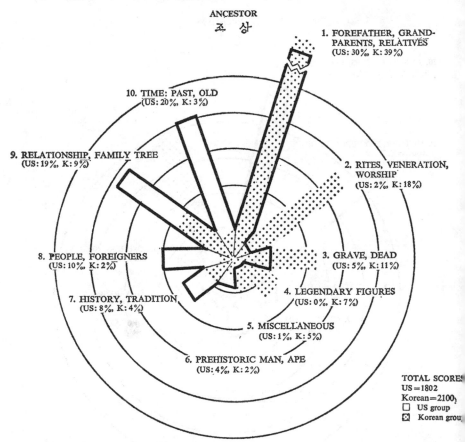

ANCESTOR
조 상

1. FOREFATHER, GRAND-
   PARENTS, RELATIVES
   (US: 30%, K: 39%)

10. TIME: PAST, OLD
    (US: 20%, K: 3%)

9. RELATIONSHIP, FAMILY TREE
   (US: 19%, K: 9%)

2. RITES, VENERATION,
   WORSHIP
   (US: 2%, K: 18%)

8. PEOPLE, FOREIGNERS
   (US: 10%, K: 2%)

3. GRAVE, DEAD
   (US: 5%, K: 11%)

7. HISTORY, TRADITION
   (US: 8%, K: 4%)

4. LEGENDARY FIGURES
   (US: 0%, K: 7%)

5. MISCELLANEOUS
   (US: 1%, K: 5%)

6. PREHISTORIC MAN, APE
   (US: 4%, K: 2%)

TOTAL SCORES
US = 1802
Korean = 2100
☐ US group
▨ Korean group

with ancestors. The American tendency to give equal weight to both grandparents can be seen in their reference to grandparents and grand-mother (US 47 + 88 = 135).

Another difference that appears within this category involves the role of age. The Koreans strongly associate ancestors with elders and seniors, while the American sample makes no reference to age.

When we examine the other elements of this category, we find a strong American association of ancestors with deceased blood relatives, foreign immigrants, historical figures, and history itself. Though blood relations are explicitly mentioned by the United States respondents, ancestors also seem to include all ancestors of the human race, including prehistoric man and apes. These strong references to time and history suggest that the American's relationship to ancestors is vague and weak. For the Koreans, ancestors are more real, more immediate persons, who in-

Table 7. Theme: ANCESTOR; meaning component: FOREFATHERS, GRANDPARENTS, RELATIVES

Responses	US groups			Korean groups			Totals	
	S	W	F	S	W	F	US	K
grandfather	47	42	37	133	157	130	126	420
great-grandfather	11	4	–	23	11	43	15	77
father	11	11	12	9	22	27	34	58
forefather	37	21	17	28	47	50	75	125
grandmother, great-grandmother	–	31	16	–	–	–	47	–
grandparent, great-grandparent	41	34	13	–	–	–	88	–
elders	–	–	–	6	42	34	–	82
senior	–	–	–	–	11	–	–	11
family, family life	55	21	14	12	6	10	90	28
forebears	16	–	–	–	–	–	16	–
predecessor	45	–	–	–	–	–	45	–
other[1]	3	7	–	–	–	23	10	23
Total	266	171	109	211	296	317	546	824
(percent)	(49)	(31)	(20)	(26)	(36)	(38)	(30)	(39)

[1] United States: uncle, parent; Korean: mother, brother, parent.

Table 8. Theme: ANCESTOR; meaning component: RITES, VENERATION, WORSHIP

Responses	US groups			Korean groups			Totals	
	S	W	F	S	W	F	US	K
worship	10	–	–	–	–	–	10	–
respect	6	–	–	27	7	–	6	34
veneration	–	–	–	37	12	35	–	84
serve	–	–	–	11	6	7	–	24
great	–	10	7	–	–	–	17	–
rite	–	–	–	105	58	35	–	198
other[1]	6	–	–	35	–	9	6	44
Total	22	10	7	215	83	86	39	384
(percent)	(56)	(26)	(18)	(56)	(22)	(22)	(2)	(18)

[1] United States: pride; Korean: authority, authoritarian, bow, *chusok*, filial duty, gratitude, solemnity.

fluence their decisions, and in this sense are a part of their daily lives. This connection is reflected by rites, veneration, worship — that is, activities that are obligations which constitute a part of the Korean's daily existence.

Koreans not only see ancestors as involving a somewhat different category of people, but their relationship to ancestors is also different from that of the Americans. A strong Korean association with ancestors is rite, as shown in Table 8 (K 198, US 0), which carries clear religious connotations, followed closely by associations with grave (K 106, US 0). According to Confucian beliefs, ancestor worship, including ritual mourning for the dead parent, is part of one's filial duty. T'ae-gil Kim (1969: 14–15) says that "the filial duty of a son does not terminate when his parents die. Both the funeral and memorial services are held to be very important parts of that duty ... the memorial service is supposed to be held not only for one's own parents but also for one's remote ancestors." The validity of these traditional concepts for the contemporary Korean has been an issue of controversy. The sizable responses in the category of rite, veneration, worship, and respect (K 384, US 39) could positively assist in the settlement of this argument.

SUMMARY

There seems to be ample evidence that even if the family is gradually diminishing in size, its role in the socialization process remains dominant, and its responsibility for maintaining cultural differences, decisive. The concomitants to the transition from extended to nuclear, from rural to urban, from simple to complex life patterns are highly influenced by family socialization, and therefore differ from one culture to another.

Family socialization, influenced by family structure, seems to have an impact on the development of the self concept and is producing culture-specific patterns in shaping the individual's relationship to his social environment. Hsu (1970) suggests that in the Chinese conceptualization, self is part of a larger kinship network, while in contrast, the American concept of self is rooted in individualism.

The results of the study provide empirical evidence supporting Hsu's hypotheses. Associations with the stimulus words ME, FAMILY, RELATIVES, and ANCESTORS show contrasting self concepts as between the American individualist "me in the world" concept and the Korean familist "me in the family" concept. The associations also show differences in the concept of family structure and intrafamily relationships. The American concept is more horizontally-structured and narrower in scope, while the Korean concept is more hierarchical and wider. The American concept is bilateral and sexually egalitarian; the Korean does not exclude female members but assigns them a less prominent status than men. The Korean seems to be more concerned with elders; the American, more with children.

The circles of relatives and their hierarchical arrangement are well-defined in the Korean mind, and relatives are conceptualized as an extension of the intimate group of family members living under the same roof. The American concept of relatives focuses more on the closer circle and tends to include only the closest family members, such as wife, husband, parents.

The extension of the concept of relatives leads to the concept of ancestors. For the Koreans, ancestors are an extension of the family and are viewed as elderly and male, that is, having the qualities that rank high in the social and family hierarchy. Although they do not exist in the physical world, ancestors represent people very much alive and present; they are worshipped, venerated, and remembered, and, thus, are an important part of the Korean's daily living. For the Americans, ancestors are people belonging to the past, historic or even prehistoric, with little or no direct relationship to the living. This association seems to underline the general American impersonal or more abstract conceptualization of ancestors, as compared to the person-centered Korean conceptualization.

REFERENCES

BLOOM, BENJAMIN S.
  1964 *Stability and change in human characteristics*. New York: J. Wiley and Sons.
BRUNER, EDWARD
  1961 Urbanization and ethnic identity in North Sumatra. *American Anthropologist* 63:50.
HAUSER, PHILIP M., *editor*
  1957 *Urbanization: Asia and the Far East*. Tensions and Technology Series. Calcutta: UNESCO (United Nations Educational, Scientific, and Cultural Organization).
HSU, FRANCIS L. K.
  1963 "Kinship and ways of life," in *Psychological anthropology*. Edited by Francis L.K. Hsu. Cambridge: Schenkman.
  1970 *Americans and Chinese: purpose and fulfillment in great civilizations*. New York: Doubleday.
KIM, T'AE-GIL
  1969 "How to harmonize the traditional moral values and present-day needs in Korea," in *Aspects of social change in Korea*. Edited by C. I. Eugene Kim and Ch'angbok Chee. Kalamazoo, Michigan: The Korea Research and Publications.
NORBECK, EDWARD
  1965 *Changing Japan*. New York: Holt, Rinehart and Winston.
SZALAY, L. B., J. BRENT
  1967 The analysis of cultural meanings through free verbal associations. *Journal of Social Psychology* 72:161–187.

SZALAY, L. B., R. D'ANDRADE
1972   Similarity scaling and content analysis in the interpretation of word associations. *Southwestern Journal of Anthropology* 50–68.
SZALAY, L. B., B. C. MADAY
1973   Verbal associations in the analysis of subjective culture. *Current Anthropology* 14:33–50.
SZALAY, L. B., C. WINDLE, D. A. LYSNE
1970   Attitude measurement by free verbal associations. *Journal of Social Psychology* 82:43–55.

Aspects of Personality in a Communal Society

JOHN A. HOSTETLER

The Hutterian Brethren who live exclusively in North America, numbering about 20,000 persons, demonstrate an impregnable sense of collective
identity. They are conspicuous for their lack of identity problems. They
do not share in the widespread symptoms of alienation and futility, nor
are they groping for meaning to ultimate questions. In a recent survey we
discovered that the individual Hutterite thinks of himself as having on the
average slightly more than 100 close friends. By contrast Rollo May has
stated that the typical American has not a single close friend.

The Hutterites are known to us as an Anabaptist, Germanic sectarian
communal group which has survived the Peasants War, the Thirty Years
War, the totalitarian religions and nationalizing influences of several
European empires, and the patriotism of the midwestern plains culture of
North America. Specialized studies have called attention to their mental
health (Eaton and Weil 1955), their prolific population growth (Eaton and
Mayer 1954), their successful large-scale agriculture (Bennett 1967), and
their effective training of the young (Hostetler and Huntington 1967).
Hutterites do not regard themselves as a rationalized experiment in communal living. They are Christian believers equating the practice of communal living with the will of God, willing to be persecuted or die rather
than compromise.

The general pattern of socialization in Hutterite society has been discussed in an earlier publication of the author (Hostetler and Huntington
1967). The life cycle is divided into clearly defined age and sex categories
in keeping with the hierarchical values of the world view. The individual
is taught to be obedient, submissive, and dependent upon human support
and contact. The goals for each stage of socialization are attainable by

virtually all Hutterites. Roles are clearly defined, and each person is rewarded by the smooth execution of his work and by the awareness that his contribution is needed by the colony. A certain amount of deviance is permitted within each of the age sets where the individual learns to relate positively to his peer group.

The thrust of this study is confined to one age stage, the "school children" in Hutterite society. Are there measurable differences between Hutterite and non-Hutterite personality patterns? From our anthropological fieldwork we are convinced there are major differences. To ascertain differences that could be demonstrated, we gave simple inventory exercises to seventh and eighth grade pupils in the schools. The samples included 70 Hutterite pupils (from 36 colonies) from South Dakota and 100 non-Hutterite children from rural South Dakota public schools. The exercises called for descriptive personal data, sentence completion, open-ended questions intended to discover attitudes toward parents, attitudes toward punishment, personal wishes, dreams, fears, and the concept of self. We chose "tests" that were relatively free from clinical or psychopathic questions since we wanted knowledge about normal personality profiles. The purpose was not only to discover what differences there were, but to see if our direct observations could be supported. The technical aspects of the analysis remain in an unpublished paper by Dennis Kleinsasser (1965) who assisted in the study. Some of the major findings follow.

ATTITUDE TOWARD PARENTS

Sentence completion exercises designed to elicit attitudes toward parents were scored in terms of "positive," "neutral," and "negative" responses. The responses of Hutterite boys tended to be neutral, rather than positive or negative, while the boys and girls in the control group tended toward extremes in their attitudes toward their parents. These results are not astonishing in the light of our knowledge of the culture. Hutterite children are socialized to obey their parents and not necessarily to show affection, nor are they to be treated as equals. In both samples girls tended to respond more positively toward their parents than did boys. There was, however, a significant difference between the response of boys and girls in the Hutterite group. Girls responded much more positively to their mother than to their father, while the response of the boys was primarily neutral toward both their father and mother. Negative response toward parents (mostly the father) was highest among the control group. Among Hutterite boys and girls there was little negative response toward parents.

Kaplan and Plaut (1956: 93) also observed a predominantly favorable attitude toward parents.

PUNISHMENT

To discover how children regarded punishment, whether they thought of HOW they were punished or in terms of WHO punished them, we asked this open-ended question: "Because Kathy (Dick) was bad she was punished by . . . ." The responses were grouped according to the presence or absence of a punitive figure or the method of punishment. The punitive figure response indicated a person who was carrying out the punishment such as father, mother, or teacher. A response indicating the form of punishment contained statements such as "he got a spanking," or "he had to stay after school." The two groups of children responded very differently (Table 1). Hutterite children mentioned the punitive figure in their re-

Table 1. Comparison of form of punishment and punitive figure responses among Hutterite and non-Hutterite children

Category	Hutterite (N–70)	Control (N–100)
Punitive figure	57	43
Form of punishment	6	54
(Non-classifiable responses: Hutterite = 7; Control = 3)		
$X^2 = 32.5$	d.f. = 1	P .001

sponses with great frequency. (In Hutterite culture it is important who punishes you, not how you are punished, for Hutterites learn to endure punishment.) The non-Hutterite children responded in terms of the form of punishment rather than the punitive figure. The differences are striking. The punitive figures mentioned by Hutterite children in order of frequency were father, teacher, and elder. In the control group "mother" was mentioned as a punitive figure more frequently than among Hutterite children.

WISHES

To discover the cognitive pattern of aspirations, the two groups of children were asked: "If you had a wish and your wish could come true, what would you wish?" The purpose was to gain insight into the attitudes, thought processes, and values of the children. Again there were striking differences in the responses. Hutterite children tended to wish for material possessions more frequently than did the pupils in the control group. The non-Hutterite children were more benevolent in their wishes in that they wished for things for their parents or friends more frequently than did the Hutterite children. The wishes of the Hutterites centered on things for themselves rather than on direct benefits to others. They wished for adventure or travel more often than did the non-Hutterite children. (From the viewpoint of the culture, the elders are right: the children have a strong desire for property, material possessions, and the desire to be selfish. From the viewpoint of the elders, the age group still needs to achieve a mature Hutterite attitude toward material possessions.) An indirect method of discovering aspirations, through dreams, tends to substantiate the persistent wish for material possessions.

DREAMS

We asked school age children in three colonies to: (1) "Write out on paper the best dream you ever had, that is, a dream you hope will come true," and (2) "Write on another page the worst dream you ever had, and one you hope will never come true. Write out as much as you can remember." The responses were grouped according to content and treated as observable behavior. No effort was made to emphasize the symbolic meaning of dreams. Our interest was in manifest content in light of the Hutterite socialization process. There was no control group for the dream analysis. The distribution of "best" dreams is shown in Table 2.

Table 2. Responses of 57 Hutterite children to "the best dream I ever had"

Category	Schmiedehof		Lehrerhof		Dariushof		Tot. resp.	
	Girls	Boys	Girls	Boys	Girls	Boys	No.	%
Wish for material possessions and candy	6		3	5	2	1	17	33
Positive social interaction (e.g. playing with friends, etc.)	4				1	1	6	11
Trips, visits, hikes	1		9			2	12	24
Going to heaven	1	1					2	4
Ending of a bad dream	1				2	2	5	10
Caught or trapped an animal				1		3	4	8
Hostility toward:								
Interviewer	2						2	4
Siblings					1		1	2
Teacher						1	1	2
Lack of ability to feel pain						1	1	2
Total	15	1	12	6	6	11	51	100

Most numerous were the wishes for "material possessions and confections." Girls responded in this manner twice as much as did the boys. Toys and candy goodies were mentioned most frequently. Next highest in the number of responses were those involving "trips and visits." The trips were usually described as traveling to the home of relatives in other colonies. Trips to nearby cities were also frequent. A considerable number of girls reported dreams of trips to the nearest village post office. Some who dreamed of visiting other colonies wished never to return.

Examples of "best" dreams are these:

A boy and I went down the hill. I ran ahead of him, and I lifted up a plate and saw a big hole of money. The boy with me ran for a pail while I watched the hole. We carried it home to the preacher's house. (Boy age 11)

I once got a camera for a present. The camera was quite big and could develop pictures in two minutes. I was very glad, but then just as I was going to take a picture, I woke up, but I was happy anyway. (Girl age 14)

I dreamed we went to Saskatchewan. It took us a couple of years to get there. The dream was happy because I have a sister down there. (Girl age 12)

The predominance of responses in the category of material possessions must again be viewed in social context. Toys, money, and candy are not denied but strongly controlled. It is not uncommon for children to receive candy and gum from adults who return from nearby towns and cities. Our field observations indicate that again and again, sweets are used as tokens of love and approval by the parent. Children strive desperately for any token of affection, and candy is such a token. It is occasionally withheld by parents when they are provoked. Sweets are also used as a substitute for personal attention. When a child asks for candy he often really wants attention. Toys are given in recognition of work well done, so sweets and toys have social meaning in relation to superiors. Thus the desire for hedonistic satisfactions and material possessions are by no means absent in the pre-adolescent Hutterite but are channelled into socially tolerated forms.

FEARS

To discover the pattern of fears among the children a direct as well as an indirect method was used. The children were asked to write answers to the question: "What are some things that scare you, things that make you afraid?" The answers given by the two groups were very different, interesting, and significant (Table 3). Hutterite children regarded animals as a

Table 3.   Response to fear: Hutterite and control subjects, by percent of category usage

Category	Hutterite	Control group	Chi-square P value
	(N–70)	(N–100)	
Mediators of threat			
Animals	55.7	16	.001
Other persons	4.3	29	.001
Parents	0.0	0	
Teacher	0.0	8	.05
Opposite sex	0.0	8	.05
Peers	0.0	5	
Adults	0.0	3	
Siblings	1.4	0	
Other people	2.9	13	.01
Natural phenomena	7.1	15	
Supernatural	10.0	2	.05
Threats: psychological, social and biological			
Loss of affiliation	0.0	2	
Exposure	4.3	5	
Punishment	1.4	1	
Unpredictable	1.4	10	.05
Injury, illness and death	1.4	8	.05
Dreams/fantasy	2.9	4	
Non-classifiable	11.4	8	

source of fear far more than did the non-Hutterite children. The fears of non-Hutterite children were largely other persons, including teachers, members of the opposite sex, and other adults. Hutterites were more afraid of supernatural phenomena than they were of other people. Children in the control group feared unpredictable happenings more than Hutterites, and Hutterite children were less afraid of bodily injury than non-Hutterites.

These findings again substantiate what is known about the culture from observation. Hutterite children live in a colony environment that is secure and predictable. They know every person in the colony and have no apparent need to fear the adults in their immediate environment. Not knowing people well or intimately may make non-Hutterite children more afraid of adults and their environment less predictable. Children who attend public school in American society are taught from grade one to avoid contact with adults who are strangers.

The indirect method of discovering fears was to ask the Hutterite children to describe "The worst dream you ever had and one you hope will never come true." The response from children in three colonies are given in Table 4. The most frequent responses were in the category of "Strange

Table 4. Responses of 56 Hutterite children to "the worst dream I ever had"

Category	Schmiedehof		Lehrerhof		Dariushof		Total	
	Girls	Boys	Girls	Boys	Girls	Boys	f	Z
Threatening or strange animals	4	3	8	2	3	7	27	48
Threatening or strange people	5	1		1	1	1	9	16
Death or injury								
to subject			1	2		1	4	7
to siblings				1		1	1	2
to family (other than siblings)					1	1	2	4
Inflicted by the subject						1	1	2
Fire (burning buildings)	1	1	1	3			6	11
Fighting or maiming of bodies (general)		1	3				5	9
Good dream that failed to come true						1	1	2
Total	10	6	13	9	5	12	56	100

and threatening animals." Snakes, bulls, and bears were the animals alluded to most frequently. Encounters with such animals were often quite vividly described and involved animals attempting to bite or devour the child, or intending to attack the child while he was in bed. Threatening or strange people did not include any colony adults, but robbers and criminals.

Of the "worst" dreams these are examples:

There was a ladder in our house. Some snakes were crawling up and down. Then they came to me and bit my foot. I couldn't sleep the whole night through. I was very frightened. (Girl age 12)

I dreamed that my mother and all my relatives died and I was left alone and had nothing to eat or anything at all. Then I awoke. (Boy age 11)

We were playing behind the shed and we heard a loud mooing sound. We went to the corral to see what happened. The wild bull was fighting with the other bulls. The wild bull looked up at us and he chased us. He caught up to us and pushed us around on the ground. Finally we got into the cow barn. Then I awoke. (Boy age 11)

The predominance of threatening animals or threatening human figures in the Hutterite dream content may reflect two aspects of the Hutterite culture. First, parents often utilize threats as a coercive measure for the purpose of attaining conformity to Hutterite mores. Threats such as "A bear will eat you" are not uncommon in parent-child interactions. Another observation, with respect to the nature of this parental threat, is intimately related to the Hutterite world view. Animals are often equated biblically with the instinctual or "id" components of the human personality. For the Hutterite, animals, in addition to the threat to physical well-being, also have a parallel threat of consummation by lusts and evils of the flesh. This association is most clearly seen in the use of the snake as a symbol, the referent being the "id" impulses of man, depicted in the Genesis account of the Garden of Eden. Hence, the threat of animal attack carries with it the threat of expulsion from the community of the chosen people; the threatening aspect of attacking animals becomes dual in nature. Perhaps this explains why there is a general disregard for the welfare of birds and wild animals in the community.

A second reason for the preponderance of animal responses may be related to situational determinants; namely, animals are simply a part of this group's environment. Girls especially are threatened by animals. Our field data show that great differences are required between the behavior of boys and girls. Males are more assertive in relation to young girls. In one colony girls have pronounced fears of strange people, perhaps directly related to the many outside visitors to the colony and the excessive cautioning the girls receive.

Hutterite culture has severe sanctions prohibiting aggressive behavior and affective expression, and there is a strong tendency toward socially patterned orderliness. The strong affective expression embodied in the dream content connotes a striking contrast. Such affective expression may merely be characteristic of the pre-adolescent developmental phase. On the other hand, these data may indicate aggressive and affective tendencies which are not permitted overt expression, and hence find expression in the dream content. The findings of Kaplan and Plaut (1956) support this notion. Their investigation revealed that Hutterite adults produced a great deal of aggressive fantasy material. In light of their findings, they felt that the general success of repressed aggression was quite remarkable within the culture.

To summarize, fears may be a reflection of the kinds of controls a culture has over various mediators of threat. Field observations indicate that in spite of the many fears involving animals, the culture has adequate control over the threat of animals. It is also interesting that Hutterite children do not frequently express fear of bodily injury, even though observations indicate that, with the constant movement of heavy machinery, hauling trucks, and other machinery, children are often in danger of being injured.

THE CONCEPT OF SELF

What conception does the communal personality have of himself in contrast to the person who is reared in an individualistically oriented culture? Most theories emphasize that the social self arises out of social interaction. We know that cultural and social interaction patterns are strikingly different in a Hutterite colony from those in the American population at large. The emergence of the social self in the process of socialization is essential in all cultures. To discover the concept of self we gave the two groups the W-A-Y (Who Are You?) exercise (Bugental and Gunning 1955: 41–46), with these instructions: "Ask this question of yourself, 'Who Are You?' Give three answers to this question that are different." This method allowed the person to structure his responses along the lines that are expressive of his needs and with virtually unrestricted freedom. The responses were tallied in twelve categories (Table 5).

Hutterite children differed from other children in the frequency of their responses on these items: age, family, occupation, group membership, and personal description. Hutterites tended to respond according to their age category more significantly than did others. This supports empirically what we have observed, that age (within sex) is the single most important determinant of an individual's placement in the colony hierarchy. Age is a major means by which Hutterites identify with their place in the order of things.

Occupation is important to the self-image. Hutterite youngsters, in comparison to control subjects, chose to define themselves in terms of work responsibilities assigned to them by the colony. That this image of self is so strong in the adolescent period, while the youngsters are still in school just prior to the assignment of adult responsibility, attests to very successful socialization. Most American young people of this age have minimal work responsibility and do not identify with an occupation.

Hutterite children identify with groups more readily than do non-Hutterite children. Being part of a group is important to them, and their answers indicate that a wide range of groups were included in their thinking. They thought not only of themselves as being a member of a religious group (Hutterite), but as a member of a family, of a state, and of a country. This way of thinking is essentially a non-individualized identification, a response that tends to play down the uniqueness of the respondent.

In personal descriptions of themselves, such as height, dress, maturity, or happiness, Hutterite children tended to be neutral rather than positive or negative. Non-Hutterites made more negative comments about themselves: they were more disparaging in their descriptions than the Hutterite

Table 5. "Who are you?" Response categories: Hutterite and non-Hutterite children, by percent and chi-square comparison

Response category		Hutterite Percent (N = 70)		Control group Percent (N = 100)	Chi-square P Value
Name		5.71		3.66	
Age		7.14		1.33	.01
Sex		7.14		6.00	
Family		9.05		5.33	
Occupation		10.00		1.66	.001
Group membership	(18.57)		(7.33)		.001
Religious affiliation		4.76		1.60	.05
General		13.81		5.66	.001
Social		4.29		1.00	
Personal description	(18.81)		(48.33)		.001
Positive affect		10.00		19.33	.001
Negative affect		1.91		16.00	.001
Physical attributes		4.76		2.66	
General		1.91		10.33	.001
Unit		0.00		1.33	
Metaphysical		8.10		3.33	
Interests and special ability		10.48		14.00	
Non-classifiable		10.48		6.33	

children. Responses that indicated an affirmation of belief or religious position (metaphysical) were greatest among Hutterite children.

Differences of the self concept between Hutterite boys and girls showed the following features: boys thought more along occupational lines than did the girls. The cleavage between male-female subcultures is affirmed by our direct observations. Boys can associate with a farm job they may retain for the better part of their life. A man's role in the colony is more clearly defined as a position of worth than the role of a woman. Much of the work of women is done on a rotating basis. The response of Hutterite boys was higher in the categories of personal description, interests, and special abilities than for Hutterite girls.

To summarize, Hutterite children think of themselves as belonging to their colony group through the recognized social order, age and sex, and through work responsibility. To remain a Hutterite is a persistent undertone. Contentment with their reference groups is dominant. Hutterite children tend to think in non-individualized terms among themselves and appear to lack the facility for individualized descriptions of themselves. The strong emphasis of the culture to control overt affective expression is reflected in the concept of the self. Self descriptions tend toward industriousness, in contrast to more hedonistic identifications among non-

Hutterite children. In short, the evidence from these measures of personality underscore the general effectiveness of Hutterite socialization patterns.

These findings are suggestive, certainly not conclusive. The reliability of the generalizations, particularly of anyone doing psychological or educational research, depends greatly on the awareness of the field worker and on the colony's acceptance of him. The young, like the adults in a Hutterite colony, are sensitive to the probing questions of the unwelcome visitor. Although they are often very free in talking with the outsider, they also know when to withhold information or to confuse him.

REFERENCES

BENNETT, JOHN W.
1967 *Hutterian brethren: the agricultural economy and social organization of a communal people*. Stanford: Stanford University Press.
BUGENTAL, J. F. T., E. G. GUNNING
1955 Investigations into self concept: II. Stability of reported self-identifications. *Journal of Clinical Psychology* 11:41–46.
EATON, JOSEPH W., J. MAYER
1954 *Man's capacity to reproduce: the demography of a unique population*. New York: The Free Press.
EATON, JOSEPH W., R. J. WEIL
1955 *Culture and mental disorders: a comparative study of Hutterites and other populations*. New York: The Free Press.
HOSTETLER, JOHN A., G. E. HUNTINGTON
1967 *The Hutterites in North America*. New York: Holt, Rinehart and Winston.
1974 *Hutterite society*. Baltimore: Johns Hopkins University Press.
KAPLAN, BERT, T. F. A. PLAUT
1956 *Personality in a communal society*. Lawrence: University of Kansas Publications.
KLEINSASSER, DENNIS
1965 "A cross-cultural investigation of adolescence in the Hutterite communal society." Unpublished paper, The Pennsylvania State University.

After Coming of Age: Adult Awareness of Age Norms

DAVID W. PLATH and KEIKO IKEDA

Socialization usually has been studied in terms of what happens to children and youth on their way to becoming adults. Once a person has learned society's grammar of conduct the process of socialization is done — or so the assumption has been — and one has "come of age." But adulthood is not a steady state. The grammar of conduct does not apply equally to all adults regardless of age. There is a timetable of appropriateness, such that standards for conduct vary as one moves through the adult life course. To the extent that this is so, socialization continues until one's dying gasp.

Adults are the most common target of ethnographic research but they seldom are studied with the socialization process in mind. (Child rearing gets investigated for what it does to the child, not for what it may also do

Our thanks to various people and institutions for aid of several sorts:

For providing us with copies of the age-norms questionnaire developed by her and her colleagues, to Professor Bernice L. Neugarten, Committee on Human Development, University of Chicago.

For field research funds, to the John Simon Guggenheim Memorial Foundation and to the Research Board and the Center for Asian Studies of the University of Illinois in Urbana-Champaign.

For help with the field phase of the study, to Professor Kōkichi Masuda and his students and research associates in the Department of Sociology, Kōnan University. In particular to Ms. Akiko Kuno and Ms. Kaori Hotta for extensive aid in the often onerous task of coding and tabulating.

For comments on an interim report, to the members of two groups: the faculty seminar on comparative cultures chaired by Professor Tadao Umesao, Institute for the Study of Human Sciences, Kyoto National University; and the Kansai area social anthropology colloquium sponsored by the same university.

An earlier Japanese-language version of this paper is in press in the journal *Kikan Jinruigaku*.

to the rearer.) One aspect of adult socialization is a shift in patterns of consciousness as the self matures and ages. And one dimension of this shift has to do with changes in a person's awareness of age norms.

If age norms merely had to be memorized like a multiplication table, then after one had come of age his awareness of the norms might remain at about the same level for the rest of his life. In fact the older one gets the more he tends to be aware of age when judging conduct. This was documented for Americans in a study done in Chicago a decade ago (Neugarten, Moore, and Lowe 1965); we found it to be true as well for Japanese whom we surveyed in the Hanshin region (Osaka-Kobe) in 1972–1973.

We here report part of the results of the Hanshin survey, compare them with the Chicago study, and comment on some questions that arise with regard to adult socialization and adult awareness.

SPANS OF SUITABILITY

Every society has its Ecclesiastes complex, its notions of the right time for almost any action in the human repertoire. One measure of right time is the actor's age, usually expressed as a span of suitable years (in Japanese, *tekireiki*). People continually make use of such spans of suitability in judging their own actions as well as those of others. "I'm 50, and that's too old for playing baseball." "She's too young to be called Grandma." A recent Japanese weekly magazine article bears the title, "Examining the age of eligibility for a company president — Mitsubishi Heavy Industries' display of rotating the leadership" (*Shūkan Asahi* May 4, 1973).

Neugarten, Moore, and Lowe found that people in the U.S. have a high degree of consensus about such spans of suitability. They also devised a handy procedure for tapping awareness of such age norms, and we replicated this procedure in the Hanshin survey. The procedure consists of stating an action and then specifying three ages at which it might occur. For example:

A woman decides to have another child
   when she's 45   (inappropriate)
   when she's 37   (marginal)
   when she's 30   (target)

The three ages are meant to indicate the outlines of consensus as to the span of suitability. At the TARGET age most persons will approve of the act. At the MARGINAL age a considerable number will disapprove. And at the INAPPROPRIATE age disapproval will be the majority view.

In questionnaire use a respondent is asked to check for each of the three ages whether he approves or disapproves of the act. Responses are given a numerical score (see Table 1).

Table 1.   Sample scores for questionaire responses

Target Age	Marginal Age	Inappropriate Age	Score
A	A	A	0
D	D	D	0
A	A	D	1
A	D	D	3

If a person approves at all three ages (A-A-A) or disapproves at all three ages (D-D-D) then to him age is irrelevant in judging the act, at least within the normal span of suitability.

If he disapproves only at the inappropriate age (A-A-D) then to him age is relevant within the normal span.

If he disapproves both at the inappropriate and the marginal ages (A-D-D) then he holds a span of suitability that is even narrower than the normal one.

Logically, other patterns of response are possible. For example a person might disapprove only at the target age (D-A-A) or only at the marginal age (A-D-A) and so on. This seldom happens, and it seems to be random. In the United States study people approved of the act at the target age more than 90 percent of the time. In our Hanshin study only 7 percent of the responses show an "irregular" pattern of any kind: further evidence of the strength of consensus regarding these spans of age suitability.

The scores may be used in two ways. First, they may be used to measure people's awareness of age norms. For example, if men consistently score higher than women, then in judging conduct men are more concerned about age than are women. Second, they may be used to measure the relevance of age norms to a domain of action. For example, if clothing behavior consistently elicits higher scores than dining behavior, then people are more insistent that we "act our age" when we dress than when we eat.

THE HANSHIN STUDY

Money and time forced us to work on a scale smaller than that of the Chicago study. But in order to bolster comparability we followed the Chicago model as closely as possible in choosing a sample, administering the questionnaire, scoring, and tabulating results.

Sample

Hanshin and Chicago samples are shown in Table 2. These are quota samples, respondents having been chosen by sex and by age. One should be cautious about extending these results to samples drawn on other criteria.

Table 2.   Hanshin and United States samples

Hanshin	Male		Female		United States	Male		Female	
	Number	Percent	Number	Percent		Number	Percent	Number	Percent
Young (20–29)	21	28	26	27	Young (20–29)	50	25	50	25
Middle (30–60)	34	46	53	56	Middle (30–55)	100	50	100	50
Old (61+)	19	26	16	17	Old (65)	50	25	50	25
	74		95			200		200	

Most of the Hanshin respondents live in cities in Hyōgo prefecture, a few in Osaka or its suburbs. Seven out of ten consider themselves to be middle class, or about the same proportion found in most national surveys (Akuto 1972: 63). Two-thirds of the men are in salaried occupations, the rest are self-employed, with the exception of six full-time students and four men who are retired. More than half of the women are full-time housewives, another one-third hold outside jobs. Almost all persons over thirty are married, or have been married, and have children.

Details of the Chicago sample have not been published. Neugarten, Moore, and Lowe say that respondents were chosen to be middle class according to combined criteria of occupation, level of education, and area of residence.

Pragmatically speaking, the Hanshin sample reflects the social origins of students at Kōnan University. Interviews were conducted by Kōnan sociology students and research associates. We assigned them quotas of respondents by sex and age but did not specify social class; instead, we encouraged them to approach kin, friends, and neighbors who seemed likely to cooperate.

This has biased the sample towards higher education. Of ten persons in the sample, five had some years of education beyond high school, four others completed high school, and only one never went as far as high school. Ministry of Education figures are not strictly comparable, but they show that of ten persons in Japan in 1968 only one had COMPLETED a university degree program, another three had completed high school, and the remaining six had never gone as far as high school (Ministry of Education 1971: 41).

Questionnaire

The instrument we used, developed by the Chicago group, contains forty-eight items, each stating an action and listing three ages. The actions are divided almost equally among three domains of conduct: family and kin, work careers, and a more general category of life-style activities such as dress and recreation. The actions also are divided almost equally among three major phases (young, middle, older) of the adult life course. In short, the procedure tries to tap age-norm awareness across the length and breadth of the adult life space.

The respondent is given the list and is asked to mark each item with his "own" opinion. When he has finished he is given a second list — the items on it are identical to those on the first — and this time asked to mark each as he thinks "most people" would respond.

In Japan, the questionnaire was administered individually to each respondent. In Chicago about half the respondents completed the procedure individually and about half in group settings; Neugarten, Moore, and Lowe say that results were the same under both procedures.

Scoring

When tabulating a person's total score we summed his scores for each of the forty-eight items. The Chicago group discarded nine items from their tabulations, and unfortunately their report does not indicate which items were omitted. Comparison would be cumbersome using raw totals, so we have converted the scores to a standard ratio.

This standard ratio is simply the raw total expressed as a percentage of the maximum possible score — like a batting average in baseball. The maximum possible score for all forty-eight items would be $48 \times 3 = 144$. If a person had the utmost concern for age in every situation, then his score would be $144/144 = 100$ percent. If his raw score were 72 his standard ratio would be $72/144 = 50$ percent.

MORE CONCERN FOR AGE IN JAPAN?

Japanese as well as Americans often get an impression that conduct is more regulated by age in Japan than in the United States. One example

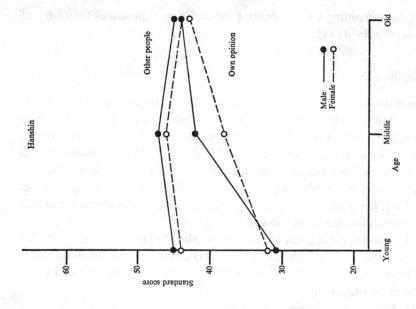

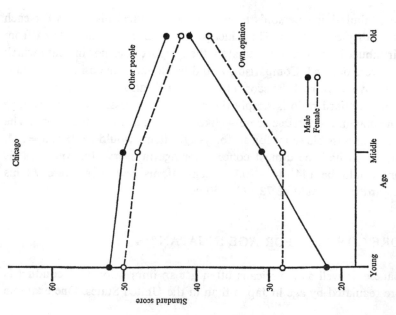

Figure 1.   Age-norm awareness in the United States and Japan

frequently cited is the way polite grammatical forms are used when speaking to a senior in Japanese. Another is the *nenkō* seniority system in large Japanese organizations. But people in the United States also usually speak with respect to a senior, although polite forms are not grammatically tagged. And seniority rules are by no means unheard-of in United States organizations. In short, a "culture-free" test is difficult to devise for such matters, perhaps impossible.

We offer that as a caution, lest Figure 1 be taken as evidence that Japanese adults are more concerned about age norms than American adults are. Figure 1 does indeed show that whether young, middle aged, or old, Hanshin people score higher on their "own" opinions than do people in the United States. The Hanshin people also sense less of a gap between their views and the views of most people, than do respondents in the United States. However, we are far from certain that this reflects any vast cultural difference; much of it may be accounted for by factors operating upon the Hanshin study.

One factor is sample bias. Hanshin respondents, we noted, have had more schooling than the national average. Are people with more years of schooling likely to be more concerned about age norms? To test this we divided the sample into two groups, those with more than twelve years of education and those with twelve years or less. As can be seen from Table 3, there is a slight tendency for people with more years of schooling to score higher, but statistical tests of significance do not confirm the difference. However, it seems possible that Hanshin scores are somewhat higher than those that would result from a random sample unbiased by education.

Table 3. Higher education = greater age awareness

Years of schooling	Average score		
	Young	Middle	Old
Own opinion			
12 years or less	30	41	43
more than 12 years	32	41.5	42.5
Most people's opinions:			
12 years or less	43.5	46	45.5
more than 12 years	46.5	47	45

Hanshin scores also may be higher than Chicago ones because of differences in the items used when computing totals (forty-eight used in Hanshin, thirty-nine in Chicago).

Then too, one cannot hold constant the language nuances and cultural contexts that are linked to an instrument of this type. We put the Chicago questionnaire into idiomatic Japanese and pretested it with several

Hanshin people. Their reactions led us to adjust the age-span in two items and to make minor substitutions in five others. "Run for President of the United States" became "run for a Diet seat." Or another example: "move to a retirement village" became "move to an old people's home" because retirement communities, familiar in the U.S., do not exist in the Japan of today.

Three statements proved puzzling in the pretest and were replaced. First was the statement that "A woman refuses to celebrate her birthday." Although birthday parties are becoming more and more popular in Japan, there is no concept of refusing to celebrate one's birthday for fear of revealing one's age. We replaced this with "A woman doesn't feel like answering when asked her age."

The second situation involved the U.S. proverb "You can't teach an old dog new tricks." We could not find a good Japanese counterpart so we replaced this with a situation familiar in Japan: "A married couple think they are old enough to serve as marital go-betweens."

Third was the notion of a young man wanting to enlist in the Navy. We tried changing "Navy" to "Self-Defense Corps" but respondents still had difficulty with the idea of wanting to enlist. So this, too, was replaced with a more common situation: "A man thinks he's old enough to rest at home on Sunday rather than take the family out."

These factors presumably would influence respondent scores for "own" and for "most people" in the same direction. However, another factor may be affecting the scores for "most people," the differing connotations of the term in American English and in Japanese. Among possible counterparts we rejected *tanin* ['others' but implying 'strangers, non-kin'] as too specific, and *ōku no hitobito* [lots of people] as too vague. We finally chose *seken no hito* ['people in society' or, more literally, 'people in the world']. It readily is associated with *sekentei* [reputation; public esteem] and implies normative judgment on the part of others in one's own society.

In any case what most strikes us about Figure 1 is that trends in age norm awareness move in much the same way across the adult life course in Japan as in the United States. Cultural differences between the two countries seem to have little influence on this pattern of changing consciousness, though cultural differences might produce great diversity if we were to contrast Japan with, say, an East African tribal society that is organized into formal age-sets.

Japan and the United States are both mass industrial societies with vast similarities in technology, standard of living, population structure, life expectancy, and pathways through the adult life course. It seems reasonable to expect broadly similar patterns of adult awareness of age.

One instance of this is the high amount of agreement among people in Japan as well as the United States regarding the major phases of the adult life course.

Neugarten, Moore, and Lowe found that most people in the United States think of middle age as centering around the decade of the 40s, and of old age as beginning in the early sixties (for women) to mid sixties (for men). Other surveys have reported the same: see the summary in Riley and Foner (1968: 311). In Japan one recent study found slightly earlier dividing lines — earlier by two or three years (*Kobe Shimbun Sha* 1973). But respondents in the study all were young adults; had older persons been included the dividing lines probably would have come later.

The dividing lines we used in Figure 1 and Table 2 are arbitrary, of course, but approximate the consensus. The Chicago group's report does not specify a dividing line between middle and old age; the study apparently had no respondents between ages fifty-six and sixty-four although the report is not clear on this point. For Hanshin we chose sixty as the dividing line. Both the traditional coming-of-older-age ceremony *(kanreki iwai)* and the modern social security system use this age as a benchmark.

Table 4. Objective versus subjective age classification

	Male Objective	Subjective	Female Objective	Subjective
Young	21	28	26	27
Middle	34	33	53	51
Old	19	13	16	17

We asked Hanshin people to class themselves into one of the three phases. Twenty-four persons (14 percent) chose a phase other than that into which years of life objectively would place them. Table 4 shows the resulting changes in cells.

Fewer women than men put themselves into a different age category, and those who do are as likely to class themselves with an older as with a younger phase. Men overwhelmingly prefer to put themselves into a younger phase, with one man of sixty-three classing himself as a young adult.

Neugarten, Moore, and Lowe did not report on subjective age classification. Other United States studies show that of ten adults, four feel that they are just as old as their years, another four feel younger, and two feel older (Riley and Foner 1968: 303).

Trends in age norm awareness do not change markedly when we recompute scores by subjective rather than objective age — see Figure 2.

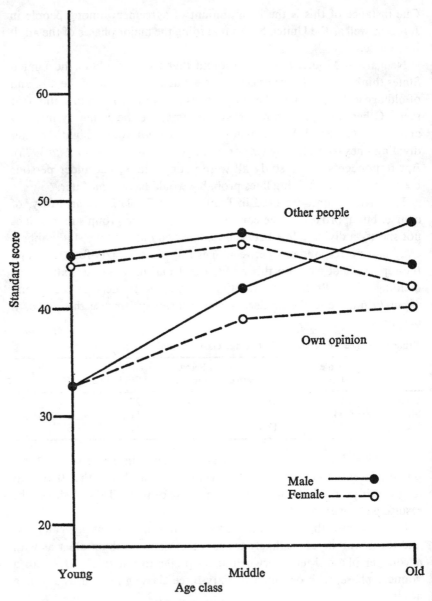

Figure 2.   Subjective age classification scores

But men's and women's scores draw together among young adults and diverge even more widely among the aged.

TRENDS IN AGE NORM AWARENESS

Neugarten, Moore, and Lowe already have noted two trends in changing age norm awareness across the adult life course. We want to add a third trend which, we think, carries the analysis a step further.

Like the Chicago group we set aside historical factors as needing separate study. We suspect that historical drift has only minor influence on life course trends in awareness. But rapid demographic change — longer life expectancy and a larger fraction of the population in higher age brackets — could dramatically alter the relevance of age in judging actions. Novels of a century ago often depict a person of fifty as senile and doddering in a way that today's novels would depict a person of seventy or eighty.

As a Person Grows Older He Pays More Heed to Age Norms

In Hanshin as in Chicago the scores for "own" opinion rise directly and steadily with age. Tested statistically by an analysis of variance the trend is reliable for both samples (F-ratio greater than 0.01).

As a Person Grows Older He Thinks that Others' Concern for Age Norms is More Like His Own

In both countries young adults think that other people are more attentive to age norms than they themselves are, but by old age this gap has closed. Chicago scores for "most people" decline across the years (F-ratio greater than 0.001) but Hanshin scores show no statistically significant trend.

Neugarten, Moore, and Lowe argue that the trend toward greater awareness of age norms comes about through cumulative learning or internalizing of society's standards. One projects this general standard onto "most people" and over the years brings his own views into line with what he thinks are the views of people in general.

Cumulative learning and responses to a "generalized other" probably are part of the process. But if the explanation is plausible it also has much of the bias that has dominated studies of socialization TO adulthood. The difference is that now one has at last absorbed the generalized other by the time one reaches seventy-one instead of by twenty-one.

The Chicago group's explanation assumes that age norms are constant or timeless; what varies is how well or how poorly a person has learned them. This is the usual sort of conformity/deviance model used to explain

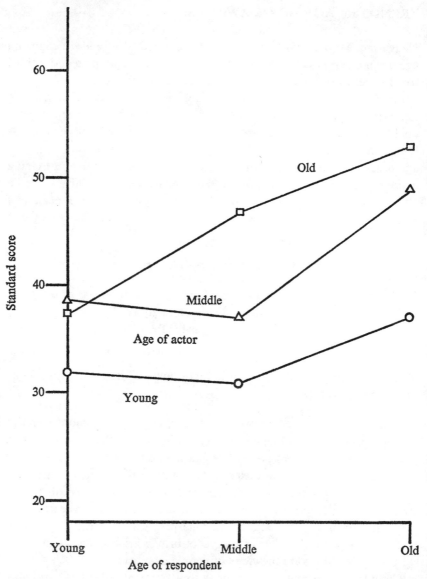

Figure 3.   Age relevance

many kinds of norm-guided behavior. Perhaps some norms are timeless, such as those regulating truth or reciprocity, fairness or honesty. But when age itself is a normative factor the norms may vary with age.

Hanshin data shown in Figure 3 indicate that, in Japan at least, the pattern of norms gives increasing relevance to age across the adult life course. This is a third trend.

The Later an Act Occurs in the Typical Life Course the More One is Likely to Regard Age as Relevant in Judging It

This comes out when scores are tabulated by topic rather than by respondent. We grouped the items into three sets, those pertaining to young/ middle/older adulthood, as determined by the target age of the action. "A woman decides to have another child" thus was classed as middle age since the target age is thirty. A second example was classed with old age: A couple move across the country so they can live with their married children

☐ at age 40

☐ at age 55

☐ at age 70

The average score for a phase then gives a measure of how much age itself is relevant in judging the actions of a person in that phase of life. Figure 3 shows the relevance of age norms during young, middle, and older adulthood as perceived by Hanshin adults in the three different phases. (In tabulating these scores we used respondents' self-classifications as to young, middle, or old.) With minor variations the pattern is consistent. Young adults think that age does not matter as much when judging an action appropriate during early adulthood as when judging an action appropriate later in life. Older adults think the same.

The implication is this: A person tends to become more aware of age norms as he gets older not simply because he has gone further in absorbing society's ideal. He does so also because the rest of the people around him, young as well as old, regard age as more and more relevant in judging his actions. He is responding not just to a timeless ideal, he is responding to a normative curve that dictates increasing attention to age as one grows older.

The conformity model leads the Chicago group to posit a kind of double standard for different ends of the life course. The argument is that old adults judge themselves by their peers because their peers come closest to society's ideal. Young adults, however, do the opposite: ignore their peers and judge instead by their elders. We think it more consistent to assume that young and old alike are responding to their peers in similar ways, but that the normative curve calls for greater age awareness on the part of the older-age self and its peers alike. Older adults are not somehow "more" socialized than younger ones, they are socialized to variant norms.

GENDER DIFFERENCE

In Hanshin as in Chicago there also is a gender difference in trends in awareness of age norms.

As They Grow Older, Men Pay More Heed to Age Norms than Women Do

Note again the curves for "own" opinion in Figure 1. Young adult women score higher than do young adult men. But in later years the male curve rises above the female curve and increases at a more rapid rate. This is statistically reliable for both Hanshin and Chicago samples (F-ratio greater than 0.01).

With regard to "most people," women's scores are lower than men's in both countries but the difference is not confirmed statistically.

Neugarten, Moore, and Lowe do not try to explain this gender difference, other than to remark that young adult women may be unusually conscious of age norms because of pressures to find a spouse while still within the "marriageable-age" bracket. Hanshin data show that:

Both Men and Women Regard Age as More Relevant when Judging Actions by Men than Actions by Women

This comes out when scores are tabulated by the sex of the actor rather than by the gender of the respondent. Of the forty-eight items in the questionnaire, twenty-four specify a female, sixteen a male; the rest do not indicate sex or specify a married couple.

The average score for statements in which the actor is male then gives a measure of the relevance of age for judging actions by men. Figure 4 shows that when the actor is male, scores tend to be higher than when the actor is female. This holds true whether a man or a woman is judging the action. Young women respondents are the one exception: they show more concern for age when judging females.

Perhaps this is further evidence that being of marriageable age induces a special consciousness of age norms in women, though the question needs much further study. In general though, as with age so with gender. If men tend to be more aware of age norms than women do, this does not mean that men are "more" socialized but rather that they are responding to a pattern of norms which prescribes more attention to age in judging the actions of males.

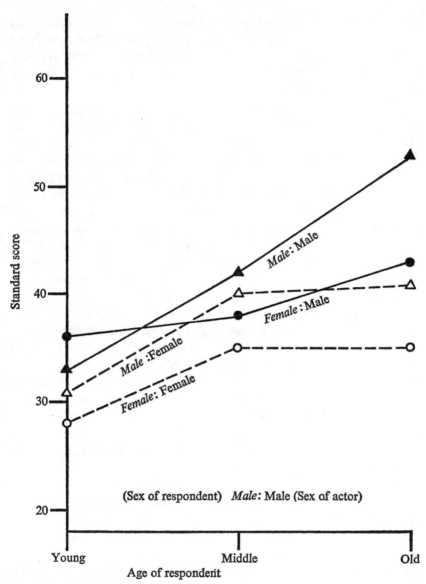

Figure 4. Sex relevance

REPRISE AND PROSPECT

Common knowledge in every society includes a timetable of proper conduct across the life course. Ever since Arnold Van Gennep coined the term early in this century, ethnographers have been attentive to the rites of passage that are part of this timetable. But the less public patterns of changing awareness that are also an important part of the human life course seldom have caught the investigator's eye. The Chicago study by Neugarten, Moore, and Lowe is path-breaking in this regard. We have tried to extend this line of inquiry and want to suggest some ways in which it might be carried further.

Neugarten, Moore, and Lowe mainly concerned themselves with socialization to age norms as a process of cumulative learning of abstract ideals imputed to "most people," i.e. to a Meadian generalized other. To this we add that age norms are not timeless or sexless. In Japan at least, the norms themselves hold that age is more relevant when judging the actions of males than of females, or of older than of younger adults.

A second point, which we only touched upon in our mention of peer influence, has to do with the salience of particular others as well as the generalized other. A person forms his views on age appropriateness in response to the views of an array of others, male as well as female, younger as well as older. Socialization across the adult years needs to be examined in light of this web of normative influence.

For example, does a person adjust his age norms more to those of his peers than to those of his seniors or juniors? Does his direction of adjustment shift with age, e.g. older people perhaps giving more weight to the views of their juniors than their peers? And HOW MUCH difference does it make when the actor being judged is male rather than female, or older rather than younger than oneself? Hanshin data suggest that a person tends to be more aware of age when judging males and seniors than when judging females and juniors. But the questionnaire was not designed to test such differences directly. Further studies should include specific contrasting judgments along these lines.

Spans of suitability also invite more careful inquiry. The Chicago instrument assumes that spans of suitability are "psychologically equivalent" even though they differ when measured in calendar years. This is reasonable enough to assume in a first-stage inquiry. But might the spans vary across the life course? Might they grow narrower in calendar years as one grows older? If so, the higher scores of older persons would then be reflecting not an increase in awareness of age but a decrease in the breadth of the spans of age significance.

It also seems likely that spans of suitability differ for different domains of action. For example spans relating to events in work careers may turn out to be more narrow than those relating to events in family careers. Occupational sociology offers some information on the former, family sociology on the latter. These, and other domains as well, need to be examined within a common framework.

Lastly, what of age norms among the very old? Do people continue to grow more and more aware of age norms after, say, age seventy? If "disengagement theory" is correct — that the very old get nudged out of active roles — then age awareness ought to decline. There should be an old-age "de-socialization" reversing the trends of the earlier years.

We have too few cases to make a good test of this with Hanshin data. The sample includes only twelve people over seventy. Assuming for the moment that these are very old (an assumption wide open to dispute) we compared their scores for "own" opinion with the scores of persons sixty to sixty-nine. Averages proved to be the same for both groups. No doubt it will be difficult to study age-norm awareness among the very old; new instruments probably will have to be devised. But the results could be a valuable test of current assumptions about socialization and awareness across the adult years.

Even after "coming of age" a person continues a lifelong process of normative steering and learning. Age norms are only a part of the vast panorama of life-course shifts in adult awareness. But even preliminary study of changing age norms is enough to suggest that human consciousness shifts not only in response to "material factors of production," it shifts also in patterned and predictable ways across the many stations of the adult life course.

REFERENCES

AKUTO, HIROSHI
    1972   "Kachi ishiki no hen'yō: shinrigakuteki apurōchi," in *Hendōki no nihon shakai.* Edited by Hiroshi Akuto, Ken'ichi Tominaga, and Takao Sofue, 15–84. Tokyo: NHK Books.
Kobe Shimbun Sha
    1973   Ryō no imēji to gengo rensō. *Kobe Shimbun Sha 55* (102) (special issue).
MINISTRY OF EDUCATION OF JAPAN
    1971   *Educational standards in Japan: the 1970 white paper on education.* Tokyo: Ministry of Education.
NEUGARTEN, BERNICE L., JOAN W. MOORE, JOHN C. LOWE
    1965   Age norms, age constraints, and adult socialization. *American Journal of Sociology* 70(6):710–717.
RILEY, MATILDA WHITE, ANN FONER
    1968   *Aging and society*, volume one: *An inventory of research findings.* New York: Russell Sage Foundation.

Delegation of Parental Roles in West Africa and the West Indies

ESTHER N. GOODY

The ethnographic literature on West Africa contains many references to the sending of children to their kin to grow up away from their own parents (Skinner 1964; Oppong 1965; Cohen 1969; Azu 1975; Goody 1961, 1966, 1970a, 1971a, 1973; Muir and Goody 1972). A number of explanations have been offered for this widespread practice, which can never be seen solely as an economic, micro-political, or kinship institution, and often seems to share aspects of all these. In all the societies for which it is reported, the fostering of children by kin also provides proxy parents in cases where the family of orientation has been scattered by the death or divorce of the parents. Such a rescue operation may be termed CRISIS FOSTERING to distinguish it from PURPOSIVE FOSTERING arranged while the family is intact, which is entered into with the intention of securing some benefit to the child, his parents, the foster parents, or perhaps to all.

Many reports on West Indian domestic and kinship organization also include a reference to sending children to kin to be looked after. Typically an infant goes to his mother's mother or perhaps to a mother's sister and is often brought up to regard this foster mother as his mother, using "mother" as a term of address for her and calling his own mother by whatever term her siblings use (see R. T. Smith 1956: 143; Clarke 1966: 142, 179; Spens 1969: 278 ff.). These accounts suggest that the rearing of children by kin in the West Indies tends to be the result of the inability of the parents to provide proper care (whether because they have no joint home or because the mother must work full time), a situation that I have called crisis fostering in discussing the West African material. However, there are also hints of purposive fostering in the West Indies; Clarke speaks of "schoolchildren" who are ostensibly taken into a household to help in exchange for food, clothing, and a chance to go to school. One such child she encountered was treated much like the other children in the house — all of whom helped with chores — but she alone did not go to school (Clarke 1966: 177). Among the Black Carib of Guatemala, González describes the sending of young boys to families in town where they take an increasing share of jobs around the house and learn both literate skills and town ways (González 1969: 54ff.). Again, Horowitz refers more than once to children staying with kin on Martinique in cases where their parents are living together (1967: 49). But on the whole the picture is one of fostering as a means of coping with children of dissolved or nonresidential unions. Indeed, M. G. Smith (1962b: 80) writes as though this were the only circumstance under which children would be sent to be reared by kin, and he treats fostering in the way he does household composition, as a reflex of the mating forms.

In both West Africa and the West Indies, then, children are sent to be reared by kin when the family of orientation cannot, for some reason, manage. And in both areas, fostering is used as a means of widening the education of a child, of providing relatives with companionship and assistance, and of strengthening ties with kin who are relatively well off. In the West Indies it appears to be crisis fostering which is most prominent, while in West Africa purposive fostering is probably more important.

The question of whether the West Indian institution is a survival from West Africa, via the slaves brought to Caribbean plantations, is not relevant at this point. I am concerned with analyzing the present constraints and supports of behavior, whatever its origin.

Although these two regions seem to have very similar institutions in respect to the rearing of children by kin, they behave very differently as immigrants in the United Kingdom. In a recent study in four London boroughs, we have documented the very high percentage of West African children sent to English foster parents (Goody and Muir 1972). Less direct information from several sources indicates that West Indians vitually never send their children to English foster parents (though the local authority may occasionally place children from disturbed or broken homes with foster parents as a welfare measure). Instead, West Indian mothers prefer to send their young children to a "nanny," who takes several children into her home from early morning until six in the evening. Payment is either on an hourly or a weekly basis and the mother is expected to do all laundry for the child and often must provide food. These women are also known as "daily minders." Probably the large majority of women who do daily minding are themselves West Indian and it appears likely (though reliable figures are not available) that the majority of children sent to them are also West Indian.

The problem I wish to pose here is this: Why should two groups with apparently similar traditional institutions for coping with children outside the natal family of orientation react in such different ways to the constraints of living in an urban environment abroad? In order to be able to answer such a question, we must look more closely at both traditional and contemporary fostering in these two areas, as well as at the circumstances of life in London for both groups of immigrants. It may be that the parents of each group are seeking different goals in coming to England and, more immediately, have different reasons for delegating the care of their children to others. Or the choice between forms of child care may simply be one of economics: one mode or the other may be more expensive and require more resources. Or it may be that we have been over-hasty in believing that the traditional forms as they appear in West Africa and the West Indies are essentially similar. Perhaps they function rather differently at a basic level, and in the immigrant situation this difference gives rise to the variations in adaptations to the new environment which we have found.

FOSTERING IN WEST AFRICA

Despite the relatively small number of West African societies for which there are detailed, numerical data on frequency and distribution of foster children, it is becoming clear that this is a pan-West African phenomenon for which no locally appropriate functional explanation will suffice. While it is perfectly true that fostering "fits" stratified societies such as the Hausa and Bornu because it is one avenue for the establishment of clientship relationships, it also exists among commoners in Gonja and among the relatively egalitarian Ga. Similarly, where wives are kept in purdah by well-to-do Muslims, the need to have a child as a link between households and with the market is pressing and is neatly met by those without children of their own by taking a foster child. But fostering is also common among pagan and Christian Yoruba, where no such explanation is appropriate. Or again, in contemporary towns and cities, one often comes across children staying with their kin, helping in the house, and attending school. But African fostering cannot have arisen as a means of avoiding expensive boarding school fees.

I first came upon fostering among the Gonja of northern Ghana, in a town with no school and where few children in the kingdom, and scarcely any adults, had had a chance to attend one. The Dagomba, also of northern Ghana, make use of fostering to train a daughter's child in the traditional skill of the paternal *dang* (Oppong 1969b). The neighboring Gonja have many of the same skills and a high incidence of fostering, but only rarely do they use the institution as the basis of apprenticeship. In the west of the kingdom, the Gonja do, however, view the sending of a son to grow up with his mother's brother as one form of arranging for the mother's care when she eventually returns in old age to her natal kin. The son already there can give her a home and can farm for her, in addition to the support which her brother is morally obliged to contribute. The spatial distribution of marriages is narrower in eastern Gonja, and a wife's retirement is less likely to mean her departure to a distant village. Perhaps for this reason, the fostering of a son with his mother's brother is much less common in the eastern divisions.

One could go on citing similarities and differences between local variations of fostering in West Africa. The general point should be clear — there is a wide range of specific reasons or functions, each of which makes excellent sense in its own context but no one (or indeed several) of which can be made to account for the widespread occurrence of institutionalized fostering of children by kin in West Africa.

Yet if one considers other cultural areas, this practice is strange enough to warrant some kind of explanation.[1] Few Europeans or Americans would readily take a sibling's or cousin's child into their home for several years, or send their own son or daughter to live with an aunt or grandparent from the age of five to adulthood. Purposive fostering, the placing of children with kin to fulfill one's obligations and at the same time gain for them the opportunity to grow up in a different family, often in a different town, does not seem to occur in Indo-European societies. There are partial equivalents of a functional kind (*compadrazgo* and other forms of fictional kinship) but rarely the actual removal of a boy or girl for his entire childhood and adolescence, as we commonly find in West African societies.

Why is there this very general difference between the two sets of societies? What kind of underlying factor is common to all the various West African groups which have different particular reasons for fostering their children,[2] groups which differ widely in language, social structure,

---

[1]   Though by no means unique, see studies of fostering and adoption in Eastern Oceania in Carroll (1970), as well as the Caribbean material.

[2]   There is another, equally important question with which I am not concerned here: What accounts for the fact that fostering is institutionalized in some West African

political organization, and religious institutions? The simple answer is that fostering reflects the claims, rights, and obligations of members of an extended kin group. Given the norm that kin need to share rights and obligations over resources, the fostering of children becomes only a special case of such sharing.

This is explicit for the Gonja of Northern Ghana. Rights of siblings over one another's children are expressed in two models. One model allocates the first daughter of a marriage to the fathers's sister as a foster daughter, in recognition of her role in establishing the bride in her new home. The father's sister will be informed of the birth of this first daughter; she should then send *kola* to the naming ceremony and provide waist beads for the little girl. When the child has reached the age of sense (*e kø kinyesheng*), the father's sister comes with a gift of cloth for the mother and for the child and takes the little girl home with her. She will remain with her aunt until she is ready to marry, suitors paying their respects both to the foster mother and the true parents. There is a term of reference for female foster parent, *tchepe*, but the child uses the term for father's sister.[3] She never calls the father's sister "mother" or ceases to call her own mother by the familiar *maa* form for mother.

The other model for Gonja fostering designates the second or third son as a foster child of the mother's brother. A man who wishes to ensure his rights over a sister's son may insist on paying the expenses of the naming ceremony which takes place seven days after birth. Otherwise he will come to "beg" for the child some time during its infancy or early childhood. As with a female foster child, the boy does not join his foster parent until he is considered old enough to "have sense," which means around the age of six or seven. Once a boy has joined his foster father he should remain until old enough to marry, learning from him the skills of farming, hunting, and house building which are necessary for all adult men. The foster father ought to help the youth to marry or he may offer him a horse or a gun rather than a wife. Thereafter the boy may either remain with his mother's brother or return to his father; among Muslims and members of the ruling estate, men virtually always return in the end

---

societies, while it appears to be absent from others? This question is more difficult than might appear, because our work in London suggests that even those groups which do not foster in West Africa are prepared to do so in the United Kingdom. In other words, the underlying factor is present in these ostensibly non-fostering groups too, but there appears to be some alternative institution which takes the place of fostering within the traditional system. But all the prerequisities are there, in both types of West African society.

[3]   Or, if with another relative, the kin term for that person is ordinarily used.

to their father's town, but commoners may opt to remain with a mother's brother. The term of reference for male foster parent is *nyinipe*, but the appropriate kinship term is used in address and not the term for father, which continues to be applied to the real father.

In practice, a wide range of relatives serve as foster parents in Gonja, but these two models are the stated forms that act as charters for other claims. Siblings all say that they own (*wø*) each other's children, which means both that they are responsible for them, and that they have claims over them. Unless there is some reason why the parents cannot manage their children, perhaps from poverty, lack of discipline, or the break-up of the natal family of orientation, the initiative in arranging fostering is usually left to the would-be foster parent. Only when he or she presses his rightful claim will the child actually be sent. Occasionally, a child is sent to an office holder or to a Quranic teacher. In these cases it is more likely to be the goals of the parent which are the critical factors.

It is characteristic of West African societies that the "sibling group" is not thought of as confined to children of the same mother and father. This inclusiveness is usually reflected in the terminology, which designates the children of sisters (in matrilineal systems) or brothers (in patrilineal systems) or of brothers and sisters (among the bilateral Gonja) as themselves siblings. For instance, Fortes (1949) writes of Tallensi brothers (*sunzøp*) as in some contexts being all members of the agnatic lineage of a man's own generation. In Gonja, ALL of a person's relatives of the same generation are either "older sibling" or "younger sibling." Claims on the children of classificatory siblings are also successfully made in Gonja, though only rarely when the relationship is more distant than that of first cousins. It would seem to be, in those cases where the terminology is open-ended and the norms of siblings' rights and obligations very generally phrased, that the recognition of claims over children serves to define the limits of effective obligation. Rearing a sibling's child has this function because, in addition to the formal moral obligation of kinship, the fostering relationship itself creates what I have elsewhere called the "reciprocities of rearing" (Goody 1971b). That is, specific, reciprocal obligations of care and support are built up during childhood; the foster parent is seen as looking after the child, feeding and training it, and these acts create a debt which the child must later be prepared to repay. Thus, where second or third order relationships might cease to be considered binding in and of themselves, when they are reinforced by fostering, a second set of obligations comes into play which is compelling in its own right. Furthermore, the fostered child grows up in a household of classificatory siblings (the foster parents' children) with whom he or she is on effective terms of full sibship, rather than the more distant relationship which exists between distant kin who meet only occasionally.

In traditional West African societies, then, fostering depended on claims made against, and honored by, kin. At the same time the sending of foster children between elementary families served to strengthen the bonds between kin by superimposing specific claims on the more general ones which tend to define the roles of distant relatives. An illuminating comparison can be made with systematically practiced cross-cousin marriage; indeed the diagram Yalman uses (Figure 1) to indicate the

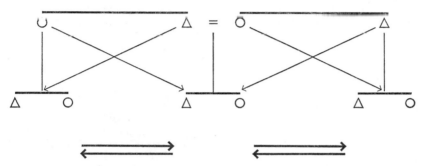

Figure 1. The interconnection and lateral extension of claims for cross-cousin marriage: Kandyan Sinalese (Yalman 1967:154).

claims of cross-cousin marriage in a Kandyan Ceylonese village would serve equally well to illustrate the claims of fostering. As with cross-cousin marriage, it would be a mistake to expect that fostering will always occur between the children of primary kin (see Goody 1973).

Recent Fostering in Northern Ghana

In Table 1 data on the relationship of foster parents are given from four different studies, representing all seven communities from eastern, central, and western Gonja. The sex of the fostered child is given in brackets for each study. Several points emerge from these figures. First, in all the studies, a very substantial proportion of foster parents come from the parental generation (between 39 percent and 59 percent). This should be borne in mind for comparison with the West Indian pattern of fostering. Next, if we compare the proportion of male and female foster children resident with a grandparent (real or classificatory), we find that it is the girls who are more likely to be sent to someone in their grand-

Table 1.   Gonja (northern Ghana): generation of foster-parent for four samples

| | Foster parent is of: | | | | |
Data from:	Grand-parents' generation	Parents' generation	Child's generation	Not kin	Total number
Buipe census[a] (children, male and female)	13 (38%)	20 (59%)	1 (3%)	0	34
Kpembe core sample[b] (children, male and female)	15 (48%)	12 (39%)	4 (13%)	0	31
Bole/Daboya sample[c] (adults, female)	39 (51%)	35 (45%)	3 (4%)	0	77
Men's marriage survey[d] (adults, male)	13 (20%)	37 (57%)	4 (6%)	11 (17%)	65
	80 (39%)	104 (50%)	12 (6%)	11 (5%)	207 (100%)

[a]   Old Buipe (1956).
[b]   These are all the fostered children in two sections of the divisional capital of Kpembe (eastern Gonja) (1964).
[c]   The Bole sample consisted of all adult women in randomly selected compounds in the western Gonja divisional capital of Bole; the Daboya sample consisted of all the adult women in nine selected compounds in the central Gonja divisional capital of Daboya (1965).
[d]   This survey was carried out in three divisional capitals of eastern, central, and western Gonja, and surrounding villages. The informants were all adult men in selected compounds (1966).

parents' generation (50 percent), while for boys this only happen 20 percent of the time. This same pattern is found in some of the southern Ghana samples. The sending of girls to a "grandmother" fits with their training in a domestic role, for they are expected to take over household tasks as well as provide companionship for the old women. Old men, on the other hand, are fed and looked after by their daughters or daughters-in-law, and a boy cannot be expected to fill a man's economic role. Finally, only in the men's marriage survey were there children sent to foster parents who were not kin. Indeed, only in two of the three communities represented in the men's marriage survey did this occur. These boys went either to join the household of a chief (six cases) or to a Quranic teacher (five cases, all in western Gonja). No girls went to non-kin in any of the communities studied.

Fostering in Southern Ghana

I must stress at the outset that most of my own work in West Africa has been with a relatively remote group, the Gonja, on whom the industrial age has hardly begun to make an impact. The coastal peoples to the south have, on the other hand, been within the orbit of European trade and all that this implies since the beginning of the sea-borne trade with Europe in the late fifteenth century. I have been able to do little work directly with coastal peoples apart from making brief surveys in four communities representing three different language groups in southern Ghana. The following remarks draw on these surveys, as well as inter-views with West Africans in London, and on two books: Oppong's *Marriage in an Akan elite* (1974) and Azu's *The Ga family and social change* (1975). Although the documentation for the coastal areas is in-complete, the picture is fairly clear.

Briefly, there appears to be a tendency to shift from fostering by kin to the arrangement of fostering with strangers who can provide either training in modern skills, or a chance to gain familiarity with urban, Western ways. In the Ewe, Krobo, and Fanti communities I looked at briefly in southern Ghana, daughters were sent to live with and "serve" women who baked bread for sale, seamstresses, and traders; sons went to fishermen, carpenters, fitters, and masons. Where such teachers were available within the kin group they were selected for preference, but in a number of cases they were not and instead an arrangement was made with a friend or someone of good reputation who could train the child. My impression was that availability of a suitable master could determine the choice of skill to which the child would be apprenticed. For Ga boys, there appears to be a similar pattern of choice between a kinsman or a local expert of good repute (Azu 1975).

For girls, in addition to skills in sewing, baking, and trading, there has evolved the institution of the housemaid. I say evolved, because there does not appear to have been anything similar in the traditional societies of West Africa, with the possible exception of girls who were lent to a creditor as surety of a debt.[4] These children (they might also be boys, though apparently this was less common) are referred to in the classical ethnographic literature as having been "pawned," and there seems to be a word in many if not all of the West African languages to distinguish this practice.[5] Such pawns worked in the household of the creditor until the debt was redeemed. There might ultimately be an agreement to let the girl be married there in exchange for cancelling the debt, but casual

[4]   A further possible exception may have occurred in traditional Yoruba society. Informants on the London Survey sometimes distinguished between a relative sent as an *alagbato* [foster child] and an *omodo* [unrelated child] who was considered of inferior status. This was likened by a few informants to a slave.
[5]   In *Gbanyito* the verb is *terma*, while the verb which applies to fostering is *belo* [to rear, or bring up].

sexual relations between the girl and her master were usually specifically forbidden.

The modern housemaid may be a relative of her master or mistress. This is preferred and is common (Oppong 1974). However, many appear to be unrelated and to have come for a few pounds paid monthly or annually to the parents of a young girl[6] or, when she is older, to the girl herself. Such girls tend to stay only a few years and then either marry or move on to some form of more remunerative employment, perhaps to an apprenticeship where they can learn a more saleable skill than housekeeping. There is a definite pattern of recruiting girls in rural areas to work as housemaids in the cities of Ghana.

It would seem that, as the skills and experiences which parents desire for their children become more diversified, they begin to look beyond their kin to find someone to train them. Fostering by kin is gradually transformed into various forms of apprenticeship and domestic service. At the same time that kin are proving less able to meet these needs, there is a movement towards limiting the acknowledgement of kinship claims by those whose own education has led to a standard of living far above that of most of their relatives. While there is evidence that parents and full siblings still successfully request assistance in regular and substantial amounts, among the educated elite there is no longer the same pattern of honoring the claims of distant kin, even when made according to traditional norms (Oppong 1969a).

Recent Fostering in Southern Ghana

The data in Tables 2 and 3 come from three very brief surveys in southern Ghana. The purpose of the surveys was to discover whether the Gonja were unusual in giving such weight to fostering by kin in the rearing of their children, or whether similar practices might be found in other West African societies. Time and resources did not allow me to spend more than a few days in either the Ewe or the Fanti community, while the Krobo survey was conducted through local assistants after I had returned to England. The main weakness of the material lies in its narrow focus. The interviews with Ewe and Fanti were necessarily conducted through an interpreter, and the central question, once the constitution of the informant's sibling group had been established, was: "Who reared ... (each sibling in turn)?" Although this was further broken down

[6] Ages can only be very roughly guessed from Busia (1950), my main source on this point. The youngest girls may be ten or twelve.

Table 2. Relationship between child and foster parent in three southern Ghana societies: boys[a]

Foster parent is of:	Societies			
	Fanti	Ewe	Krobo	Total
Grandparental generation	0	2 (18%)	1 (1%)	3 (2%)
Parental generation	39 (75%)	7 (64%)	53 (74%)	99 (73%)
Child's generation	11 (21%)	2 (18%)	11 (15%)	24 (18%)
Not kin	2 (4%)	0	7 (10%)	9 (7%)
	52 (100%)	11 (100%)	72 (100%)	135 (100%)

Table 3. Relationship between child and foster parent in three southern Ghana societies: girls[a]

Foster parent is of:	Societies			
	Fanti	Ewe	Krobo	Total
Grandparental generation	8 (17%)	6 (23%)	2 (3%)	16 (11%)
Parental generation	26 (54%)	10 (38%)	41 (60%)	77 (53%)
Child's generation	6 (12%)	7 (27%)	10 (14%)	23 (16%)
Not kin	8 (17%)	3 (12%)	17 (24%)	28 (19%)
	48 (100%)	26 (100%)	70 (101%)	144 (99%)

[a] These data are based on interviews in which the rearing histories of all members of the informant's full sibling group were recorded. In Ewe and Fanti communities the informants were selected from people known to my sponsors, and they form what can only be described as an arbitrary sample. The Krobo sample consists of all adults in every tenth compound on selected streets of the two largest Krobo towns. The figures exclude fifty-six cases in which the generation of the foster parent could not be determined, although he or she was stated to be a relative.

by periods in infancy, childhood, and adolescence, a full exploration of the rearing situation was not possible. I am persuaded that the Krobo interviewers confined themselves almost entirely to the formal interview schedule. Informants were adults, and the information thus refers to childhood of from twenty to sixty years ago (dating from 1972).

What I did not anticipate in planning these surveys was the shift from kin to non-kin fostering. Hence when exploring the vocabulary of child rearing in the vernacular in order to standardize the questions prior to interviewing, I did not ask about how such apprentice-fostering was referred to. The figures in Table 2 particularly, on the non-kin fostering of boys, do not fit with observations on the sending of boys to learn such skills as carpentry, driving, automotive mechanics, and so on. While this may be a very recent pattern, it seems more likely that informants did not consider these apprenticeships as "rearing" when the master was not a kinsman. Those few cases which do appear in Table 2

may be the ones in which a change of residence occurred in the context
of apprenticeship, thus more closely approximating the kinship fostering
pattern, in which the foster parent expects to have the domestic services
of the child as part of the relationship.

In these southern Ghana samples a substantially higher proportion of
girls than boys is sent to non-kin foster parents. Some of these girls are
learning trades like baking or sewing, while others are acting as housemaids. The fact that they were considered as being reared by their
mistresses may be related to the domestic nature of the skills they were
learning and to the undoubted fact that their training involves helping
their mistress in her household work as well as, in some cases, learning
a particular skill.

Both boys and girls in the southern Ghana samples are sent relatively
infrequently to grandparents to be reared. The contrast with the figures
for Gonja (northern Ghana) is pronounced (Table 4), and the difference

Table 4.   Generation of foster parent: comparison of northern Ghana (Gonja) and
southern Ghana, combined samples.

	Foster parent is of: Grand-parents' generation	Parents' generation	Child's generation	Not kin	Total number
Gonja	80 (39%)	104 (50%)	12 (6%)	11 (5%)	207 (100%)
Southern Ghana	19 (7%)	176 (63%)	47 (17%)	37 (13%)	279 (100%)

between this pattern and that of the West Indian samples is extreme
(Table 7). There are some differences between the different southern
Ghana samples in frequency of fostering by the grandparental generation
which I cannot adequately discuss here. There is a regular tendency for
girls in all samples to go more frequently to their grandmothers than
boys to their grandfathers. This, as I suggested in discussing the Gonja
data, seems likely to be related to the domestic nature of the fostered
girl's training.

The great majority of the boys in the southern Ghana samples went to
a sibling of either the father or the mother (73 percent). This preference
for a foster parent of the parental generation appeared in some of the
Gonja samples, and it is much clearer here. For the girls in the southern
Ghana sample also, the parental generation provided by far the largest
class of foster parents (53 percent), with the next largest group being
unrelated (19 percent). A substantial minority of both boys and girls
(18 percent and 16 percent, respectively) went to an elder sibling (own or

classificatory). These proportions are much higher than the 6 percent average for the Gonja samples and very likely reflect the fact that older siblings who are educated or have learned a trade are more likely to be seen as able to contribute to a child's development than older siblings belonging to the pre-industrial, pre-bureaucratic world of northern Ghana in the first half of the twentieth century.

While both southern and northern Ghanaian samples reflect a preference for selecting foster parents from the parents' own generation, there is a relatively greater emphasis in the north on sending a child to a grand-parent and in the south on making use of siblings and unrelated foster parents. At the time these children were being fostered, between 1910 and 1950, northern Ghana scarcely participated in the economic differen-tiation and educational stratification of modern society. The south, on the other hand, had begun to enter the age of technology.

In seeking to understand the shift away from grandparents as foster parents in favor of siblings and strangers, the critical factor is the balance between fostering as a reflection of rights vested in kinship roles and fostering as a mode of education. Both these aspects coexist in traditional Gonja fostering (Goody 1973). However, with a shift to sibling and non-kin fostering the element of kinship rights becomes secondary to the educational functions of fostering. A child is not sent to an elder sibling (and certainly not to a stranger) because they have a RIGHT to a lien on the child's labor and companionship. On the other hand, this was a significant element in the request for a foster child in traditional Gonja.

It would appear that in the modern world of southern Ghana, rights vested in kinship roles have become less compelling than the need to help children to make their way in the new occupational and social milieu. Indeed, the shift probably reflects the diminishing role played by the senior generation in helping youth to become established in the adult world. Instead of age in itself leading to positions of importance, relatively restricted skills, especially those based on advanced education, become the critical factor. In all the Ghanaian samples there is a pronounced emphasis on fostering by parents' siblings. This emphasis reflects recipro-cal rights and obligations acknowledged between both full and classifica-tory siblings.

I have argued thus far that traditional fostering by kin, while it ful-filled many specific functions which varied with the form of each society, also reflected the strength of claims which members of a kin group could successfully make on one another. As the skills demanded for full participation in an increasingly diversified economy grow more complex, with success in school and the training of new crafts of growing importance, it is no longer possible for just any adult to provide the model and the training which are necessary for the child to take his place in society. Where no kinsman is available, an arrangement for the child's education must be made on another basis. The usual pattern is that the child's labor over a period of several years pays for the training he reccives, though a lump sum may be given to the teacher at the beginning or at the end of the training period.

In this transformation of the traditional institutions of fostering we see two aspects emphasized: (1) the experience is sought for the child as a way of helping prepare him for a more successful adulthood and (2) the labor of the child is a major part of the recompense for the training received, but money may pass either to the "teacher" or to the parents, in lieu of the kinship obligation which would once have sufficed. If there is a highly educated member of the family, a teacher or a clergyman, or one who is in another kind of important job, he will often be asked to take on children, since it is felt that he is in a position to give them a better training than others would be. It is not only specific skills which are sought but a facility with the written and spoken word and with Western ways.

Fostering by West Africans in London

How is all this related to the fostering of children by West Africans in London? There are many practical reasons why fostering might appeal to this group: they often live in cramped conditions and do not have room for small children; the mother may need to work full time to help support the father's studies; often, the mother is herself trying to train in addition to her job and, thus, needs to be free in the evenings; the father is usually studying as well as working and needs a quiet home in which to read; many mothers are training as nurses and need to be free for night duty or even to live in the hospital. Yet English or American parents in a similar situation would simply not consider fostering a child with strangers as an appropriate solution.

It should be made clear that West African parents are often distressed to have to part with their very young children, and they take elaborate pains to ensure that the families to whom they go are clean and kind and that they will feed and care for them properly. But basic assumptions of the two cultures differ. A cultural paradigm as to the appropriateness of delegating child rearing underlies West African thinking on this subject. And, though there is evidence that Europe once shared at least some of the same ideas,[7] it has ceased, with the influence of writings of psychologists from Freud to Bowlby, to seem credible to the West. One part of the explanation of the high incidence of fostering by West Africans in London, then, is that parents, who are trying to fill several other roles as well, share a cultural view of parenthood which approves of delegating certain aspects of this role.

Another part of the explanation lies in the traditional definition of fostering as character building, as an educational process. This educational side of fostering has been increasingly emphasized in recent years as the institution has been adapted to modern conditions. When faced with a child care problem in England, the West African parent asks: How can I arrange both for the care and for the education of my child? Since it is very young children who constitute the main problem,[8] language and domestic culture are the primary things the child is expected to learn. A number of parents in our intensive study commented explicitly on the advantage they hoped their children would gain at school from having spoken English as a first language.

A different sort of light is shed on this aspect of fostering in England by a question which we asked the parents on the extensive survey: "If you were living in West Africa now, or when you go back, would you consider fostering your child?" While some parents replied that they would have to do so if a relative was in need, the great majority said that there were no circumstances under which they would do this. And much the most common reason given was: "There is no one there better able to rear him than we are." That is, relative to their kin and the people they knew, these budding elites did not feel there was anyone who could train their children any better than they could themselves. Yet this judgment apparently does not apply in the United Kingdom, for, while living in London, 50 percent of this sample of nearly 300 couples had either previously fostered a child with an English family (25 percent) or were currently doing so (25 percent). Their firm rejection of fostering in

---

[7] Morgan (1944), in writing about the Puritan family in seventeenth-century New England, records the placing of daughters in the houses of relatives and friends to learn housecraft, while apprenticeship began at eleven or twelve and lasted for a minimum of seven years, with the master having complete control over the movements of the youth, in and out of working hours. See also Ariès (1962:374) on the prevalence of sending children out to wet nurses in France in the seventeenth century. Systematic searching would almost certainly reveal many more examples from a period when the boundaries of the family were not yet so tightly drawn as they are in our society today.
[8] See Muir and Goody (1972) and Goody and Muir (1972) for a discussion of the developmental cycle of West African immigrant families and the resulting high incidence of births among student parents.

West Africa ostensibly included "all circumstances" and thus ought to be comparable with the situation of very real objective strain under which many lived in London. But even allowing for a certain amount of idealization, it is clear that West African parents feel they are getting something of worth through fostering their children with English parents, which fostering in West Africa would not secure. These advantages are mainly defined as a greater facility with the language and a greater ease with Western institutions, both of prime importance to a highly upwardly mobile group.

West African Fostering in Different Contexts

I have very briefly considered the distribution of children in fosterage in three very different West African contexts. First, we saw that in Gonja society, where education and occupational differentiation are very little affected by industrialization, children go almost always to kin. Exceptions are found only among boys, who sometimes are sent to Quranic teachers and occasionally to office holders. Forty percent of the children go to a foster parent of the grandparental generation, while about half go to kin of the parental generation — that is, to a parent's real or classificatory sibling.

The second context was contemporary southern Ghana, where apprentice fostering is becoming important. Here masters are still sought among kin for preference, but differentiation of skills may make this impossible. Apprentice fostering affects both boys and girls, but exists side-by-side with fostering for more diffuse objectives. Children are also sent to educated relatives in the hope that they may receive both an improved education and perhaps advantages in securing work later. Here foster parents are seldom of the grandparental generation, and children most often go to a sibling of the parent or, in a substantial number of cases, to non-kin.

The final situation in which we have found fostering of children by West African parents is among the temporary immigrants to London. Here the fostered children are much younger, reflecting the absence of domestic help or relatives in the household to assist with the care of infants and toddlers. There are no relatives available to serve as foster parents in London[9] and children all go to strangers, and indeed to

---

[9]   In fact a surprising number of West African couples do have one or two relatives in the United Kingdom, but as they are also there in order to study and must work to support themselves, they are not available as foster parents.

non-West African couples who care for them in exchange for a weekly payment.

These data reflect a clear progression from fostering by kin to fostering by strangers which shows a close similarity to apprenticeship. They also suggest a decreasing reliance on the grandparental generation in situations in which fostering is viewed as a means of securing skills or advantages for the child. Admittedly the situation of immigrants to London is an extreme one, but perhaps all the more revealing for that, especially when contrasted with the response of West Indians to objectively similar circumstances.

FOSTERING IN THE WEST INDIES

There are a few references in the ethnographic literature on the West Indies to the sending of children to live with kin even though their natal family of orientation is still intact and forms a co-residential unit. González writes of the "loaning" of children between compounds as sometimes being based on kinship ties, and this seems to include children of intact families (1969: 52–53). Sanford also refers to "loaning" of children and it seems likely that in some of these cases the parents are living together (1971: 100). Horowitz specifically mentions that parents may send a child to a relative from an intact conjugal household (1967: 49). There are also clear indications that children are sent to stay with non-kin who are in a position to offer them a better start in life than their own parents. Clarke's data from three very different communities in Jamaica show a substantial proportion of children living with neither parent; over the three communities the average is 18 percent (see Table 5). Nearly one-third of these fostered children are living with non-relatives. In the poorest community (Mocca) almost half the fostered children are with non-kin, while nearly all those from prosperous Orange Grove are with relatives. But although Orange Grove children are seldom sent out to live with non-kin, Clarke reports that more unrelated children come to live in Orange Grove homes than was the case in the other communities studied (1966: 178).

The sending of children to middle- and upper-class white and Creole families in the hopes that they will receive an education and assistance in finding a secure occupational niche is also reported by González for the Black Caribs of Guatemala (1969: 53ff.) and Sanford for the Carib and Creole population of a British Honduras community (1971: 94–95).

Yet despite these references, purposive fostering with kin and with

Table 5.   Children in three Jamican communities living with neither parent; percent living with kin and with non-kin; percent of all children living with foster parents (Clarke 1966: Appendix 5)

| | Fostered children living with: | | | | Total fostered children | Total children in community | Percent all children fostered[a] | Percent all children fostered by non-kin |
| | Kin | | Non-kin | | | | | |
	Number	Percent	Number	Percent				
Orange Grove	20	90	2	10	22	296	7	1
Sugar Town	65	72	25	28	90	318	28	8
Mocca	14	54	12	46	26	133	19	9
All three communities	99	72	39	28	138	747	18	6

[a]   It is not clear from Appendix 5 whether the children enumerated are those in each community or all the children born to adults living in each community. I nevertheless include the comparison to give some indication of the proportions of children being reared by relatives and non-kin.

strangers seems to account for a relatively small proportion of the children who are reared apart from both their parents in the Caribbean area. Again from Sanford's figures, 59 percent of her instances of "child keeping" (205 cases) I would classify as crisis fostering, with another 13 percent (forty-six cases) as probable crisis fostering. If we include the latter group, then something like 72 percent of her cases were due to the inability of the parents to rear the child themselves (Sanford 1971: 82). As Sanford points out, this classification is based on reasons given after the fact and cannot but represent bias of some sort. Unfortunately, there are few figures of which I am aware which enable a distinction to be drawn between crisis and voluntary fostering in the Caribbean area.[10]

Although additional figures are lacking, the burden of the descriptive material on the West Indian area is clearly that children are most often placed with a pro-parent because their parents have no home in which to care for them. These may be children of transient unions, "outside" children whose presence in a conjugal household is not welcome, or children whose parent or parents must work in a city or abroad and cannot care for them as well. For some such reason the parents cannot cope and some pro-parental figure has to be found.

The multifunctional quality of fostering in the West Indies is precisely what we find in traditional West African societies, and the adaptations in

[10]   To do so on the basis of whether or not the child's parents are living together at the time of inquiry is not satisfactory, because in at least some cases the family of orientation is likely to have dispersed following the fostering arrangement.

West Africa to Western industrial changes are echoed in those described
for the Caribbean. Yet the working out of the pattern is subtly different.
Not only does a relatively higher proportion of crisis fostering seem to
characterize this area, but fostering among kin seems more likely to mean
the rearing of a child by a parent's own parent rather than, as in West
Africa, by a wide range of classificatory relatives, particularly parents'
siblings.

It is in societies based on cognatic descent systems, or with weak unilineal descent groups that fostering appears to flourish in West Africa.
West Indian societies are cognatic, with a few weakly unilineal (e.g.
M. G. Smith 1962a). Despite this similarity, the range of kin who participate is wider in West Africa than in the West Indies. What is interesting
for the comparison of fostering in the two areas is that these collateral kin
are, in West Africa, seen as having a claim on children to foster. Furthermore, they are ready to acknowledge requests to take children which are
phrased in terms of kinship ties.

Sanford refers to anxiety over dependability of kinship bonds among
the Creole and Carib peoples of British Honduras (1971: 108). But the
bonds of which she is speaking are those linking primary kin, that is, full
and half-siblings and parents and children. And, given the dispersal of
half-siblings in different households in the town, the extended absence
of fathers, and the periodic absence of many mothers, this is perhaps not
surprising. It is a case of a dispersed core, with very little in the way of
back-up institutions.

The comparable situation in West Africa finds the paternal half-
siblings usually located in a single compound (this will be the case with
maternal half-siblings in a matrilineal system like Ashanti). The same
compounds contain a number of elementary families, linked by senior
members of a kin group who usually recognize one person as their formal
head. This person in turn represents the compound to the community,
acting on behalf of the individual members on such public occasions as
life crisis rituals or serious litigation.[11]

Should the child's own family of orientation break up, there is a double
safety net. On the one hand there are the two on-going residential groups
in which the parents have birth status rights, into either of which he will
be welcomed; and on the other there are the kinfolk living elsewhere who
have a claim on him and an obligation to care for him if this becomes
necessary. Fostering does sometimes occur within a residential complex
of several domestic groups. In Gonja, this happens most often when an

[11] See Fortes (1969: Chapters IX, X) for an especially clear account of the compound
as a mediating structure in Ashanti.

elderly mother is assigned one of her granddaughters as a companion and a runner-of-errands. But on the whole, fostering occurs between compounds and very often between villages. By this I mean that the parents are living in a different compound or village from that of the foster parent, and that these are their regular homes. In Gonja, and I believe in other West African societies too, the fostered child moves between fixed points (domestic groups, though not necessarily based on a conjugal unit), and these fixed points are embedded in a nexus of wider institutions — kinship, jural, ritual, political — into which the child is introduced in a systematic way, and as a member of his residential group.

To an outsider, it seems as though the fostered child in the West Indies has only his foster home as a secure base.[12] And further, that however strong the bonds between parent, child, and foster parent, this is in effect an isolated unit. Even where domestic groups are gathered into larger aggregates (as among Black Caribs in Guatemala, González [1969]), there is not the pattern of extra-domestic institutions into which these larger groups are integrated.

Thus, fostering in West Africa leads the child out from the domestic and local group of the parents, but this remains his primary base and he or she remains the child of this compound, of this village, and of these particular parents. One minor index of this continuity in Gonja is that kinship terminology does not alter with fostering. The child and the foster parent use the same kin terms as before, and the child continues to call only his own parents by the fond terms for "mother" and "father." The major index of the lack of change in status through fostering is that a man is eligible for no new offices by virtue of residence with his foster parent and remains eligible for whatever offices were open to him in his natal community; inheritance is not altered by fostering relationships, though a fond foster parent may give gifts *inter vivos* to a foster child.

In contrast, there seem to be two themes in West Indian fostering. First, the child may be sent "outside" to unrelated foster parents, usually in a quasi-servant role, but with the intention that he learn urban middle-class ways and get an education. If this is successful, then as an adult he

---

[12] This is partly a function of the age at which a child is sent to foster parents. In West Africa this tends to be around five to seven, often referred to as the time when a child begins to "have sense." In the West Indies, on the other hand, the pattern seems to be to place an infant with a foster mother in order that the mother can work to support herself and the child and be free to try to form a stable union. In the latter case, the child knows no other home than that of the foster parent, though the mother may visit it regularly.

will be in a good position to support his parents. There may be a breaking of ties with natal kin, and an attempt to pass into middle-class society. If the child fails to secure an education or effective occupational skills, he will be thrown back onto his own kin and class. The second theme is the fostering grandmother. Here the child is returned to the mother's home, which may or may not still be her primary base. If the mother has established a separate conjugal household, it is likely to be with a man who is not the child's father, and the majority of writers on the West Indies seem to agree that "outside" children are not welcome in the conjugal home (see especially Clarke 1966: 174). If, as in Sanford's community in British Honduras, the parents are both away working, there IS no conjugal home to which the child can relate. The result appears to be a very strong relationship with the fostering mother. Several authorities have noted that she is apt to be called "mother" while the real mother is referred to by her name, and treated as a sister. Sanford suggests that it can go much further than this. Writing of a woman who reared a younger brother and sister, she says:

This woman receives from her younger siblings the reverence and the regular acquiescence to her authority over them that a mother would receive. ... Their attitudes are almost a caricature of the respect for authority which is a strongly evidenced characteristic of social relations in Stann Creek. No matter that they are both quite old and responsible themselves, their sister is the elder and she is loved, feared, and obeyed in all respects as if they were children. She is their psychic mother (1971:133–134).

Yet Sanford insists that the keeping of children by Creole and Carib peoples in British Honduras is not a form of adoption and gives as evidence the fact that the mother's right to reclaim her child is recognized as overriding any promise she might have made to the fostering parent (1971: 92–94, 125). Interestingly enough, this is discussed in the context of the treatment of parent and foster parent by the grown foster child. A girl who sent gifts only to her foster mother and not to her real mother was criticized for forgetting the woman who bore her and looked after her in infancy. Sanford remarks that the girl would not have been able to withstand these criticisms if she had been living in the community, but as she was working abroad they did not affect her. Another woman affirmed that if either of the two boys she had reared should turn out well (i.e. become well off), she would see to it that the mother shared in her good fortune. As these examples suggest, it appears to be the fostering mother in the first instance who benefits from the assistance of grown children, but the mother is seen as having a residual claim, though this may be difficult to enforce and may depend on the goodwill of the foster parent.

Such dual responsibility can be seen as arising, on the one hand, from the moral obligation which links genetrix (and genitor) and offspring, regardless of their subsequent relationship, and on the other hand through the reciprocities of rearing which arise from the dependency of infancy and childhood, and the emotional and moral claims this makes on the child in adulthood. The same dual obligations exist for the West African foster child, but there are two important differences in their form. First, the moral obligations towards his biological parents are augmented by the fact that they also provide him with his place in adult society, since this is (or was in traditional times) implicit in birth status. This very strong pull back to one's natal kin is recognized by the Gonja who say that a son will always return eventually to live with his father. Anyone could provide instances of this happening, even in middle age. The rights and obligations arising out of bestowal of birth status may be seen as STATUS RECIPROCITIES.

Secondly, there seems to be much less emphasis on children as a form of security in old age in West Africa. With Sanford, I suspect that this may be because of the insecurity of the West Indian situation rather than because West African parents do not look to their children for comfort in old age. But in the African context there is a wider range of relatives with whom one may find support, and perhaps more important, old age in many societies is a time when both men and women are highly respected for their wisdom and skill.[13] Nor, in most traditional societies, were adult sons likely to disappear regularly for the major part of their working lives. In the West Indies both the migration of young adults out of the country, or to distant centers of employment, and the absence of a strong extended kin group leave the older folk without a sure means of support and companionship in old age.

In the West Indies, then, the fostering of children appears to be associated with a narrower range of kin ties. The foster child is often without an alternative home and grows up very strongly identifying with his foster mother: her home is his home; there is little to pull the foster child back to his own parents, although he owes them respect and support too; and adults, particularly women, may depend very greatly in their old age on the support of their youngest "child," who is very likely to be a foster child. Indeed, it would seem that by fostering her daughters' children a woman can effectively extend her own period of

[13] The coming of Western technology and education is altering this rapidly. When wisdom is learned at school, the elders are at an increasing disadvantage.

child rearing so that it lasts not until middle age but through to old age.
Sanford speaks of women "building their empires as mothers" by appro-
priating their daughters' children (1971: 99; see also Clarke 1966: 180–
181).

The importance of the grandmother as foster parent in the West Indies
can be seen in Table 6. The figures for British Honduras and Jamaica also
reflect the pattern of sending children to non-kin, presumably in apprentice fostering.

Table 6. West Indian fostering relationships: generation

	Foster parent is of: Grand-parental generation	Parents' generation	Child's generation	Not kin	Total number
Dominican rural village[a]	130 (89%)	10 (7%)	—	6 (4%)	146 (100%)
British Honduras coastal village[b]	156 (55%)	34 (12%)	6 (2%)	89 (31%)	285[b](100%)
Three Jamaican communities[a]	74 (54%)	21 (15%)	2 (1%)	39 (29%)	136 (99%)

[a] From Spens (1969).
[b] From Sanford (1971). I have omitted category "other kin" ($n = 64$) in calculating
percentages, as this could not be assigned to any generation. The figures in the above
table thus represent percentages of those classifiable by generation from Sanford's data.
[c] From Clarke (1966: Appendix 5). I have considered only children living with neither
parent.

The other point to note from Table 6 is the very low proportion of foster
parents of the parents' own generation. There are some cases in each
sample, but the figures are very low in comparison with those for grandparents.

West Indians in London

These comments are based on a pilot study carried out by Spens and a
West Indian (Dominican) assistant in a London suburb, where there is a
small Dominican enclave. They draw also on West Indian ethnographies,
and on Spens' close knowledge of Dominica. They must, however, be
considered as tentative findings rather than as the results of a full-scale
study.

The trip to England is in a sense a further extension of the emigration
in search of work which takes West Indians from the farm to the local

sugar plantation, on to the towns and cities or on to the fruit, tobacco, or sugar estates on other islands or the mainland of central America. Puerto Ricans holding United States passports go to the United States in search of work. Those from the ex-British colonies come, or used to come, to England. Many, both men and women, leave a child behind with a mother or sister, and some men come promising to bring over wives and children. Those who reunite their families in England often add to them, while others find a spouse and start a family. The jobs they are able to get are those which English workers avoid, such as industrial cleaning, railwaymen, bus conductors, and unskilled and semi-skilled factory work — jobs which pay poorly and require few skills. Since both husband and wife are almost certainly committed to sending money home regularly, both must work.

The pattern of illegitimate first (and often second) pregnancies is very clear among the families in the pilot study. Seven out of nine women had borne their first child before marriage, and three were still not married several years later. Illegitimacy of their first-born is not equally characteristic of all Dominican women, however. Again and again these women explain that they came to England because they had a child (or several children) to support and they could not do this successfully on the island. Thus emigrants to London appear to be selected from those who have difficulty meeting their responsibilities under the conditions of low wages and high unemployment on Dominica. Mothers of illegitimate children are prominent in this group and probably account for the large majority of single women who come to work in England. All those in the pilot sample had left their illegitimate children with kin on Dominica. One of the women had come with her husband, but again for much the same reason — to work and earn a better standard of living. This couple left their first child behind with the wife's mother so that they could both work full time. This is exactly the reasoning given by single women for leaving a child with its grandmother: "If I had to look after the child I couldn't work so much, and that is why I came to England."

But for the single woman with a child to support, work has an added meaning: she must send money to the woman in whose care she has left the child. This person is almost always the mother's mother. The money is seen as fulfilling two obligations. In the first place, the care of her child places an extra burden on the grandmother. And secondly, the daughter feels responsible for helping the mother herself with cash if she possibly can. There is, however, a subtler pressure on a woman to contribute to her child's support: if she is the one who provides money for daily necessities and for such extra expenses as the clothes and celebration of First Communion, then she has a much clearer claim to the child's affection and loyalty later on. She has been a proper mother, even though circumstances forced her to leave the child to be reared by others. This is of very great importance in the mother's eyes. One woman whose mother died just before she left for England left her daughter with the child's godmother. She did this very reluctantly, and insists that she has always continued to send money for her support, because the godmother would like to adopt the girl and she does not want to lose her. In another case the mother had sent money for the maintenance of her son while he was being looked after by his father's mother. She was careful to continue these payments in order to retain her rights in the child, and later was able to take him to live with her.

A woman feels differently about the child she has left with her own mother. My impression is that this is usually a temporary arrangement in the beginning, "until I am able to send for the child in England." Whether the grandmother views it in this way is unclear. Significantly, two of the women in our sample had encountered serious resistance from their mothers when seeking to bring to England the children left in their care. Each had had to leave her child there for some time longer, and one ended by having to return to the West Indies to resolve the matter there. Thus the mothers do not from the first consider that they are turning a child over to his grandmother "for good." However, this is often the outcome of fostering by the maternal grandmother, either because she effectively resists returning the child, of because the mother is never in a position to send for him.

The grandmother's position is very much strengthened by the fact that a child left with her in infancy grows up knowing her as its mother and calling her "Mama," while calling its own mother by her first name and often treating her like an older sibling. Interestingly enough, this even happens when the mother is present in the household. One of the Forest Gate women had lived with her mother after the birth of her first child, going out to work while the grandmother looked after the baby. The child grew up calling the grandmother "Mama" as its mother did, and calling the mother by her first name, as the grandmother did. The mother describes the situation as "like I was the big sister." It didn't worry her at the time and after some years she left her son with his grandmother and come to England where she married and had two more children. When the boy joined her in England he still refused to call her "Mama" and at this time she minded very much and tried unsuccessfully to change the pattern which had been established in his infancy. There is another instance in our small pilot sample of this same pattern — a son who grew up calling his grandmother "Mama" and who in this case refused to admit that his own mother WAS his mother.

Women are very ambivalent about losing children to their mothers in this way. On the one hand they feel extremely grateful that the grandmother was able to care for the child at a time when they could not do so. This places the mother doubly in her own mother's debt: first there were the reciprocities of rearing built in during her own infancy and childhood; now there is a second set which links child, mother, and grandmother. In this situation the continued residence of the child with its grandmother in adolescence and adulthood is seen as one way of looking after the grandmother in her old age, one way of fulfilling the obligation felt towards her. One of the women in the pilot study, still unmarried and with four children, said that she sometimes regrets having had so many children, as: "No man will marry you with four children. They are scared of the responsibility." However she went on to say that whenever she thinks this way, she remembers her mother, how she needs the children, and what a help they are to her. The eldest boy is now seventeen, has a job, and in addition makes a vegetable garden for his grandmother. The others fetch wood and water and run errands. She expects them to look after her mother in her old age. So she is glad she had the children, since her mother needs them. "But," she added, "they must also give me some sort of respect as well."

And here is the crux of the matter. A child who feels primary obligations towards his grandmother and treats his mother like a big sister cannot be depended on by the mother in her later years in the same way as one she has reared herself. The reciprocities of rearing are laid down between child and grandparent, not between parent and child, and concern about whether children will care for their parents in old age is very real.[14] Mrs. M's first child was born in Dominica and was acknowledged by the father, who could not marry the mother as her family was "lower" than his. The girl has been raised by a sister of Mrs. M's mother, and even now is staying with her since Mrs. M's husband does not want the child in their home. Mrs. M is pleased that her daughter shows great fondness and respect for her foster mother, but she only hopes "that R... will not neglect me in my old age, when she is bigger and able to help herself." The Dominican interviewer comments that in her opinion the girl will not let Mrs. M down because she is conscious of her mother's goodness towards her. The interviewer is here referring to the fact that

[14]   It was Dr. Spens who made me realize the depth of this.

Mrs. M has always sent money to help with her daughter's maintenance and has kept in touch with her.

The concern over whether a child will feel obliged to care for a parent in old age when reared by someone else is most clearly seen when the foster parent is not the maternal grandmother. This is probably because the mother feels a strong obligation towards her own mother, which she can fulfil through her child, and, also, because the bond between mother and grandmother is close enough that the child identifies the two women and can reasonably be expected to give the mother, too, some respect when she is old. But when the foster parent is a stepmother or godmother, then women become really anxious that they will lose their right to the child's sense of obligation in old age. In one of the sample families, the husband and wife had virtually separated but still occupied the same house. The mother was determined to try to maintain this arrangement, as otherwise she feared she would lose her children. She wants to look after them when they are small so that they can care for her when she is old. She thinks they will do this, except perhaps the eldest girl who is against her.

None of the West Indian children in the pilot study had been sent to English foster parents, and indeed London informants specifically deny that they would ever do this. Sending very young children to a nanny, that is a woman who looks after them locally during the day, is a fairly common practice. Ideally women prefer to stay at home when their children are very young, but this is not always possible. Some who must work manage by taking an evening job when the husband can be at home with the children. Others make use of either West Indian or English daily minders (nannies) with whom they leave the children between eight and nine o'clock in the morning and five or six in the evening. School-age children are often "latchkey" children who return to an empty house and may even be expected to start the supper for a working mother.

ECONOMIC ASPECTS OF FOSTERING AND DAILY MINDING IN LONDON

To what extent is the preference of West Indian parents for daily minding rather than fostering with English families a matter of economic necessity? The range of costs for daily minding in London (at 1970 prices) starts below that for fostering, but there is an area of overlap. The less expensive foster parents charge no more than the more expensive daily minders. There are additional costs in both forms of care: for daily minding —

food (usually supplied by the parents), laundry, twice-daily fares on bus or underground, and, of course, clothing; for fostering — occasional lump sums for clothes, new shoes, etc., and the expense of visits.

It is worth noting that although the West Africans in London are on the whole much better educated than the West Indians, the jobs they are able to find are very often the same. Both tend to take unskilled or semi-skilled jobs in transport, the post office, or factories. Hence many West Africans are not materially better off than West Indians. Although virtually ALL West Africans are in London as students, only 11 percent of the extensive sample were mainly supported by loans, student grants, or money from home. The families in one of the two groups in the intensive phase of the West African Immigrants study, the Ibo, were receiving no money from home and were instead trying to send money to kin who had lost homes and jobs as a result of the Biafran war. Overall, the Ibo families tended to delegate their parental roles less frequently than the others, but this applied equally to fostering and daily minding. Despite their financial straits, there were Ibo families who fostered their children in English homes.

When discussing the relative advantages of fostering and daily minding with West Africans the choice generally turned on factors other than expense. Daily minding was preferred because parents could check up on the minder's standard of care and for convenience, if there was a good minder near the mother's place of work. It was disliked because of crowded conditions, poor care, and constant travel. Fostering was disliked due to difficulty of checking on the foster parent's care of the children (parents are expected to give notice of visits beforehand) and because of the difficulty and expense of frequent visits. Fostering was preferred to daily minding because of the home atmosphere — the children were thought to get more attention and be treated more like their own children by a foster parent; there was no need to take and fetch the children every day (often in the dark and cold); and the mother was free in the evenings to study or work the night shift.

Fostering can be considerably more expensive than daily minding, and a few West African families are undoubtedly better off than virtually all West Indians. Yet these differences do leave a considerable area of overlap, where there are West Africans who are as hard up as the typical West Indian family, but who still prefer to foster their children rather than send them to a daily minder. While there is probably an economic element in the choice between the two modes of care, impoverished West African parents do foster their children. Nor can this factor account for the explicit rejection of English foster homes by West Indian parents.

COMPARISON OF CONTEMPORARY PATTERNS OF FOSTER-ING IN WEST AFRICA AND THE WEST INDIES

We noted that there were two themes, one dominant and one sub-ordinate, in West Indian fostering. The main theme is the caring for a child by the maternal grandmother when the mother is for some reason unable to do so herself. The secondary theme is the sending of a child to non-relatives in apprentice fosterage. Both are reflected in the summary figures for the West Indies in Table 7 (drawn from the totals of Tables 4 and 6), where by far the majority of foster parents are found in the grandparental generation, while the next largest category consists of non-kin. This pattern contrasts strongly with the relative lack of emphasis on the mother-daughter-granddaughter chain in West Africa.

Table 7. Comparison of northern Ghana, southern Ghana, and West Indian fostering relationships — by generation of foster parent (from totals of Tables 4 and 6)

| | Foster parent is of: | | | | |
	Grand-parents' generation	Parents' generation	Child's generation	Not kin	Total number
Population:					
Northern Ghana	80 (39%)	104 (50%)	12 (6%)	11 (5%)	207 (100%)
Southern Ghana	19 (7%)	176 (63%)	47 (17%)	37 (13%)	279 (100%)
West Indies	360 (64%)	65 (11%)	8 (1%)	134 (24%)	567 (100%)

If we take the southern Ghana situation as reflecting a degree of occu-pational and social differentiation roughly equivalent to that in the West Indies,[15] we find that the great majority of related foster parents are in the parents' generation, that is, they are collateral rather than lineal kin. While the figures suggest that the resort to non-kin in ap-prentice fosterage is less pronounced in the Ghanaian samples, observa-tions do not entirely support this finding. This may be because non-kin fostering is increasing rapidly at present, while the figures refer to the childhood of informants who were adults in the mid-1960's. Fostering by non-kin is definitely more common in southern Ghana than in the north, where several samples had no instances, and the overall incidence is substantially below that in the south and markedly lower than the figures for the West Indies. We have suggested that this is probably

---

[15] Southern Ghana lacks, of course, the racial differentiation which plays such a central part in West Indian stratification. I would not wish to imply that this is not of great importance in determining the available avenues of social mobility in the two culture areas, but the West Indian data come from black and colored populations, and thus the discussion is necessarily limited to this stratum.

related to the greater occupational and social differentiation in the south, itself a response to increasing urbanization and industrialization.

But why should there be such a striking contrast between the West Indian preference for fostering by maternal grandmothers and the West African pattern of sending children to collateral kin of both parents? The analysis of West Indian material has indicated that two factors are critical in accounting for this bias. On the one hand, mothers are very often in need of someone to care for an infant while they work or establish a stable conjugal union. The woman on whom a mother has the strongest claim for such service is her own mother. On the other hand, older women are extremely anxious about what will become of them in old age, and one kind of provision they can make is to continue mothering children after their own period of childbearing has ended. The children they have the strongest claim to are pre-marital children of the daughters (and less often, of their sons). Finally, the needs of daughter and mother coincide: the latter is seeking to gain an additional child, the former to delegate the care of an infant.

The dynamics behind the sending of children to be reared by their parents' siblings in West Africa are entirely different. Parents believe that they are likely to spoil their own child, while a relative will be more demanding. The purpose of (non-crisis) fostering is the education of the child as well as the fulfilment of kinship obligations which are recognized between full and, often, between classificatory siblings. To the extent that foster parents in the grandparental generation are seeking domestic services rather than supplying training in adult skills,[16] the preference for collateral kin also reflects the educational aspect of fosterage.

Finally, it should be emphasized that only very rarely are men stipulated as foster parents (or keepers) in the West Indies, while the West African data show a rough balance between male and female foster parents. This I take to reflect the essentially NURTURANT role of West Indian fosterage except where older children are sent to non-kin. The utilization of male foster parents in West Africa corresponds to their function in training boys both in adult skills and manly virtues.

The differences reflected in Table 7 result in a distinctive "shape" to fostering in West Africa and in the West Indies which may be summarized as in Table 8.

[16]   This assumption is only partly warranted in a West African context. A father's father may still be relatively young and actively engaged in his trade. On the other hand, many grandparents are sent foster children to provide companionship and small services when they become old and infirm.

Table 8.   Summary of characteristics of fostering in West Africa and the West Indies

West Africa	West Indies
Strong element of purposive fostering by kin	Emphasis on crisis fostering by kin, purposive fostering by non-kin
Most foster parents are in parents' generation (i.e. collateral kin)	Most foster parents are in grand-parental generation (i.e. lineal kin)
Male foster parents are common	Male foster parents are rare
Model of fostering stresses the claims of foster parent	Model of fostering stresses the needs of parent and child
Fostering kin are not necessarily primary kin of parents	Fostering kin tend to be primary kin of parents
Fostering links siblings' children (lateral linkage)	Fostering links generations (lineal linkage merging mother and her siblings with their children)
Fostering does not change birth status identity; status reciprocities unaltered	Fostering may change birth status identity informally; no status reciprocities operate

COMPARISON OF CHILD CARE ARRANGEMENTS BY WEST AFRICANS AND WEST INDIANS IN LONDON

What then can we say about the observed difference between West Indians who refuse to consider placing their children with English foster parents while in England, and the West Africans who favor this form of arrangement? We have seen that both groups must make some arrangements for their young children to allow them to pursue the goals for which they have come so far. And while economic factors would favor a higher incidence of fostering among West Africans than among West Indians, these factors are not sufficient to account for the complete rejection of English foster parents by the latter group. Further, it is clear that both groups share the premise that delegation of some aspects of the parents' roles may be in the best interests of both parent and child.

I would suggest that the difference lies in the cultural meaning of fostering for the two groups. For West Indians, the rearing of a young child by another woman involves the transfer of at least some (if not all) aspects of motherhood, including all the loyalties and obligations that arise out of childcare in the early years. So long as this transfer is used to reinforce the ties between a woman and her own mother, it is tolerated as necessary, though we have seen that feelings here may also be ambivalent. But to risk the loss of a child to a complete stranger — which is the implication of sending it to live with another family — is simply unthinkable. The care offered by English foster parents is not seen as offering any advantages to compensate for the threat to the ties which the child would feel obliged to honor as an adult.

For West Africans, the meaning of fostering is different. Traditionally, children were not sent away as infants, and a foster parent is not seen as a substitute mother, but rather as providing character training and instruction. Where fostering occurs between kin, it is recognized as fulfilling (and creating) rights and obligations, but these in turn reinforce existing ties of a secondary nature rather than create a new set of primary ties (as happens between the West Indian child and the foster parent who becomes a "psychic mother"). The delay of fostering in West Africa until the child "has sense" at six or seven is consistent with this pattern of augmenting existing ties rather than creating a new set of primary bonds. Early rearing reciprocities are already established between the mother and child and are reinforced by status reciprocities linking the child to both parents. Only the later reciprocities of rearing, based on training in adult skills, remain as a basis of bonding. When the parental roles are under strain in an immigrant situation, the West African response is also consistent with the traditional pattern. The roles of father and mother are seen as firmly established and not as liable to threat in a caretaking situation. The fostering experience is perceived as providing a service to parents and their children and as being primarily educational and custodial in function (as no kinship obligations are involved in fostering by strangers).

CONCLUSIONS

In West Africa, kinship fostering is evolving into apprenticeship on the one hand and residential formal education on the other. To end with a speculation, I suggest that much the same pattern may have occurred in Western Europe with the development of a more complex division of labor. The relevant factor in occupational differentiation is that it becomes increasingly difficult to find a master of the required trade among one's kin. Apprenticeship then becomes an obvious alternative and is clearly associated with movement into the city and away from kin. Where trades are restricted to a closed group, especially a kin group, the picture would obviously be altered and information from caste-based societies would be critical here. Again, the centralizing of advanced literate skills in religious foundations which exclude family life (and hence cannot supply their own recruits) is another critical case which would reward study in the context of educational fostering. Like apprenticeship, formal education takes over some of the functions of fostering in less complex societies, functions which themselves include the provision of a link between the nuclear family and wider structures beyond.

REFERENCES

ARIÈS, P.
  1962 *Centuries of childhood: a social history of family life.* Translated by R. Baldick. New York: Knopf.
AZU, D. G.
  1975 *The Ga family and social change.* African Social Research Documents. Leiden: Africa-Studiecentrum.
BUSIA, K. A.
  1950 *Report on a social survey of Sekondi-Takoradi.* London: Crown Agents for the Colonies on behalf of the government of The Gold Coast.
CARROLL, V., *editor*
  1970 *Adoption in Eastern Oceania.* Honolulu: University of Hawaii Press.
CLARKE, E.
  1966 *My mother who fathered me* (second edition). London: Allen and Unwin.
COHEN, A.
  1969 *Custom and politics in urban Africa.* London: Routledge and Kegan Paul.
FORTES, M. F.
  1949 *The web of kinship among the Tallensi.* London: Oxford University Press for the International African Institute.
  1969 *Kinship and the social order.* Chicago: Aldine.
GONZÁLEZ, N. S.
  1969 *Black Carib household structure.* Seattle: University of Washington Press.
GOODY, E. N.
  1961 "Kinship, marriage and the developmental cycle among the Gonja of northern Ghana." Unpublished doctoral dissertation, Cambridge University.
  1966 Fostering of children in Ghana: a preliminary report. *Ghana Journal of Sociology* 2:26–33.
  1970a "Kinship fostering in Gonja: deprivation or advantage?" in *Socialization: the approach from social anthropology.* Edited by P. Mayer. London: Tavistock.
  1970b "The Kpembe study: a comparison of fostered and non-fostered children in eastern Gonja." Unpublished report, Social Science Research Council. London.
  1971a Varieties of fostering. *New Society* (August 5): 237–239.

1971b "Forms of pro-parenthood: the sharing and substitution of parental roles," in *Kinship*. Edited by J. Goody. London: Penguin Books.

1973 *Contexts of kinship: an essay in the family sociology of the Gonja of northern Ghana*. Cambridge: Cambridge University Press.

GOODY, E. N., C. L. MUIR

1972 "Factors related to the delegation of parental roles among West Africans in London." Unpublished report, Social Science Research Council. London.

HOROWITZ, M.

1967 *Morne-paysan: peasant village in Martinique*. New York: Holt, Rinehart and Winston.

MORGAN, EDMUND S.

1944 *The Puritan family, religion and domestic relations in 17th century New England*. Boston: The Trustees of The Public Library.

MUIR, C. L., E. N. GOODY

1972 Student parents: West African families in London. *Race* 13:329–336.

OPPONG, C.

1965 "Some sociological aspects of education in Dagbon." Unpublished master's thesis, Institute of African Studies. Legon, Ghana.

1969a Education of relatives' children by senior civil servants in Accra. *Ghana Journal of Child Development* 2(2).

1969b A preliminary account of the role and recruitment of drummers in Dagbon. *Research Review* 6:38–51. Institute of African Studies, Legon, Ghana.

1974 *Marriage in an Akan elite*. Cambridge: Cambridge University Press.

SANFORD, M. S.

1971 "Disruption of the mother-child relationship in conjunction with matrifocality: a study of child-keeping among the Carib and Creole of British Honduras." Unpublished doctoral dissertation, Catholic University of America, Washington, D.C.

SKINNER, E. P.

1964 Intergenerational conflict among the Mossi: father and son. *Journal of Conflict Resolution* 5:55–60.

SMITH, M. G.

1962a *Kinship and community in Carriacou*. New Haven: Yale University Press.

1962b *West Indian family structure*. Seattle: University of Washington Press.

SMITH, R. T.

1956 *The Negro family in British Guiana*. London: Routledge and Kegan Paul.

SPENS, T.

1969 "Family structure in a Dominican village." Unpublished doctoral dissertation, Cambridge University.

YALMAN, N.

1967 *Under the bo tree*. Berkeley: University of California Press.

To Be Treated as a Child of the Home: Black Carib Child Lending in a British West Indian Society

MARGARET SANFORD

Vern Carroll (1970: 14–15) and Ward Goodenough (1970: 391) have suggested that the analysis of transactions in parenthood (adoption and fosterage) can make an important contribution to the anthropological theory of kinship. Some preliminary directions for such an analysis, in a West Indies society, are suggested in this study. First of all, the analysis of kinship and of transactions in parenthood must proceed together. Child lending and child dispersal among West Indies peoples cannot be understood without a background reference to marriage and kinship among these people (Goodenough 1970: 408).

Unfortunately, so far as the West Indies is concerned, although some considerable effort has been expended in attempts to explain family, marriage, and kinship there (Simey 1946: 80; Frazier 1939: 142–144; Henriques 1969: 113; Cohen 1956: 670–683; Davenport 1961: 446; Rubin 1961: 63; Blake 1961: 156; R. T. Smith 1956: 142; see also Rubin and Zavalloni [1969: 123–126] for a concise summation of the theoretical situation with regard to mating, marriage, and family practices heretofore thought of as "West Indian," and González [1969] who has presented a reconceptualization of "matrifocality" which takes into account the data from areas outside the West Indies), it is precisely in these areas that we still meet difficulties in analysis. Goodenough's definition of "marriage" (1970: 12–13), shows promise in helping us sort out the mating phenomena, and yet there remain questionable areas, to be discussed below.

I wish to thank my colleague, Franklin Takei, for his generosity in reading and criticizing this paper.

The data from which the paper is drawn were collected in the year 1969 while I was engaged in ethnographic field work among the Black Carib of British Honduras, under the guidance of Michael Kenny of the Catholic University of America in Washington, D.C.

We now have a great deal of information on marital, sexual, family, and domestic relations among West Indies peoples, but little or no agreement on what it all means. Matrifocality, once the prime explanatory focus, is now seen to be present in widespread areas of the world under a number of conditions which are not peculiar to the specific situation, historical or present-day, among West Indian peoples. Moreover, "matrifocality" as it is now conceptualized does not in fact describe the situation of kinship among West Indian peoples or among North American blacks. Under examination matrifocality fades away as being of any great importance in explaining kinship. Matrifocality in British Honduras (the British West Indies society from which I draw my data) is more an ideal situation than a real one, and has more to do with linking siblings than with tying children to a mother (Sanford 1971; cf. Stack 1970).

Thus, despite the plethora of data which we now have, there is still missing some unifying principle by which we may organize it. In this study I shall discuss child lending as a SOCIALIZATION IN RECIPROCITY, offering this value as a unifying concept around which to group the various phenomena of mating, marriage, parenthood, family, and kinship.

Kinship and the reciprocal obligations which nurture and maintain friendly relations among kin are very much interrelated in the West Indies society of British Honduras. To paraphrase Roger Keesing (1970: 31), "When we can understand friendship, we may be able to understand kinship."

RECIPROCITY AND KINSHIP

Lending of children and "giving" of children among the West Indian population of British Honduras cannot be understood apart from the generalized, society-wide value for reciprocity in social relationships. The idiom of kinship is called upon to explain or sanctify a transaction or expected behavior. I shall describe some of the mutual expectations in social life to give the frame or background against which to discuss in greater detail the transactions in parenthood — the lending and "giving" of children.

Reciprocity in Courtship

Young girls and boys after puberty do not mingle freely in social life except at school. For most of the young people the terminal point in this association is at graduation from elementary school at the age of perhaps fourteen. Comparatively few go on to secondary school and most of the secondary schools are segregated by sex. Thus, the young people after about fourteen years of age have little social contact with the opposite sex except on the street. Girls are less frequently sent on errands by their parents as they progress beyond the age of puberty. Boys, if they are not apprenticed or employed, are permitted or even encouraged to live a street life presumably in the hope they will find an occupation or some kind of productive engagement. Girls attend the cinema in groups, and there they may pair off with some favorite boy, perhaps having made the appointment earlier in a quiet way to avoid notice by their parents or the adult townsfolk. Meetings between young people are definitely clandestine. Parents try to guard their girls from social contacts with men or boys, and they are filled with consternation, surprise, and outrage when the girls become pregnant, as they do more often than not, in their middle to late teens.

The high frequency of early premarital pregnancy among West Indian peoples, despite the vigilance of the parents and guardians to prevent it, and despite the real desire of the girls themselves to avoid giving birth to illegitimate children, stands as an unexplainable phenomenon unless the value for reciprocity is taken into account: it implies that giving establishes a tie to the receiver, obligating the recipient not only to accept the gift but to bestow a return gift at some suitable time.

Blake has noted that the girls she studied in Jamaica engaged in sexual intercourse with men upon the bestowal of rather minor gifts, such as a chocolate candy bar (Blake 1961: 89–90). She implied that the transaction was then complete. I believe that this is a false view, and that the giving and receiving of small gifts are merely preliminary moves looking toward the establishment of a possibly enduring relationship — perhaps legal marriage or concubinage. Men are permitted to engage in multiple concurrent marital relationships, to be discussed below, so that a young girl is justified in believing that a man is sincere in his approach to her. Trial matings precede legal marriages, just as they precede less prestigious marital arrangements. I believe girls are seldom "taken advantage of." Even though they may be rather young, say fourteen years of age, their sexual partners are usually mature men — men who could provide for a mother and child. This circumstance has been seen as an exploitation of the young girls. I believe, on the contrary, that the power of the gift is as much used by the young girl as by the man. Contraceptives are not used by young girls, not because they do not know about them, but because their use would betray a lack of trust and thus interfere with a developing interpersonal relationship. Whether the relationship is discontinued or maintained after the girl becomes pregnant depends upon the strength and quality of the relationship which has developed rather than upon her pregnancy.

If pregnancy is not followed by a marital relationship of some kind — if the man does not "take care of" the young mother — it is rather because they were incompatible in some way, or because the prospective "in-laws" were disagreeable and rejecting. The nearer parents approach upper class levels the less likely they are to accept a marital status less than legal marriage. They are also less likely to permit their daughters to marry men of a lower class than theirs. The parents prefer an illegitimate grandchild to marriage of a daughter to a man of lesser social standing. They do not permit their daughters to set up any kind of continuing relationship with such a man. The child produced by their daughter is taken and raised as their own.

The offer of a gift of food by a man to a woman, no matter how trifling its value, may imply that the man offers a closer relationship which may then lead to a sexual relationship. Acceptance of the gift may imply willingness to entertain the idea of becoming closer friends. The meaning varies, of course, with the situation and the status of the people involved. A woman securely mated to a man who spends time with her and "maintains" her can accept a small fruit from a neighbor man, and both may realize there will be no further development. She would not accept such a gift offered in private, and she risks the gossip of her townsfolk when she accepts it publicly. I saw a woman reject with asperity the offer of a banana from a neighbor man. He was passing by on his bicycle and stopped to chat. People live outdoors in British Honduras, so this interchange was in full public view if the neighbors were looking upon the scene, as they no doubt were. This woman's mate had gone to the United States some three months before and had sent no money back. The woman was in a state of wounded feelings and of panic as to how to maintain herself and her four children, not the progeny of her mate. The man who stopped to chat and all the neighbors were well aware of the situation, and the angry rejection of the gift was clear public announcement that she still remained faithful to her mate, even though he might have decided to leave her. There were three other women in the town with whom the mate had had continuing marital relationships, and each woman was watching for signs in the behavior of the others.

The man who offered the gift went off on his bicycle protesting, with wounded innocence, the woman's rejection, as if he had not meant the gift to have any further consequences. And indeed he may have been teasing in a rather spiteful way, having no intention of pursuing the matter, but trying to elicit from this poor woman a public admission that she was in the market for another mate.

Failure to send money back to maintain mates and children seems to be a common behavior on the part of men who migrate for work. Even married men, much as the marriage tie seems to be respected, are inclined this way. Some men may be quite faithful in this respect, but one hears more of men who are not. When they receive no remittance from a migrating mate, women justly fear that he has decided to leave them. In explanation of this behavior, it should be understood that the primary duty of a man is to his mother and sisters. Legal marriage to a woman presumably places her on the same level as a sister so far as economic obligations are concerned. A marital relationship of lesser status than marriage entails increasing obligation on both sides the longer it lasts, provided the mutual exchange is faithfully pursued. Thus, newly entered upon relationships entail rather minor obligations on the part of a man for the maintenance of his mate. Her maintenance is the duty of her siblings or her parents. If children are born to the two, then he has the duty to supply food, money, clothing, and school fees for the children only. The woman with whom a man lives has a greater claim upon his money and food, in that she washes and irons his clothes and prepares food for him. This exchange of duties is so strong a symbol of relationship that when one side fails to perform, or for some reason cannot perform, the relationship is ended. Men who for one reason or another prefer not to live with any one of their mates may call upon their mothers or sisters to cook for them and to wash their clothes. In exchange the men provide food and small sums of money to the sister or mother. Men who have gone to a distant place to find work must of course have someone to cook and wash for them, and this leads more often than not to their acquisition of another mate. The women who are left behind have every right to feel apprehension. They cannot perform their side of the exchange and from the experience of many other women in this position they know what the likely outcome will be. It is the woman with whom a man lives and makes the meaningful exchanges who has prior call upon his earnings.

So demanding of reciprocity is this exchange that a woman whose mate leaves her for another, even though she may rightfully claim support for their joint progeny, sometimes refuses to accept such support because the man would then expect sexual privileges to continue even though he no longer lives with her. The woman's status would be diminished thereby from partner in a "lady-gentleman" relationship to that of a woman who engages in a visiting relationship. If she is prideful and has kin to help her, she will refuse such an arrangement by refusing to accept "maintenance" for the children.

After a failed trial mating, a man has the duty to supply the expenses for the birth of his child and a layette. He may be called upon for needs of the mother for food or clothing until she is able to work again. He could be asked to provide for the child until it is grown, perhaps fourteen years of age. But this seldom happens. After a child is about a year old, if his parents are not still mates, his needs are met by someone else. If the mother has entered a marital relationship with another man, the genitor of the child is wary of approaching the house where the family lives, and the bringing of gifts to the child is even more likely to arouse resentment and misunderstanding on the part of the new mate. The genitor of the child then stays clear of the house. His sisters or his mother may bring gifts to the child, thus acknowledging and maintaining a kinship tie.

At the death of a mother her children are sent to her mother or to her sister. Her mate is not expected to keep the children even though several may be their joint progeny. For example, a woman died in childbirth. She had been living in a lady-gentleman relationship, and the child at whose birth she died was the third by her gentleman. She also had three earlier-born children. The first child was mentally defective and had lived from birth with the woman's mother. Her next two children were by different men. These two had lived with the mother and her gentleman and their joint progeny. When the woman died, her father went to the city and brought the children back to the woman's mother to be cared for. The gentleman sent nothing for the care of the children, nor did he visit them, although he made some gestures indicating kindly feelings toward them — his new mate sent a letter saying they would try to get together a few dollars to send at some indefinite time in the future. The genitor of one of the older boys wanted to take the child into his own home, but the woman had extracted a promise from her mother that she would not permit it. The genitor sent clothing for the boy, but would give the grandmother no help in the way of money or food. He was trying, said the grandmother, to entice the boy away from his grandmother's household (where food was scarce) by inviting him to eat as often as he liked at his and his wife's house.

Eligibility for Parenthood

Young men and women in British Honduras are eligible to produce children as soon as they are physically capable of doing so. It is considered an unfortunate happening but not illegal. The infants are not taken away from them. But a very young couple is not eligible to start a conjugal family and live together in a separate house, except at lower levels of social status and even there only in rare instances.

The infants produced by young women before they have entered a stable union (or if a trial union breaks up before the child is born) are kept by the mother's mother or some very close woman relative of the mother. If both the mother and the father are very young, sometimes the father's mother or some very close woman relative of the father keeps the child. About two-thirds of the outside children in this category that I found in 1969 (Sanford 1971: 88) were being kept by the mother's relatives and about one-third by the father's relatives.

If the father of the child is able to support the young mother and child it would not be illegal for the young couple to engage in any one of the forms of marital union, with her parents' consent. But this is not done except in a very few instances. I saw one lady-gentleman relationship in which both parents were very young, the mother about fourteen years of age and the father about eighteen. This young man and his very youthful "lady" and their infant lived in a small shack across the road from the young man's blind adoptive mother, to whose needs he still ministered.

I also heard that in a smaller town to the south some very young girls had been permitted by their parents to go and live with the men who had impregnated them. All these exceptions to what I believe to be the general rule were among Carib people of lower class. The well-acculturated Caribs, those who emulate the upper-class Creole behaviors, follow the general rule. The very young are not ineligible for producing offspring, but they are not to be burdened by their care. Someone else takes over the duty of raising the child, takes the responsibility for his nurture and care. This person then becomes the child's psychic mother and has the rights of a mother to his loyalty, his labor, and his affection. She has the right to lend him to others or to give him away to another relative or to strangers. This latter right is subject to ratification by the genetrix, or to rescinding.

A very young genitor or genetrix has few duties or responsibilities to offspring when the child is young. As the child matures, some duties with respect to its care may be taken over by its genitor or genetrix.

Girls are not permitted to enter stable unions until they are well beyond puberty, somewhere between eighteen and twenty-six. Girls express the feeling that they should "do something" for their mothers or be established in a job before they settle into a marital relationship.

The same attitude is seen and encouraged in young men. They do not want to marry or enter any marital union until they are established in a career or trade or have a reasonable expectation of being able to support a family. Boys are depended upon to see to it that their mothers and sisters are provided for before they take on the responsibility of a mate or wife.

Marriage

Criteria for deciding whether a sexual mating is to be considered a marital relationship in a cross-cultural sense have been set forth by Goodenough:

[Marriage is] ... a transaction and resulting contract in which a person, male or female, corporate or individual, in person or by proxy establishes a continuing claim to the right of sexual access to a woman — this right having priority over rights of sexual access others currently have or may subsequently acquire in relation to her (except in a similar transaction) until the contract resulting from the transaction is terminated — and in which the woman involved is eligible to bear children (1970: 12–13).

Goodenough's suggestion (1970: 19–21), that a number of Caribbean mating situations would qualify as marriage by his definition, is borne out quite clearly by my data. I do not believe there has ever been any argument among observers that the lady-gentleman relationship should be considered a marital union, albeit consensual. But some of the other forms of mating such as the visiting or friending relationships have been and still are a problem to classify.

In applying Goodenough's criteria I find some difficulty in drawing sharp distinctions between what is marriage and what is not, for there are trials which produce children but no marital union. Are these to be considered short-time marriages even though they were clandestine? Then again, a clandestine relationship comes into the open and fits Goodenough's criteria for a marital union. I would think that we should call both of these "trial marriages" — one succeeded and the other failed.

The relationships which I have classified as clandestine are probably not marriage, not only because they are not public, but also because the question as to whether the man expects a privileged sexual relationship with the woman is not determinable. If the woman becomes pregnant, and if the man recognizes the child as his progeny, then we could call this marriage. But it would be indistinguishable, so far as the public is concerned, from trial marriage.

There appears to be a trial period in the early stages of all the types of marital relationships, including legal marriage. A young man and woman might have intentions to marry, but before they get to the altar it may develop that they are incompatible. The fact that the girl is pregnant makes no difference. They will not marry or live together if they are not congenial. Only if they are mutually agreeable does the marriage proceed. In many cases the young bride is well along in pregnancy at the time of the wedding.

In other cases the man and woman start living together as lady and gentleman, and after a time, perhaps a year, perhaps thirty years, they marry. Whether progeny have arrived or not seems to have little to do with the decision to marry at the earlier stages of the mating. At the later stages, the offspring themselves are frequently the instigators of the marriage, as this raises their prestige.

In real life the situation is complicated by the fact that almost everyone is involved in several kinds of matings, the women serially and the men both serially and concurrently. There are few marriages or lady-gentleman relationships which have not been preceded by one or more of the other kinds of matings. And there are few men who limit themselves to one kind of marital relationship at a time. There is a double standard which limits a woman's sexual activities to one partner at a time, but leaves the man at liberty to engage in as many other marital relationships or casual sexual relationships as he pleases.

Forms of Marital Unions

Table 1 sets forth the various forms of mating and marriage among the West Indian peoples of British Honduras, the Carib, and the Creole.

Legal marriage is the most prestigious form of marital union in British Honduras and it is the only one called "marriage" or in which the partners refer to each other and are referred to by others as "husband" and "wife." (British Hondurans speak English.)

Legal marriage creates a greater weight of responsibility on the part of the man for the economic support and care of the woman than the other forms of mating, and it remains as a kin tie even though the partners have long since parted and have no living issue. The husband may return to his wife when he is sick and old to be cared for and given a funeral at his death. This kind of lifetime obligation, which remains in effect despite the erosion of distance, time, and neglect, is a characteristic of mother-child, brother-sister relationships, but not of any marital union at its beginning except legal marriage. Lady-gentleman relationships may develop ties as durable as the brother-sister relationship but this comes with time and

Table 1.   Mating and marriage among the West Indian people of British Honduras

		I. Mating relationships	II. Local terminology	III. Terms of reference	
(A) Prestige ranking categories	Public	Legal marriage	Marriage	My husband — my wife	(B) All Trial Marriages
		Lady–gentleman relationship	Living the concubine life	My gentleman — my lady	
	Clandestine-Open Secret-Public Passage of time moves these from clandestine to public and enhances individual prestige	*Visiting relationships — regular* A woman still living in parental household receiving visits from: An otherwise unmated man A previously mated man A concurrently mated or married man		My gentleman — my lady My boy — my girl My friend	
		A woman living in an independent household receiving visits from: An otherwise unmated man A previously mated man A concurrently mated or married man			
	Clandestine	*Visiting relationships — irregular* Multiple concurrent visiting relationships (man visiting) Casual sexual relationships (man visiting) Multiple concurrent visiting relationships (woman visiting) Casual sexual relationships (woman visiting)			

mutual cooperation rather than as the result of a contract at the beginning of the relationship.

The ceremony of legal marriage creates kin links between families of the partners which in other forms of union are developed over a long time of mutual cooperation in economic, household, and parental duties. Lady-gentleman or visiting relationships which have no living issue are considered to have created kin links between the pair only after they have endured for some time. The raising of children together, even though they are not their joint progeny, strengthens the tie between a man and woman.

For a woman, legal marriage confers rights to which she is ordinarily entitled only by having been born sister to a man, or by having lived in faithful concubinage over a long period of time. For a man, legal marriage creates more duties toward a woman but few rights beyond those which he has in lesser forms of mating. One right which a man acquires by legal marriage is control over any property in land or money which a woman may have in her own name. These circumstances cause legal marriage to be considered rather dangerously burdensome to a man while conveying no advantage beyond other lesser forms of marriage except for its value as a sign of high status. For a woman the rights and privileges which she gains in marriage far outweigh the disadvantages. Marriage, I believe, is feared by men because it is viewed as upsetting the balance, overburdening oneself with relationships which have a quality of falseness in that they have no background of time and history of mutual accommodations and helpfulness.

Legal marriage was once characteristic only of upper-class Creoles or whites. It is now being entered into more frequently as the middle class expands. Before 1954 there were very few salaried positions available for British Hondurans. Since the accession to internal self-government the former colony has taken over clerical details which once were handled in Great Britain. As their economic status improves the young are willing to take on the added responsibility which marriage entails. Many marry women who also have government jobs, which of course is advantageous since the income is doubled. Marriage is not only a result of better economic conditions, however. It is a symbol of rising social standing. In the past two generations, whenever a Carib was able to get a teaching position he would very often marry, even though the salary was quite small.

For the major portion of the West Indian population, the less prestigious forms of marital relationships are engaged in, particularly at preliminary stages. The couple may marry, perhaps a year, perhaps thirty years after the beginning of the relationship. Pregnancy or the birth of children have little to do with the decision to marry. Most frequently it is a matter of prestige which propels the couple into legal marriage. For example, one of the many rules of a certain social club is that the women who join, or even women guests who dance at the Christmas ball, must be married, or must be "young ladies." The definition of a young lady is that she still lives under her parents' roof and is not engaging in any of the forms of marital union. Invitations to the Christmas ball of this club are highly prized among the Carib. Some couples marry during the preceding week in order that the woman may go to the dance. Men may be members of the club and dance at Christmas no matter what their marital status.

Another influence toward legal marriage at later stages of life is that of progeny of the pair who want to raise their own status, as mentioned above.

The woman who is married legally behaves in a manner strikingly different from that of other women. She carries herself with self-conscious dignity when she walks in the street. Most of the time she remains at home and sends children on any necessary errands. She is quiet and subdued, withdrawn, cold, and stiff. To the outsider, some of the women lead amazingly restricted lives in a society noted for its exuberant gaiety and gregariousness. It seems a heavy price to pay for a rise in status, but some appear quite willing to pay it. One woman, wife of a town leader, told me with evident pride that she had seldom left her house since her marriage twenty years before.

Visiting relationships range from those which are very close to lady-gentleman relationships to those which are very close to casual sexual relationships. The partners do not live together. The man visits the woman in her parental home or in an independent household owned by the woman. If this relationship continues over a long period of time and there are offspring it may become a lady-gentleman relationship with all the appropriate rights and duties. If the man is upper class Creole or white and has legitimate offspring, his illegitimate offspring share in his estate unless some legal steps have been taken to see to it that only his legitimate offspring inherit. Otherwise all offspring are entitled to share.

Identification of, Acknowledgment of, and Claim to Paternity

For legally married men or those engaged in a lady-gentleman relationship there is no question as to paternity of the children. But for the lesser forms of marital union and for trial unions there are certain ways of acknowledging or claiming paternity.

A man acknowledges paternity by providing a layette and money for the midwife or physician. He provides whatever the mother may ask for in maintenance of the child until the mother is able to work again. After that time the man may maintain certain rights as genitor by providing money for the child's school fees, buying his books or a new set of clothing such as a new school uniform. If the man continues to provide help to maintain the child beyond the time when the mother can work, he thereby maintains a right to sexual congress with the mother, unless or until the mother is engaged in another marital union. Thus, as we have seen, a woman may refuse offers of money or goods from the child's father if she wants to break off relations with him. For this reason a man hesitates to visit or bring gifts to the child if the mother has entered a marital relationship with another man. He does not give up his rights as father by not bringing gifts in this case, for he may send gifts through his mother or sister.

Naming the Child

A legally married man has the demand-right to have his wife's children registered in his surname. A genitor in other forms of marital union has a privilege-right to have his child registered at birth in his surname. The mother can deny this privilege and have her child registered in her surname.

Perhaps in recognition of this difference in rights, the regulations having to do with birth registration require a man to present himself along with the mother of his child at the registration office if he is not legally married to the mother and if he wants the child given his surname. The mother alone cannot give the child the father's surname if she is not married to him legally. A woman once legally married can give her future children the marriage partner's surname, however, even though the two may have been separated early in the woman's childbearing career and the children obviously sired by others.

If the man who presumes himself the genitor does not present himself at the registration office, this does not invariably mean he denies parentage nor does it invariably mean that he will refuse to help support the child, although these are both possibilities. It may mean that the mother is angry with the father and proceeds to the registry without him. It may mean that the father is away from home. In this land where migration for labor is so frequent it happens that many men are absent from their home villages at the time of a child's birth. Finally it may mean only that it is inconvenient for the father to present himself at the registry.

If, for whatever reason, it is desirable to change the surname to that of the genitor, this can be done easily at a later time. Both parents must present themselves to the authorities.

Thus, if a man prefers not to admit parenthood, and the relationship between him and the mother has not been public and exclusive, then he can avoid any or all the duties of parenthood including the bestowing of his surname.

Apparently, this is not a frequent occurrence, for the status of genitor is rather prized. But it happens sometimes, for example, when the man is embarrassed somehow by the birth of the child. For example, if he has been courting another woman with whom he would like to set up a stable marital relationship, then he may wish to deny fatherhood at the time the child is born. Not bestowing his surname and not publicly recognizing his fatherhood, however, does not prevent him from later helping the mother maintain the child. Helping the mother in maintaining the child serves as a retroactive acknowledgement of paternity.

Whether or not the surname of the child is later changed legally to that of his father depends on the relationship between the mother and father, on how many mothers of his children he must consider, on how many children he has and their sex, and on what advantages he will gain or lose by changing the name. As a man grows old he is likely to look for a male heir to "carry on his name," and he might consider changing the name of one of his sons. But this desire has to be balanced against the annoyance this action might cause among the other women who are mothers of his children. If all his sisters predecease him, one or more of these former mates may later provide for him when he is ill or too old to provide for himself. In case the old man is not sure the woman and male child are able and willing to take over such responsibility it behooves him to "keep all his options open" by refusing to offend the other women. There are some old men who balance among three or four women, exchanging the signs and symbols of a renewed or continuing marital relationship in a somewhat tentative way, not willing it seems to settle upon any one to the exclusion of the others. Changing the name of one of the children could upset such a balance.

To return to the naming of a child at birth, the more usual situation is that a child is given his genitor's surname even if little else. A man may claim the right to give his name to his child even though he and the mother are separated. His power to enforce the claim is meager, but the mother is ordinarily quite willing that the child be registered in the name of its father. This is a minor concession on her part even though she may have parted with the father and have antagonistic feelings toward him, for she may register the child in one name and call him by another. After he has been called by this name long enough it may become a legal name. Growing children sometimes informally change their names to something else, and this change, too, may in time be legalized.

The name a child goes by, then, has not so much to do with the name he was registered by at birth as with the name of the family he is close to as he grows up. A young boy of my acquaintance was known by the surname of his mother's mother who lived in the same town, rather than by the name on his birth certificate, the surname of his father whom he had never lived with and who had no kin in the town. Even when both mother's and father's families live in the same town, however, the child takes the name of that side of the family that cares for him. Changing the name in this case does not cut the child off from legal or social connection with the other kin.[1]

---

[1]   An Afro-American naming system has been described by Richard and Sally Price (1972), among the Saramaka Maroons of Surinam. The naming practices among the Black Carib of British Honduras are not nearly so well institutionalized.

Psychic Motherhood

The affect which develops between a woman and the children she cares for from birth or early infancy is a prominent part of the definition of motherhood among the Afro-American peoples of British Honduras. The physical mother in a number of cases (twenty-five percent of a sample selected to show the least number of children in this category [Sanford 1971]) is absent from the household in which her progeny are raised for a significant part of their infancy and youth. The woman who nurtures the children is called "mother" and she refers to the children as "my son," or "my daughter," even when, as sometimes happens, the physical mother is and has been a resident of the same household. The children refer to the physical mother and address her by her given name in the latter case.

Another woman referred to "my mother," but addressed the woman in question as "Aunty." The biological relationship of the older woman to the younger was father's sister. She and her twin brother had been given as infants to their father's sister. When the young woman produced her first child, he was taken in his first year by "Aunty." The younger woman said that she gave her first child to her mother because her mother no longer had her, and the boy would make up for the loss.

A woman acquires certain rights to a child when she has nurtured it, rights which are honored by the physical mother and allowed to grow stronger, or which are nipped in the bud when it suits her desires and convenience. These are the right to the child's presence, his loyalty, and his help in household chores. At a later stage the nurturer will have rights to the productive labor of the youth and adult. In her old age she will have rights to support, to companionship, and to have at least one of the descendants of the individual she has raised living in the house with her and tending to her needs.

To a certain extent the woman who has allowed her rights to a child to lapse, as it were, by allowing another woman to care for it, never quite loses them all, for she can call upon her progeny for help in her old age, and the progeny are quite faithful in this respect if they are still living in fairly close proximity.

A woman who allows someone else to raise her children very often takes other people's children to raise, usually one at a time in a series. As soon as one is well along toward puberty another is taken.

For about a quarter of the population, then, each person has two mothers, his genetrix and the woman who raised him. He has rights and duties with respect to both of these women. But the mother he lives with is the one to whom he owes household help as a child and economic help as a youth and adult. This difference in duty emerges in cases where the two mothers live in close proximity or the same household. In the case mentioned above, in which a woman gave her first-born child to her "mother," she later returned to the same town with her seven later-born children and lived on the mother's property in a separate house. They lived in the same "yard," but there was only very limited economic cooperation between them. They did not constitute a domestic group. The first-born child of the younger woman had no duties in the care of his younger half-siblings. These duties and responsibilities were on the shoulders of the eldest child of the seven, another boy, who had lived from birth with his genetrix. The eldest child whom she had given to her "mother" owed household duties only to the woman raising him. This boy, somewhere between ten and twelve years of age in 1969, helped the older woman by peddling foods she had made to sell, and also by peddling sweet ices on commission, an elementary form of entrepreneurship. A boy of this age or even older, as long as he lives with his mother, is expected to bring home his earnings and receive spending money in return.

A genetrix, then, has the right to give her child to a relative or even to a stranger, and she thereby disposes of her rights to his presence and household help. She also is likely to lose some of her rights to loving attention of the child. Some of her rights may lapse from non-use. This is a well-recognized possibility, and in cases where the mother wants to retain some of the affectional ties for herself she returns to retrieve the child.

A woman who is raising a child, or with whom the child has been left, is expected to keep reminding a child of its physical mother. She is expected to help the genetrix keep affective hold of the child. If the woman who keeps the child is a mother's mother or a mother's sister, the mother does not fear so much losing the affection of the child. Proxy mothers of a more distant relationship are more often suspected of trying to gain more rights than they are entitled to by gaining the affections of the child.

In a case in which a husband and wife loaned one of their girls to the wife's sister, because she had no children of her own, the mother, as the daughter came to maturity, demanded on several occasions that the girl come back to live with her. At one point she refused to give the daughter enough money to pay for a tonsillectomy on the grounds that as long as she insisted on remaining with the mother's sister the sister should pay for this. The sister did pay the medical expense. Later, the daughter wanted to marry, and the mother went to the priest and informed him that the girl was not yet eighteen. This was true, and since by British Honduras law a girl of her age had to have the consent of her parents, the marriage could not proceed.

This was one of the very common instances in which one of the parties of a family argument tries to use national law and the authority of the courts to contravene a customary law. If this situation had been brought to a court, I believe the mother's sister's right as guardian by customary law might very well have been upheld, since the courts often find some way to uphold local customary rights. The priest in the end was persuaded to let the girl marry.

This was a case in which the married couple, parents of the girl, lost the right to deny their daughter permission to marry. They lost this right not only because they permitted the girl to live for a long period with another woman during which time strong affective ties developed, but because they failed to maintain their own affectional ties, not only with her but with the woman keeping her. When they tried to reinstate their rights, the affection which the girl had developed for her "other mother" stood in the way.

The rights of the genetrix to companionship, affection, loyalty, to physical labor of the child, and to economic support by progeny, both male and female, are all-encompassing. Any or all of these may be delegated to others, but the delegation is presumed to be temporary. Theoretically, the rights may be reinstated at any later time.

In actuality, there are certain contingencies in which the genetrix's rights are lost to her: (1) the child may choose between his genetrix and his social mother in cases of dispute, and (2) a written paper given to the foster parent by the genetrix at the time she bestows the child is thought to prevent a genetrix from reclaiming it. But it appears that the child's right to choose is accorded greater weight by courts of law and by custom than the contents of the paper.

Rights of a genetrix to reclaim a child can be eroded, then, by a keeper who engages the affections of a child for a sufficiently long time, and who wants to alienate the child from its genetrix.

The rights of a genetrix and psychic mother to economic help from children apply to girls as well as to boys. Physical distance can erode the rights of the mothers, or rather can give a child the opportunity to avoid his or her duty.

Favorite Children

Children learn very early the value of reciprocal exchanges, not only of affection but of the symbols of stronger interpersonal attachments. Each mother has a favorite child on whom she depends for important services. This child is often the eldest of a set of siblings living with their mother, a girl or boy who tends the siblings while the mother is absent, cleans the house and yard, and sells home-baked foods.

The sense of responsibility and of consequence which such a child exudes is almost palpable as he sells bread or sweets for his mother, or stands behind the counter in a shop, or attempts to find transportation to the clinic for a sick mother or granny. Rather important family business is entrusted to growing children, both boys and girls, and the contributions of these children are recognized, respected, and praised. The favorite children gain self-confidence and flourish as they practice adult roles.

Children are frequently given the right to choose the household in which they will live. A grandmother or mother's sister's house, sometimes standing in close proximity, can be run to when a child has displeased his mother. A grandmother in this position is very likely to form a special attachment to one of the children and to make him her favorite child. He will start spending more and more time in the other household until finally the arrangement may be "formalized." He will be loaned to the granny by his parents.

TRANSACTIONS IN PARENTHOOD

Lending of Children

Children are loaned by their parents most often to close kin or neighbors, usually as a result of an interpersonal relationship already established between the adult and child. There are mutually beneficial goods and services exchanged between the adult and child, but the most important exchange appears to be affection to the adult and respect to the child. The child performs household chores, runs errands, and in general serves as an extra pair of eyes and ears for the householder, very much as the favorite child does for his mother. The householder provides food, clothing, and whatever else the child needs. The child then has the gratifying position of being the favorite child. He may indeed be the only child of the house, and his value and importance in the establishment are enhanced thereby.

One of the most dependable ways of gaining such a role is to start acting out some of the appropriate behaviors with an adult who has no children in the house. The child discovers in practice how to call forth the desired response in another. He finds out how behaving as a child of the grown-up inspires that grown-up to act as a parent to him. Children at rather young ages start practicing the appropriate behaviors. A child of three regularly "takes his tea" (eats his meals) at his mother's sister's house a block or so away from his grandmother's house, to which he returns to play and sleep with his siblings. This is not only permitted but is encouraged by all as precociously enterprising on his part.

A little girl of about six or seven years of age appeared at the door of an older woman living alone by preference, I believe. She did not really need a child, and if she had, she could have called upon neighbors for one. The woman described the girl's pitiful appearance, sores on her face, and worn clothing. The child hung about, ate there, and the two enjoyed each other's company very much. Finally one day the little girl took her clothes from her mother's house and put them in the old woman's house. The woman felt she had to send her back home, but the little girl returned again and again to "take care of" the woman. As they walked down the road the little girl guided her to safe places to walk. Although the woman was far from doddering and was quite capable of seeing and avoiding mud puddles, still she was charmed by the child's precocity in playing the role of protector and friend. The little girl was then loaned to the older woman.

In my experience it was the middle children who sought other households and other adults to attach themselves to. It was never the eldest in a group of children living together nor the youngest.

Boys are loaned to uncles who are school teachers to go with them to their posts in the "bush." Elementary schools are located in isolated areas, and the Carib people have occupied these posts for various reasons which we need not discuss here. Unmarried teachers have in the past been loaned a nephew to help them with household work and to serve as companions. The two would go to the location at the beginning of the fall term and not emerge until the next summer. Very often such a boy would later become a teacher himself. Obviously these experiences turned out to be apprenticeships, despite what they may have been considered at the beginning.

Boys and girls are frequently loaned to priests and nuns. The schools in British Honduras are operated by churches although they are supported by government funds. Some boys are granted "scholarships" to be educated at the secondary school in Belize. They are supplied with room and board and books, and in exchange they perform duties around the schools and churches.

The practice described above apparently has a long history. There is documentary evidence for its having taken place as early as the beginning of the nineteenth century. The motive of the government and the church officials was to train emissaries to the Carib people. We can only guess at the motives of the parents who sent their sons to Belize for this purpose. One can assume that the parents recognized the benefits to their sons in social status advancement. One can also assume that it is similar to the motives which seem to be current today — a generalized value for education in the dominant culture, a learning which it is hoped will benefit the child in his later life.

Apprenticeship as a Form of Reciprocity

Apprenticeships to service occupations and in such skills as cattle-tending, tailoring, barbering, and carpentry are as often as not entered by children on their own initiative in much the same way as they attach themselves to other households. Sometimes the parents arrange for the apprenticeship, but the most satisfactory and successful apprenticeships are those which are initiated by the children themselves. As I asked older men about their early experiences, it appeared with some regularity that the first apprenticeship their fathers or mothers arranged for them was for one reason or another unpleasing to them. They chose their own and were satisfied.

Little boys, it appears, make many trials at occupations. They go from one to another until they find one or more that they like, and then if they are persistent enough and useful enough to the adult worker, the arrangement may be formalized — a young boy is taken into the household and the workman behaves as parent to him. He then becomes a specialist in this particular occupation. But a more important generalized skill he has shown himself to have gained is that of establishing and maintaining interpersonal relationships — primary relationships that can be useful to him.

Lending of Children at a Distance

Children are sometimes taken to a distant city by their parents to find a rich householder who will take them. The merchants of Belize were in the past quite accustomed to having people knock on their doors with children to be placed. The phrases of presentation fell into a pattern: "I give you this child — I know you will take good care of him. He will be treated as a child of the home, fed, clothed, sent to school and to church. In return he will do for you what a child can." On the face of it this is an employment contract, and to the receiver of the child it appears to have been precisely that. To the givers, however, there was much more to the transaction. They expected, I believe, that the child would gain something of a generalized nature, some experience in another milieu. When I was able to elicit a verbalization of the expected "good" to be gained by the child it was often expressed as the learning of English. A Carib's first language is the Amerindian Carib language. Those living in Spanish-speaking areas next learn to speak Spanish. It is indeed true that the learning of English is extremely useful to a child. But I believe the bestowing parents expect more. They expect the "given" child to take on Creole attributes — the attributes of a much higher social rating. The child is expected to make something of it. Far from being got rid of by his parents, he is being put into position to make his fortune, to use his position for personal enrichment. To the bestowing parent the arrangement is an incipient patron-client relationship. It is up to the tiny client to be so useful and so ingratiating to his patron that the patron will be induced to bestow greater and greater advantages as time went on.

Some children are "given" in infancy to neighbors, friends, or even to strangers. The recipients sometimes hope and believe that these are out-right gifts. They may try to formalize the transaction by demanding a "paper" from the mother indicating that she will not try to reclaim the child later. Despite all verbal and written agreements, the mothers return later and try to take back their "given" children. If the children are still very small, too young to make a choice, the mother takes them away, even by force. If the child is old enough to choose, perhaps beyond seven or eight years of age, he decides. In cases of dispute, the local court upholds the child's right to choose. If a child chooses its genetrix in preference to the woman who has raised him from an infant, this is a severe humiliation to his foster mother, *prima facie* evidence of her failure to maintain the kind of interpersonal relationship with the child which would have caused him to choose to stay with her. A large proportion of the children asked to choose will remain with the foster parent, and the mother respects this choice.

In conclusion, I invite attention to the resemblance between successful matings, successful transfers of children to parent surrogates, and to successful kinship relations. A mating begins with the exchange of the symbols and activities appropriate to a successful marital relationship. Kin relations are accompanied by friendly relations and appropriate exchanges if they are active. All depend upon the establishment and the maintenance of interpersonal relationships of mutual affection and respect, evidenced by a constant reciprocal flow of material and non-material benefits.

Kinship is rather widely spread and weakened by the mating and marriage customs, combined with the retention of all known biological kin within the system. This results in a large number of possible kin ties for each individual, but the overlap of kin ties among a set of individuals is correspondingly increased. Kin ties therefore are only opportunities for the enterprising. Friendship is equally as important as kinship, and when friendship and kinship are combined the tie is much strengthened. Several observers have noted a form of pseudo-kinship which is called upon to explain and justify very close friendly relations.

When young children are taken to the city and "given" to rich householders, the transaction is couched in terms which clearly imply an understanding that they are to be treated the same as the offspring of the householder. The child is expected to learn, if he has not already learned, how instrumental relations are established and maintained and how his behavior as a child of the keeper inspires in return an obligation in the keeper to behave as a parent to him.

REFERENCES

BLAKE, JUDITH
    1961   *Family structure in Jamaica.* New York: The Free Press of Glencoe.
CARROLL, VERN
    1970   *Adoption in Eastern Oceania.* Honolulu: University of Hawaii Press.
COHEN, YEHUDI
    1956   Structure and function: family organization and socialization in a Jamaican community. *American Anthropologist* 58:644–868.
DAVENPORT, WILLIAM
    1961   Family system of Jamaica. *Social and Economic Studies* 10:420–554.
FRAZIER, E. FRANKLIN
    1939   *The Negro family in the United States.* Chicago: University of Chicago Press.
GONZÁLEZ, NANCIE SOLIEN
    1969   *Black Carib household structure.* Seattle: University of Washington Press.
GOODENOUGH, WARD H.
    1970   *Description and comparison in cultural anthropology.* Chicago: Aldine.
HENRIQUES, FERNANDO
    1969   *Family and colour in Jamaica* (second edition). London: MacGibbon and Kee.
KEESING, ROGER
    1970   "Simple models of complexity: the lure of kinship," in *Kinship studies in the Morgan centennial year.* Edited by Priscilla Reining, 17–31. Washington, D.C.: The Anthropological Society of Washington.

PRICE, RICHARD, SALLY PRICE
1972   Saramaka onomastics: an Afro-American naming system. *Ethnology* 11:341–367.
RUBIN, VERA
1961   "Family aspirations and attitudes of Trinidad youth," in (Second) *Caribbean conference for mental health. Children of the Caribbean: their mental health needs*, 59–68. San Juan, Puerto Rico: Department of the Treasury.
RUBIN, VERA, MARISA ZAVALLONI
1969   *We wish to be looked upon.* New York: Teachers College Press, Columbia University.
SANFORD, MARGARET
1971   "Disruption of the mother-child relationship in conjunction with matrifocality: a study of child-keeping among the Carib and Creole of British Honduras." Unpublished doctoral dissertation, Catholic University of America, Washington, D.C.
SIMEY, T. S.
1946   *Welfare and planning in the West Indies.* Oxford: The Clarendon Press.
SMITH, R. T.
1956   *The Negro family in British Guiana.* London: Routledge and Kegan Paul.
STACK, CAROL B.
1970   "The kindred of Viola Jackson," in *Afro-American anthropology.* Edited by Norman E. Whitten and John F. Szwed, 303–312. New York: The Free Press.

Who Raises Black Children: Transactions of Child Givers and Child Receivers

CAROL B. STACK

The Black community has long recognized the problems and difficulties which all mothers in poverty share. Shared parental responsibilities among kin have long been the response. As kinsmen change residence, children may be dispersed in households which do not include their biological mother. Many children growing up in The Flats, an urban Black community in the Midwest, move back and forth from the households of their mothers to households of close female kin. The woman who temporarily assumes the kinship obligation to care for a child acquires the major cluster of rights and duties ideally associated with "motherhood."

This participant-observation study of urban poverty and the domestic strategies of urban-born Black Americans whose parents had migrated from the South to a single community in the urban North concentrated on family life among second generation urban dwellers who were raised on public welfare. Its purpose was to explore the ways in which parental responsibilities distribute socially, and to draw out the criteria by which persons are entitled to parental roles.

Child keeping corresponds to general characterizations of fosterage (Carroll 1970; Goody 1966; Keesing 1970a; Sanford 1971). Keesing and Sanford have defined fosterage as the housing of a dependent child in a household which does not include the mother or father. Carroll views fostering in more specific terms as a temporary obligation of kinsmen to take care of one another's children. Goody contrasts kinship fostering in crisis situations to the rights of kinfolk to take children and rear them apart from their own parents.

The responsibility of caring for children in The Flats is a kin obligation. It is not necessarily a role required of a single actor. Rights in children are delegated to kin who are participants in domestic networks of cooperation. In 1970 four-fifths of the children in The Flats were being raised by their mothers. One-fifth of the children were living with adult kin rather than with their mothers.

Table 1.   Frequency of child keeping, AFDC data

	Frequency	Percentage
Children raised by biological mother	559	81
Children raised by adult female kin	127	18
Children raised by non-kin	8	1
	694	100

Within a network of cooperating kinsmen, there may be three or more adult women with whom, in turn, a child resides. In this cycle of residence changes, while younger children usually sleep in the same household as their mother, the size of the dwelling, employment, and many other factors determine where older siblings sleep. Although patterns of eating, visiting, and child care may bring mothers and their children together for most of the day, the adult woman immediately responsible for a child changes with the child's residence. The residence patterns of children in The Flats have structural implications for both the ways in which rights in children distribute socially and also the criteria by which persons are entitled to parental roles.

From the point of view of the child, there may be a number of women who act as "mothers" towards them; some are just slightly older than the children themselves. A woman who intermittently raises a sister's or niece's or cousin's child regards their offspring as her grandchildren as much as children born to her own son and daughter.

The number of people who can assume appropriate behaviors ideally associated with parental and grandparental roles is increased to include close kinsmen and friends. Consequently, the kin terms "mother," "father," "grandmother," etc., are not necessarily appropriate labels for describing the social roles. Children may retain ties with their parents and siblings and at the same time establish comparable relationships with other kinsmen. There is even a larger number of friends and relatives who may request a hug and kiss, "a little sugar," from children they watch grow up. But they do not consistently assume parental roles towards those children.

DOMESTIC ARRANGEMENTS

People in The Flats generally view child keeping as a part of the flux and elasticity of residence. The constant expansion and contraction of households and the successive recombinations of kinsmen residing together require women to care for the children residing in their household. As households shift, rights and responsibilities in children are shared.

The following passages provide examples of some circumstances which require mothers to sleep in households apart from their children, and which require co-residence kinsmen to take care of one another's children. These examples show how misleading it is to regard child keeping apart from residence, alliance, and daily exchanges of other kinsmen in the domestic network of the child.

The responsibility for providing care, food, clothing, and shelter for children in The Flats is diffused over many kin-based household units. While household boundaries are elastic and frequently change, cooperative networks generally maintain the same participants over time.

Most of our kin lived in two apartment buildings which were joined together. I decided it would be best for our five children if we moved in too. My husband's mother had a small apartment, her sister had one in the basement, and another brother and his family took a larger apartment upstairs. My husband's brother was really good to us. He got the kids things they wanted and controlled them too. All us women kept the kids together during the day. We cooked together too. It was good living.

Close kin may fully cooperate in child-care activities during periods of time when they are not co-resident. In addition, individuals may insist upon joining a household in order to help raise children.

Even when me and my two sisters were pretty young my mother had a hard time keeping track of us. My grandmother was old then and receiving a pension and some help from her son. She decided to move in with us to "bring us up right." She stayed on about four years, but she and my mother didn't get on, they fought a lot. All our kin in The Flats was helping us out and we didn't want for nothing. One of my uncles kept us and fed us every Thursday and Sunday night, another uncle got us all our clothing. We was really being kept good.

Kin networks change with birth and death. Likewise, natural processes and events in the life cycle of individuals create new child-care needs and new household alignments. Fluctuations in interpersonal relationships over the life cycle account for changes in the residence of children. It is not uncommon for young children to reside in the home of rather aging kin, who eventually become too old to care for the children.

I was staying with my great-grandfather [momofa] for the first five years of my life, but he just got too old to care for me. My mother was living in The Flats at the time, but my "daddy" asked my mother's brother and his wife to take me cause he really trusted them with me. I stayed with them and their three kids, but my mother came by and took care of us kids lots of times. When I was about nine years old my mother got married and from then on I stayed with her and her husband and he gave me his name.

Occasionally adolescents decide on their own that they want to live with a kinsman other than the one with whom they are residing. Boys, for example, who have maintained a close relationship with their natural father may choose to go and live with their father.

When my brother was about half grown his father started buying him clothes. When he was sixteen he decided to go stay with his father who lived right down by the center of town. He's been staying with him ever since.

When a young girl becomes pregnant, the closest adult female kin of the girl or of the unborn child is expected to assume partial responsibility for the young child. Usually rights in such children are shared between the mother and appropriate female kin. If the mother is extremely young she may "give the child" to someone who wants the child — for example to the child's father's kin, to a childless couple, or to close friends.

I ran away from home when I was fourteen. I ran off to Chicago first and then to The Flats. The friends of kin who took me in had two sons. I gave birth to the oldest boy's baby, but I was in no way ready for a baby. The baby's grandmother [famo] wanted the baby so I gave the baby to her and she adopted her as her own.

Children are sometimes given to non-kin who express love, concern, and a desire to keep a child.

My girl friend had six children when I started going with her, but her baby daughter was really something else. I got so attached to that baby over about two years that when her mother and I quit, I asked if she would give the baby to me. She said fine, and my "daughter" has been living with me, my mother, my grandmother, and my sisters and brothers ever since. My daughter is ten years old now. She sees her mother now and then, and her father takes her to Church with him sometimes, but our family is really the only family she's ever had.

Entering a new marriage or consensual relationship, a woman with children often temporarily disperses her children among kin (Goody 1966; Midgett 1969).

My old man wanted me to leave town with him and get married. But he didn't want to take my three children. I stayed with him for about two years and my children stayed in town with my mother. Then she told me to come back and get them. I came back and stayed.

Just as the beginning of a male-female relationship can split a mother from her children, the end of a marriage or consensual union may cause a family to separate.

I left my husband 'cause I knew he had been fooling around. After that my family was really split in parts for a while. I sent my three oldest children to stay with my husband's aunt [humosi], my middle girl stayed downstairs with my husband's mother, and my two youngest stayed here with my mother.

The intricacy of the involvement of kinfolk in one another's lives is a recurring theme which emerges in descriptions of residence changes during childhood. Bonds of obligation, alliance, and dependence among kinsmen are created and strengthened in a variety of ways. Goods and services are the main currency exchanged among cooperating kinsmen. But in the process of giving and receiving, children are sometimes regarded as chattel: they may be transferred back and forth, borrowed or loaned. Consequently it is not uncommon for individuals to talk about their residence away from their mother as a fact over which she had little or no control. For example, one may insist upon "taking" a child to help out.

My mother already had three children when I was born. She had been raised by her maternal great aunt [momosi]. After I was born my mother's great aunt insisted on taking me to help my mother out. I stayed there after my mother got married and moved to The Flats. I wanted to move there too, but my "mama" didn't want to give me up and my mother didn't want to fight with her. When I was fourteen I left anyway and my mother took me in.

When my youngest daughter got polio my mother insisted on taking her. I got a job and lived nearby with my son. My mother raised my little girl until my girl died.

A mother may request or require kin to keep one of her children. An offer to keep the child of a kinsman has a variety of implications for child givers and receivers. It may be that the mother has come upon hard times and desperately wants her close kinsmen to temporarily assume responsibility for her children. Kinsmen rarely refuse requests to keep one another's children, and yet they recognize the rights of kinsmen to take children and raise them apart from their own parents (Goody 1966). In the latter situation, individuals allow kinsmen to actively create alliances and obligations towards one another which may be called upon in the future.

The uncontrollable spectrum of economic and legal pressures from outside society constitutes the external forces acting upon domestic groups. Unemployment, migration, welfare requirements, housing shortages, high rents, eviction, and prison necessarily lead to a change in residence. Disasters and calamities such as death, murder, accident, and fire also require residence changes. Most often these changes are closely related to the need for child-care arrangements (Stack 1970).

People in The Flats are evicted from their dwellings by landlords who want to raise rents, tear a building down, or rid themselves of tenants who complain about rats, roaches, and plumbing. The landlord can then rent to a family in such great need of housing that they will not complain for a period of time. When families are evicted, other kinsmen usually take them in. Such moves alter the residence of children and the adults who acquire authority over them.

Soon after we moved to The Flats me and my kids were evicted. The landlord said he was going to tear the building down and build a parking lot. He never did. The place is still standing and has folks living in it today. My husband's mother and her husband took me and the kids in and watched over them while I had my baby. We stayed on after her husband died, and my husband joined us.

Individuals fail to pay their rent for many reasons: they may be temporarily "cut off aid" if the welfare office has some reason to be suspicious of their eligibility; some portion of the rent money may be given to a kinsman who is not on aid in order to help him through a crisis or illness; and money loaned to kin or friends may not be returned in time for the rent. People receive eviction notices almost immediately after they fail to pay the rent.

My oldest sister was cut off aid the day her husband got out of jail. She and her husband and their three children were evicted from their apartment and they came to live with us. We were in crowded conditions already. I had my son, my other sister was there with her two kids, and my mother was about going crazy. My mother put my sister's husband out 'cause she found out he was a dope addict. He came back one night soon after that and murdered my sister. After my sister's death my mother couldn't face living in Chicago any longer. One of my other sisters who had been adopted and raised by my mother's grandmother [famo] visited us and persuaded us to move to The Flats where she was staying. All of us moved there — my mother, my two sisters and their children, my two baby sisters, and my dead sister's children. My sister who had been staying in The Flats found us a house across the street from her own.

Murder, accidents, and personal injury resulting from fights within the community coincide with ghetto life, overcrowded conditions, unemployment, and poverty. Likewise, bad housing conditions and unenforced housing standards result in hazardous living conditions.

My son set fire by accident to our place one night when the gas lines sprung a leak. We had to move. The place belonged to my husband's sister-in-law's grandfather. We had been living there with my husband's mother, his brother's children and our eight children. My husband's father lived in the basement 'cause he and his wife were separated.

Overcrowded dwellings and the impossibility of finding adequate housing in The Flats have long-term consequences on where and with whom children live.

I married my first baby's father when the baby was three months old. We couldn't find or afford a place of our own, so we moved in with my husband's mother and her old man and my husband's brother.

My brother stayed with my aunt [mosi] and her husband until he was ten, 'cause we didn't have enough room — but he stayed with us most every weekend. Finally my aunt moved into the house behind ours with her husband, her brother, and my brother and my other brothers and sisters and I lived up front with my mother and her old man.

The above passages illustrate the various circumstances of residential changes which lead to child keeping and shared responsibilities of child care. It might appear that the events described above contribute to a rather random relocation of individuals in dwellings, and a random distribution of the rights individuals acquire in children. But this is not the case. Individuals constantly face the reality that they may need the help of kin for themselves and their children. As a result they anticipate these needs, and from year to year they have a very clear notion of which kinsmen would be willing to help. The calculation is simple because it is an outcome of calculated exchanges of goods and services between kinsmen. Consequently, residence patterns and the dispersing of children in households of kin are not haphazard. This issue is taken up in the following section in which the norms and expectations of folk fosterage are compared with the statistical patterns of fosterage in The Flats.

STATISTICAL PATTERNS

From time to time most of the adults involved in this study had been fostered by kinsmen. Some of their own children are currently residing in the homes of kinsmen, have been kept by kinsmen in the past, or may join the household of a close kinsman in the future. These are alternatives which enable parents to cope with poverty; they are possibilities which every mother understands.

Information on the frequency of fosterage collected from Aid for Dependent Children (AFDC) case histories shows that one-fifth of 694 dependent children were assigned to the welfare grant of a close female kinsman other than their mother. This means that the adult female responsible for the child is not the child's mother. Table 2 shows the frequency of fostering based upon AFDC case histories, and the relationship of grantees to AFDC children on their grant, and in their households.

Table 2.   Frequency of child keeping, AFDC data

Relationship to grantee	Frequency	Total	Percentage
Children raised by biological mother	559	559	81
Children raised by adult female kin:			
Younger sibling	34		
Sibling's child	34		
Grandchild	24		
Other kin	35	127	18
Non-kin	8	8	1
	—	—	—
		694	100

These statistics on the frequency of fostering are in fact much lower than actual instances of child keeping in The Flats. According to the AFDC case histories, 81 percent of the dependent children are being raised by their own mothers, and 18 percent by close female kinsmen. Grantees must claim that a dependent child is residing in their household in order to receive benefits for the child. But my personal contact with individuals whose case histories make up the statistical survey clearly shows disagreement between the record and actual residence patterns. Mothers temporarily shift the residence of their children in response to changes in their own personal relationships, illness or pregnancy, or housing problems. Dependent children, and the funds for these children, are dispersed into households of cooperating kinsmen. In the process of switching the residence of children, mothers or grantees rarely report these residence changes to the welfare office.

The variance between the statistics and actual residence patterns is also demonstrated in detailed life histories of adults and children involved in the study. The residential life histories[1] of children show that at least one-third of the children have been "kept" by kinsmen one or two times during their childhood. Consequently the frequency of child keeping in The Flats is higher than the AFDC statistics indicate. The lower limit of child keeping in The Flats may be 20 percent, but the range of child keeping is between 20 percent and 35 percent.

Important factors which show the relationship between patterns of child keeping and the daily domestic organization of cooperating kinsmen are the age, status, and geographical location of the mothers of dependent

[1]   Residence life histories are detailed chronological accounts of the residence changes from birth to the present (Stack 1970). For each move or change in household composition, I gathered data on (1) the age of the person for each residence change, (2) the situation which precipitated the move [context], and (3) the kinship links between members of each newly-formed household.

children assigned to grantees who are not the child's mother. Field observations of 139 dependent children who are assigned to a grantee other than their mother revealed that practically one-half of those children's mothers generally resided in the same dwelling as their child. Many of those mothers were teenagers when their first child was born. At the time of the survey only 6 percent of them were under eighteen. Table 3 shows the status and location of biological mothers whose dependent children were assigned to AFDC grants of female kinsmen. According to the female kin now responsible for the children (Table 3), only 8 percent of the mothers had actually deserted their children. Three-fourths of the biological mothers of these children were living in The Flats at the time of the survey. They resided intermittently in the grantee's household, the household of a kinsman, or from time to time in a separate residence with male or female friends.

Table 3.   Status and location of biological mother

Status and location of biological mother	Frequency	Percentage
Married adult (over 18) Resides in grantee's house	34	24
Adult: lives in The Flats	34	24
Unmarried adult Resides in grantee's house	19	14
Mother deserted child	11	8
Married or unmarried minor Resides in grantee's house	9	6
Not ascertainable	32	24

The examples above point to the confusion which can arise when statistical data are interpreted out of context. Statistical patterns do not divulge underlying cultural patterns. This confusion between statistics and cultural patterns underlies most interpretations of Black family life.

Another clear example of this confusion is the assumption that Black children derive all their jural kin through females. Widely popularized statistics on female-headed households have contributed to the classification of Black households as matrifocal or matriarchal and to the assumption that Black children derive nothing of sociological importance from their father. In fact, 69 percent of the fathers of AFDC children recognized their children and provided them with kinship affiliations.

A further demonstration of the importance of the kinship links a child acquires through his mother and father is given in patterns of fostering. In the preceding section we saw that couples, mothers with children, and children continually join the households of the kinsmen. Table 4 shows the residence of children temporarily fostered in households of kinsmen at one point in time.

Table 4.   Patterns of child keeping, AFDC data

	Frequency	Percentage
Mother's kin	57	74
Father's kin	20	26
	77	100

Analysis of changes that have occurred in the residence of children in The Flats over the past fifty years is provided in residential life histories. The data show the residence patterns of children being fostered during time changes in the domestic groups in a community (Otterbein 1970). Table 5 shows residence patterns of children kept in the households of kinsmen based on information derived from life histories of adults and children.

Table 5.   Laterality of child keeping, residence histories

	Frequency	Percentage
Mother's kin	43	69
Father's kin	19	31
	62	100

The ratio of children kept in the homes of kinsmen related through a child's mother or father is approximately similar in Table 4 and Table 5. Although the majority of children in this study lived with their mother or her kin, based on the statistical study of AFDC case histories, one-fourth of the fostered children lived with their father's kin; based on life histories, one-third of all children fostered are living with their father's kin.

Expectations and mutual demands of kinsmen are rarely fulfilled to satisfaction. But individuals in The Flats have a fairly clear notion of which kinsmen they can count on in times of crisis or stress. When mothers apply for AFDC benefits for their dependent children they are required to list, in rank order, whom they expect to raise each of their children if they die or are unable to maintain custody of the child. The responses of mothers in Table 6 reflect their "expectations" regarding which kinsmen would be willing and able to raise their child.

When asked by welfare workers who they would expect to raise their child in the event of their own death, mothers of 228 children named their own blood relatives; mothers of 76 children named the child's father's kin. The agreement between the expectations of adult females regarding child keeping and the statistical patterns of child keeping over the life cycle is striking.

Table 6. Laterality of child keeping expectations, AFDC data

	Frequency	Percentage
Mother's kin	222	73
Father's kin	83	27
	305	100

Black family life has been continually characterized as "broken" and "disorganized." But it is clear that the individuals involved in this study are aware of the choices, criteria, and norms regarding fostering in The Flats. They understand their child keeping practices to the extent that their expectation regarding the laterality of fostering approximately predicts the correct statistical patterns of fosterage.

TRANSACTIONS IN PARENTHOOD

The purpose of this section is to explore the ways in which rights in children distribute socially, and to draw out the criteria by which parents are entitled to parental roles. Discovering the criteria by which kin are eligible to assume parental roles is not an easy task. One must identify the cultural nature of folk rights and duties in relation to children and then observe when and by whom these behavior patterns are assumed. The content of rights and duties in relation to children differ cross-culturally; residents in The Flats find it difficult to spell out particular rights and duties in children. The elaboration of rights pertaining to children is best elicited from observed scenes.

Scenes in which rights in children are in conflict must be analyzed in terms of the social context in which they occur. The social context of situations includes at least the following considerations: the participants present, the specific life histories of the participants, the socially meaningful occurrences which preceded the event, and the rules which come into play. The scenes described below reflect tension or conflict among kinsmen over rights in children. These scenes provide a basis for identifying parental behaviors which may be shared.

The first scene takes place on the front porch of a house which Georgia, thirty, and her three children share with Georgia's Aunt Ethel, fifty, and

Ethel's boy friend. Just before the incident occurred, Georgia and Ethel had fought over the division of housework and the utility bills. Aunt Ethel was angered at Georgia's lack of respect, and her unwillingness to support her with the AFDC benefits Georgia received for her children. Georgia was willing to pay the rent but insisted that Ethel's boy friend pay the utilities and that Ethel take over more of the cooking and housework.

Following the argument, Ethel's brother dropped by to visit. Ethel, her boy friend, and her brother sat in the sunshine on the porch. Georgia and her children joined them. Georgia's daughter Alice was bothered by her first loose tooth. Alice continued whimpering on the porch as she had for most of the afternoon.

SCENE I

Aunt Ethel yanked Alice's arm, drawing Alice nearer to her on the porch. Trouble over Alice's loose tooth had gone far enough. Ethel decided to pull the tooth. Without nudging it to see how loose it really was, Ethel fixed her fingers on the tooth and pulled with all her strength. Alice screamed with fear, kicked, and tried to bite her aunt. Alice's mother, Georgia, sat near by, her tense body and bulging eyes voicing silent resistance to her aunt's physical act. After some moments of the struggle passed, a friend who happened to be visiting said, "Maybe the tooth isn't ready, Ethel," and Ethel let the child go. Georgia's tensed face and body relaxed as her daughter sprang into her arms in tears. Georgia turned to her friend, her eyelids lowered, expressing relief that her friend's quick words had stopped Ethel's performance.

Georgia had lived in the same household with her mother's sister Ethel for most of her life. Ethel helped Georgia's grandmother raise Georgia. After the grandmother's death, Ethel assumed responsibility for Georgia. Georgia's mother lived close by, but she had nine other children to raise on her own. Ethel has been married twice, but she never had any children. She refers to Georgia as her daughter even though she did not become head of the household in which Georgia was raised until Georgia was thirteen. In recent years Georgia has been much closer to her mother than to her aunt. Nevertheless, Ethel regards Georgia's children as her own grandchildren.

Ethel's assertive behavior with regard to Alice was not an isolated event. In Georgia's presence, Ethel frequently demonstrates the right she holds to love, discipline, and even terrify Georgia's children. Ethel feels intense love, obligation, and bitterness towards Georgia's children. Not so long ago Georgia left her children with Ethel and ran off with a serviceman. When Georgia returned six months later she complained that Ethel had neglected her children, their clothes, their hair, and had not fed them well.

In the context of the previous fight between Ethel and Georgia, Ethel's action is partly a performance. Ethel is demonstrating the rights which she shares and may be expected to assume in relation to Georgia's children. Ethel forcefully attempted to pull Alice's tooth. She was angered by Georgia's arrogance just minutes before. In response, Ethel strongly asserted and strengthened the rights she has in Georgia's children, rights which she simultaneously shares with Georgia.

Commenting on the event, Georgia said, "Whatever happens to me, Ethel be the person to keep my kids. She already kept them once before. My mother, she ain't in no position to take them with all of her own, and I wouldn't have Aunt Flossie take them noway." The event disturbed Georgia. She didn't want to sit quietly and allow her child to be hurt. But she found herself powerless to act considering her expectations that Ethel might be required to nurture her children.

The second scene takes place during a train ride to Chicago. It includes some of the same participants as those in the first scene. Kin to Ethel and Georgia rode the train together for a Fourth of July celebration with relatives. The group traveling together included Ethel's sisters Wilma and Ann, their children and grandchildren, and Georgia and her children — fourteen children in all.

SCENE II

The three sisters, Ethel, Wilma, and Ann, sat toward the rear of the train, dressed fine for the occasion, ignoring the children's noise. Georgia sat across from them with her girl friend. A coke bottle struck against the iron foot railing broke into pieces. Shrieks of laughter traveled from seat to seat where most of the small children — all cousins — were sitting together in the front of the train. Instantly Ethel walked forward to the front of the train by Wilma's young boy and began beating him harshly with her handbag. Then, showing she meant business, Ethel grabbed the boy next to the window who was laughing and gave him a few sharp slaps on the cheek. Wilma paid no attention the the cries of her two young boys. But when Ethel returned to her seat, Ann told her, "Don't you lay a hand on my granddaughter."

Throughout the trip Ethel shouted, beat, and teased the children. Her sisters enjoyed the train ride and generally ignored the children. But Ethel's rights regarding each of her sister's children are not equivalent. From time to time Ethel helped Wilma raise her children, including Georgia. Ethel has cared for or lived with Georgia's children for the past five years. Her rights in Wilma and Georgia's children are recognized by both the mothers and the children. During the train ride, in the presence of her sisters and her niece, Ethel demonstrated her right to discipline the children of these kin. Likewise, the children observed the authority Ethel had over them.

On the other hand, Ethel's sister Ann had been married and was living fairly well. Ann was not an active participant in the domestic network of the sisters: she did not participate in the daily flow of exchanges among the sisters, and, more often than not, Ann avoided exchanges of services which might obligate her to her sisters. Ann's daughters are self-support-ing adults. It is quite unlikely that Ethel, Wilma, or Georgia would be expected or required to raise Ann's granddaughters. In fact, Ann and her daughters consider themselves "better" than Ethel and Wilma. Usually Ann does not even allow her granddaughters to play with Wilma's children except for short periods of time. Rights over children come into conflict indicating who is excluded from parental rights in children. The third scene provides an example of who is not eligible to assume parental behavior patterns.

Vilda, Ann's daughter and Ethel's niece, had the opportunity to get a job she wanted. But she had to begin work immediately. Ann was working and Vilda had difficulty finding someone to care for her daughter Betty, aged four. She asked her cousin Georgia to take care of her daughter during the day and offered to pay Georgia $10.00 a week.

SCENE III

Betty cried and put up a fuss at breakfast because she didn't want her mother to go to work and she didn't want to stay at her Aunt Georgia's house. Betty said that Georgia beat her and yelled at her. Vilda and her mother, Ann, took the child to Georgia's house together that morning. They told Georgia that they didn't want her to yell or lay a hand on Betty.

This incident clearly communicated to Georgia that her cousin did not respect her and did not consider her an equal. Georgia made a big issue over this event to her friends and close kin. She said that Ann and Vilda were spoiling Betty and that "Betty was nothing but a brat." In turn, Georgia was unwilling to share rights in her children with Vilda and Ann. During the following summer during a large family barbecue with many kin and friends present, Georgia made this clear.

SCENE IV

Georgia's daughter took a hot poker from the fire and ran after the younger children threatening them. Ann quickly took the poker away from her niece and slapped her. Georgia jumped into the scene, grabbed her daughter from Ann and said, "You won't let me touch your granddaughter, so don't you tell my child what to do."

Although it is common for rights in children to be distributed among close female kin in The Flats, Scene IV shows that standards other than kin criteria are operative. Ann is not an active participant in the domestic network of her sisters; she and her husband are both employed and economically secure. Ann is the adult female kin least likely to be willing to accept responsibility for her nieces, nephews, and grandnieces and nephews.

Scenes I and II are examples of circumstances in which a cluster of parental rights (the discipline of children, administering folk cures, etc.) are shared by the biological mother with eligible kin who are common members of her household. There are, however, circumstances in which clusters of rights and entailing behaviors are transferred from one individual to another. In these situations, mothers still retain the folk and legally jural right to acquire physical custody over their child if the right is disputed, the right to take their child as heir, and the rights of cognatic descent. But the major cluster of behavioral entailments of parenthood are shared or transferred to the woman currently raising the child.

When a child resides with its mother, the ordering of jural rights of motherhood is unimportant. But when a child resides with other kinsmen, the parental rights in the child are redistributed. In these cases, parental rights are shared among eligible kinsmen, but the hierarchy of rights in children is reordered. Descent, inheritance, and physical custody are folk and legal jural rights the biological mother has claim to by virtue of her having borne the child. She retains these rights when her child resides with other kinsmen.

Within the folk system of shared parental rights in children, time and intent play an important role. How long a child resides in a household apart from his mother may determine the extent to which the mother, in the eyes of the community, retains or transfers rights in the child to the responsible female. Likewise, whether the biological mother views the situation as a permanent or a temporary response to her personal problems is an important factor.

In Scene V a young mother, Violet, married and moved to another state with her husband and her two youngest children by a previous union. She left her two older daughters with their grandmother (momo), Bessie, because at the time the couple could not afford to take them along. Violet intended the situation to be temporary, but it lasted over seven months. Before Violet left the state she told Bessie not to let her children see their father. Violet feared that the father would try to acquire custody of the children by claiming that the mother had deserted them. After about seven months Violet learned through gossip that her children were spending a lot of time with their father and had been staying with him on weekends. She took the train back home as soon as she could in order to get her daughters and take them to her new home out of state.

SCENE V
Violet was angered by her mother's decision to let the granddaughters stay with

their father every weekend. She told her mother, "You wasn't sposed to let him see them." Bessie said to Violet, "You ain't doing nothing for your child — the child's lucky her father and his kin take an interest in her."

Two issues complicate this situation. While Violet was living in The Flats with her children, she was willing to have her children's father buy their clothes and take them places. At least once a month the children would spend the weekend with their father at his sister's house. But when the father began "keeping house" with a new girl friend, Violet became very jealous and told her friends, "The girl wants to take my babies from me."

The issue of paternity is a further complication in this scene. The father considered himself father only to Violet's oldest child. Violet told her second born child that she and the oldest child had the same daddy. The father's kin showed much more concern and responsibility towards the oldest child and teased Violet, saying, "Soon, girl, you going to push all your children off on him." When Violet was in town she demanded that this man treat her two oldest children as his own. One time the second child became very emotionally upset when the father said to her, "I ain't your daddy." Violet was afraid that in her absence he would say it again, or hurt the child. Although Violet's mother, Bessie, was aware of both of these issues, Bessie decided that while she was responsible for her grandchildren, she would decide what was best for them. Bessie exercised the rights she acquired in her grandchildren when Violet left town and left her children.

The conflict between Violet and Bessie over this issue was so great that Violet returned to town to regain physical custody of her children. Late one winter evening, she rode the Greyhound Bus into The Flats with winter coats for her two daughters. She took a cab to her mother's home, woke her daughters, put on their coats, and took the same cab back to the bus station. Within two hours Violet and her daughters were on the way out of town. The father had no knowledge of what had happened until several days later. He made no attempt to contact Violet.

Violet did not have enough money with her to buy tickets to travel out of the state. In fact, she only had enough money to buy one-way tickets to Chicago. She and her daughters took the bus to Chicago and she called one of her closest girl friends, Samantha, to pick them up at the bus station. Violet and her daughters stayed with Violet's friend, Samantha, and her three children for nearly a month.

Violet and Samantha considered themselves kin. They lived down the street from one another while they were growing up, attended the same schools, and dated boys who were close cousins or best friends. Five years ago, just after Samantha gave birth to her second child, she became very ill. Violet insisted upon "taking" Samantha's year-old son to help Samantha. Scene VI was told to me by Violet three years following the event.

SCENE VI

That day I went over to visit Samantha, I don't know how the good Lord tell me, since I hadn't been seeing her for some time. The last old man she had didn't like me, so I stayed away. He sure was no good. Left her right before the baby come.

I went over to her place. She had a small, dark little room with a kitchen for herself and those two babies. The place look bad and smell bad. I knew she was hurting. I took one look around and said to her, "Samantha, I'm going to take your boy." I hunted up some diapers and left the house with her year-old son. She didn't come by my place for over a month, but her younger sister brought me a message that Samantha was feeling better. A week or two later she came by to visit. Her boy hardly knew her. She came by more often, but she still seemed pretty low. I told her one day, "Samantha, I don't have any sons, just daughters, so why don't you just give me this boy." She said that if he didn't favor his father so much she'd let me keep him, but she was still crazy over that man. Her boy stayed with me three or four months, then she came and got him. Soon afterwards she moved to Chicago with her two kids and her new old man.

When friends in The Flats have good social dealings with one another they often call each other by kin terms and conduct their social relations as if they were kinsmen. Close kin form alliances with one another to cope with daily needs. Close friends assume the same style of dealing with one another. Samantha and Violet shared an exchange of goods and services over the years and lived up to one another's expectations. They obligated, tested, and trusted one another.

The exchange of children, and short-term fosterage, are common among female friends. Child-care arrangements among friends imply both rights and duties. Close friends frequently discipline each other's children verbally and physically in front of each other. In normal times, and in times of stress, close friends have the right to "ask" for one another's children. A woman visiting a friend and her children may say, "Let me keep your girl this week. She will have a fine time with me and my girls. She won't want to come back home to her mama." This kind of request among kin and friends is very difficult to refuse.

Among friends, temporary child exchange is a symbol of mutual trust. Furthermore, given the fragility of the social and economic conditions of poverty, friends use this privilege as a performance. It provides a means of acquiring self-confidence in the presence of others. For example, when a woman "takes" a friend's child, she may walk around town to "show off" to others how much her friend must trust her to give her the child.

Likewise, as a field worker, I found that people began accepting my trust and respect for them when I began to leave my son with them for an hour, a day, or overnight. After such an event, kin and friends of the person who had "kept" my son would be sure to tell me that they saw my boy with their kin.

Temporary child care services are also a means of obligating kin or friends for future needs. Women may ask to "keep" the child of a friend for no apparent reason. But they are, in fact, building up an investment for their future needs. From this perspective it is clear that child keeping in The Flats is both an expression of shared kin obligations towards children and an important feature of the distribution and exchange of the limited resources available to poor people in The Flats.

JURAL IMPLICATIONS

The scenes in which conflicts arise between kin over rights in children provide a basis for pinpointing the patterns of rights and duties in relation to children in The Flats.[2] From the viewpoint of the white middle class, the kinship term "mother" is an idealized combination of behavioral roles expected to be assumed by a single person (Keesing 1969). In striking contrast, the scenes just described are illustrations of a sharing among close kinsmen of obligations towards children.

Close female kinsmen in The Flats do not expect a single person, the natural mother, to carry out by herself all of the behavior patterns which "motherhood" entails. When transactions between females over the residence, care, and discipline of children run smoothly, it is difficult for the field worker to clarify the patterns of rights and duties to which kin and non-kin are entitled. But scenes in which these rights and duties come into conflict show which behaviors may be shared.

Keesing (1970b: 432) suggests that "where the division of behaviors usually performed by a single actor among two or more actors follows lines of cleavage established by and standardized in the culture, then we are dealing with separate 'social identities.'" Goodenough (1965: 3) has defined social identity as "an aspect of self that makes a difference in how one's rights and duties distribute with respect to specific others." A kin term such as "mother" entails a cluster of social identities which we will define as distinguishable social position. A set of appropriate behavior

---

[2]   This section reflects theoretical advances in the analysis of transactions in parenthood (Goodenough 1970) and role analysis (Goodenough 1965; Keesing 1969, 1970a, 1970b).

patterns applies to each social position; and more than one person can occupy the same social position at the same time (Keesing 1969, 1970b). For example, if two or more women customarily assume behavioral roles towards individual children which could be performed by a single actor, then these women occupy a social position which has behavioral entailments with respect to those children.

Scenes from the preceeding section illustrate patterns of rights and duties toward children in The Flats and furnish examples of social positions which kinsmen occupy with respect to one another's children. As stated earlier, it is impossible to elaborate fully the rights and duties toward children in a culture. But from scenes in which these rights come into conflict, some of the following more apparent social positions stand out (Keesing 1970b).

a. Provider
b. Discipliner
c. Trainer
d. Curer
e. Groomer

These social positions represent the composite of typical parental behaviors which may be shared primarily among a child's close female kinsmen. They are categories of behavior which have predictable, non-jural rights and obligations.

Economic PROVIDERS are expected to share in providing subsistence and scarce goods, daily meals, food stamps, a bed, a blanket, clothes, and shoes. DISCIPLINERS are allowed to participate in the control of children. At their own discretion they may beat, threaten, terrify, blame, or scare children for unacceptable social behavior. TRAINERS not only discipline but teach moral values and respect for adults. They instruct by example, teaching children the consequences of their acts. If a child is found playing with fire, a trainer may strike a match, holding it close to a child's skin in order to teach the consequences of playing with fire. CURERS provide folk remedies for physical ailments. They have the right to attempt to heal rashes, remove warts, pull teeth, and cure stomach ailments of children. A GROOMER has the obligation to care for the physical appearance of children, wash and press hair, bathe children, wash clothing, and check children's bodies for rashes and diseases. In addition to eligible adults, older female siblings are also expected to groom their younger siblings.

Let us now turn to the criteria by which persons are entitled to assume these social positions. Adult females who share parental rights in children are recruited from participants in the personal domestic network of the child's jural mother. This includes cognatic kin to the mother, the child, and close friends. But the rights that eligible kinsmen or close friends share in one another's children are not equal. Other factors such as economics and interpersonal relationships within domestic networks come into play. A detailed look at scenes from preceding sections provides important clues about eligibility.

Consider Scene I. What factors underlie the mutual expectations that Ethel and Georgia share concerning Ethel's rights in Georgia's children?

a.   Ethel raised Georgia and assumes grandparental rights in Georgia's children.

b.   Ethel assumed full responsibility for Georgia's children when Georgia abandoned them and left town temporarily with a serviceman.

c.   The behavior patterns which Ethel assumes with respect to Georgia's children are appropriate independent of whether or not they are co-resident.

d.   In the presence of others Ethel frequently exhibits the rights she shares in Georgia's children and Georgia acknowledges these rights.

It appears that Ethel is demonstrating the rights which she shares and may be expected to assume in Georgia's children. Georgia's own words reinforce this interpretation: "Whatever happens to me, Ethel be the person to keep my kids."

Scenes II, III, IV, and VI illustrate that standards other than kin criteria effectively exclude individuals from assuming parental rights in children. Close friends who are active participants in domestic networks may be expected to "keep" children. On the other hand, relatives who are not participants in the domestic networks of kinsmen are not eligible to assume parental roles.

a.   Ann was not a participant in the domestic network of her sisters.

b.   Ann is excluded from parental rights in her sister's and niece's children.

c.   Ann's sisters do not have parental rights in Ann's children or grand-children.

These situations show that even siblings' rights regarding sisters' children are not equivalent.

Kin and friends in domestic networks establish mutual ties of obligation as they bestow rights and responsibilities upon one another. As these responsibilities are met with satisfaction, the depth of the involvement between kinsmen and between friends increases. Simultaneously, females acquire reciprocal obligations toward one another's children and rights in them. As responsibilities toward specific children are amplified, females are ultimately allowed to occupy parental roles toward children which are recognized by both adults and children. When women consciously perform duties as PROVIDER, DISCIPLINER, TRAINER, CURER, and GROOMER, then they have accepted the reality that they may be required to nurture these children. These are the women who come to be next in line to nurture and assume custody of the children to whom their obligations apply.

Our concern up to now has not been with jural motherhood itself, but the criteria by which rights and duties in children distribute socially and may be delegated to other kinsmen. At this point it is necessary to take a close look at Goodenough's definition of jural motherhood.

If we try to define jural motherhood by the kinds of rights and duties comprising it, we are in trouble, as the societies we have already considered reveal. For the ways in which rights in children distribute socially and the very content of the rights themselves vary considerably cross-culturally. We are dealing with a jural role, then, but can identify it cross-culturally not by its content but by some constant among the criteria by which people are entitled to the role (1970: 24).

With the foregoing in mind, we may say that jural motherhood consists of the rights and duties a woman has claim to in relation to a child by virtue of her having borne it, provided she is eligible to bear it and provided no other disqualifying circumstances attend its birth (1970: 25).

Potential nurturers of children share or transfer non-jural rights in children in the process of child keeping. Individuals do not acquire rights of jural motherhood in the temporary exchange of children. But some child-keeping situations which were intended to be temporary became permanent. And child keeping can ultimately involve the transfer of jural rights in children.

There is no specific time period after which child keeping becomes a permanent transfer of jural rights in the eyes of the community. The intentions which the jural mother makes public, the frequency of her visits, the extent to which she continues to provide for the child, and the extent to which she continues to occupy all of the social positions of parenthood are all factors in folk-jural sanctions over rights in children.

Some mothers whose children are being kept by kin or friends eventually stop visiting and providing goods and services for their children. In such cases, the child keeper may ultimately become the jural parent in the eyes of the community. Later attempts by the biological mother to regain custody of her child may be met with disapproval, threats, and gossip within the domestic group.

In the eyes of the community, individuals who acquire jural rights in children have the jural right to make decisions over the subsequent transfer of custody of the child. In the following situation a great-grandfather "kept" his great-granddaughter for eight years. During this time the mother showed little concern for her daughter, and the great-grandfather came to be considered the jural parent. When the grandfather decided that he was too old to care for the child, the mother wanted the child back. But the grandfather decided to give custody to another relative whom he considered more responsible. This decision was supported by their kinsmen.

I was staying with my great-grandfather [momofa] for the first five years of my life, but he just got too old to care for me. My mother was living in The Flats at the time, but my "daddy" asked my mother's brother and his wife to take me 'cause he really trusted them with me.

Folk sanctions concerning the transfer of jural rights in children are often in conflict with the publicly sanctioned laws of the state. The courts are more likely to award child custody to the biological mother than to other kinsmen. Individuals in The Flats operate within the folk and legal system. Mothers have successfully taken close kinsmen such as their own mother or aunt to court in order to regain custody of their natural children. But such acts are strongly discouraged by kinsmen who regard children as a mutual responsibility of the kin group. Children born to the poor in The Flats are highly valued, and rights in these children belong to the networks of cooperating kinsmen.[3] Shared parental responsibilities are not only an obligation of kinship, they constitute a highly cherished right. Attempts of outside social agencies, the courts, or the police to control the residence, guardianship, or behavior of children are thwarted by the domestic group. Such efforts are interpreted in The Flats as attempts on the part of the larger society to control and manipulate their children.

REFERENCES

CARROLL, VERN, editor
   1970   Adoption in eastern Oceania. Honolulu: University of Hawaii Press.
GOODENOUGH, WARD H.
   1962   Kindred and hamlet in Lakalai, New Britain. Ethnology 1:5–12.
   1965   "Rethinking status and role," in The relevance of models for social anthropology. Edited by M. Banton. London: Tavistock.
   1970   Description and comparison in cultural anthropology. Chicago: Aldine.

[3]   Rivers (1924) makes a strikingly similar statement in his book, Social organization. He says that "A child born into a community with societies or clans becomes a member of a domestic group other than the family in the strict sense."

GOODY, ESTHER
  1966   Fostering of children in Ghana: a preliminary report. *Ghana Journal of Sociology* 2:26–33.
KEESING, ROGER M.
  1966   Kwaio kindreds. *Southwestern Journal of Anthropology* 22:346–355.
  1969   On quibblings over squabblings of siblings: new perspectives on kin terms and role behavior. *Southwestern Journal of Anthropology* 25:207–227.
  1970a Kwaio fosterage. *American Anthropologist* 72(5):991–1020.
  1970b "Toward a model of role analysis," in *A handbook of methods in cultural anthropology*. Edited by R. Cohen and R. Naroll. New York: Natural History.
MIDGETT, DOUGLAS K.
  1969   "Transactions in parenthood: a West Indian case." Unpublished manuscript, University of Illinois.
OTTERBEIN, KEITH F.
  1970   The developmental cycle of the Andros household: a diachronic analysis. *American Anthropologist* 72(6):1412–1419.
RIVERS, W. H.
  1924   *Social organization.* New York: Knopf.
SANFORD, MARGARET SELLARS
  1971   "Disruption of the mother-child relationship in conjunction with matrifocality: a study of child-keeping among the Carib and Creole of British Honduras." Unpublished Ph.D. dissertation, The Catholic University of America, Washington, D.C.
STACK, CAROL B.
  1970   "The kindred of Viola Jackson: residence and family organization of an urban Black American family," in *Afro-American anthropology: contemporary perspectives*. Edited by Norman E. Whitten and John F. Szwed, 303–312. New York: The Free Press.

The Functionally Extended Family in Lebanon and the Effects of Its Solidarity on the Mental Health of the Individual

ANEES A. HADDAD

The major objective of this research is to investigate the relationship between perceived family vertical (intergenerational) solidarity and individual mental health or psychological well-being within the culture of a Middle Eastern society, namely, Lebanon. In pursuit of this goal, a multi-dimensional approach to both family solidarity and mental health is used throughout the study.

Two general questions are investigated:

i. What is the relationship between perceived family intergenerational solidarity and psychological well-being?

ii. How do background factors such as sex, religion, generational membership, and socio-economic status influence the relationship?

Based on a detailed review of the literature (Haddad 1971), the central postulate of the study is that: "The greater the perception of family vertical solidarity, the greater the mental health or psychological well-being." Four background variables were assumed to be of significance; hence four hypotheses were tested:

i. "The correlation between solidarity and psychological well-being for males will be higher than the correlation for females";

ii. "The correlation between solidarity and psychological well-being for G_1 (grandparental generation) will be higher than the correlation for G_2 (parental generation) and G_3 (adult children's generation);'

iii. "The correlation between solidarity and mental health for Christians will be higher than the correlation between solidarity and mental health for Mohammedans";

iv.   "There will be no difference between social classes in the correlation of solidarity with psychological well-being."

Lebanon was chosen as the arena for this research because of its "functionally extended family" (Farsoun 1970: 257). Though Lebanon must be considered a modern, advanced society, the family still plays the most important role in all aspects of secular and religious life. How far an individual advances in his economic status, educational attainments, government appointments, and a host of other areas will depend mostly on his family of orientation. The family name is an important ascribed status in Lebanon.

Furthermore, Lebanon's population, evenly divided between Christians and Mohammedans, affords a maximum degree of variability of attitudes toward the family between these two world religions not available anywhere else (Gulick 1965: 1). With a higher rate of divorce among Mohammedans, it is expected that the Christians will perceive a higher degree of family solidarity and that there will be less association between family solidarity and psychological well-being for Mohammedans than for Christians.

Lebanon also presents a unique situation for the study of male-female contrasts, especially in status and role. While the Lebanese female is more educated and Western-oriented than her counterpart in any other Arab country, the male is still predominantly the master, both within and outside the family. It is expected, therefore, that the female will be higher than the male in her perception of family solidarity but that there will be a higher association between family solidarity and psychological well-being for the male than for the female.

This study analyzes the data gathered from forty-nine, six-member, three-generational families which were chosen for this purpose by a sampling technique to insure approximately equal sex, religious, generational, and social class representation. The total number in the purposive sample was 294. Interview schedules were used by trained interviewers in Lebanon.

THE CONCEPT OF SOLIDARITY

The concept of solidarity has had an extensive background of usage in the literature of sociology and social psychology. Many writers have stressed the importance of the concept for the analysis of group and social system phenomena. If one were to equate, as some do, the concepts "integration," "cohesion," and "solidarity," one would find that these concepts have been recognized and studied by social scientists for centuries.

This study focuses on the issue of solidarity within the family. It is assumed that just as on the macro-societal level integration, solidarity or cohesion is an important prerequisite for the proper functioning of society, so it is with any social subsystem, including the family. According to Parsons (1968:40), "the family is the 'primordial' solidary unit of all human societies. Indeed, in the most primitive, kinship, which includes much more than the nuclear family, is the mode of organization of ALL solidarity." Khaldun (1958: 29–30), Durkheim (1893), Brown (1965: 74), Merton (1957: 315), Thibaut and Kelley (1967: 247), Cartwright and Zander (1960: 92), Deutsch and Krauss (1965: 55), and many others discuss the importance of solidarity to group life.

Social psychologists have attempted to define solidarity in precise terms. Some have dealt with the elements of human cohesiveness, others have dealt with its effects. Homans (1950) posited three basic human interaction processes: similarity, sentiment, and solidarity. "Similarity" referred to those elements of behavior which interacting persons did in similar ways, upon which they felt a consensus. "Sentiment" had to do with the expression of emotional feeling, or affect. "Solidarity" had to do with associative behaviors (Bengtson, Olander, and Haddad 1971:10).

The importance of solidarity to the family can be divided into two areas: (a) horizontal solidarity, which includes intragenerational relations; and (b) vertical solidarity, which encompasses intergenerational interaction. The literature is very rich in intragenerational family relations. For all practical reasons, all marriage research dealing with spouse relationship can be placed in this category (see Haddad 1971: 25–27, for a brief review of such research).

Relatively less of the family literature deals with vertical relations between two generations, and far less with vertical relations between three generations. But as Streib and Shanas (1965: 469) point out:

The analysis of intergenerational relations is a focus of growing interest. Psychology, social psychology, and sociology have contributed much work to the study of relations between parent and young child, but very little empirical research has been done on the relations between retired parents and their adult children.

Litman (1969: 2) suggests that "an intergenerational approach to family research ... allows examination of not only the interaction of family members but the totality of intra-familial trans-actions as well as within the context of historical time ... families and family members, within and throughout the three phases of the life cycle."

THE FAMILY AND MENTAL HEALTH

This research deals with interpersonal integration in the family subsystem and with intrapersonal integration only as a psychological well-being sequence of interpersonal solidarity. It offers, therefore, a means of understanding mental health in part as a function of family interaction. Ackerman (1958: 11) spotlighted the bridge that connects the family and mental health of the individual with these words: "We must, it seems to me, acknowledge the fact that mental health cannot be understood within the limited confines of individual experience... A broader approach to mental health must embrace the dynamics of the family group as well."

It is the thesis of this research that the perception of family relationships, as manifested in high family solidarity, will show high association with a survey measure of psychological well-being. This is a position assumed by Sherman also (1967: 216–221) in his research on "intergenerational discontinuity and therapy of the family." He stresses the importance of family cohesiveness and mental health.

Another finding that shows the linkage between family integration and mental health is that of Albee (1965: 3). He first reviews the research which demonstrates that the rate of psychopathology increases when the integrity of the family is destroyed or damaged and that it is low where the stability and strength of the family is high. He then presents his findings: "Children from well-integrated families have very low life-long rates of mental disorder, and children from broken or emotionally disrupted families have high subsequent rates." He goes on to state the following:

We already know that the most significant contributing factor to emotional disorder is to be found in disrupted, disturbed, and unhappy family relationships and that these in turn reflect profound problems in our society... Children who grow up in homes characterized by insecurity, stress, and impoverished emotional relationships are a very high risk group (1965: 6).

"There is the challenge," as Ackerman has put it (1958: 12), "to discern the role of family patterns and values in the mental health of the individual." The individual is "a mirror image, a microcosm of his family group" (1958: 7).

MEASURING INSTRUMENTS

In order to test the proposition that there is a direct and positive relationship between family vertical solidarity and psychological well-being, the concepts "family solidarity" and "psychological well-being" had to be operationalized through empirical measures. An extensive review of the literature (Haddad 1971: 75–85) confirmed Handel's own conclusion (1967: 3) that:

The nature of family cohesion or integration is thus a central topic, and the reader will not take long to discover that no simple unidimensional scale or index is adequate to tell us what we need to know to understand such phenomena ... The phenomena push us, at least at this necessarily early stage, toward the conceiving of KINDS of integration.

From a wealth of theoretical background the following three levels of integration were developed to arrive at an index of family vertical solidarity.
1. *Associational Solidarity: Activity Level.* A scale was designed to measure associational solidarity which includes: (a) intergenerational face-to-face communication (e.g. "talk over things that are important to you"); (b) intergenerational media communication (e.g. "telephoning," "writing letters"); and (c) intergenerational common activities (e.g. "commercial and other recreation such as movies, picnics, swimming, hunting, etc."). The frequency of interaction was measured and ranges from "very frequent" to "never" on a four-point scale.
2. *Affectual Solidarity: Sentiment Level.* A scale was designed to measure the following facts of intergenerational affectual solidarity: (a) expressions of love, (b) respect, (c) appreciation, (d) recognition, (e) acceptance, (f) understanding, (g) trust, and (h) fairness.
3. *Consensual Solidarity: Value Level.* A scale was designed to measure agreement of views between generations within the same family concerning society's five major institutions, namely: (a) the economy, (b) the polity, (c) the family, (d) the school, and (e) religion.

It is important to note that in order for the research design to be complete, questions were asked of each generation concerning its "integrative" measures with the other two generations. Therefore, G_1 (grandparent) was asked about his relations with G_2 (parent) and G_3 (adult child) in a descending order; while G_2 was asked about his relations with G_1 and G_3; and finally, G_3 was asked about his relations with G_1 and G_2.

Since this was a pioneering effort at measuring family tri-generational vertical solidarity, two forms of the solidarity scale were developed, the long form and the short form. The long form was composed of 24 Associational items, 53 Consensual items, and 28 Affectual items — a total of 105 scale items. The short, or global, form was composed of only 12 items. The global items were summary items. The scales were pretested using 40 junior college subjects. (Since then the instrument has been administered to over 400 members of three-generation American families.) The correlation (r) between the long and the global forms was .87. This means that the global form, the short form, explained 76 percent of the variance of the long form.

Taking the data from Lebanon and making a check on one of the long forms, namely, the Affectual Solidarity Scale, and its global counterpart, we found that they correlate at .70. In view of this, and because analyzing each of the long scales is a separate study by itself (a study now being carried out), we felt it was justifiable to use the short form in the present analysis. Therefore, the Global Family Solidarity items were used in analyzing the data.

While special scales to measure family vertical solidarity were specifically developed and tested for this research, no effort was made to develop similar scales to measure mental health or psychological well-being. Out of several attempts by social scientists at measuring "mental health," it appeared that Bradburn's formulation (1965, 1969) and operationalization would be the most adequate for this study. His research centered on the nature of mental health and its relation to behavior. When he operationalized the concept, he used several dimensions also. Three of these dimensions were used in this study, the first two of which were said by Bradburn (1965: 56; 1969: 110) to have been the most important measures of psychological well-being. The three dimensions are:

1. *The Affect Balance Scale.* This scale has two sub-scales, the Positive Affect Scale and the Negative Affect Scale. It consists of ten statements of emotion as to whether the respondent during the past month felt lonely or remote, on top of the world, bored, depressed, restless, pleased about his accomplishments, and so on.

2. *The Worry Extensity Scale.* This scale is composed of twelve questions as to whether the respondent worried during the past few weeks about debts, sexual problems, health, growing old, world situation, neighborhood events, moving ahead in the world, some member of the family, and so forth.

3. *The Avowed Happiness Scale.* This scale consists of six questions, the first four of which deal with whether the respondent felt he was very happy, pretty happy, and not too happy; how his life was today as compared with five years ago (happier then, not as happy then, about the same); whether he wants his life to continue much the same way, change in some parts, or change in many parts; and whether he was doing pretty well or not too well in getting the things he wants from life. The last two questions of the scale were addressed only to those who were married and had children, since they deal with marital happiness and satisfaction in the parental role.

DEMOGRAPHIC PROFILE OF THE SAMPLE

Of the 49 complete six-member, three-generational families (294 subjects) that provided data for this study, there were 153 males and 141 females. There were 98 subjects to each of the three generations. The sample was composed of 146 Christians, 143 Mohammedans, and 5 undeclared.

According to the indices of an official Lebanese Commission of Economics (IRFED), this sample was composed of 47 percent in the lower-income categories, 41 percent in the middle-income categories, and 12 percent in the upper-income groups. 158 of the respondents had only elementary school education, 58 had secondary school education, and 26 had college or university education. At the time of the interviewing, 127 were unemployed (65 in G_1, 25 in G_2, and 37 in G_3). Forty-four had part-time employment (11 in G_1, 10 in G_2, and 23 in G_3); and 78 were fully employed (10 in G_1, 46 in G_2, and 22 in G_3).

The mean age of the 98 young respondents was 19.3 years. Fifty of them were 100 percent financially dependent on their parents, and only 16 were 100 percent independent. The rest were partially dependent. Of the 58 total respondents that reported secondary education, 45 were members of G_3 (27 males, 18 females); and of the 26 total respondents that reported college or university education, 14 were members of G_3, and 9 were members of G_2.

MAJOR FINDINGS

The central postulate of the research that "the greater the perception of family vertical solidarity, the greater the mental health or psychological

Table 1. Pearsonian correlations of family solidarity and mental health — total

Solidarity	Affect Balance	Positive Affect	Negative Affect	Worry Extensity	Avowed Happiness
Affectual	.16	.02	− .18	− .12	.16
Consensual	.18	.09	− .16	− .13	.17
Associational	.09	.11	− .01	− .06	.15
Total Global Solidarity	.20	.10	− .16	− .14	.22

N = 294

With an N of 294, *r* achieves statistical significance at the .05 level when it reaches .11 or greater; and at the .01 level when it reaches .15 or greater.

214 ANEES A. HADDAD

well-being" received weak but consistent support. It was found that 80 percent of those high on family solidarity were also high on psychological well-being. Even though the magnitude of the correlation coefficients was not very high (see Table 1), every sign of the twenty correlations was in the expected direction. Therefore, Family Vertical Solidarity was related to all five measures of Psychological Well-Being.

There are four hypotheses regarding the effect of background variables on the relationship of family solidarity and mental health. These will be presented with the appropriate findings regarding each:

a.   *Sex.* The data support the hypothesis that "the correlation between solidarity and psychological well-being for males will be higher than the correlation for females." Of the twenty correlations possible between family solidarity and psychological well-being, the males are higher than females on thirteen (see Table 2).

b.   *Generational Membership.* The data do not support the hypothesis that "the correlation between solidarity and psychological well-being for G_1 will be higher than the correlation for G_2 and G_3." In fact, G_3 (the adult children) emerge as showing the highest correlations of the three generations. In Multiple Regression Analysis, the correlation coefficients for G_3 are consistently and substantially higher than those for either G_1 or G_2 (see Table 3).

c.   *Religion.* The hypothesis that "the correlation between solidarity and mental health for Christians will be higher than the correlation between solidarity and mental health for Mohammedans" was also supported by the data (see Table 4). The correlation coefficients between Affect Balance and Solidarity were as follows: Affectual .06 for Mohammedans, .27 for Christians; Consensual .13 for Mohammedans, .21 for Christians; Associational .05 for Mohammedans, .11 for Christians; and Total Global Solidarity .11 for Mohammedans, .27 for Christians.

d.   *SES.* The data support the hypothesis that "there will be no difference between social class in the correlation of solidarity with psychological well-being" (see Table 5).

In sum, the data would suggest that the highest association of Family Vertical Solidarity and Psychological Well-Being would be found among a group of Lebanese who were young, male, and Christian. It is important to note that though the magnitude of the correlations and differences may not have been great, the consistent direction seems to be important and significant.

Table 2. Pearsonian correlations of family solidarity and mental health — by sex

Solidarity	Affect Balance		Positive Affect		Negative Affect		Worry Extensity		Avowed Happiness	
	Male	Female	Male	Female	Male	Female	Male	Female	Male	Female
Affectual	.21	.15	.10	-.07	-.17	-.24	-.17	-.06	.26	.03
Consensual	.18	.20	.13	.02	-.11	-.21	-.13	-.11	.13	.21
Associational	.11	.12	.15	.09	.00	-.06	-.11	-.02	.18	.11
Total Global Solidarity	.23	.22	.18	.02	-.13	-.24	-.19	-.07	.26	.17

Table 3. Pearsonian correlations between types of solidarity and measures of mental health — by generation

Solidarity	Affect Balance			Positive Affect			Negative Affect			Worry Extensity			Avowed Happiness		
	G_1	G_2	G_3	G_1	G_2	G_3	G_1	G_2	G_3	G_1	G_2	G_3	G_1	G_2	G_3
Affectual	.10	.23	.22	-.06	.05	.17	-.16	-.26	-.10	-.20	-.09	-.13	.19	.03	.23
Consensual	.13	.04	.39	-.05	-.05	.31	-.19	-.09	-.18	-.12	-.21	-.24	.11	.21	.33
Associational	.11	.00	.21	.17	.09	.12	.01	.08	-.14	.04	-.11	-.17	.22	.09	.15
Total Global Solidarity	.17	.12	.37	.05	.04	.27	-.16	-.11	-.19	-.13	-.18	-.24	.26	.14	.32

$N = 294$
With an N of 294, r achieves statistical significance at the .05 level when it reaches .11 or greater; and at the .01 level when it reaches .15 or greater

Table 4. Pearsonian correlations of family solidarity and mental health — by religion

Solidarity	Affect Balance		Positive Affect		Negative Affect		Worry Extensity		Avowed Happiness	
	Moham-medan	Chris-tian	Moham-medan	Chris-tian	Moham-medan	Chris-tian	Moham-medan	Chris-tian	Moham-medan	Chris-tian
Affectual	.06	.27	.03	.05	−.10	−.31	−.08	−.15	.13	.21
Consensual	.13	.21	.10	.05	−.06	−.34	−.05	−.19	.13	.16
Associational	.05	.11	.17	.05	.11	−.10	.06	−.18	.01	.26
Total Global Solidarity	.11	.27	.12	.07	−.01	−.30	−.02	−.24	.11	.29

Table 5. Pearsonian correlations of family solidarity and mental health — by SES (social-economic status)

Solidarity	Affect Balance			Positive Affect			Negative Affect			Worry Extensity			Avowed Happiness		
	U	M	L	U	M	L	U	M	L	U	M	L	U	M	L
Affectual	.08	.36	.18	−.06	.18	−.01	−.16	−.29	−.24	−.14	−.14	−.26	.28	.04	.21
Consensual	.35	.04	.22	.11	.00	.05	−.39	−.04	−.34	−.27	−.06	−.16	.22	.02	.18
Associational	.15	.16	.03	.16	.13	.03	−.06	−.09	.00	−.13	−.03	−.09	.15	.26	.17
Total Global Solidarity	.25	.28	.20	.09	.16	.03	−.26	−.21	−.22	−.23	−.11	−.23	.28	.18	.26

N = 294
With an N of 294, r achieves statistical significance at the .05 level when it reaches .11 or greater; and at the .01 level when it reaches .15 or greater

OTHER FINDINGS

Using the Affect Balance Scores as an indicator of psychological well-being, it was found that in all three generations, males had higher scores than females. In a higher-to-lower rank order of the six-member families, they ran as follows: son, father, mother, grandfather, daughter, and grandmother (see Table 6).

Table 6. Rank order of generation and sex on affect balance — mean scores

Generation and Sex	Mean Affect Balance
G_3 — Male	5.54
G_2 — Male	5.08
G_2 — Female	4.82
G_1 — Male	4.71
G_3 — Female	4.66
G_1 — Female	4.45

The young generation had higher mean scores than the middle generation, which in turn had higher scores than the old generation. And on all five items of the scale, the males scored higher than the females.

The old generation had highest scores on feeling lonely, and the second generation highest on feeling depressed, with the third generation highest on feeling restless.

In terms of the Worry Extensity Scale, the middle generation appeared to be worried most about debts and work; the young generation about sex; the old generation about health and growing old. Females in all generations seem to be worrying more than males about sex, health, and old age.

It was also found that, contrary to prediction, it is not age but sex that is a better predictor of psychological well-being. In all age groups, it was the female who had lower psychological well-being than the male. The sex variable looms high in importance when dealing with psychological well-being.

SUMMARY

The major goal of this research was to investigate the relationship between perceived family vertical (intergenerational) solidarity and individual psychological well-being in Lebanon using a three-generational sample. A structural-functional orientation underlies the theoretical framework: the family is seen as a human group, centered around the institutions of marriage and parenthood, whose function it is to serve as a buffer between the individual and the extra-familial stresses and strains that impinge on him. Consequently, the major postulate of the study posits a direct and positive relationship between family solidarity and mental health.

The basic hypotheses of the study revolve around four specifying demographic variables: sex, religion, generation, and social-economic class. The relationship of these variables both to perceived family solidarity and to psychological well-being was investigated.

A multidimensional approach was followed to operationalize both family solidarity and mental health. The first was measured by three sub-scales specifically developed for this research: (1) Associational, (2) Consensual, and (3) Affectual Solidarity; the second was measured by the following scales of psychological well-being developed by Bradburn: (1) Affect Balance, (2) Positive Affect, (3) Negative Affect, (4) Worry, and (5) Avowed Happiness.

Forty-nine six-member, three-generational families were chosen by a purposive sampling technique to insure approximately equal sex, religious, generational, and social class representation. The total sample was 294 Lebanese. Interview schedules were administered by eight trained interviewers.

Data indicated support for the central thesis of the research that there is a positive association between perceived family solidarity and measures of psychological well-being, though the correlational coefficients were not high. There were twelve positive coefficients to be expected between Family Solidarity and (1) Affect Balance, (2) Positive Affect, and (3) Avowed Happiness; and eight negative coefficients between Family Solidarity and (1) Negative Affect, and (2) Worry Scale. All twenty correlations in the matrix were found in the expected direction.

The hypotheses concerning (1) sex, (2) religion, and (3) SES were supported. The correlation between family solidarity and psychological well-being was higher for males than for females, and higher for Christians than for Mohammedans. There was no significant difference in the correlations by social class (as measured by income). The hypothesis concerning (4) generation was not supported. Contrary to the hypothesis, the correlation was highest for the young generation rather than the old.

In sum, the general findings of this research would suggest that, in Lebanon, Family Vertical (intergenerational) Solidarity and Psychological Well-Being are most related in youth rather than the elderly, in males rather than females, and in Christians rather than Mohammedans.

REFERENCES

ACKERMAN, N. W.
1958 *The psychodynamics of family life.* New York: Basic Books.

ALBEE, G. W.
1965 "A critical look at social work's approach to mental disorders." Speech to Cleveland Area Chapter, National Association of Social Workers. October 25.

BENGTSON, V. L., E. B. OLANDER, ANEES A. HADDAD
1971 "The 'generation gap' and aging family members." Paper presented for discussion at the annual meeting of the National Council on Family Relations, Estes Park, Colorado, August 25–28.

BRADBURN, N.
1965 *Reports on happiness.* Chicago: Aldine.
1969 *The structure of psychological well-being.* Chicago: Aldine.

BROWN, R.
1965 *Social psychology.* New York: The Free Press.

CARTWRIGHT, D., A. ZANDER, *editors*
1960 *Group dynamics: research and theory.* New York: Harper and Row.

DEUTSCH, M., R. M. KRAUSS
1965 *Theories in social psychology.* New York: Basic Books.

DURKHEIM, EMILE
1893 *De la division du travail social.* Paris: F. Alcan.
1951 *Suicide.* Glencoe: The Free Press.

FARSOUN, S. K.
1970 "Family structure and society in modern Lebanon," in *Peoples and cultures of the Middle East.* Edited by L. E. Sweet. New York: The Natural History Press.

GULICK, J.
1965 Old values and new institutions in a Lebanese Arab city. *Human Organization* 24:1–7.

HADDAD, ANEES A.
1971 "The effects of generation, religion, and sex on the relationship of family vertical solidarity and mental health in Lebanon." Unpublished Ph.D. dissertation, University of Southern California, Los Angeles.

HANDEL, GERALD, *editor*
1967 *The psychosocial interior of the family.* Chicago: Aldine.

HOMANS, GEORGE C.
1950 *The human group.* New York: Harcourt, Brace, and World.

KHALDUN, I.
1958   *The muqaddimah: an introduction to history*. Translated by F. Rosenthal. New York: Pantheon Books.

LITMAN, T.
1969   Health care and the family: a three-generational analysis. *American Sociological Review* 28:9–21.

MERTON, R.
1957   *Social theory and social structure*. New York: The Free Press.

PARSONS, T.
1968   "The normal American family," in *Sourcebook in marriage and the family* (third edition). Edited by M. Sussman. Boston: Houghton Mifflin.

SHERMAN, S.
1967   Intergenerational discontinuity and therapy of the family. *Social Casework* 48:216–221.

STREIB, B., E. SHANAS
1965   *Social structure and the family: generational relations*. Englewood Cliffs, N.J.: Prentice-Hall.

THIBAUT, J., H. KELLEY
1967   *The social psychology of groups*. New York: John Wiley and Sons.

Differential Enculturation and Social Class in Canadian Schools

ELEANOR W. SMOLLETT

A November afternoon at Spruce Crescent School, in a prairie city in Canada. A group of fashionably dressed, eight-year-old, middle-class children sit before their teacher, Miss Simms. A bright, well-equipped third-grade classroom. Miss Simms explains that today they will begin work on their Christmas pictures. They will draw with crayons again today, as they did such a good job on their last set of crayon drawings.

She explains the task. They will do, altogether, two Christmas pictures each, one today in crayon, one next week in paint. One picture will be on the religious side of Christmas, such as a manger scene, the wise men, or the like (henceforward referred to in class as "the manger picture"), the other on Santa Claus (St. Nicolas) or something on the non-religious side (henceforward referred to as "the Santa Claus picture").

"Now, you have two choices," she declares. "You can do either the manger picture or the Santa Claus picture this week — as you like. Then you will do the other one next week."

Miss Simms now asks for suggestions on various ways to deal with these subjects — "What else could we put in the picture to fill up the space around Santa Claus?"

The children begin to draw. Miss Simms walks about, making suggestions, answering questions. "Do the figures first, Janet, then the background."

Several children begin to put questions to Miss Simms, exploring the boundaries of their choices. "Can we do it in pencil?" asks Tom. "No, do it in crayon," says Miss Simms, "it must be in crayon." Little Brenda whispers to another child: "... hard to do manger in paint; ... try it in crayon first." "Miss Simms," asks Brenda, "can I make both pictures of the manger?" "No," says Miss Simms, "you have a choice — one subject for one picture, one for the other." "Can both pictures be in crayon?" asks a boy. "No." Brenda tries again: "Miss Simms, can I make both pictures about the manger if I put Santa Claus in both of them?" Miss Simms walks to another part of the room without responding. After several minutes, Brenda begins to draw.

Small events of classroom life like this — varied, recombined, repeated — constitute a significant aspect of the enculturation process in classrooms. The underlying patterns in these events accustom the children to the work habits and styles of thought and behavior appropriate to North Americans of their particular social class. These events serve as models for many things ranging from habits of interaction with peers or supervisors at work to ways of defining knowledge, its acquisition and uses, to ways of defining problems and making decisions.

THE ILLUSION OF CHOICE

This particular small event illustrates a process I have observed over and over again in middle-class schools[1] — the cultivation of an illusion of choice.

The parents of these Spruce Crescent school children occupy managerial and professional positions — they are civil servants, middle-echelon business managers, doctors, lawyers, engineers, professors. The teachers and principal at the school expect that most of the children will go on to a university and occupy positions similar to those of their parents. They must know that they and their activities are "nice" and "well done," that they have reached their positions in life through "merit" in a system of "free competition," and that they have a certain life style, a certain occupation, and, of course, a certain government as a result of their own, individual, "free choice." At the same time, since they are not the upper class, they must learn to accept externally prescribed boundaries on the range of their "free choices," and externally formed definitions of the alternatives they choose among, while still considering themselves "decision makers" and free individuals in a "free society."

---

[1]   To those readers who are not familiar with North American education, it should be explained that school populations, at least in urban areas, are drawn from specific residential neighborhoods, and that urban residential neighborhoods are relatively homogeneous as to class. Therefore, one can refer to certain schools as "middle-class schools," others as "working-class schools," etc.

A Multiple-Choice World

The process of creating an "illusion of choice" as a significant feature of classroom life is most striking in middle-class schools, but some aspects of this process are not restricted to them but prevail throughout public education. One of the earliest school experiences of all North American children, for example, is the "multiple-choice test" — this is an examination (usually short) of the form:

Underline the correct answer; choose one only.

$2+2=$
a) 0
b) 4
c) 3
d) 1

or:

The most densely populated country in East Africa is:
a) Kenya
b) Tanzania
c) Uganda
d) Ethiopia

or:

The government of the U.S.S.R. today is run by:
a) Mongols
b) Czars
c) Communists
d) Slavs

Such tests frequently come soon after a lesson in which the "correct" (expected) answer is stated or implied in a text. School children, of every social class, spend so much time during their classroom life answering multiple-choice tests that the meaning of this experience needs to be examined.[2] Perhaps it is true, as educators would suggest, that these tests

---

[2] When counseling university students regarding their selection of classes, I usually start by asking them to give an idea of what they are interested in, what they would like to study. Invariably they reach for the University Calendar, at which point I tell them

are used so frequently for their ease of correction. But perhaps, as part of the enculturation process, they reflect something more profound — the frequency with which decision-making has a "multiple-choice" character. That is, individuals are free to make the "best choice" from among a prescribed set of alternatives. They have freedom to choose which television channel to watch (without freedom to influence the nature of broadcasting), freedom to choose between one doctor and another (without freedom to choose the character, purpose and organization of medical practice), freedom to choose between one candidate and another or one party and another in an election (without freedom to define the issues at stake). Life in such a society presents people with a multiple-choice world, but one in which the very definitions and limits of the alternatives presented define and break up and structure social reality and social possibilities.

Learning the Primacy of Proper Form

It should be noted that something else is being taught as well. Children are learning to attend to form — "I am choosing" — rather than substance (the nature and limits of the choices).

For example, to return to the drawing lesson in Miss Simms' classroom, most of the children have made their "choices" between Santa Claus and the manger without question, and have carried out the assignment. Miss Simms calls them each to the front of the room to show their pictures to the class, and tells each one: "Good," or "Nice," or "Well done." She makes no reference to the content of their pictures, just as — earlier in the day — she had made no reference to the content of stories they wrote, for which she meted out similar praise. They had produced a product that satisfied the form specified. Particularities of content, of the substance of the work done, were not considered significant enough to merit discussion.

All school children are taught this. Middle-class children are taught it more persistently. In middle-class occupations (such as middle-echelon management), after all, it is most often the carrying out of proper form that matters. POLICY is set above; PRODUCTION is carried out below. Proper form, in the sense of "regulations" and "procedures," is a necessity

---

to forget about what is listed in the Calendar for a moment and just tell me what they might LIKE to study. This usually causes them to panic. They find it inconceivable that anyone should request that they articulate any desire without supplying them with a list from which they can CHOOSE a desire. Twelve years of multiple-choice enculturation MUST be a factor in this expectation.

for industrial production. To implement it, there must be a corps of middle-level personnel that is thoroughly schooled in the sanctity of "regulations," and can therefore be relied upon to translate policy into action without questioning the content of that policy, and to do it reliably and accurately.

Control

All of these attitudes are encouraged in middle-class schools through a style of control that is subtly different from that found, for example, in working-class schools in the same city. I do not mean to suggest that classroom life in middle-class schools is totally different from that found in working-class schools; they have much in common, and the difference is one of degree. But the differences are sufficiently patterned to be quickly apparent.[3]

For example, in working-class schools, children are most often told what to do in a direct, overt manner. They are instructed: "Now, class, take out your workbooks. Johnny, close your book; I didn't say to open them yet. Now, open to page 63, and do Exercise 6." This relationship is simple. The teacher tells the children what to do and reprimands them if they disobey or anticipate her instructions. The teacher of working-class children is often very concerned that they be "disciplined." As she freely explains in conversation, she is convinced that this will be necessary for their future occupations. However, the working-class actually learns its kind of disciplines primarily on the job, out of the material necessities of production, and has less need than middle-class children to master "rules of behavior" while in school. More often than not, a working-class child's response to the middle-class teacher's attempts to teach him "discipline" in the abstract is good-natured insolence.

The teacher in the working-class school is usually not very worried about the students' precise achievement level, since she doesn't consider them to be college bound.[4] Accordingly, she doesn't always expect uniform "right answers" in discussion, say of literature or social studies, but allows a certain amount of imagination, and even humor.

[3] This account is based on observations in three working-class and three middle-class schools, several days at a time, over three successive years. In each school, rotating pairs of observers recorded in detail the events of the day in each of a number of classrooms. The observers, including the author and her students, had subsequent discussions with principals and teachers in these schools.

[4] For evidence that they are indeed NOT college bound, but will be channeled into "terminal" or "vocational" secondary schools, and for good analyses of differential enculturation by social class, see References listed at end.

By contrast, middle-class classrooms are as remarkable for their relative (and sometimes total) lack of laughter as they are for their lack of overt control of behavior. Control is both subtle and absolute. It is achieved, in part, by the timing of activities, particularly in the case of the younger children who might be most inclined to be restless.

In Miss Simms' third grade class, for example, activities rarely last longer than a few minutes. Teacher explains the mechanics of the activity and, very often, the choices available. The children begin work. Before they can lose interest in the task (or develop any thoughts of their own on the subject matter, or begin to elaborate in any way on the defined alternatives the teacher has offered), the activity is over, and the children are listening to teacher again in order not to miss her description of choices for the next activity. Often, the next one involves different kinds of materials or a different location, so that the children must re-orient themselves; by the time they have done so, and before they can become restless, it is again over. In this manner they are gently led through the day, by a teacher who speaks to them with sweet and quiet voice, believing that they are "choosing" one activity after another, being given explanations of how to carry out this or that choice, rarely being given a straightforward order or reprimand, kept in control with subtle precision, while being regularly told that they are "doing very well."

Attitudes Toward Work

Part of the enculturation process involved here is the nurturing of some typical middle-class attitudes towards work, i.e. that good jobs are ones that are made up of a variety of activities, and better yet, where one can choose these activities oneself. The converse is the over-riding fear of the middle class of jobs that entail long stretches of continuous, unvaried activity (defined as "boring"), and having a boss "tell you what to do." The latter two attributes are considered to be typical of factory labor, a fate considered worse than death by the middle-class. (It is interesting to note that the office jobs that many of these middle class children will occupy are in fact closer to the embodiment of the twin evils they fear so much than are real factory jobs.)

The Making of Data Processors

There are a number of published works analyzing the content of textbooks and other curricular materials, but little research has been done on the subtle, yet profound effects of the forms of much of this material.

For example, the exercises school children spend their days completing are replete with examples of how they are trained to ignore the real issues in a discussion. For instance, the children are presented with a "reading comprehension" exercise – a three paragraph story about whaling, followed by multiple-choice questions to test "comprehension." The subject is introduced by a few remarks about whales — they are large mammals, larger than elephants, who frequent the cold waters of the North Atlantic near Scandinavia and so on. The substance of the selection then begins — a description of the nature of the work of whalers, past and present. A detailed account is given of how whaling used to be done, and how the work has been modified with the introduction of mechanized equipment. The multiple choice "comprehension" questions then proceed to ask whether whales are smaller, larger, or the same size as elephants (woe to the child who wonders what species or age of whale is in question!), and whether they are found in the North Atlantic, South Atlantic, or Mediterranean.

Similar questions are asked about other readings, so that children learn to remember certain kinds of information about what they read — anything that refers to quantity or size, anything that specifies location, or dates, and the like — and to ignore the essential subject matter.

They become very skilled at recognizing and extracting this kind of information, and develop a certainty (reinforced by good grades) that this is the only sort of information that is of any importance. Critical thinking about the content or significance of material? No. But they become experts at extracting and processing data. Again, many of the jobs in middle-level management and the professions require just such narrow skills, and habits of thought that optimize such skills.

LIBERALIZING REFORMS

What kinds of changes occur when "reforms" are introduced into North American school systems by professional educators? The kinds of reforms one attempts depend, of course, on how one defines the problems to be solved. For example, educators observe that individual children in any classroom, no matter how much they are classified in "ability groups" learn particular material at different rates. This is perceived as a "problem" which is described as children "interfering with each other's progress," holding each other back. The children have, of course, been set against each other by the process of competitive grading, in which only a limited number can "earn" good grades (translated later into good salaries), and in which each child learns that his gain must therefore be another's loss. Under these conditions, different rates of learning cannot be accommodated by encouraging children who learn mathematics, for instance, more quickly, to work with and help those who are "slower" in this subject. The "slow" children are instead seen as "holding back" others, and the solution that is called for is a school in which each child is "free" to learn "at his own speed." Conditions for this kind of "individualized learning" have been created in some of the "open area" schools that have been established in a number of cities.[5]

These "open area" schools are large, warehouse-like structures, built without interior dividing walls, i.e. without separated classrooms within them. The stated purpose of this design is to facilitate impermanent groupings of children — to make it easier to re-group children, according to their "ability" and "achievement" levels, into different groups for each subject (classroom walls are said to be an obstacle to this). A group of children gather with a teacher in an area furnished with movable tables and chairs. Materials (books, maps, programmed learning kits, etc.) are kept in resource areas, from which they are borrowed for use.[6]

It is fascinating to observe how this restructured physical environment is utilized in practice. Along with the new buildings and their furnishings, the knowledge industry has sold these school systems an enormous quantity of instructional kits and audio-visual devices to "facilitate individualized learning programs." The floor space in the school is thus jammed with equipment of all kinds — boxed kits, audio-visual equipment, tables and chairs, shelves and files, and more shelves and files. The children appear dwarfed when they move about among it all. The school resembles a factory floor — interestingly, teachers refer to the instruction area as "the floor." There is much equipment for production, and there is much din as files and lockers are opened and shut, voices hum, groups move about, a film projector somewhere emits its sound track.

---

[5]   These remarks are based on observations in an "open area" school in Florida, and one in a western Canadian city.

[6]   Storing materials in this way is said to make it possible for children who are working on a project to cross the lines of subject areas [disciplines] and make use of materials from history, mathematics, and so on that might all be related to one project. In our observations, nothing of the kind resulted at all:

(a)   because children had no time to work on such interdisciplinary projects; all their school time was tied to "individualized" instruction, and

(b)   because only teachers or pupils specifically sent by them signed out and returned materials.

In the midst of all this, children are working (or sitting, often listlessly, looking around), and they are indeed working individually. As teachers freely admit, given the noise level it is impossible for a teacher to speak to more than two or three children at a time. There is thus no classroom group — no consistent group of children and teacher — with its own social structure, style of interaction, common habits and assumptions. Consequently, there is no more process of children learning from each other's recitations and from the teacher's response to others (nor any possibility of children who haven't learned to read learning from what they hear).

Instead, a set of tasks is assigned to each child (or sometimes to several together). These tasks are established on the basis of "diagnostic tests" (to discover the areas in which the child is "lacking" — i.e. plurals, multiplications, etc.), which determine a "prescription" for the child (as if areas in which he is not yet educated are like illnesses to be cured). Usually, these prescriptions consist of a set of printed cards, coded as to achievement levels, selected from one of a variety of programmed instruction kits. These kits are, in effect, like textbooks on reading, social studies, math, etc., broken down into a number of separate printed cards — several at each "level" — on each of which a text is printed, together with some "self-testing" questions.[7]

In such a school, the role of the teacher is reduced to that of a foreman in production. Her role is to distribute the raw materials (the programmed cards, film strips, etc.) to the children, and to explain to them how to process the materials — i.e. the form of the task; she does NOT explain the subject matter — that is left to the "experts" who wrote the programmed material. She explains the method of studying the passages given, how to look up the answers to the (usually multiple choice) self-test, how to make corrections, when to go on to the next step. She walks about the room, picking up materials from those children who are finished and waiting, distributing other materials, answering questions about their use. As one teacher explained: "My job is to teach the children to follow complex instructions, which is probably the most important thing they can learn in school." Perhaps, with regard to enculturation for the attitudes necessary in the work place in capitalist society, she is quite right.

The children do follow their instructions and fill up their answer sheets — each one all alone; they are atomized, isolated from each other's

---

[7] Most current educational "reforms" are infused with "McLuhanist" dogmas about books being passé, about the magical advantages of audio-visual materials and "computer-like" instructional kits. Instead of learning the joy of discovering and becoming absorbed in a book, students develop "skills" in manipulating "teaching materials."

learning, the ultimate in the achievement of capitalist individualism — each moving along, "succeeding" at his own speed, by himself and for himself.

What about differences in social class in these open area schools, these reformed schools that, just like "free schools" of the Summerhill type, create "freedom" by preventing individuals from "interfering" with each other? One thing is clear — the inadequate education provided for working-class children can readily be explained away in the context of open area schools. It is a simple matter. Each child progresses at his "own speed." His "own speed" is determined by tests written in middle-class dialect about subject matters familiar to middle-class children. Naturally, middle-class children will appear to be at higher "ability" and "achievement" levels on these tests and will be assigned "faster" levels of work. The fact that older children of working-class background often remain locked in the most elementary levels of most subjects can be readily explained by reporting that they are "moving along at their own speed," thus absolving the school of any responsibility for the lack of progress made by these children.

The open area school is in many ways the liberal educational reformer's answer to the subtle constraints on choice represented by Miss Simms' classroom, and to the more obvious constraints in the "old-fashioned" autocratic classroom.

As enculturation, it also helps to elevate personal physical mobility into the realm of absolute good. To stay in one place is bad. (Even if it's a good place to be.) To move around is good. (Even if there is no place worth going to.) A generation of middle-class North American youth is perhaps beginning to recognize the profound middle-class nature of the "hippie" ethic of the last decade. "We were moving around more, and enjoying it less."

Of course, the sense of freedom embodied in limitless physical mobility is an illusion in middle-class life, just as it is in the open area school. Most managers, salesmen, engineers (as well as many workers in extractive industries, transport, etc.) must declare their willingness to "re-locate" as a condition of employment. The freedom to move about turns out in fact to be the freedom of huge corporations to deploy their managerial work-force as flexibly as they wish.

APOLOGIA

This paper has touched upon several interrelated topics. Within the confines of a few pages, it is neither possible to fully document nor even to present an exhaustive analysis of the material included. The paper is intended merely to be suggestive of the role of school life in differentially enculturating children to the behavior, expectations and attitudes appropriate for their position in the social class structure.

REFERENCES

BUTTRICK, JOHN
1972 Who goes to university in Ontario. *This Magazine is About Schools* 6:81–100.
FORD, JULIENNE
1969 *Social class and the comprehensive school.* London: Routledge and Kegan Paul.
LEACOCK, ELEANOR B.
1969 *Teaching and learning in city schools.* New York and London: Basic Books.
PARK SCHOOL COMMUNITY COUNCIL
1971 Class bias in Toronto schools. *This Magazine is About Schools* 5:6–35.
PORTER, JOHN A.
1965 *The vertical mosaic: an analysis of social class and power in Canada.* Toronto: University of Toronto Press.
SAVORY, LINDA
1972 Organizing English parents in Point St. Charles, Montreal. *This Magazine is About Schools* 6:6–30.

On the Origin of the Socialization Process

THOMAS R. WILLIAMS

This discussion is concerned with comprehending the origin of the socialization process.[1] It begins with a brief account of changes in basic assumptions that have occurred following evaluations of recently discovered fossil evidence for human biological and cultural evolution. The discussion then moves to a consideration of the meaning of these changes for research on the origin of contemporary human behavior processes, including socialization. The third part of the discussion is concerned with a brief review of definitions, concepts, and theoretical approaches used in studies of the socialization process, in terms of recent changes in basic assumptions about the nature of human biological and cultural evolution. The discussion concludes with a summary of present understanding of the origin of the socialization process.

I.   Beginning in the late 1940's, under the stimulus of new concepts and theoretical views from fields as diverse as physical anthropology, genetics, paleontology, mathematics, and electronic engineering, a number of scholars have suggested that the evolutionary transition from hominid to *Homo sapiens* and the development of *Homo sapiens* personality structure and behavior forms probably occurred as a con-

A draft version of this paper was presented on March 29, 1973, to a symposium on the socialization process at the 52nd Annual Meeting of The Central States Anthropological Society in St. Louis, Missouri. Drafts of this work have been read by Margaret Mead, Judith K. Brown, Gerald Erchak, Alan Peskin, and Bruce T. Grindal. However, I am solely responsible for the contents of this work.
[1]   It is very important that readers clearly understand that this paper is not primarily concerned with the specific mechanisms of human biological evolution or with the particular consequences of such mechanisms in the evolution or the

sequence of a series of complex interactions between evolving hominid biology and forms of emerging cultural behavior. This major theoretical insight has been expressed in the publications written or edited by Hallowell (1950, 1953, 1954a, 1954b, 1956, 1959, 1960, 1961, 1963, 1965, 1967), Campbell (1966), Chance and Mead (1953), Count (1958), Dobzhansky (1962, 1963a, 1963b), Dobzhansky and Montagu (1947), Etkin (1963), Geertz (1962, 1964), Kurth (1962), LaBarre (1954), Mead (1944, 1945, 1947a, 1947b, 1947c, 1947d, 1949, 1954a, 1954b), Montagu (1951, 1962), Robinson (1961), Roe and Simpson (1958), Spiro (1954), Spuhler (1959), Waddington (1960), and Washburn (1950, 1960). The term CYBERNETIC has been applied (cf. Williams 1972b) to the theoretical model for describing the nature and products of the interaction process between evolving hominid biology and emerging cultural behavior. This model is based on an assumption that, beginning in the late Miocene to the early Pliocene epochs (i.e. sometime prior to 5.5 million years before the present) and running through most of the Pleistocene geological epoch until perhaps 50,000 to 60,000 years before the present, a dynamic and mutually dependent interaction process between evolving hominid biology and emergent forms of cultural behavior led to the synthesis of the biological and behavioral complex typical of *Homo sapiens.*[2]

---

development of specific human structural features (e.g. bipedalism, the opposable thumb, etc.). This paper does not examine the details of the evolutionary genetic or structural processes involved in the transitions from ape to early man (from Hominoids to Hominids) or from early to modern man (from *Homo erectus* to *Homo sapiens*). Thus, recent studies in primate behavior and molecular biology (cf. Kohne 1970; Goodman 1963; Goodman, Barnabas, Matsuda and Moore 1971; Lancaster 1968b; Wilson and Sarich 1969; Sarich 1970; van Lawick-Goodall 1968, 1970, 1971; Washburn 1972b) that appear to demonstrate that man and the chimpanzee are behaviorally and structurally very similar, and which have been used to construct a primate "phylogenetic tree" and to estimate the "genetic distance" between man and other primates, are not described here or commented upon in detail. Similarly, I am not directly concerned here with data such as those from recent field and laboratory studies that indicate that both chimpanzees and gorillas are "ground living" knuckle-walkers rather than being arboreal primates, and that therefore a basic evolutionary question now is, "how did a ground living, knuckle-walking creature become a biped?" rather than the previous question of, "how did an arboreal ape come to the ground and become a biped?" (cf. Washburn 1972a: 164). Such concerns and questions, whether arising from studies in molecular biology or in the relationship of data from primate field studies to evolutionary changes in primate structure, are not a central topic of interest in this discussion of the possible origin of the human process of socialization. This work should not be read as an exercise in physical anthropology, describing the details of the evolution of human biology, or the nature of specific mechanisms involved in the evolutionary development of human biology.

[2]   There have been some recent major changes in the techniques and results of

The formulation of the major features of this theoretical model has depended on a rejection of a long-standing assumption in evolutionary studies that it was unlikely that major behavior changes would ever precede significant biological changes in an animal population as a consequence of the operation of the processes of natural selection, population intermixture, isolation, or genetic drift. However, by the mid-1940's, the discovery and studies of new fossil hominid remains, particularly those of the Australopithecines, had made it apparent that during the course of the evolution of the hominids of the late Miocene and Pliocene epochs, body structure was directly affected in both "form" (i.e. anatomy) and "function" (i.e. physiology) by a whole range of new hominid behavior forms, including the making and using of tools and various social activities such as family life, hunting, and the defense of a local population. Washburn appears to be the first scholar to understand fully and to demonstrate the broad theoretical implications of a rejection of the assumption that in the course of hominid evolution behavior always had depended upon and followed from body form.

Prior to the discovery and approximate dating of the Australopithecine fossil materials, and their associated cultural remains, physical anthropologists generally had assumed that most *Homo sapiens*-like behavior, and especially tool making and use, could not have occurred until the brain had evolved to nearly its present average size of 1,450 cc. But, by the late 1940's, evidence from continuing studies of Australopithecine materials suggested to Washburn (1950) and some others (cf. Montagu 1951) that this was an incorrect assumption. Today, we know that Australopithecines possessed of brains less than one-half the average size of *Homo sapiens sapiens* regularly made and used tools at least 1.75± million years before the present, perhaps 2.61± million years before the present (Leakey 1969, 1970, 1973) or even as long ago as 4± million years before the present (Howell 1968, 1969). The evidence now available from Australopithecine sites at Olduvai, Omo, Lake Rudolph, and elsewhere in East Africa clearly indicates that small-brained, bipedal hominids behaved regularly in ways that

---

dating various geological epochs. Thus, the Pliocene epoch now is believed by some geologists to have begun about 5.5 million years before the present. My primary concern here is to provide a reasonable estimate of a singularity in evolutionary time for a possible beginning of the cybernetic interaction process between evolving hominid biology and emergent forms of cultural behavior. I am not concerned with tracing the development of geological dating techniques or the details of specific arguments among specialists in geological dating as to exactly when a particular geological epoch began or ended.

formerly had been supposed to depend entirely on a very much larger brain and other more complex body fetaures, including a general anatomy similar to the *Homo sapiens* hand, wrist, and forearm. Washburn (1950, 1960) had grasped the great theoretical significance of the evidences that major behavioral changes, such as tool making and use, produced in evolving hominids significant structural changes in the shape and size of the face, head, brain, teeth, and hands. But Washburn did not at first fully appreciate the CYBERNETIC nature of the hominid evolutionary process and so understand that the theoretical model was not, as he suggested, [BEHAVIORAL CHANGE → STRUCTURAL CHANGE] but rather [BEHAVIOR ←→ STRUCTURE].[3]

However, Washburn's proposal (cf. 1968a, 1968b, 1971, 1972a, 1972b) that forms of emerging cultural behavior, including tool making and use, had directly shaped the course of hominid structural evolution, opened the way for rejection of the assumption that in the course of the evolution of the hominids, since earlier populations appeared to be more "primitive" or "simpler" in their structure, they probably were "simpler" in their behavior than *Homo sapiens*, while more "modern" or "advanced" body structure, as possessed by *Homo sapiens*, not only reflected a much later evolutionary appearance, but also the potential for much more complex forms of behavior. The evidence from studies of the Australopithecines clearly indicates that it is very difficult to judge accurately the ways fossil hominids may have behaved on the basis of their seemingly more primitive structural features.[4]

II.   The abandonment of these two assumption in studies of human evolution means that it is now possible to conceive of the appearance and the long-term existence of complex behavior processes, such as socialization, or social organization, law, religion, art, and so on, among hominids whose structure only generally resembled that of contemporary man. Rejection of these assumptions in studies of hominid evo-

[3]   See Bajema (1972, i.p.) for some refinements of this cybernetic conceptual model.
[4]   The rejection of the assumption that, in the course of hominid evolution, structural change always preceded behavior change, which was derived from studies of fossil materials, has received independent support from comparisons of protein macromolecules of modern chimpanzees and man by King and Wilson (1975) and their conclusion that the evidence from biochemical studies indicates that while the "genetic distance" between chimpanzees and man is very small (corresponding to the genetic distance between sibling species of fruit flies or other mammals) the substantial anatomical and behavioral differences between man and chimpanzee indicate that "macromolecules and anatomical or behavioral features of organisms can evolve at independent rates" (King and Wilson 1975: 115).

lution has also made it possible to look at contemporary non-human primates as possibly exhibiting some rudimentary behavior forms that perhaps were characteristic of early hominids (cf. King 1971).[5] As a consequence of these greatly altered theoretical views, it is no longer necessary to regard *Homo sapiens sapiens* behavior forms or processes, such as socialization, as having no direct antecedents or precursors in the behavior of other types of animals ancestral to contemporary man.

Until recently, it has been common for research concerned with the socialization process to proceed as if this process were limited solely to contemporary man.[6] This does not mean that there has been an absence of discussion concerning the origins of human behavior processes, including socialization. The writings of many late nineteenth and early twentieth century scholars reflected a belief that studies of "savage" peoples, as well as primates and some other "social animals," might provide clues to the development of major forms and processes of human behavior, including the socialization process. But such cultural evolutionary theories became untenable in the decades following World War I as a consequence of the development of historical and functional theories and studies, culture area studies, and demonstrations of the severe logical problems inherent in theories of human behavior based on the practice of comparing examples from supposedly "savage" and "primitive" cultures with those taken from more "advanced" civilizations and cultures. Thus, for nearly half a century, research and theory concerned with the origin of human behavior processes, including socialization, was greatly limited by an inability to become fully informed by new empirical evidences and revised theories from physical anthropology, ethology, genetics, and other disciplines

---

[5] King (1971) notes, as does Washburn (1968a, 1971, 1972a, 1972b), that many of the behavior forms once thought to be unique to modern man have now been observed in free-ranging primates, and particularly among chimpanzees. Chimpanzees use objects in hitting, prying, digging, gathering food, and in play (cf. Lancaster 1968b; van Lawick-Goodall 1968, 1971) and regularly engage in cooperative social action while hunting food. These facts, which have caused great interest among anthropologists and others must be viewed in the context of the logical caution that it does not at all follow that the evolutionary transition from hominoid to hominid forms involved behavior identical to that now documented among chimpanzees. It is possible that "object use" among contemporary chimpanzees developed as a feature of chimpanzee behavior subsequent to the separation of Pongidae and Hominidae.

[6] For instance, see the discussions of Aberle (1961); Brim (1968), R. Burton (1968), Child (1954), Clausen (1968), Elkin (1960), Elkin and Handel (1972), Goslin (1969), Greenberg (1970), Greenstein (1968), Mayer (1970), McNeil (1969), and Whiting (1968).

concerned with understanding animal evolution and behavior. However, it is necessary to exercise considerable caution in the use of such data and theory in studies of the origin and development of particular human behavior forms or processes. For instance, there is a body of data and theory in an area of physical anthropology that has been termed "primate socialization" that must be considered with some skepticism and used with a modicum of doubt concerning the logic, assumptions, and definitions employed by individuals specializing in such studies. It appears that such research might be more appropriately termed as "animal (or primate) learning" and be discussed through use of particular phylogenetic modifiers, that is, as Pongidae learning, Hylobatindae learning, and so on, when discussing particular kinds of primates, or other animals.

This follows from the fact that there is no creditable scientific evidence for the existence of a cybernetic interaction process between biology and culture, or for the specific products of such a process in the forms of behavior or behavior processes, among any other animals than members of two of the three genera (i.e. *Australopithecus* and *Homo*) of the Hominidae or human family.

It is important to note that while "field" (or naturalistic observation) and "experimental" (or laboratory and zoo) studies of animals provide important insights into the specific nature of species-characteristic behavior forms, reflexes, drives, and capacities in a wide variety of animals ranging from fish through ducks, geese, gulls, rats, cats, and dogs to monkeys and apes (cf. Eibl-Eibesfeldt 1970; Klopfer and Hailman 1967) such research has not established the existence of a cybernetic interaction process between the biology of particular animals and an emergent, or developed, system of culture other than in the human family. Thus, recent field studies and accounts which have been termed as "primate socialization" (cf. Burton 1972; Chalmers 1972; Lancaster 1972; Ransom and Rowell 1972; Sugiyama 1972; Itani 1972; Mitchell and Brandt 1972) do not offer basic insights into the origin, development, and current nature of a cybernetic interaction process between biology and culture among macaques, vervet monkeys, baboons, chimpanzees, or other non-human primates. Contemporary accounts of "primate socialization" actually are focused upon the process of learning by particular kinds of primates. Thus, when "primate socialization" is defined as "... the sum total of an individual's past social experiences, which in turn may be expected to shape its future social behavior..." (Poirier 1972: 8), what really is being described and defined is learning, or any modification of behavior by an animal — any animal — based on its experience.[7] Hence accounts termed as "primate socialization" are misleading, since they provide data and conclusions that are not germane to an understanding of the human process of socialization.

III. Anthropologists have used both the terms SOCIALIZATION and EN-CULTURATION to refer to the process of cultural transmission. In a 1963 paper, Mead noted the major theoretical problems caused by confounding these terms, and proposed that it is vital to distinguish between abstract statements of empirical reference concerning intergenerational transmission of culture that are universally valid (i.e. socialization) and abstract statements of empirical reference concerning intergenerational transmission of culture valid only for a specific culture, or a group of related cultures (i.e. enculturation).

Mead suggests that the concept of socialization be defined as a process involving a set of species-wide requirements, or demands, made on humans as they learn a system of culture and that the concept of enculturation be defined as the process through which humans learn one culture in all of its historical uniqueness and local particularity. On the basis of Mead's definitions, we would no longer seek to generalize to all cultures from data concerning the ways culture is transmitted and learned in only one culture, or in a group of closely related cultures. It seems clear now, on the basis of only limited research using these conceptual distinctions (cf. Williams 1972a, 1972b), that the prototypical features of the socialization process are not to be derived from description and analysis of the details of the transmission and learning of one culture. Rather, it is necessary to systematically abstract valid statements concerning cultural transmission and learning from studies in all cultures, or in at least an adequate sample of cultures known to be linguistically and culturally distinct (cf. Naroll and Cohen 1970; Goodenough 1970; Honigmann 1972).

Distinguishing between the concepts of socialization and enculturation in this manner means that research and the building of theory can be focused more clearly. Thus, if we are concerned with studies of the process of enculturation, we begin with a clear understanding that we are describing and analyzing details of a behavior process shaped in one society through a long period of time by significant events such as war, migration, and epidemic disease, and by the factors of ecology,

---

[7] The concept of learning is usually defined in psychology as "a relatively permanent modification of behavior resulting from reinforced practice" (CRM 1970: 688).

language, technology, social relations, demography, and culture change. And, as we proceed with comparative studies of cultural transmission and learning in a large number of different cultures, we can concentrate on a search for common features of that process, understanding that these abstract features will have a configuration (i.e. "shape") imparted through their being part of many different enculturation processes. Thus, valid generalizations concerning the socialization process will depend on the abstraction of general statements from descriptions of many different kinds of enculturation processes. Precise methods will need to be developed to insure that the abstraction of general statements from different and contrasting enculturation processes fully accounts for the demands of a rigorous scientific logic and the special demands made in such work, such as attention to "Galton's question" (cf. Naroll and Cohen 1970).

Recently I have used Mead's conceptual distinctions as the basis of a theoretical model (Williams 1972b) for research on the origin, development, and nature of the socialization process. This model begins with the assumption that our investigations of the contemporary socialization process must explicitly account for the facts of its evolutionary origin and development. And this model rests upon an assumption that as we move back through evolutionary time in studies of the socialization process, we eventually arrive at a SINGULARITY (or critical period) where hominid populations lived entirely in a state of "natural ecology," that is, where the system of mutual relations between evolving hominids and their environments was not shaped, altered, or directed in any synthetic or processed manner. Then, from that singularity in hominid evolution, which now can be estimated as being between 5± and 3± million years before the present, there was a lengthy time of transition from a completely natural hominid ecology to a fully "cultural ecology," that is, when the system of mutual relationships between evolving hominids and their environments was regularly shaped and directed by cultural transmission and learning. This theoretical model for the origin and development of the socialization process involves use of the concept of an on-going cybernetic feedback between evolving hominid biology and emerging forms of culture. It also involves the use of the concept that it is possible to postulate a typical *Homo sapiens sapiens* behavior process as a property of life among hominids whose structure was only generally similar to that of contemporary man.

It seems that, in thinking about the origin of the socialization process, one major barrier to the appearance of this process in early hominid evolution was a lack of a specific way for hominids to provide for, or to enhance, a wide-spread social sharing of the products of individual life experiences and use of their capacities for reflection, cognition, insight, understanding, and learning. But there would have been increasingly greater naturally selective advantages for evolving hominid populations to be able to draw upon the products of various individual capacities and life experiences to promote group survival and reproduction. In contemporary man, the capacity for reflection involves symbolic anticipation of future events on the basis of past and present life experiences, and acting in ways that will affect anticipated future events. Hominids capable of reflecting on their life experiences and settings would have increased their individual ability to survive in a natural ecology. But a heightened individual capacity for reflection, or any other capacity, would not have contributed to the survival and reproduction of whole populations of evolving hominids. It would have been only at that time when the specific products of use of individual hominid capacities or life experiences were shared generally throughout a population, allowing the "least able" individuals to share in and to benefit from the heightened capacities and life experiences of the "most able" individuals, that hominid populations could benefit from any increased or developed capacities possessed by individuals.

The appearance and development of a symbolic communication system, based on language and its surrogates, seems to have provided a means for widespread sharing of the products of individual capacities and life experiences, both within and between generations of evolving hominid populations. The topic of language origin and development is being intensively debated at present (cf. Washburn and Dolhinow 1972). But it seems clear that among the hominids the gradual emergence and use over a period of some 5 or more million years of a symbolic communication system and capacity provided a mechanism for both intra- and inter-generational sharing of the products of individual hominid capacities and life experiences, and enabled whole populations of evolving hominids to benefit from the concepts, understandings, and insights of the most cognitively able individuals to the ultimate gain of the entire population, particularly in terms of its survival and reproduction.

And so it seems clear that the socialization process had its beginnings when individual hominids began sharing and transmitting the cumulative products of their own capacities and life experiences to their offspring and the young of other hominids. Undoubtedly, such intra- and inter-generational sharing had a fitful start and was probably not a regular feature of evolving hominid life for a very long period of time after the appearance of the hominids. However, this does not mean that hominid adults were not transmitting many different types of data and information to their offspring prior to the development and regular use of a capacity for symbolic communication. It seems probable that hominids were possessed of fairly well developed capacities for reflection, cognition, and so on before the advent of a language system. Thus it is possible that for a long period the products of adult hominid capacities and life experiences were transmitted and shared socially through non-linguistic means. Recent field studies of various types of contemporary animals (e.g. "red" deer, tigers, wolves, chimpanzees, gorillas, and gibbons) appear to indicate that hominid young could have shared in the products of use of individual hominid adult capacities and life experiences through direct observation of, reflection upon, and imitation of the patterned behavior forms of adults. And, as the early hominid young took on these products of the use of capacities and of life experiences by members of the adult generation, whether by direct instruction through the use of a language system and capacity or through use of other capacities joined with direct observation and imitation, their responses to parents and parent surrogates may well have further stimulated adult hominid efforts to transmit and share the products of their own capacities and life experiences, and so set in operation the characteristic reciprocal aspect of contemporary socialization. This reciprocity is the feature of the modern socialization process in which parents, or their surrogates, are stimulated to active participation in cultural transmission by the active responses of the infant and child to the actions of the adults, so that a mutually dependent feedback process develops surely and consistently between the socializing acts of an adult and the specific responses of an infant and child (cf. Williams 1972a: 67–102).

IV.   On the basis of a comparative study of reports of enculturation processes in a sample of 128 cultures, I have abstracted and defined (Williams 1972a, 1972b) a number of specific structural and functional features that I believe comprise the basic nature of the contemporary socialization process. I also have proposed a conceptual plan for considering the association of these features in a dynamic system. The usefulness of this preliminary effort to define the nature of the contemporary socialization process systematically is limited by a number of factors, including (1) the size of the sample, (2) the fact that many cultures in the sample have had some type of known linguistic and cultural contact, and (3) the incomplete nature of the basic descriptions of enculturation in many cultures used in the sample. The results of this effort to define the current nature of the socialization process are also directly affected by the limited conceptual devices and procedures for abstraction of data of enculturation in ways that do not "decontextualize" or render such data meaningless because of the techniques employed in abstraction and comparison. The usefulness of this effort is further limited by lack of knowledge concerning the origin and development of the socialization process.

I do not know whether or not the specific structural and functional features of the contemporary socialization process have remained unchanged through the time of the existence of that process and have been associated through the whole time of the existence of the socialization process in the ways these structural/functional features now seem to be interrelated, or whether these structural/functional features have their origin in the same or different manner and at the same time or a different time in the course of hominid evolution.

It seems to me that one way to examine these questions is to search for evidence concerning the origin and development of the socialization process in the record of hominid evolution. At present, such evidence is quite limited and difficult to discern; clues to the evolution of behavioral processes and forms are difficult to detect in straightforward reporting of human fossil and early cultural remains. Yet recent changes in basic assumptions concerning hominid evolution have at least made it possible to search for such evidence, if it does exist, and to begin to think systematically about its meaning for the origin and development of the contemporary socialization process.

What, then, can be said at this time? I believe that the socialization process probably had its origin in the period between 5± and 3± million years before the present as a consequence, or perhaps a part of, a cybernetic interaction synthesis between evolving hominid biology and emerging forms of culture. The empirical evidence available at present does not provide for more than the formulation of tentative hypotheses concerning the dominant events and dynamic mechanisms in the course of the origin and development of the socialization process. However continued attention to this question, in terms of available empirical evidence from studies of hominid evolution and particularly fossil evidences, seems likely to lead to a new comprehension of the role and meaning of the process of socialization in human life.

REFERENCES

ABERLE, D.
1961   "Culture and socialization," in *Psychological anthropology*. Edited by F. L. K. Hsu, 381–399. Homewood, Ill.: Dorsey.

BAJEMA, C.
1972   Transmission of information about the environment in the human species: a cybernetic view of genetic and cultural evolution. *Social Biology* 19:224–226.

i.p.   "Differential transmission of genetic and cultural (non-genetic) information about the environment: a cybernetic view of genetic and cultural evolution in animal species," in *Evolutionary models and studies in human diversity*. Edited by R. J. Meier, C. Otten, and F. Abdel-Hameed. World Anthropology. The Hague: Mouton.

BRIM, O., JR.
1968   "Socialization: adult socialization," in *International encyclopedia of the social sciences*, volume fourteen. Edited by D. Sills, 555–562. New York: Macmillan and The Free Press.

BURTON, F.
1972   "The integration of biology and behavior in the socialization of *Macaca sylvana* of Gibraltar," in *Primate socialization*. Edited by F. Poirier, 29–62. New York: Random House.

BURTON, R.
1968   "Socialization: psychological aspects," in *International encyclopedia of the social sciences*, volume fourteen. Edited by D. Sills, 534–545. New York: Macmillan and The Free Press.

CAMPBELL, B.
1966   *Human evolution*. Chicago: Aldine.

CHALMERS, N.
1972   "Comparative aspects of early infant development in some captive cercopithecines," in *Primate socialization*. Edited by F. Poirier, 63–82. New York: Random House.

CHANCE, M., A. MEAD
1953   Social biology and primate evolution. *Symposia of the Society for Experimental Biology* 7:395–439.

CHILD, I.
1954   "Socialization," in *Handbook of social psychology*, volume two. Edited by G. Lindzey, 655–692. Reading, Mass.: Addison-Wesley Press.

CLAUSEN, J., *editor*
1968   *Socialization and society*. Boston: Little, Brown.

COUNT, E.
1958   The biological basis of human sociality. *American Anthropologist* 60:1049–1085.

CRM BOOKS
1970   *Psychology today*. Del Mar, Calif.: CRM Books.

DOBZHANSKY, T.
1962   *Mankind evolving*. New Haven, Conn.: Yale University Press.

1963a Cultural direction of human evolution: a summation. *Human Biology* 35:311–316.
1963b Evolution: organic and superorganic. *The Rockefeller Institute Review* 1 (2).

DOBZHANSKY, T., M. F. A. MONTAGU
1947　Natural selection and the mental capacity of mankind. *Science* 105:587–590.

EIBL-EIBESFELDT, I.
1970　*Ethology: the biology of behavior.* New York: Holt, Rinehart and Winston.

ELKIN, F.
1960　*The child and society: the process of socialization.* New York: Random House.

ELKIN F., G. HANDEL
1972　*The child and society.* New York: Random House.

ETKIN, W.
1963　Social behavioral factors in the emergence of man. *Human Biology* 35:299–310.

GEERTZ, C.
1962　"The growth of culture and the evolution of mind," in *Theories of the mind.* Edited by J. M. Scher, 713–740. New York: The Free Press of Glencoe.
1964　"The transition to humanity," in *Horizons of anthropology.* Edited by Sol Tax, 37–48. Chicago: Aldine.

GOODENOUGH, W.
1970　*Description and comparison in cultural anthropology.* Chicago: Aldine.

GOODMAN, M.
1963　"Man's place in the phylogeny of the primates as reflected in serum proteins," in *Classification and human evolution.* Edited by S. L. Washburn, 204–234. Chicago: Aldine.

GOODMAN, M., J. BARNABAS, G. MATSUDA, G. MOORE
1971　Molecular evolution in the descent of man. *Nature* 233:604–613.

GOSLIN, D., *editor*
1969　*Handbook of socialization theory and research.* Chicago: Rand McNally.

GREENBERG, E.
1970　*Political socialization.* New York: Atherton.

GREENSTEIN, F.
1968　"Socialization: political socialization," in *International encyclopedia of the social sciences,* volume fourteen. Edited by D. Sills, 551–555. New York: Macmillan and The Free Press.

HALLOWELL, A.
1950　Personality structure and the evolution of man. *American Anthropologist* 52:159–173.
1953　"Culture, personality and society," in *Anthropology today.* Edited by A. L. Kroeber, 597–620. Chicago: University of Chicago Press.
1954a The self and its behavioral environment. *Explorations* 2 (April): 106–165.

1954b "Psychology and anthropology," in *For a science of social man.* Edited by J. Gillin, 160–226. New York: Macmillan.

1956 The structural and functional dimensions of a human existence. *Quarterly Review of Biology* 31:88–101.

1959 "Behavioral evolution and the emergence of the self," in *Evolution and anthropology: a centennial appraisal.* Edited by B. Meggers. Washington, D.C.: Anthropological Society of Washington.

1960 "Self, society and culture in phylogenetic perspective," in *Evolution after Darwin,* volume two: *The evolution of man.* Edited by Sol Tax, 309–371. Chicago: University of Chicago Press.

1961 "The protocultural foundations of human adaptation," in *Social life of early man.* Edited by S. L. Washburn, 236–255. Chicago: Aldine.

1963 "Personality, culture and society in behavioral evolution," in *Psychology: a study of a science,* volume six. Edited by S. Koch, 426–509. New York: McGraw-Hill.

1965 "Hominid evolution, cultural adaptation and mental dysfunctioning," in *Transcultural psychiatry.* Edited by A. V. S. de Reuck and R. Porter, 26–54. Boston: Little, Brown.

1967 *Culture and experience.* New York: Schocken.

HONIGMANN, J.
1972 *Method in cultural anthropology.* Chicago: Rand McNally.

HOWELL, F.
1968 Omo research expedition. *Nature* 219:567–572.

1969 Remains of Hominidae from Plio-Pleistocene formations in the Lower Omo Basin, Ethiopia. *Nature* 223:1234.

ITANI, J.
1972 "A preliminary essay on the relationship between social organization and incest avoidance in non-human primates," in *Primate socialization.* Edited by F. Poirier, 165–171. New York: Random House.

KING, G.
1971 "The use of living species in the reconstruction of hominid behavioral evolution." Unpublished Ph.D. dissertation, University of California, Berkeley.

KING, M. C., A. C. WILSON
1975 Evolution at two levels in humans and chimpanzees. *Science* 188:107–116.

KLOPFER, P., J. HAILMAN
1967 *An introduction to animal behavior: ethology's first century.* Englewood Cliffs, N.J.: Prentice-Hall.

KOHNE, E.
1970 Evolution of higher-organism DNA. *Quarterly Review of Biophysics* 3:327–375.

KURTH, G., editor
1962 *Evolution und Hominization.* Stuttgart: G. Fischer.

LA BARRE, W.
1954 *The human animal.* Chicago: University of Chicago Press.

LANCASTER, J.
  1968a "Primate communication systems and the emergence of language," in *Primates: studies in adaptation and variability*. Edited by P. Jay, 439–457. New York: Holt, Rinehart and Winston.
  1968b On the evolution of tool-using behavior. *American Anthropologist* 70:56–66.
  1972 "Play-mothering: the relations between juvenile females and young infants among free-ranging vervet monkeys," in *Primate socialization*. Edited by F. Poirier, 83–104. New York: Random House.

LEAKEY, R.
  1969 Early *Homo sapiens* remains from the Omo River region of southwest Ethiopia. *Nature* 222:1132.
  1970 Fauna and artifacts from a new Plio-Pleistocene locality near Lake Rudolph in Kenya. *Nature* 226:223.
  1973 Evidence for an advanced Plio-Pleistocene hominid from East Rudolph, Kenya. *Nature* 242:447–450.

MAYER, P.
  1970 *Socialization: the approach from social anthropology*. London: Tavistock.

MC NEIL, E.
  1969 *Human socialization*. Belmont, Calif.: Brooks-Cole.

MEAD, M.
  1944 Cultural approach to personality. *Transactions of the New York Academy of Sciences*, series 2, 6:93–101.
  1945 "Research on primitive children," in *Manual of child psychology*. Edited by L. Carmichael, 735–780. New York: Wiley.
  1947a Age patterning in personality development. *American Journal of Orthopsychiatry* 17:231–240.
  1947b The concept of culture and the psychosomatic approach. *Psychiatry* 10:57–76.
  1947c The implications of culture change for personality development. *American Journal of Orthopsychiatry* 17:633–646.
  1947d On the implications for anthropology of the Gesell-Ilg approach to maturation. *American Anthropologist* 49:69–77.
  1949 "Character formation and diachronic theory," in *Social structure*. Edited by M. Fortes, 18–34. Oxford: Clarendon Press.
  1954a *Culture patterns and technical change*. Paris: UNESCO.
  1954b Cultural discontinuities and personality transformation. *Journal of Social Issues* 8:3–16.
  1963 Socialization and enculturation. *Current Anthropology* 4:184–188.

MITCHELL, G., E. BRANDT
  1972 "Paternal behavior in primates," in *Primate socialization*. Edited by F. Poirier, 173–206. New York: Random House.

MONTAGU, M. F. A.
  1951 *An introduction to physical anthropology* (second edition). Springfield, Ill.: Thomas.

248 THOMAS R. WILLIAMS

MONTAGU, M. F. A., *editor*
1962 *Culture and the evolution of man.* New York: Oxford University Press.

NAROLL, R., R. COHEN, *editors*
1970 *A handbook of method in cultural anthropology.* Garden City, N.Y.: Natural History Press.

POIRIER, F., *editor*
1972 *Primate socialization.* New York: Random House.

RANSOM, T., T. ROWELL
1972 "Early social development of feral baboons," in *Primate socialization.* Edited by F. Poirier, 105–144. New York: Random House.

ROBINSON, J.
1961 The Australopithecines and their bearing on the origin of man and of stone tool making. *South African Journal of Science* 57:3–13.

ROE, A., G. SIMPSON, *editors*
1958 *Behavior and evolution.* New Haven, Conn.: Yale University Press.

SARICH, V.
1970 "Primate systematics with special reference to Old World monkeys," in *Old World monkeys.* Edited by J. R. Napier and P. H. Napier, 175–226. New York: Academic Press.

SPIRO, M.
1954 Human nature in its psychological dimensions. *American Anthropologist* 56:19–30.

SPUHLER, J.
1959 Somatic paths to culture. *Human Biology* 31:1–13.

SUGIYAMA, Y.
1972 "Social characteristics and socialization of wild chimpanzees," in *Primate socialization.* Edited by F. Poirier, 145–163. New York: Random House.

VAN LAWICK-GOODALL, J.
1963 "Feeding behavior in wild chimpanzees," in *The primates.* Edited by J. Napier and N. Barnicot, 39–48. Symposia of the Zoological Society of London 10. London: Zoological Society.
1964 Tool using and aimed throwing in a community of free-living chimpanzees. *Nature* 201:1264–1266.
1967 *My friends, the wild chimpanzees.* Washington, D.C.: National Geographic Society.
1968 The behaviour of free-living chimpanzees in the Gombe Stream Reserve. *Animal Behaviour Monographs* 1:161–311.
1970 "Tool-using in primates and other vertebrates," in *Advances in the study of behaviour,* volume three. Edited by R. A. Hinde and E. Shaw, 195–249.
1971 *In the shadow of man.* Boston: Houghton Mifflin.

WADDINGTON, C.
1960 *The ethical animal.* London: G. Allen and Unwin.

WASHBURN, S.
1950 The analysis of primate evolution with particular reference to the

origin of man. *Cold Spring Harbor Symposia on Quantitative Biology* 15:67–77.
1960 Tools and human evolution. *Scientific American* 203:63–75.
1968a *The study of human evolution.* Condon Lectures, University of Oregon. Eugene, Ore.: University of Oregon Press.
1968b Behavior and the origin of man. *Rockefeller University Review.*
1968c "Speculations on the problem of man's coming to the ground," in *Changing perspectives on man.* Edited by B. Rothblatt. Chicago: University of Chicago Press.
1971 "On the importance of the study of primate behavior for anthropologists," in *Anthropological perspectives on education.* Edited by M. L. Wax, S. Diamond and F. O. Gearing, 91–97. New York: Basic Books.
1972a Evolution of human behavior. *Social Biology* 19:163–170.
1972b "Primate studies and human evolution," in *Primates in biomedical research.* Edited by G. Bourne. New York: Academic Press.
WASHBURN, S., *editor*
1961 *Social life of early man.* Chicago: Aldine.
1963 *Classification and human evolution.* Chicago: Aldine.
WASHBURN, S., V. AVIS
1958 "Evolution of human behavior," in *Behavior and evolution.* Edited by A. Roe and G. Simpson, 421–436. New Haven, Conn.: Yale University Press.
WASHBURN, S., P. JAY DOLHINOW, *editors*
1968 *Perspectives on human evolution I.* New York: Holt, Rinehart and Winston.
1972 *Perspectives on human evolution II.* New York: Holt, Rinehart and Winston.
WASHBURN, S., C. LANCASTER
1963 "The evolution of hunting," in *Man the hunter.* Edited by R. B. Lee and I. DeVore, 293–303. Chicago: Aldine.
WASHBURN, S., J. LANCASTER
1971 On the evolution and the origin of language. *Current Anthropology* 12:384–385.
WHITING, J.
1968 "Socialization: anthropological aspects," in *International encyclopedia of the social sciences,* volume fourteen. Edited by D. Sills, 545–551. New York: Macmillan and The Free Press.
WILLIAMS, T.
1972a *Introduction to socialization: human culture transmitted.* St. Louis: Mosby.
1972b "The socialization process: a theoretical perspective," in *Primate socialization.* Edited by F. Poirier, 207–260. New York: Random House.
WILSON, A., V. SARICH
1969 A molecular time scale for human evolution. *Proceedings of the National Academy of Sciences* 63:1088–1093.

PART TWO

Infant Vocalization: Communication Before Speech

MARGARET BULLOWA, JAMES L. FIDELHOLTZ, and
ALLAN R. KESSLER

Understanding the development of communicative skills in infancy is for both practical and theoretical reasons an urgent problem today. We have come to believe that optimal human development depends to a large degree on the development of communication and especially on speech, the vocal component of language. We trace many social, educational, and psychiatric maladaptations to failure in this sphere. It is therefore important that we understand the underlying processes on which each person builds his speech capacity.

We must be clear in distinguishing between communication and language (Jakobson 1969: 81, 90). Communication is the more inclusive term. Communication is carried on by means of signs. For humans, we may

... make a distinction between prelinguistic, linguistic, and postlinguistic signs. PRELINGUISTIC SIGNS are those which occur in the child's behavior before it speaks, or which later, even in the adult, are independent of language signs. LINGUISTIC SIGNS are those which occur in a language considered as a system of interpersonal signs restricted in their possibility of combination. POST-LINGUISTIC SIGNS are signs which owe their signification to language but which are not themselves elements of language (Morris 1964: 58).

The data base was collected under National Institute of Mental Health research grant M–04300 (1960-1965). Recent work and this paper originate from the laboratory of the Speech Communication Group of the Research Laboratory of Electronics, Massachusetts Institute of Technology, Professor Kenneth N. Stevens, director under grant NB 04332 from the National Institutes of Health. We wish to thank Glenn Aker, T. Berry Brazelton, Judith T. Irvine, Estill Putney, Raymond Stefanski, and Kenneth N. Stevens who read portions of the text and gave us the benefit of their suggestions. We also thank Mrs. Hedy Kodish who typed the manuscript.

The most familiar sign system for human communication is the linguistic one which is basically manifest in speech, a vocal-auditory modality. Some other modalities of human communication are visually perceived body movement, touch, and smell. In infancy, before speech and language have developed, the vocal-auditory channel is already operative. We have every reason to believe that this mode is already adapted to communication, i.e. that it can transmit and receive in a systematic way signals which serve a communicative function.

The dictionary (*Webster's* 1967:367) defines communication as "... the act of imparting, conferring, or delivering from one to another ...." All members of the animal kingdom communicate. In ethology (the study of animal behavior) "... a communicative event occurs when one individual establishes a social relationship with another through the use of a signal [a display]" (Smith 1965:405). It is not our intent to offer rigorous definitions of such terms as communication or social relationship but to employ these concepts in their usual broad meanings.

The human infant communicates about his internal state through signals, which Morris (1964) calls prelinguistic signs. It is this aspect of communication we believe the human infant shares with other animals. In addition, the infant is interacting with adults who are concurrently producing both linguistic and prelinguistic signs to which infants appear to respond. We believe this is the analogue of signal or "display" as used by ethologists (Ficken and Ficken 1966: 644; Wilson 1972: 56). This signaling interaction between infants and adults provides a foundation for socially appropriate communication patterns. For example, for adult conversation, Argyle and Kendon (1967) and Kendon (1970) have described the characteristics of alternation of vocalization, posture, social distance, and eye contact, all prelinguistic aspects of communication. Bateson (1971) has shown that from a few weeks of age, infant-adult vocal interaction has characteristics of similar form. For instance, infant and adult tend to wait for one another to finish vocalizing when face to face, one to two feet apart with intermittent episodes of eye contact. These are the kinds of concepts we will discuss.

Many of the sounds we hear from infants are simply inevitable concomitants of physiological activities. In studying communication among adults, linguists tend to exclude such sounds (coughs, hiccoughs, burps, etc.) from consideration because they are clearly not part of the linguistic code. However, folk psychology often notes the significance of these sounds, and psychiatrists are likely to assign communicative value to them. Given the current state of knowledge of the human infant's entire communicative system, we feel we need to attend, for our study of potential communication, to all the vocal sounds that are produced. We also need to take note of the behavioral responses of caretaking adults, even those produced without awareness. In the study of infant vocal behavior the distinction between relatively automatic physiological sounds and others thought to be prelinguistic signs, such as a "hunger cry," is not always clearcut. Even in older babies, as linguistic sign-using emerges, it may be that prelinguistic and linguistic signs are not always clearly distinguishable. For example, observers of early language acquisition sometimes report mixed utterances in which babbling sounds unintelligible to adults appear (Bloom 1970:22).

The communicative behavior of human infants is in some ways more reminiscent of animal communication than of adult language. Both human infants and animals can impart information about their own current condition and intention, and neither, so far as we know, can make reference to the distant past or future, or state a proposition (Hockett 1960). Both are essentially creating signals. For both, when we speak of the "meaning" of vocalization, we refer to meaning in a basic biological sense (Smith 1965). Our use of "meaning" belongs to semiotics (Sebeok 1968).

When language provides the capability, people communicate relatively more by speech than by action. Speech can take over the function of direct action for the purpose of communication. "Much of man's life involves linguistic contacts, and many of the activities which appear as motor acts in lower species appear linguistically in man" (Freedman 1967: 182). This process can be seen developing as the infant and then child masters more communicative modes. The child learns to ask for something instead of grabbing or reaching for it. Within the repertoire of communicative behavior, the infant produces proportionately more with his body than the adult. As differentiation (defined from the adult viewpoint) increases in all modes, the balance shifts away from more massive body action toward more subtle use of the body in relation to speech. A number of students of non-verbal communication have shown for adults the intimate tie-in between speech and motion of other parts of the body. Condon and Sander (1974) have recently demonstrated that one- and two-day-old infants respond with synchronous body movement to adult speech in the same manner as adults (see "Non-Verbal Communication" section below)

Even recently scientists and physicians were denying that infants communicate with their caretakers with any specificity beyond the general expression of comfort and discomfort states. It was up to the caretaking adult to guess or discern from the accompanying situation what the infant needed (Spock 1968: 183). More recently, however, some pediatricians and other scientists have been willing to take infants seriously and to investigate the old wives' tale that they can be understood and communicated with. Some, but not all, mothers in our culture seem to be aware of the things we are considering, and so are some child care professionals. We do not know how this knowledge is attained, nor whether it is always available but suppressed by our culture.

We believe the first step toward understanding a social process is to observe and describe it. The way in which it is observed, the sampling technique, the relationship between observer and observed, as well as the theoretical frame of reference, all influence our perception of what is going on and our interpretation of it. By applying observation techniques from several disciplines in this study, we hope to decrease the bias of our perceptions and to expand the range of our interpretations.

We will first describe our data base and discuss its appropriateness to the problem we are investigating. Then we will discuss the relevance of certain disciplines and how we are drawing on them for our research. Finally we will make recommendations for further research, in particular how anthropologists and ethnologists could contribute to this area.

DATA BASE[1]

We are looking at data from the first few months in the lives of five infants from white, non-academic, middle-class families living in the Boston area. The parents had used English exclusively all their lives. Since these infants were born to mothers already enrolled in the Maternal-Infant Health study[2] at the Boston Lying-In Hospital, we have records of each of the pregnancies in more detail than is usual in clinic records.

---

[1]   This data base has been described previously in Bullowa, Jones, and Bever (1964, reprinted 1970 in *Cognitive development in children: five monographs of the society for research in child development*, 385–391. Chicago, University of Chicago Press; and 1971 in *The acquisition of language*, edited by Ursula Bellugi and Roger Brown, 101–114. Chicago, University of Chicago Press); and in Margaret Bullowa, Lawrence G. Jones, and Audrey Duckert, 1964, "The acquisition of a word," *Language and Speech* 7(2):107–111; and in Margaret Bullowa, 1970, "The start of the language process," in *Actes du Xe congrès international des linguistes, Bucarest, 28 août–2 septembre 1967*, volume three, 191–200, Editions de l'Académie de la République Socialiste de Roumanie.

[2]   The Maternal-Infant Health Study was the name for the local Boston unit of the Longitudinal Study on Perinatal Factors of the (then) National Institute for Nervous Diseases and Blindness. It was a prospective study based on over 50,000 births.

We also have access to the observations of that study group during deliveries, in the neonatal period, and periodically thereafter. We have results of a neurological examination at four months and of EEG's (electroencephalograms) taken in the neonatal period for each infant. We have every reason to consider all of these infants organically intact.

Each of the infants we studied was the mothers' firstborn. This selection was made because in pilot work with the second child of another family we had found the interaction in the household to be too complicated for us to deal with in our initial study.

We usually managed to be present in the delivery room and to tape-record the birth cry. Within an hour of birth the infant was examined using the Brazelton Neonatal Behavioral Assessment Scale (1973) — in the stage to which it had been developed at that time: the early 1960's. This was documented on tape and with 100 feet of black and white sixteen-millimeter silent film showing spontaneous behavior, neurological tests, and important responses in an interactional situation. During the hospital stay two or three more neonatal assessments were done by our "child development team" (see p. 259), and the baby was observed with the mother during two feedings using our "vocal observation" technique.

The vocal observations (illustrated in Plates 1 and 2) consisted of continuous half-hour tape and film recordings taken weekly in the infant's home. The tape utilized two parallel tracks. On one track we recorded from an ElectroVoice 664 microphone (cardioid pattern) aimed in the infant's direction from our apparatus stand several feet away. This inevitably picked up environmental noise as well as human voices. We felt this to be appropriate because this is the sound environment in which the infant has to develop auditory perceptual capacities. M. Bullowa recorded on the other track a running commentary on and description of the ongoing scene. This was done in the presence of the subjects by whispering into a microphone embedded in a "Hushaphone"[3] which effectively kept her voice from being heard in the environment. Whispering was necessary in order to prevent leakage of sound from her throat. The descriptions were free-form with no precoding because we did not know what information would prove relevant.[4] A patterned electronic signal was placed on this descriptive sound track every five

[3] "Hushaphone" is the trade name for a device used to shield a telephone mouthpiece so that the speaker's voice does not leak into the environment. We embedded a crystal microphone in one and added urethane foam for greater sound absorption. We found that the whispered voice was so well shielded that we felt no constraint on describing the behavior of subjects in their presence.

[4] When M. Bullowa was contemplating the development of a method of field observation and recording, she wished to devise a way of describing ongoing behavior of

seconds, both in order to segment the data on both tracks for indexing, and for synchronization with the film.

A film frame (sixteen-millimeter black and white double X) was taken by a Kodak Ciné Special camera every half-second; thus the half-hour could be recorded on a standard 100-foot reel of film. The film was taken under room lighting to avoid the stimulating effect of flood lighting. Because the pictures were taken as single frames and the film was forced in the developing, most of the pictures are sharp and a great deal of detail can be read from them.

It is possible to synchronize tape and film in the laboratory or to study either separately. Each of the three streams of data can be analyzed separately and related through the segmental indexing system. The field descriptions have been transcribed onto sheets ruled to correspond with the segmentation. The lexical content of adult speech picked up by the open microphone has also been transcribed onto such sheets. Interesting portions of the vocal output of our subjects can be transferred to a special tape accepted by the sound spectrograph[5] and analyzed. Film can be studied one frame at a time, pulsed by hand, or at a selected rate from one to twenty-four frames per second by use of an L-W 224A Flickerless Projector.[6]

The original plan was to follow these infants from birth to thirty months of age. For three of the five this was accomplished, and all were followed for at least seven months so that we have data obtained by this method for the first six months of life for five normal first-born American infants.

Such data gathering lends itself to certain kinds of investigation and precludes others. No experimental intervention would have been compatible with our objective: to record the natural history of language development. In the fieldwork phase we would have wished to be non-participant observers, but this was in practice impossible. Rather than behave in a stilted manner, which would have distorted the behavior of

infants and children in their own homes and their interaction with their parents. The intention was to describe the observations in free form, but as objectively as possible. As an aid to accomplishing this objective it was decided to do the first longitudinal recording in a family which was monolingual in a language unknown to her. It was expected that the combination of a strange culture and lack of linguistic clues would make her a better observer and it probably did. But she found very soon that she could understand a great deal of what was going on between members of the Chinese family being visited weekly.

[5]   A sample sound spectrogram is shown in Plate 3. It displays energy at various frequencies over time.

[6]   The L–W Flickerless Projector is a modified Kodak Analyst Movie Projector which makes it possible to view film at slow speeds without flicker.

our subjects, we interacted with them during recording when they initiated it. This usually was confined to brief interchanges which are easily identified in the data.

For a first approach to the vocal aspects of communicative development, our once-a-week schedule is probably closely enough spaced to bring out the general outline. We took a second observation each week in one family using tape only and found, on the basis of listening, that the sounds on the second tapes did not yield new kinds of information. When we feel we have a complete inventory of infant vocalization and of behavioral units, it would be worthwhile to make closely spaced prolonged observations[7] with attention focused on communicative behavior, as Wolff (1959) and others have focused on other developmental issues.

In addition, we have records for each infant from "developmental" examinations taken once a month in their own homes.[8] The developmental observers were T. Berry Brazelton, a pediatrician with special research interest in infancy and child development, and Grace C. Young, a developmental psychologist. They interviewed the mothers on developmental and other events since the last visit, observed spontaneous behavior, and used developmental tests and schedules, including Gesell (1940) summaries. Thus this team made a twofold attempt to understand the development of each infant. On the one hand, through free-flowing observation they investigated how the mother and infant interacted with one another and with the observers, and noted how they dealt with being observed. On the other hand, in the structured situation of the Gesell tests they subjected the pair to the stress of a performance situation. They considered not only the success but also the quality of the performance.

[7] M. Bullowa has tested the feasibility of prolonged observation by dictating field notes on home observation of an infant into a shielded microphone for twelve hours with one two-hour break during the infant's nap. She experienced almost no voice fatigue from the whispered speech. Four- or five-hour sessions would be practical. The major problem would be transcription time and analysis of the large amount of data which would be generated.

[8] The developmental observations were documented with tapes and 100 feet of silent black and white ciné film. The hand-held camera was a Bolex Rex with Pan Cinor zoom lens. The same audio-visual technician who participated in the "vocal observations" took these developmental recordings. We strove to minimize the number of different people from our study group in contact with the studied families. During the major part of the fieldwork (1961–1964) two undergraduate psychology students from Northeastern University, Edward Basinski and William Weiner, alternated as audio-visual technicians.

RELEVANT DISCIPLINES

Child Development

Child development has roots both in the medical discipline of pediatrics and the academic field of psychology. By a variety of methods the investigators in this field concern themselves with the child as a developing organism. There is a tendency to fragment the field according to focus (cognition, personality, physical growth, etc.), and there is no unified theory. There is always concern with progress from one stage or phase to another in the course of development from neonate (or even from fetus) to adolescent and adult. Two principal modes of study are employed. The same individuals may be followed over time in respect to one or more characteristics. This is known as "longitudinal" study. Our data base belongs to this tradition. The other method is called "cross-sectional." Similar data are gathered from samples of children at different ages, and the succession of ages is expected to yield a developmental sequence. Individual characteristics are averaged out.[9]

The observations of our child development team (pediatrician and psychologist) were partly traditional and partly innovative. The use of Gesell (1940) summaries month by month makes it possible to compare our five children with developmental norms from Gesell and his co-workers based on a large number of intensively studied infants. On the other hand, some of the examination methods used by Dr. Brazelton were among those used in the development of his Neonatal Behavioral Assessment Scale (1973). Our method of vocal field observation and recording, while drawing on many sources, was in its entirety innovative.

Up to now there have been two main trends in the study of infant vocalization as child development. One is based on an attempt to classify spontaneously occurring infant vocal sounds using categories based on adult language with little regard for use or context. The other, while attending to, or rather producing, context, elicits the sounds for study by experimental means, thus insuring that the infant's output is in response to the desired stimulation, such as pain or hunger. The former method applied at a linguistic segmental level has produced disappointing results. This is mainly because the adult categories utilized are not relevant to early infant vocal activity.

As an example of the former method in the tradition of phonetic recording and analysis of spontaneous vocalization, the studies from Irwin's child development laboratory in the 1940's are among the best

---

[9]   Whati s often not realized or understood in the application of such cross-sectional results is that idiosyncratic but normal developmental sequences are also averaged out.

known. A summary of thirty of Irwin's published papers is contained in the encyclopedic article "Language development in children" by McCarthy (1954: 507–509). The vowels and consonants found among infant sounds were classified phonetically, and relative frequencies over time were studied.

Vocalization by infants has been recognized as part of socialization. Rheingold, et al. found that three-month-old institutionalized infants could be induced to increase their vocal responses when offered social reinforcement (smiling, vocalizing, caressing). They remark

> ... the speech of the infant, if only in a social situation, can be modified by a response from the environment which is contingent on his vocalizing. Hence, what happens after the infant vocalizes has been shown to be important ... If the results can be extended to life situations, then mothers might be able to increase or decrease the vocal output of their children by the responses they make when the children vocalize (Rheingold, et al. 1959).

Caudill (1972), who made comparative studies of mother-infant interaction in Tokyo and Washington using fixed schedules for recording, included vocalization, categorized as happy and unhappy, among the behaviors he studied quantitatively. He found American infants at three to four months of age to have a higher level of vocalization, particularly of happy vocalization, than Japanese infants from comparable backgrounds. He discussed the difference in terms of culture-specific styles of child care. This study and Rheingold's both point to the bearing of the infant's environmental context on at least the quantitative aspects of vocal output.

The experimental approach when combined with acoustic analysis has yielded increasingly precise descriptions of the acoustic nature of infant vocal output under given conditions. This method makes it possible to detect significant deviations from normal performance, and this knowledge is applied in medical diagnosis of neonatal pathology. Karelitz (and Fisichelli 1962), a pediatrician working in association with psychologists, was a pioneer in this field. The painstaking studies of a group of Scandinavian pediatricians, linguists, and acoustic engineers (Lind 1965; Wasz-Höckert, et al. 1968) produced a great deal of information not only about what the newborn sounds like but also how the sounds are produced. These studies provide a model for correlated vocal and behavioral investigation.

Ethology

The fields of comparative psychology and ethology treat communication as a facet of animal behavior. Comparative psychology developed in America while ethology originated in Europe with Konrad Lorenz. The ethologist studies behavior by observing members of his target species in their natural habitat and, if necessary, in captivity. In the past he used a notebook and pencil and perhaps a watch to record behavior and behavior sequences as they occurred. He tried to achieve as complete as possible an inventory of the behaviors he observed (cthogram; cf. Eibl-Eibesfeldt 1970: 10) and to improve his precision in defining and recording behavior. He often made sketches to help in the construction of what he had seen. With technological advances he has added photographic (Eibl-Eibesfeldt 1970: 11) and acoustic recording techniques to his repertoire so that he can review sequences at will and free himself from "real time" for the purpose of analysis. When studying a developmental sequence he has to determine an observation schedule which will allow him to catch the stages of development. As in child development studies, the ethologist may choose a "longitudinal" or a "cross-sectional" model, although these terms are not used.

In the study of animal behavior by ethologists, a recognizable unit of communicative behavior is called a "display." This consists of a relatively fixed sequence of movements and is usually directed toward one or more conspecifics. It is considered to have a communicative function (Smith 1965: 405). The primate call shares the message aspect of the display of which it forms a part. Thus the message may be deduced from the call even when the visual aspect of the display cannot be observed for some reason, e.g. dense foliage. Some ethologists believe that the message is always about the state of the vocalizing animal at the time of vocalization (Smith 1965:405). Thus it would correspond with the display to which it belongs. Even an alarm call would not be interpreted in the human terms, "There is a predator," but rather something like, "I'm agitated on account of danger." Nevertheless, a great deal of information is carried in calls and displays. Besides identifying the emitter, the display and call specify whether or not the displaying animal is in an agonistic state vis-à-vis the recipient and what it is likely to do next.

A display may be vocal behavior perceived by audition as well as motor behavior perceived by vision. In the literature on primate behavior the term "call" is used for all vocal behaviors. This is different from the general ethological literature, especially on birds, where calls are distinguished from song, and each is thought of as a display in itself. Because we are considering a primate species, we will stick to primate usage and refer to calls as components of, or associated with, displays.

Smith has arrived at some generalizations about vertebrate displays.

He writes, "Displays do not resemble the words of our languages ... Most display messages make the behavior of the communicator to some degree more predictable to the recipient" (1969: 145). He discusses the difficulties of deducing messages from displays and points out that "... the complete range of uses of a display must usually be known before the message the display carries can be determined ..." (1969: 146). All displays include identification of the sender and "probability of occurrence of each behavioral act specified by a display" (1969: 146), but he notes that "some displays are not graded and indicate only a range of probabilities; a recipient then needs contextual sources as an aid in predicting relative probabilities" (1969: 146). In addition to these two kinds of "modifiers," present in all displays, a number of categories of behavior such as attack, escape, and association are encoded. One type of message, the "bond-limited subset" specifies acts occurring between parents and offspring as well as between mates and within other "bonded groups" (1969: 146). We would expect, if this categorization of message types holds for the "prelinguistic signs" of humans, that most of the messages of early infancy would fall in this category.

A classification of the causation of primate calls (not message types) is given by Andrew (1962). This leads to a list of situation categories. This is an unusual approach in ethology as Andrew himself acknowledges. Andrew says ethology has "tended to relate all components of displays to major drives, such as aggression, fear or sex" (1962: 297). This had led to classifying "... the different calls into such functional categories as 'warning call' or 'threat call'" (1962: 296). Andrew proposes the following method for analyzing the causation of primate calls: "The method followed has been to study the form of calls by means of sound spectrographs, and then to discover in how many situations a particular form of call occurs" (1962: 296). We have been applying this procedure to our study of early infant vocalization as a means of entry into the early phases of the human infant's communicative system.

Andrew's Group 2 category contains situations which lead to relatively low intensity calls and is defined as

An encounter with a social fellow after brief separation from him, under circumstances in which no attack is feared ... Such encounters may be divided into: (a) perception of the fellow at a distance and (b) an encounter with close bodily contact and often mutual grooming. A third situation (c) in this group is that of an infant searching for the nipple (1962: 296).

He describes some human infant vocalizations in this category:

"Human infants will give long grunts or segmented grunts [laughter] at the sight of a known face. It is not known yet in detail what relation these bear to the soft grunts sometimes given when searching for the teat" (1962: 301).

He goes on to state:

All of the calls described above, which are given in true greeting [i.e. which are evoked by the perception of a social fellow after separation irrespective of social rank], could be thought of as calls first evoked during contact with the mother which have been extended progressively to other social fellows (1962: 301).

There are precedents for applying the methods of the ethologists to human developmental problems. Prechtl, a physician trained by Lorenz in ethological methods, has spent years in the observation of neonates and infants. In a paper on crying during the first nine days of life he emphasized that "The infant's cry is a communication signal ..." (Prechtl, Theocell, Gramsberger, and Lind 1969:142) and concludes, "Stochastic analysis of cry patterns in newborn infants may supply data which correlate with development and with neurological findings" (1969: 150). He has paid special attention to neurological function and is responsible for defining states of arousal as basic to all other descriptions of human infant behavior (Prechtl and Beintema 1964). His five-place scale includes "crying" as the state of maximal arousal. The coding of arousal states, once learned, is quite simple. It would be useful for this method to become routine in field observation of infants by anthropologists. Such coding is included in the Brazelton scale.

More recently, especially in Great Britain, zoologists are turning to "ethological" studies of children. Their first publications are based mainly on observations of children in nursery school classes. At least two books appeared in 1972 (Blurton Jones; McGrew). Blurton Jones is now engaged in the study of infants in their own families. In Cambridge, England, an ethologically inspired "longitudinal study of mothers and babies" (Richards and Bernal 1972) is under way which has already produced a paper on crying and maternal response during the first ten days of life (Bernal 1972).

Non-Verbal Communication

In addition to inspiration from the ethological approach to the study of communicative behavior, we have built on the work of a number of investigators in the behavioral context of human speech. This leads into an area sometimes referred to as non-verbal communication. Actually this terms implies a degree of separation which fails to do justice to the integration between speech and the motor behavior in which it is embedded. It is this close integration which makes speech part of a total communicative act in which the entire motor apparatus participates in an hierarchically structured way.

This has been studied from both ends of the hierarchy. For example, Condon and Ogston (1967) have taken a microscopic view and by painstaking frame-by-frame analysis of sound film taken at rates up to forty-eight frames per second, have shown that the speaker moves in synchrony with his own speech — not just with words and syllables but with even smaller (segmental in the linguistic sense) components. Condon and Ogston have also demonstrated that a listener moves in synchrony with the speech of the person he is attending to (1967: 229). Condon and Sander (1974) have recently shown that neonates at one day and two days of age move synchronously with the speech of caretaking adults. It is this kind of attention to the relation between vocal and non-vocal behavior that we believe will provide fruitful results in the elucidation of infant communicative acts.

Working from the "macro" end of the hierarchy, Scheflen (1965) and Kendon (1972) have delineated larger behavioral frames into which various levels of discourse fit. People signal the beginning and end of their discourse by major postural shifts involving joints around the pelvis (Scheflen 1964: 321). Within these positions the change of topic (paragraph level) is signaled by a definite but less comprehensive shift in motor activity.

All the advance in this area depends on very painstaking study of ciné-film and, recently, of video tape. The phenomena dealt with require slowing down, repeated viewing, and precise coding. An advance was made in the management of filmed behavioral data when Birdwhistell's laboratory developed a method of printing serial numbers from a second negative ("B roll") on each frame of film to be studied (van Vlack 1966). Condon (personal communication) has used this method with film and has adapted it to video by including a chronometer in the background when he takes video tapes. These methods contribute to the possibility of rigorous study of recorded visual data.

Ekman and co-workers have developed a computerized method for handling non-verbal behavioral data coded from video (Ekman, et al. 1969). Frame numbers are assigned by computer as a way of segmenting and indexing the tapes so that any position on the tape can be uniquely identified, viewed on command, and its already coded data displayed. This system facilitates data storage and retrieval and makes comparisons efficient.

Ethnology

We have thought of our study as falling within the scope of ethnology as well as comparative ethology. Primate ethology suggests seeking the meaning of vocalizations in other motor behaviors with which they are associated and understanding these communicative behaviors by seeing how they function in relation to the behavior of other members of the species; it suggests examining their communicative functions. When we started this study in the early 1960's we had to seek elsewhere, possibly in ethnology, for clues as to how to recognize the organization of behavior based on data recorded serially on film. Film had not been the ethologist's tool. In field ethology, units of behavior have become recognizable through prolonged observation, description, and testing until they can be named and coded directly. Social scientists are not used to segmenting much of human behavior in this way. Certain ritualized actions are easy to recognize. Greetings, for instance, stand out clearly (Kendon and Ferber 1973). But people are so convinced of the freedom and flexibility of their own behavior that they do not find it "natural" to break up the "stream of behavior" into small units.

In general, ethnologists have not used the concept of organizing observed behavior hierarchically.[10] Rather, descriptions dealt with behavior as goal-directed: the completion of an artifact, the performance of a ritual. In relation to communication, the focus was not on communicative process, or on analyzing systems of human interaction, but was directed toward decoding language and other symbolic systems.

We might mention an attempt of an anthropologist to deal with the hierarchical structure of social behavior. In Bock's study (1962) of Micmac society, an attempt was made to apply Pike's "unified theory of behavior" (1967) to ethnological description. We attempted to apply this method to our data but could find no way to get it to accommodate the temporal flow of events at the finer level of detail we were using. We suspect that once the management of the full range of detail in the description of human behavioral data has been developed, probably through computerized data management, it will be possible to link it to some such schema as Bock's for higher orders of social organization.

We have sought a model in anthropological film with little success. We expected that ethnology, a field which has specialized in the observa-

[10]   Recently, under the rubric "ethnomethodology," an approach to the segmentation of behavior has come to grips with this problem: e.g. Harold Garfinkel (1967); Harold Garfinkel and Harvey Sacks (1969); and John J. Gumperz and Dell Hymes 1972.

tion of "naturally" occurring human behavior, and which has recently contributed fine film studies of aspects of exotic cultures, would have ready-made techniques to offer for our film analysis. This turned out to be a false hope. Bateson and Mead's *Balinese character* of 1942 seemed to presage good things. Here were studies of child development in cultural context based on closely spaced Leica shots and simultaneously recorded field notes in great detail. It was coming close, but not quite close enough, to the contexts for vocalization we wish to establish. Anthropological film making has taken another direction. It has tended to deal with events at a high level of abstraction, presenting a single supposedly representative sequence for each type of behavior considered. But in order to abstract from the actual "performances" a description which concentrates on only the emic aspects of the behavior, it is necessary to have at least several instances to compare. We also found that indexing of "raw footage" of ethnological film is at a very gross level in the hierarchy of behavior, usually at the level of instrumental activity (Eibl-Eibesfeldt 1970: 412).

An example of a use of anthropological film which approaches the material in a way to bring out characteristics of action is the collection of dance sequences assembled for the "choriometric" part of the Canto-metrics Study (Lomax, Bartenieff, and Paulay 1968). Their "effort-shape" analysis is concerned with qualities of movement rather than with segmentation. In the reported study they use their method to apply uniform coding to films of dance from many cultures.

Byers (1972) is another anthropologist who attends to film analysis in great detail and includes the sound track in his analysis. He has utilized available raw footage taken by others to explore ideas on the border between anthropology and the field of non-verbal communication.

It is quite ironical that anthropology, a field which is consciously and avowedly concerned with "enculturation," has traditionally paid scant attention to infancy, the most important period of enculturation. Notwithstanding considerable lipservice to the subtleties and pervasiveness of the socialization process, anthropologists have all too often confined their attention in this area to the direct teaching of rituals at puberty, the oral tradition of poetry, and other such overt matters, while neglecting until quite recently very detailed studies of the interaction of infants and very young children with adults.[11]

In the field it has been customary for the ethnologist to become a

---

[11]   Until recently the outstanding exception has been the field studies of Margaret Mead.

participant observer in the culture he is investigating. At the opposite extreme, recently Schaeffer (1970), an anthropologist working with Scheflen in a cross-cultural study of normal family interaction in urban United States, studied observations recorded by remote control from a robot video camera. We have chosen an intermediate course, the minimally participant observation described earlier (see "Data Base" section). We feel that this degree of participation with our subjects is appropriate to our purpose. It allows us immediate access to what is going on. The observer speaking into the shielded microphone appears to the subject family to be like someone talking into a telephone. This is tolerated in our culture and discourages social interaction. We recognize that any observation, even with a remotely controlled recorder, cannot help but affect the subjects to some degree. We can, if necessary, identify at least the overt evidence of reactions to us in the data.

Linguistics

Linguistics as applied to language acquisition has little to offer to the study of early infant vocalization. As Crystal (1972: 1) points out, "Research into children's language has been almost exclusively segmental and verbal." In an earlier era in the study of infant vocal sounds, an attempt was made to classify sounds as vowels and consonants and to transcribe the sounds either in orthography or in the International Phonetic Alphabet (see "Child Development" above). This was before the technology for magnetically recording and storing sound had been applied to infants (Lynip 1951). By now it is clear not only from the nature of the sounds, but from the anatomy of the infant vocal tract (Lieberman, et al. 1972; Bosma, Truby, and Lind 1965) that young infants are not capable of producing the full range of adult speech sounds. On the other hand, such terms as cooing, mewing, etc. (as used, for instance, by Gesell 1940) are too subjective to be useful for our purpose.

One of the few linguists who has given serious attention to the "non-segmental" aspects of early infant vocal behavior is Crystal (1970). In his recent review (1972), "Non-segmental phonology in language acquisition," he supplies an exhaustive review and critique of the literature in this sphere. Under non-segmental phonology he subsumes "intonation, stress, rhythm, speed of speaking, and the many effects loosely referred to as 'tone of voice'" (1972: 1). After pointing to the terminological chaos in all aspects of the field, he defines vocalization as "any vocal sound pattern produced by an infant for which there is no evidence of language-specific contrastivity" (i.e. which is not linguistic) and considers the sound patterns "biologically controlled" (1972: 6). For him, intonation "refers to a system of non-segmental linguistic contrastivity which varies primarily in terms of pitch direction and pitch range" (1972: 6). This precludes his using the term intonation in relation to vocalization, and he suggests "melody" to refer to the auditory correlate of fundamental frequency variation in vocalization (1972: 6). He calls for studies to determine the characteristics of infant vocalization and recommends acoustic specification. He also recommends cross-cultural studies to search for points of divergence from early biologically controlled sound patterns which he appears to consider universal.

Lieberman (1967: 41) states that infants: "communicate by means of sound from the moment of birth onward ... The infant cry has a characteristic pattern. The pattern is apparently innately determined and is a characteristic human attribute." He describes the fundamental frequency contour of the infant cry and relates it to his concept of "breath-group" which he has studied by relating acoustic to physiological data (subglottal air pressure) in adults (1967: Chapter 3).

A useful tool for the study of infant sound is the sound spectrograph, an instrument devised for the analysis of adult speech sounds.[12] It produces a permanent record of energy at various frequencies in temporal sequence (see Plate 3 for an example of a spectrogram). Despite the fact that our vocal samples were obtained in a noisy environment, a practiced eye can detect patterns produced vocally by infants, even in the presence of background noise and adult vocalization.

How much can be learned from spectrographic analysis of infant vocalization has been demonstrated by the Scandinavian groups mentioned above in the "Child Development" section (Lind 1965; Wasz-Höckert, et al. 1968). These interdisciplinary workers have focused a great deal of technical skill on the study of the birth cry, pain cry, hunger cry, and "pleasure" cry. The latter three were produced experimentally. Not only have they studied spectrograms and defined acoustic parameters for the cries they have studied, but also they have worked out in detail the relation between phases of sound production and configurations of the vocal tract as shown on serial X-rays, phases of the respiratory cycle, and subglottal pressure changes. They have followed these intensive studies on "normal"

---

[12] The sound spectrograph gives a great deal of information to the linguist and acoustic engineer but is an expensive and specialized instrument found in only a few laboratories. The oscilloscope, a much more universally available instrument, can be used to assist in extracting information about timing, intensity, or pitch, any of which may be useful for special purposes.

cries with comparative studies on sounds produced in certain severe pathological conditions of the newborn (Vuorenkoski, Wasz-Höckert, et al. 1971; Michelsson 1971) and have shown that these can be differentiated by ear (Vuorenkoski, Lind, et al. 1971). They have stopped short of studying the full range of infant vocal communication because this was not their aim. We have found their spectographic work very suggestive and are extending it to spontaneous sounds produced in the course of the infant's ongoing interaction with his caretakers.

INFANT VOCALIZATION

Until recently the neonate was seen by psychologists as a purely reflex animal, responding to most stimulation with random activity except for a few well-defined responses to specific maneuvers such as the Moro [extensor] reflex to jarring the surface on which the supine infant is resting. Intensive study of human neonates in recent years has led to a very different view. The cognitive organization of the newborn has been investigated in many laboratories with findings which show a great deal of sensorimotor organization already functioning. For instance, visually guided reaching for an object in the midline can be demonstrated at seven to fifteen days (Bower 1972). This had not been thought to occur until the fourth month of life. Because the neonate cannot show this performance when lying down, he had not been credited with this capacity. This is only one among many suggestive findings, but gives an idea of the level of capacity available and makes more plausible a view of the young infant as an active participant rather than the passive, simple-reflex-dominated organism we had become used to considering him.

Devereux (1964: 267) describes how, among the Mohave, "... even fetuses about to be born as well as twin infants and nursing babies are believed capable of understanding, and responding to, rational verbal admonition even though they are manifestly incapable of speech." It would be of some interest to determine, in cultures with such different attitudes from ours toward infant understanding, whether infants in fact begin babbling or talking at an earlier age than in Western societies. As far as we know, no one has investigated carefully the actual development of language in babies of Mohave culture or of similar cultures, so it is difficult to do more than speculate about the significance of these Mohave beliefs.

A related result of our studies and others is that babies in fact can communicate (or at least indicate) more things than most adults in our culture expect them to. Therefore it is not unreasonable to expect that in an environment of greater expectation and encouragement an infant's vocal and verbal development might be speeded up relative to that in Western societies, and possibly even some sequential differences might show up. One of our babies, whose parents were especially verbal and tended to include her in family conversations from the time when she was able to sit in a highchair at the dining table, began talking relatively earlier than other babies whose development we followed, and whose parents did not treat them in this way. Our data, however, are only suggestive on such issues. A wide and representative sample would be necessary in order to eliminate the complicating factor of individual differences to which this isolated example could be ascribed.

In another case from our data, one child's father began to understand him to be speaking and responded to him on this basis several weeks sooner than his mother did. We attribute this difference to a difference between the parents in their attitudes toward their son. The father expected his son to exhibit competence in many spheres; the mother, on the other hand, was always skeptical about accomplishment until it was unmistakable. In general, however, we must be careful to distinguish individual differences (in ontogenetic development and in behavior and attitudes of one or both parents) from cultural differences.

Let us look at what the newborn does which may be considered communicative. Traditionally we are most aware of his "telling" us when he is hungry or in pain, both states of strong discomfort. Pain and hunger cries have been the subject of much investigation, including detailed studies of their acoustic characteristics. Less attention has been focused on the communication of comfort and the seeking of social interaction. Sleep has been considered the best evidence of comfort, but in fact a satisfied and comfortable baby, after the first few days of recovery from the vigorous experience of birth (and in our culture very often also recovery from the chemical sedation received via the placenta), shows kinesthetically by snuggling into a warm soft surface that he is comfortable, whereas in discomfort he is likely to arch away.

Non-cry vocalization is usually said to begin around one month of age. But in our data we find from the first days on a large range of sounds produced, often of low intensity. Many of these do not seem to be associated with discomfort. It is likely that much of this has been overlooked because it is so much less prominent than the characteristic sharp, loud discomfort sounds. After identifying the characteristic infant sounds associated with social interaction (Bateson 1971), we were able to recognize a very brief example of this sound on a tape taken at six days and then found that the corresponding film showed typical though fleeting adult-infant social interaction.

The obviously distressed infant's sounds are relatively well known as are those of the socially interacting infant. In view of Andrew's analysis of primate calls (see "Ethology" section), it is doubtful that this represents the full range of what the infant can communicate about vocally.

It is for this reason that we are undertaking a survey of the infant sounds occurring on our tapes. We are trying to establish relationships between categories of infant sound (studied spectrographically) and behavioral and interactive situations. From simultaneously dictated notes and films we are able to reconstruct the context and behavior of which the vocalization formed a part. In other words, we are considering infant vocal sound to be the "call" aspect of "displays," as in some recent primate studies.

While we do not know of any similar approach to the elucidation of human infant vocal sounds, there are models in studies of primate vocalization. One which is particularly pertinent is a study of the vocal development of Japanese rhesus monkey infants, one hand-raised by the investigator, Rumiko Takeda, and the other by its own monkey mother (Takeda 1965, 1966). Takeda found initially six "vocal stocks" and traced their development through differentiation or extinction throughout thirty weeks' observation. She felt that she could identify the vocalizations both by listening and in relation to specific situations, and that she had identified the precursors of the adult monkey vocalizations classified by other Japanese investigators. She relates parts of her classification to sounds described by Hayes (1952) in the hand-rearing of the chimpanzee, Vicki. Takeda alludes in her paper to parallels with human infant vocalization (1966: 113) and in private conversation has said that she felt similar processes were taking place in the subsequent rearing of her own two children. This needs to be verified or disproved by more disinterested observers.

A study is currently in progress on vocal development in chimpanzees by Plooy (1972). He and his wife are working with the colony well studied by Jane van Lawick-Goodall (1968) in the Gombe Preserve in Tanzania. The longer time spans involved in chimpanzee development, compared with monkeys, make it necessary for the Plooys to record from a number of young of known ages. They are aided in their work by the already existing knowledge of the behavioral repertoire of this species, to which they have added previously unobserved items.

In the current state of our knowledge of early communication, one way of judging whether a behavior should be considered communicative is to observe the interpersonal situation in which it occurs and the behavior of all participants in that interaction. One might suppose that in the young infant, discomfort crying is an automatic accompaniment of internal distress, perhaps for the purpose of discharging tension, and only incidentally a signal to caretaking adults. Close observation of instances, however, shows that even in distress an infant can be busy with social interaction. A crying sequence, probably caused by discomfort from an overstuffed belly, is in our data. The twenty-eight-day-old infant was propped extended across his father's lap (see Plate 3). The cries came in a rhythmic series of sobs and wails. The film frames at half-second intervals showed the infant's and father's faces oriented toward one another despite the infant's crying with his eyes closed part of the time. The father turned his head away for one second (first frame). When his gaze returned to his son's face (second frame), the baby had turned his face away, and it took another second for him to turn back and re-establish mutual gaze (fourth frame).

While mutual gaze is certainly not the only situation in which communication between infant and adult occurs, when mutual gaze does occur (Robson 1967) even naive observers "feel" that it signifies communication. It is the earmark of "proto-conversation" as described by Bateson (1971: 171). We can therefore feel reasonably confident that when eye-to-eye contact is mutually sought, the activity accompanying it is tagged for communication. Setting eye contact as a criterion would lead to gross underestimation of communicative activity, but when it is present we feel confident that we have genuine examples of such activity.

Eye-to-eye contact sets a limit on interpersonal orientation and distance. Between adult and infant this distance is approximately one and one-half feet (see Plate 4). Based on what we know about infant vision, this is the distance at which the adult's face is in sharpest focus for the infant. When psychologists test babies with visual test objects, they use this fact in deciding where to place the stimulus.

Because we do not yet have a firmly established behavioral inventory for the human infant and his parents, we have had to devise a model for coding and analyzing behavior from which it is possible to derive such an inventory. At the lowest level in this behavioral hierarchy is the single pulse of sound. Because of the sparseness (two frames per second) of our photographic images, we cannot establish the rest of the behavioral pattern at this level of detail from our data. The work of William Condon (Condon and Ogston 1967: 225–229) on speech-body synchrony assures us that there is such a correlation. Even with our own two-frames-per-second film data we are able to see that the onset of prominences in the infant's vocal output are associated with onset or change in direction of gross movement.[13]

We doubt that single sound pulses will yield specific messages. It is quite likely that similar pulses occur in different higher order elements which are quite dissimilar in total configuration and effect, just as a small number of distinguishable phonetic elements are used in many combinations in adult speech.

We have designated as "passage" a unit of complex behavior which includes both auditory and visual information for the receiver. We view our term "passage" as the ethologist's "display," but always with both kinesic and acoustic components. One of the most difficult tasks is to specify how to recognize a passage. Sometimes this is made easy by an apparent segmentation based on pauses with or without change of "speaker." This was the case with an analyzed sequence of proto-conversation activity between a three-and-one-half-month-old boy and his mother. There were bursts of vocal activity separated by silences longer than any pauses occurring within the bursts. Even though the infant's activity was all of the same general kind, a "natural" segmentation emerged (see Figure 1).

The next higher level of organization is passage context. At this level we attend also to interactant behavior. For the passage just described, the mother and infant were face-to-face, and the mother vocalized between infant vocalizations. These are two of the main characteristics of the passage context which led to classifying this interaction as "proto-conversation" at the next higher level: social context. Because for our present purpose instrumental activities are considered as social contexts, it is possible for two or more to co-occur. A proto-conversation may be going on while the mother is undressing her baby for his bath. Of course still higher levels of hierarchical organization could be specified, but under the conditions of our observation this would serve no useful purpose because the next higher level would always be the context of our visit to the household with two observers and equipment.

CONCLUSION

We believe that it is important to understand human communication at

[13]   This statement is based on a frame-by-frame analysis of a continuous two-minute segment of simultaneously recorded tape and film with continuous spectrographic analysis of all the infant vocal sound occurring during this period. We selected this portion for intensive study because the infant was vocalizing almost all the time with considerable variety. In the analysis, the data from each frame of film was lined up with the point on the voiceprint at which it was taken.

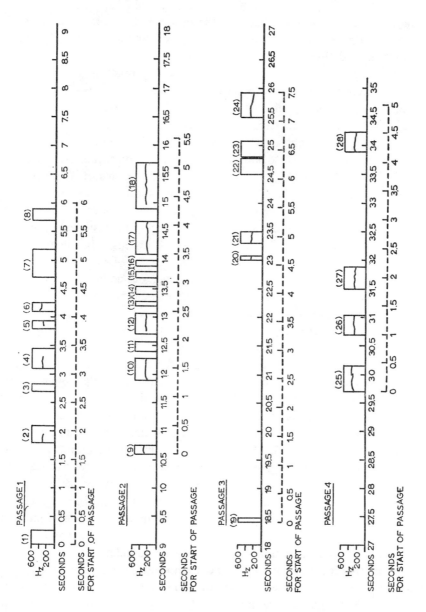

Figure 1. Diagram showing relative duration and timing of infant sounds during a stretch of "proto-conversation" at three and one-half months of age. Sounds are grouped into "vocal passages." Sound Number 19 could perhaps be considered a separate passage but was arbitrarily assigned to passage Number 3. The width of rectangles shows the duration of sound on the time scale shown on the baseline. The height of the rectangles has significance. Lines drawn within the blocks show the form of the contour of fundamental frequency when harmonic structure is present in the spectogram. Where no pitch line is shown, the sound lacked harmonic structure

its basic level as it exists between the infant and his caretakers in early extra-uterine life. Without this knowledge we cannot hope to solve many practical and theoretical problems. On the practical side, we need this knowledge in order to optimize child-rearing practices for "normal" infants and to design better practices for handicapped ones. We need this knowledge to solve problems in psychiatry and in education. Theoretically we need to understand the communication in this early period in order to gain insight into the processes of language acquisition, of language universals, of socialization, and of enculturation.

The kind of knowledge we need is of a very precise sort. We will need a great deal more of the kind of exacting close examination of the communicative activities in which infants participate, such as those we have been engaged in (but with more dense sampling of the visual component). General impressions will not give us this knowledge. It will require a great deal of help from modern technology (e.g. low cost portable video recording equipment) in recording, analyzing, and compiling at least the audio-visual data (and eventually data involving other sensory modalities such as touch, pressure, and smell). It will require investigation into developmental anatomy, physiology, and especially into rhythmic activity. We know quite a lot about the neonatal situation but very little about how and how fast it changes. Also required will be field recording in many cultures and subcultures to sort out universals from culture-specific elements. We would recommend that field recording on film or video tape be done in such a way as to facilitate close-grained audio-visual analysis. It will take long hours of looking, listening, and acoustic analyzing to define the behavioral units at successive hierarchical levels so that they can be identified and perhaps eventually, if we can learn to specify them with enough precision, be sorted out automatically.

This is an enterprise which should be of interest to anthropologists and ethnologists because it is basic to an understanding of the transmission of culture from generation to generation. Both infants and adults contribute to enculturation through their communicative activities. We propose that it is this basic level of communication shared by infants and adults which makes possible enculturation, including the acquisition of the mother tongue. There are certainly many variants in the details of parent-infant interaction from culture to culture. What all have in common may represent what is basically human and essential to human survival. We hope anthropologists will share in this investigation.

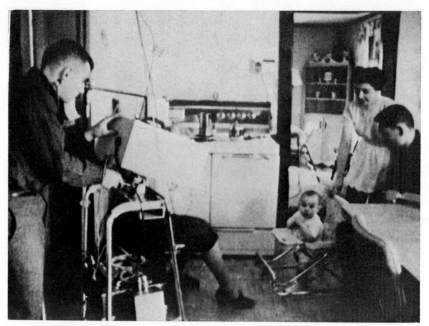
Plate 1. Field observations method for "vocal observation." Observers: audio-visual technician (behind apparatus stand) and "observer" (partly hidden by camera box) with a subject family in their kitchen

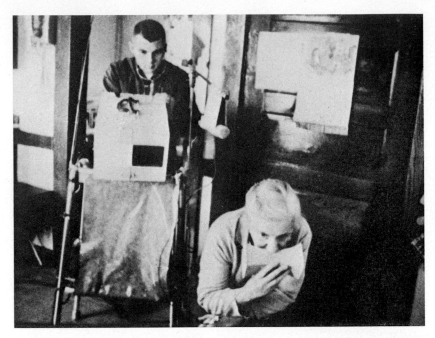

Plate 2. Field observation: as seen by subject family. Technician monitors tape and keeps camera (enclosed in sound insulated box) and microphone (shock-mounted on boom on apparatus stand) directed toward infant by sighting through view finder at right rear corner of box. Observer (seated on camp stool) dictates whispered description of ongoing activity and interaction into Hushaphone-shielded microphone

Plate 3. Five successive film frames from vocal observation when infant was twenty-eight days old. (Picture has been cropped to fit space). Arrows indicate approximately where frame was taken in relation to sound spectrogram of infant's cry shown below. The sound spectrogram is narrow band (45 Hz filter), and the frequency range is 0–3500 Hz. The diagram under the spectrogram shows on the same time scale the form and the value in Hertz (Hz) of the fundamental frequency of each of the four sounds (Numbers 11–14 given in parentheses on the diagram) in this "vocal passage." The time scale (below) is in seconds. The first picture shows the father, with his crying son on his lap, looking away from the baby's face (his face and eyes and the baby's had been oriented toward one another) toward the kitchen where his wife is preparing food for the baby. This frame was taken before the beginning of this spectrogram. The baby's facial orientation is toward where his father's was. In the second frame, which coincides with the first sound in the passage, the father's face and gaze have returned to his pre-glance position, but by now the baby has moved his head toward the father as shown by the greater exposure of hair visible. The third frame comes at the beginning of the fourth and last sound of the passage, a long drawn-out wail which shows a rising-falling-rising-falling pitch contour and clear harmonic structure. Father and baby have not yet re-established eye contact. By the fourth frame, midway through the wail, contact has been re-established through slight readjustments by both of them. In the meantime the father's left hand has started the movement (Frame 3) which will enable him to reposition the baby (Frame 5). Frame 5 occurs at or slightly after the termination of vocal sound

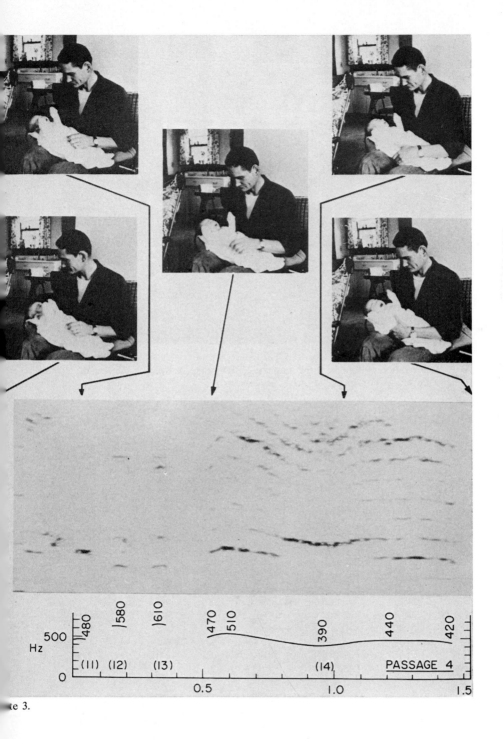

te 3.

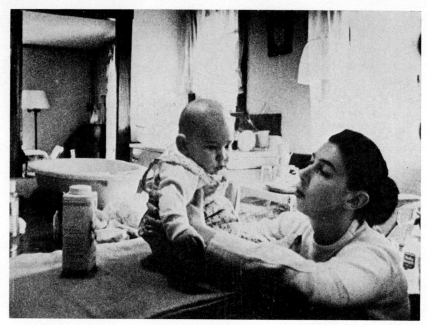

Plate 4. Single film frame (cropped at top) from observation M032: during proto-conversation. Infant is three and one-half months of age. Graininess of blown-up picture does not appear on projection screen

REFERENCES

ANDREW, R. J.
  1962   The situations that evoke vocalization in primates. *Annals of the New York Academy of Sciences* 102:296–315.

ARGYLE, MICHAEL, ADAM KENDON
  1967   "The experimental analysis of social performance," in *Advances in experimental social psychology*, volume three, 55–93. New York: Academic Press.

BATESON, GREGORY, MARGARET MEAD
  1942   *Balinese character: a photographic analysis.* New York: New York Academy of Sciences.

BATESON, M. C.
  1971   The interpersonal context of infant vocalization. *Quarterly Progress Report 100* (January 15, 1971):170–176. Research Laboratory of Electronics, Massachusetts Institute of Technology.

BERNAL, JUDY
  1972   Crying during the first ten days of life and maternal responses. *Developmental Medicine and Child Neurology* 14:362–372.

BLOOM, LOIS
  1970   *Language development: form and function in emerging grammars.* Cambridge, Massachusetts: M.I.T. Press.

BLURTON JONES, N. G., *editor*
  1972   *Ethological studies of child behaviour.* London: Cambridge University Press.

BOCK, PHILIP K.
  1962   "The social structure of a Canadian Indian reserve." Unpublished doctoral dissertation, Harvard University.

BOSMA, JAMES F., H. M. TRUBY, JOHN LIND
  1965   "Cry motions of the newborn infant," in *Newborn infant cry.* Edited by John Lind, 61–92. Uppsala: Almqvist and Wiksells.

BOWER, T. G. R.
  1972   Object perception in infants. *Perception* 1:15–30.

BRAZELTON, T. BERRY
  1973   *Neonatal behavioral assessment scale.* Clinics in Developmental Medicine 50. Spastics International Medical Publications. London: William Heinemann Medical Books. Philadelphia: J. B. Lippincott.

BULLOWA, MARGARET
  1970   "The start of the language process," in *Actes du Xe congrès international des linguistes, Bucarest, 28 août–2 septembre 1967*, volume three, 191–200. Bucharest: Editions de l'Académie de la République Socialiste de Roumanie.

BULLOWA, MARGARET, LAWRENCE GAYLORD JONES, THOMAS G. BEVER
  1964   *Development from vocal to verbal behavior in children.* Monographs for the Society for Research in Child Development 29 (1).

BULLOWA, MARGARET, LAWRENCE GAYLORD JONES, AUDREY DUCKERT
  1964   The acquisition of a word. *Language and Speech* 7(2): 107–111.

BYERS, PAUL
1972   "From biological rhythm to cultural pattern: a study of minimal units." Unpublished doctoral dissertation, Columbia University.
CAUDILL, WILLIAM
1972   "Tiny dramas: vocal communication between mother and infant in Japanese and American families," in *Mental health research in Asia and the Pacific*, volume two: *Transcultural research in mental health*. Edited by W. P. Lebra. Honolulu: The University Press of Hawaii.
CONDON, WILLIAM S., W. D. OGSTON
1967   A segmentation of behavior. *Journal of Psychiatric Research* 5:221–235.
CONDON, WILLIAM S., LOUIS W. SANDER
1974   Neonate movement is synchronized with adult speech: interactional participation and language acquisition. *Science* 183:99–101.
CRYSTAL, DAVID
1970   "Prosodic systems and language acquisition," in *Prosodic feature analysis*. Edited by P. Leon, 77–90. Montreal: Didier.
1972   "Non-segmental phonology in language acquisition: a review of issues." Preprinted manuscript for the First International Symposium on Child Language Acquisition, Florence, Sept. 1972.
DEVEREUX, GEORGE
1964   "Mohave voice and speech mannerisms," in *Language in culture and society*. Edited by Dell Hymes, 267–271. New York: Harper and Row.
EIBL-EIBESFELDT, IRENAUS
1970   *Ethology, the biology of behavior*. New York: Holt, Rinehart and Winston.
EKMAN, PAUL, WALLACE V. FRIESSEN, THOMAS G. TAUSSIG
1969   "VID-R and SCAN: tools and methods for the automated analysis of visual records," in *The analysis of communication content*. Edited by George Gerbner, Ole Rittolsti, Klaus Krippendorff, William J. Paisley, and Philip J. Stone, 297–312. New York: Wiley and Sons.
FICKEN, ROBERT W., MILLICENT S. FICKEN
1966   A review of some aspects of avian field ethology. *The Auk* 83:637–661.
FREEDMAN, DANIEL G.
1967   "A biological view of man's social behavior," in *Social behavior from fish to man*. Edited by William Etkin, 152–188. Chicago: University of Chicago Press.
GARFINKEL, HAROLD
1967   *Studies in ethnomethodology*. Englewood Cliffs, N.J.: Prentice-Hall.
GARFINKEL, HAROLD, HARVEY SACKS
1969   "On formal structures of practical actions," in *Theoretical sociology: perspectives and developments*. Edited by John C. McKinney and Edward Tirejakian. New York: Appleton.
GESELL, ARNOLD
1940   "The first years of life," in *The first five years of life: a guide to the study of the preschool child*. By Arnold Gesell, et al., 16–28. New York: Harper and Brothers.

GUMPERZ, JOHN J., DELL HYMES
1972 *Directions in sociolinguistics: the ethnography of communication.* New York: Holt, Rinehart and Winston.

HAYES, C.
1952 *The ape in our house.* New York: Harper and Brothers.

HOCKETT, CHARLES F.
1960 The origin of speech. *Scientific American* 203:88–96.

JAKOBSON, R.
1969 "Linguistics in its relation to other sciences," in *Actes du Xe Congrès international de linguistes,* volume one. Bucharest: Editions de l'Académie de la République Socialiste de Roumanie.

KARELITZ, SAMUEL, VINCENT R. FISICHELLI
1962 The cry thresholds of normal infants and those with brain damage. *Journal of Pediatrics* 61:679–685.

KENDON, ADAM
1970 Movement coordination in social interaction: some examples described. *Acta Psychologica* 32:100–125.
1972 "Some relationships between body motion and speech," in *Studies in dyadic communication.* Edited by A.W. Siegman and B. Pope, 177–210. Elmsford, New York: Pergamon Press.

KENDON, ADAM, ANDREW FERBER
1973 "A description of some human greetings," in *Comparative ecology and behaviour of primates.* Edited by R.P. Michael and J.H. Crook, 591–668. New York and London: Academic Press.

LIEBERMAN, PHILIP
1967 *Intonation, perception, and language.* Cambridge, Massachusetts: M.I.T. Press.

LIEBERMAN, PHILIP, EDMUND S. CRELIN, DENNIS KLATT
1972 Phonetic ability and related anatomy of the newborn and adult human, Neanderthal man, and the chimpanzee. *American Anthropologist* 74:287–307.

LIND, JOHN, *editor*
1965 *Newborn infant cry.* Uppsala: Almqvist and Wiksells.

LOMAX, ALAN, IRMGARD BARTENIEFF, FORRESTINE PAULAY
1968 "The choreometric coding book," in *Folk song style and culture.* Edited by Alan Lomax, 262–273. Washington, D. C.: American Association for the Advancement of Science.

LYNIP, A. W.
1951 The use of magnetic devices in the collection and analyses of the pre-verbal utterances of an infant. *Genetic Psychology Monographs* 44: 221–262.

MC CARTHY, DOROTHEA
1954 "Language development in children," in *Manual of child psychology* (second edition). Edited by Leonard Carmichael, 492–630. New York: John Wiley and Sons.

MC GREW, W. C.
1972 *An ethological study of children's behavior.* New York and London: Academic Press.

MICHELSSON, KATERINA
1971 Cry analyses of symptomless low birth weight neonates and of asphyxiated newborn infants. *Acta Pediatrica Scandinavica.* Supplement 216.

MORRIS, CHARLES
1964 *Signification and significance.* Cambridge, Massachusetts: M.I.T. Press.

PIKE, KENNETH L.
1967 *Language in relation to a unified theory of the structure of human behavior* (second revised edition). The Hague: Mouton.

PLOOY, F. X.
1972 *Yearly Report May 1971 – May 1972.* Unpublished document. Netherlands Foundation for the Advancement of Tropical Research (WOTRO), grant number w84-66.

PRECHTL, HEINZ, DAVID BEINTEMA
1964 *The neurological examination of the full term newborn infant.* Clinics in Developmental Medicine 12. London: Spastics International and William Heinemann.

PRECHTL, H. F. R., K. THEOCELL, A. GRAMSBERGER, J. LIND
1969 A statistical analysis of cry patterns in normal and abnormal newborn infants. *Developmental Medicine and Child Neurology* 11:142–152.

RHEINGOLD, HARRIET L., J. L. GEWIRTZ, HELEN W. ROSS
1959 Social conditioning of vocalizing in the infant. *Journal of Comparative and Physiological Psychology* 52:68–73.

RICHARDS, M. P. M., JUDITH BERNAL
1972 "An observational study of mother-infant interaction," in *Ethological studies in child behaviour.* Edited by N. Blurton Jones. London: Cambridge University Press.

ROBSON, KENNETH S.
1967 The role of eye-to-eye contact in maternal-infant attachment. *Journal of Child Psychology and Psychiatry* 8:13–25.

SCHAEFFER, JOSEPH
1970 "Videotape in anthropology: the collection and analysis of data." Unpublished doctoral dissertation, Columbia University.

SCHEFLEN, ALBERT E.
1964 The significance of posture in communication systems. *Psychiatry* 27:316–331.
1965 *Stream and structure of communicational behavior.* Behavioral Studies Monograph 1, Eastern Pennsylvania Psychiatric Institute. Philadelphia: Commonwealth of Pennsylvania.

SEBEOK, THOMAS A.
1968 "Goals and limitations of the study of animal communication," in *Animal communication.* Edited by Thomas A. Sebeok, 3–14. Bloomington: Indiana University Press.

SMITH, W. JOHN
1965 Message, meaning and context in ethology. *The American Naturalist* 99:405–409.
1969 Messages of vertebrate communication. *Science* 165:145–150.

SPOCK, BENJAMIN
1968   *Baby and child care* (revised edition). New York: Pocket Books.
TAKEDA, RUMIKO
1965   Development of vocal communication in man-raised Japanese monkeys, I: from birth until the sixth week. *Primates* 6:337–380.
1966   Development of vocal communication in man-raised Japanese monkeys, II: from the seventh to the thirtieth week. *Primates* 7:73–116.
VAN LAWICK-GOODALL, JANE
1968   "A preliminary report on expressive movements and communication in the Gombe stream chimpanzees," in *Primates: studies in adaptation and variability*. Edited by Phyllis C. Jay, 313–374. New York: Holt, Rinehart and Winston.
VAN VLACK, JACQUES D.
1966   "Filming psychotherapy from the viewpoint of a research cinematographer," in *Methods of research in psychotherapy*. Edited by Louis A. Gottschalk and Arthur H. Auerbach, 15–24. New York: Appleton-Century-Crofts.
VUORENKOSKI, V., J. LIND, O. WASZ-HÖCKERT, T. J. PARTANEN
1971   Cry score: a method for evaluating the degree of abnormality in the pain cry response of the newborn and young infant. *Speech Transmission Laboratory, Quarterly Progress and Status Report* 1:68–75.
VUORENKOSKI, V., O. WASZ-HÖCKERT, J. LIND, M. KOIVISTO, T. J. PARTANEN
1971   Training the auditory perception of some specific types of the abnormal pain cry in newborn and young infants. *Speech Transmission Laboratory, Quarterly Progress and Status Report* 4:37–48.
WASZ-HÖCKERT, O., J. LIND, V. VUORENKOSKI, T.J. PARTANEN, E. VALAMME
1968   *The infant cry: a spectrographic and auditory analysis*. Clinics in Developmental Medicine 29. London: Spastics International Medical Publications.
Webster's dictionary
1967   *Webster's new twentieth century dictionary of the English language* (second edition). New York: Publisher's Guild.
WILSON, EDWARD O.
1972   Animal communication. *Scientific American* 227:52–60.
WOLFF, PETER H.
1959   Observations on newborn infants. *Psychosomatic Medicine* 21:110–118.

Language, Paralanguage, and Body Motion in the Structure of Conversations

STARKEY D. DUNCAN, JR.

This paper reports findings from a program of research on the structure of face-to-face interaction (Goffman 1963) in dyadic conversations. The research was designed to discover and document some of the building blocks or components of conversations, and the rules or relationships specifying how these components are properly combined. In a sense, the goal has been a "grammar" of conversations.

In searching for interaction structure, our research strategy may be compared to that of linguists seeking basic phonological, syntactic, and semantic elements in a given language and seeking rules for the respective uses of these elements. There are, however, three important differences between traditional linguistic research and the research to be reported here.

1. *Broad Inclusiveness of Behaviors Considered* Every effort was made to minimize *a priori* judgments as to the communicational role of the many different behaviors exhibited by persons in interaction. No assumptions were made regarding which of these behaviors might be more "central" than the others or which might serve to "modify" the others. The

This study was supported in part by Grants MH-16,210 and MH-17,756 from the National Institute of Mental Health and by Grant GS-3033 from the Division of Social Sciences of the National Science Foundation. Susan Beekman, Mark Cary, Diane Martin, George Niederehe, Ray O'Cain, Thomas Shanks, Cathy Stepanek, and Andrew Szasz contributed to the transcriptions and data analysis. I am indebted to Dick Jenney, Wayne Anderson, and the client, who generously consented to serve as participants in this study. Portions of this paper are based on findings reported in Duncan (1972, 1973).

relative contributions to face-to-face interaction of language, paralanguage (Trager 1958), and body motion, as well as of specific behaviors within each of these modalities, was taken as one of the important questions being considered. Consonant with Hymes (1967), the position was taken that the question of what is communicative should be regarded as problematic, the object of investigation. Accordingly, careful transcriptions were made of a wide range of behaviors within paralanguage and body motion, as well as within language (including intonation), and these transcribed behaviors were jointly considered in the analysis.

2. *Focus on Interaction*   It was the structure or organization of the interaction that was primarily being sought rather than the structure exemplified in the behaviors of any single communicator. Using data gathered from videotapes of dyadic conversations, the research focused on the effects of one participant's actions upon the actions of the other, and the manner in which the two participants coordinated their respective behaviors in the interaction (Scheflen 1968). This relative emphasis appears to be a sharp departure from traditional linguistic concerns. As Jaffe and Feldstein (1970: 2–3) have pointed out: "The serious study of dialogue patterns makes one poignantly aware that the largest unit dealt with in contemporary linguistics is at most the monologue ..." They quote Jakobson (1964) to the effect that pure monologue is extremely rare in nature, entirely absent in many societies, and, where present, exists in highly specialized forms, such as prayer or ceremonial speeches. This research attempted to place both speech and other modes of communication in their natural interactive context.

3. *Nature of Organization Not Modeled on Language*   The object of the research being the organization of conversations, it was not appropriate to assume *a priori* the nature of the organization being sought. In particular, care was taken not to attempt any one-to-one mapping of interaction phenomena onto grammatical forms of English, the language used in the interviews studied. Certain minimal assumptions were made, however: (a) the elements of the organization were taken to be discrete and (b) the structure of the organization was assumed to be hierarchical. Relationships obtaining between discrete elements of the organization were described in terms of discrete functions (Klir 1969) in order to preserve the greatest possible generality of formulation.

SPEAKING TURNS

In the case of this research, interaction structure in dyadic conversations was approached through phenomena related to the taking of speaking turns. The results to be described below suggest that these phenomena play an important part in, among other things, the integrating of the respective actions of co-participants in dyads by providing orderly, conventional means (a) for smoothly exchanging the speaking turn, thereby avoiding excessive simultaneous talking, and (b) for marking important segmental units, not only in the stream of communication of one participant but also in the interaction itself.

While there has not been extensive discussion of speaking turns in the literature, the phenomenon has not gone unnoticed by investigators. Goffman (1967: 33–34) commented on integrating mechanisms in general and on speaking turns in particular: "In any society, whenever the physical possibility of spoken interaction arises, it seems that a system of practices, conventions, and procedural rules comes into play which functions as a means of guiding and organizing the flow of messages."

Kendon (1967) dealt in detail with the role of gaze direction in the exchange of speaking turns. Scheflen (1968) discussed turn-taking as one of a number of communication mechanisms in face-to-face interaction which serve the function of integrating the performances of the participants in a variety of ways. Schegloff (1968: 1076) proposed the "basic rule for conversations: ONE PARTY AT A TIME" (original emphasis), and discussed some implications of this rule. Yngve (1970: 568) has commented that the orderly taking of speaking turns "is nearly the most obvious aspect of conversation."

Jaffe and Feldstein (1970: 6) studied temporal patterns of speech and silence in dyadic conversations. Their findings suggested to them "... further interactional rules that govern the matching of speech rates of the participants, the prohibition of interruption, and the requirement for properly timed signals that acknowledge understanding and confirm the continued attention of the listener." They quote Sullivan (1947), who observed careful taking of speaking turns in conversation between chronic mental hospital patients, and Miller (1963), who suggested that turn-taking is a language universal.

Leighton, Stollak, and Ferguson (1971) found more interrupting and simultaneous talking in the interaction of families waiting for psychotherapy than in the interaction of "normal" families.

The term "turn-taking" has been independently suggested by Yngve (1970) and in a personal communication from Goffman, June 5, 1970.

SOURCE OF DATA

Method of Collection

INTERVIEWS   The results to be reported were based on meticulous transcriptions of speech and body motion behavior during the first nineteen minutes of two dyadic conversations, as recorded on videotape.

The first conversation was a preliminary interview held at the Counseling and Psychotherapy Research Center at the University of Chicago. This preliminary interview is part of the routine intake procedure at the Counseling and Psychotherapy Research Center, and the client was a regular applicant for therapy. A preliminary interview was chosen for intensive transcription of communication behaviors, because within a rather compressed period of time a wide variety of types of interaction may be encountered — from simple information giving, such as address, etc., to the more emotionally laden discussion of the client's reasons for applying for therapy. At the same time, there is a strong intrinsic motivation for the interview, namely an application for therapy, thereby avoiding the more artificial experimental situation in which unacquainted subjects are brought together and asked to discuss anything which might be of mutual interest.

The client was in her early twenties, working as a secretary, and had not completed college. The therapist-interviewer was a forty-year-old male, an experienced therapist, who had been doing preliminary interviews for many years.

The second conversation was between the therapist who participated in the first conversation, and a second male therapist, also forty years old. The two therapists were good friends and had known each other for about ten years. Their interaction was relaxed and lively. The topic in this case was another client whom the first therapist had seen in a preliminary interview, and whom the second therapist had at that time seen in therapy for two interviews.

The preliminary interview will be designated as Conversation 1, and the second, peer interaction, will be designated as Conversation 2. The client will be designated as Participant A; the preliminary interviewer, B; and the second therapist, C. Thus, the participants in Conversation 1 were A and B; and the participants in Conversation 2 were B and C.

VIDEOTAPING   To videotape the interactions, the camera was placed so that both participants in each interaction were fully visible from head to foot on the tape at all time. No zoom techniques or other special focusing

effects were used. A single camera was set up in full view of the participants. The camera and tape were left running prior to the participants'
entry into the room and were not touched again until after the interview.

TRANSCRIPTION   For this study, the principal requirements for the transcription were those of maximum breadth and of continuity (no breaks or
interruptions). Maximum breadth is desirable in analysis because it is not
yet known which behavioral cues are the primary mediators of any given
communication function. And continuity of transcription permits the
complete analysis of sequences of events — the basic concern of this study.

Elements of Behavior

PHONEMES
1. *Segmental Phonemes*   Transcription of segmental phonemes, which
describe the way syllables are pronounced within the framework of the
English sound system, followed the scheme developed by Trager and
Smith (1957). The segmental phonemes were the least important components of the study.
2. *Suprasegmental Phonemes*   The suprasegmental phonemes are commonly referred to as intonation. They include the phenomena of stress,
pitch, and juncture. The Trager/Smith scheme for transcribing suprasegmental phonemes was used, with minor modifications identical to those
described in previous studies by this writer (Duncan and Rosenthal 1968;
Duncan, Rosenberg, and Finkelstein 1969).

PARALANGUAGE   Paralanguage refers to the wide variety of vocal behaviors which occur in speech but which are not part of the sound system of
language, as traditionally conceived. Comprehensive catalogs of paralinguistic behaviors have been compiled by Trager (1958), Crystal and Quirk
(1964), and Crystal (1969). Any one speaker will probably use only a
small fraction of the total behaviors available. The following list, which
uses Trager's (1958) terminology, includes only those behaviors which
play a part in the turn system: (a) intensity (overloud — oversoft);
(b) pitch height (overhigh — overlow); and (c) extent (drawl — clipping
of individual syllables). The terms in parentheses define the anchor point
for each behavioral continuum. A wide variety of paralinguistic behaviors was actually encountered in the two dyads and included in the transcriptions.

BODY MOTION   In contrast to paralanguage, there was for body motion no available transcription system which could be readily applied to our videotapes. This situation led to a transcribing method based on the behaviors actually found in each interview. The transcription system for the first interview was created by first making an inventory of the movements used by the two participants, and then assigning either arbitrary or descriptive labels to these movements. This system was then applied to the second interview, after expanding it to include new movements observed in the second interview.

While there is no pretense that the resulting transcription system is able to encompass all movements occurring in this culture, every attempt was made to include all movements observed in the dyads under study. The transcription was in this sense comprehensive. Included were: (a) head gestures and movements (nodding, turning, pointing, shaking, etc.) and direction of head orientation; (b) shoulder movements (e.g. shrugs); (c) facial expressions, such as could be clearly seen; (d) hand gestures and movements of all sorts (each hand transcribed independently); (e) foot movements (each foot transcribed independently); (f) leg movements; (g) posture and posture shifts; and (h) use of artifacts, such as pipe, facial tissue, papers, and clip board.

COORDINATION OF BODY MOTION AND SPEECH TRANSCRIPTIONS   Speech syllables were used to locate all transcribed events. Thus, the movements of both participants in an interview were located with respect to the syllables emitted by the participant who happened to be speaking at the time, or to the pause between two syllables.

THE SPEAKING-TURN SYSTEM

The speaking-turn system consists of the following elements: (a) two sets of postulated states, the respective sets representing adjacent levels within a single hierarchy, and (b) a set of hypothesized signals which aid participants in conversations in the coordination of action with respect to the states, among other things. There are several sets of rules applying to various aspects of the system. These rules will be described in conjunction with the aspects to which they apply.

Turn-System States

PARTICIPANT STATES   Two mutually exclusive discrete states are posited for each participant in a dyadic conversation: speaker and auditor. A SPEAKER is a participant who claims the speaking turn at any given moment. An AUDITOR (Kendon 1967) is a participant who does not claim the speaking turn at any given moment.

INTERACTION STATES   The next higher hierarchical level in the system — that of interaction state — may be obtained by jointly considering the respective states of each participant at any given moment. Following logically from the two participant states, there are four possible interaction states within the context of the system.

1.   *Speaker — Auditor*   One participant claims the speaking turn; no such claim is made by the other participant. In this interaction state the speaker continues his turn uninterrupted by the auditor.

2.   *Auditor — Speaker*   This interaction state is identical to the one above, except that the participants have exchanged the speaking turn. The participant who had previously been the speaker has now switched to the auditor state; and *vice versa*. When this exchange is accomplished without passing through the interaction state of simultaneous turns (below), a smooth exchange of the speaking turn is said to have occurred.

In the proposed turn system, the display of a turn signal by the speaker marks points in the interaction at which the auditor may appropriately switch to the speaker state, claiming the turn.

3.   *Speaker — Speaker (Simultaneous Turns)*   Both participants simultaneously assume the speaker state, claiming the speaking turn. This interaction state represents a breakdown of the turn system for the duration of the state. No attempt is made in the proposed turn system to explain the manner of resolution of such a state, that is, which of the participants will continue claiming the speaking turn and which one will relinquish his claim, reverting to the auditor state. Meltzer, Morris, and Hayes (1971: 401) report some interesting findings on one mode of resolution, based on techniques of "social psychophysics."

"Simultaneous turns" is used here instead of the more usual term "simultaneous talking." Within the turn system there may be instances of simultaneous talking not considered to be simultaneous turns. As will be described below, the auditor responding in the back channel (Yngve 1970), such as "m-hm" or a head nod, does not constitute a claim for the turn. An auditor back-channel response, when it overlaps with the speaker's verbalizing, would therefore be a case of simultaneous talking by the two participants, but not of simultaneous turns. Jaffe and Feldstein (1970) have shown that simultaneous talking in a dyad tends to be quite brief in duration, the mean duration being less than .5 seconds.

Simultaneous turns may be caused by a violation of the system on the part of either participant. The previous speaker may fail to relinquish his turn after displaying a turn signal and after the auditor's subsequent claim of the turn. Or the previous auditor may suddenly interrupt by claiming the turn in the absence of the speaker's turn signal.

4.   *Auditor — Auditor*   The previous speaker may display a turn signal and cease talking, thereby apparently relinquishing his turn, and the previous auditor may fail to claim the turn. The result would obviously be silence for the duration of that state. Experience suggests that this fourth logical possibility of the two participant states does occur in conversations, but because it was not observed in our corpus, it will not be considered further in this discussion.

Signals in the Turn System

A set of discrete signals provides a means by which participants may coordinate (a) the switching of their respective states (i.e. the smooth exchange of the speaking turn) and (b) other actions related to turns.

In this section the appropriate display of, and response to, the signals will be discussed. In the next section the display of each signal will be defined, and the behavioral composition of each signal will be described.

For the speaker, there are three signals: (a) a turn signal, (b) a gesticulation signal, and (c) a within-turn signal. For the auditor, there are two signals: (a) a back-channel signal and (b) a speaker-state signal.

SPEAKER TURN SIGNAL   The auditor may claim the turn when the speaker displays a turn signal. In proper operation of the system, if the auditor so claims the turn in response to the signal, the speaker is obliged to relinquish immediately his claim to the turn. When the speaker is not displaying the turn signal, however, auditor claims of the turn are inappropriate, leading to simultaneous turns.

The turn signal is permissive, not coercive. The auditor is not obliged to claim the speaking turn in response to the display of the signal by the speaker. The auditor may alternatively communicate in the back channel, or remain silent.

SPEAKER GESTICULATION SIGNAL   This signal by the speaker serves to negate any turn signal concurrently being displayed. The display of the gesticulation signal virtually eliminates claims to the turn by the auditor. Because of the effectiveness of the signal, it was impossible to evaluate from the data whether or not auditor claims of the turn, during display of the gesticulation signal by the speaker, tended to result in simultaneous turns. The gesticulation signal does not similarly affect the auditor's responding in the back channel.

SPEAKER WITHIN-TURN SIGNAL   This signal was used by the speaker, apparently to mark the end of units of his discourse on a hierarchical level immediately lower than that of the speaking turn. Appropriate auditor response to these units would be a back channel communication. Once again, this signal was permissive, not coercive. The auditor was not obliged to respond in the back channel upon every display of the signal.

AUDITOR BACK-CHANNEL SIGNAL   The auditor's communicating in the back channel does not constitute a turn or claim of a turn. The back channel provides a means by which the auditor can give useful feedback to the speaker during the course of his turn. Auditor back channels not infrequently overlap with the speaker's verbalization. These occurrences are considered instances of simultaneous talking, permissible within the system, as contrasted to simultaneous turns, which are not permissible.

Auditor back channels are systematically related to the speaker's within-turn signal, in a manner described below. Auditor back channels may also be used in response to turn signals, in lieu of the auditor's taking the speaking turn. But the pattern of auditor back-channel response to turn signals is quite different from (a) auditor back-channel response to within-turn signals and (b) auditor turn-claiming response to turn signals.

SPEAKER-STATE SIGNAL   This signal marks a participant's shift from the auditor to the speaker state. The signal is characteristically found at the beginnings of turns, but not at instances of auditor back channels. In addition, it is possible that this signal is further used within turns to mark the beginnings of within-turn units. At this writing, however, analyses of this possibility have not been completed.

The proposed turn-system states and signals are shown in their hierarchical arrangement in Figure 1. Elements of the system combine to form higher-level elements, according to the discrete functions (Klir 1969) indicated in italics. These discrete functions represent many of the "rules" operating in the turn system.

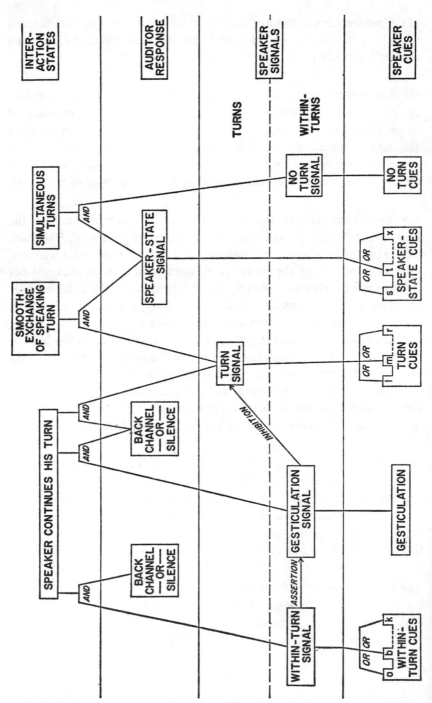

Figure 1.   Proposed organization of turn-system states and signals

Display and Behavioral Composition of the Signals

Each signal in the turn system is composed of a set of behavioral cues. Like the signals themselves, the cues are considered to be discrete.

DEFINITION OF SIGNAL DISPLAY   With the exception of the gesticulation signal, more than one cue was identified for every signal in the system. The display of a signal was in all cases defined as the display of at least one of its constituent cues.

For those signals having multiple cues, two or more of its cues were frequently conjointly displayed, their onset being either simultaneous or in tight sequences. The display of such larger numbers of signal cues or of particular combinations of these cues was not taken to alter the fact that the signal in question was being displayed. In several cases, however, the conjoint display of two or more cues was found to have interesting effects on the actions of the *vis-à-vis*, as will be described below.

EXHAUSTIVENESS OF CUE LISTS   Although pains were taken in the analysis to document as carefully as possible the participation of each of the cues in its respective signal, no claim is made that these cues necessarily represent an exhaustive inventory. Further, undetected cues may be present in the conversations subjected to analysis, as well as in other conversations in this culture. A more complete list might be obtained through a dialect survey which included behaviors in paralanguage and body motion, in addition to those in language.

SPEAKER TURN SIGNAL   The turn signal was defined as the speaker's display of at least one of a set of six discrete cues.
1. *Intonation*   The use of any pitch level — terminal juncture combination other than 2 2/ at the end of a phonemic clause. (These terms and notations follow those of Trager and Smith (1957).) Thus, the cue is defined as being displayed in a clause having some rising or falling properties either in the terminal juncture or in the pitch level on the final syllable. Clauses having such a rising or falling quality will be referred to as "intonation-marked clauses" in the discussion below.
2. *Drawl*   Paralinguistic drawl on the final syllable or on the stressed syllable of an intonation-marked clause.
3. *Termination of Gesticulation*   The termination of any hand gesticulation (Kendon 1967) used during a speaking turn or the relaxation of a tensed hand position (e.g. a fist) during a turn.
    To account for the gesticulations observed in the two interviews, it

seems sufficient to define gesticulations as those hand movements generally away from the body which commonly accompany, and which appear to bear a direct relationship to, speech.

Specifically excluded from the definition of gesticulation are self-adapters and object-adapters (Ekman and Friesen 1969). Self-adapters involving the hands are movements in which the hand comes in contact with one's own body, often with the appearance of grooming. Examples observed in our conversations would be: rubbing the chin, scratching the cheek, smoothing the hair, brushing off the pants leg, and picking lint (real or imaginary) from the socks. Highly similar behaviors, termed "self-manipulatory gestures," were also studied by Rosenfeld (1966). Examples of movements considered to be object-adapters in our conversations would be maintaining one's pipe, rubbing the arm of the chair, adjusting paper on a clipboard, and taking a facial tissue.

4. *Sociocentric Sequence*   The utterance of one of several stereotyped expressions, typically following a more substantive statement. Examples are "but uh," "or something," and "you know." The term "sociocentric sequence" was coined by Bernstein (1962), who commented on these expressions in another context. These expressions do not add substantive information to the speech content that they follow. Instances in which the auditor proceeded to take his speaking turn during the completion of a sociocentric sequence are not considered to be a state of simultaneous turns in the conversation. Rather, such an act is considered to be an instance of permissible simultaneous talking.

5. *Pitch/Loudness*   A drop in paralinguistic pitch and/or loudness in conjunction with a sociocentric sequence, as compared to the level of these behaviors at the end of the immediately preceding phonemic clause. When such paralinguistic drops were transcribed for phonemic clauses not involving a sociocentric sequence, this cue was not considered to have been displayed.

6. *Syntax*   The completion of a grammatical clause, involving a subject-predictate combination.

SPEAKER GESTICULATION SIGNAL   This signal was considered to be displayed when one or both of the speaker's hands were engaged in gesticulation, as defined above. Self- and object-adapters do not operate as gesticulation signals. Cessation of the gesticulation signal constitutes a speaker turn cue (Number 3 above). It should be noted that much speech is not accompanied by gesticulation and therefore neither the gesticulation signal nor its coordinate turn cue would be applicable for that speech. This is the only signal in the turn system characterized by a single cue.

SPEAKER WITHIN-TURN SIGNAL   A within-turn signal is defined as the speaker's display of at least one of a set of two discrete cues.

1. *Shift of Head Direction Toward the Auditor*   The speaker's turning his head towards the auditor, from a previously "away" position. While this behavior is intuitively regarded as a change in gaze direction, difficulties with reliability in transcribing gaze direction (von Cranach 1971) have forced the use of the more reliable head direction behavior.

2. *Syntax*   The completion of a grammatical clause, defined exactly as for the turn cue (Number 6 above).

BACK-CHANNEL SIGNAL   A back-channel signal might be displayed by either speaker or auditor. In this paper data will be presented with regard primarily to auditor back channels. The definition of the signal is the same regardless of who displays it. The signal is defined as the display of at least one of a set of five discrete cues.

1. *M-hm*   This expression is used to stand for a group of readily identified, verbalized signals. Included in the group are such expressions as "m-hm," "yeah," "right," and the like and Kendon's (1967) examples of "yes quite," "surely," "I see," and "that's true." Most of the "m-hm" signals may be used singly or in repeated groups, as in "yeah, yeah."

2. *Sentence Completions*   Not infrequently in our materials an auditor would complete a sentence that a speaker had begun. In such a case he would not continue beyond the brief completion; the original speaker would continue with his turn as if uninterrupted. Sentence completions have been independently reported by Yngve (1970). Example: C (second therapist, above): "... eventually, it will come down to more concrete issues ..."; B (first therapist): "As she gets more comfortable;" C: "and I felt that ...."

3. *Request for Clarification*   Contrasting with sentence completions are brief requests for clarification. Such requests were usually accomplished in a few words or in a phrase. Example: C: "... somehow they're better able to cope with it." B: "You mean these anxieties, concern with it?"

4. *Brief Restatement*   This back-channel signal is similar to the sentence completion, except that it restates in a few words an immediately preceeding thought expressed by the speaker. Example: C: "... having to pick up the pieces;" B: "the broken dishes, yeah;" C: "but then a very ...."

5. *Head Nods and Shakes*   Head nods and shakes may be used alone or in company with the verbalized back-channel signals. Head nods may vary in duration from a single nod to a rather protracted, continuous series of nods.

On the basis of modality used, we may distinguish the vocal back-channel cues (Numbers 1–4 above) from the visual back-channel cue (Number 5).

It may be useful to mention other terms which have been used to refer to various subsets of the cues described above. Fries (1952), in a study based on recorded telephone conversations, used the term "conventional signals of attention to continuous discourse." Kendon (1967: 44), in a study of British subjects in conversations, found a general class of "accompaniment signals" which were divided into two subclasses: (a) an "attention signal proper in which p appears to do no more than signal to q that he is attending and following what is being said …" and (b) a "'point-granting' or 'assenting' signal. This most often takes the lexical form of 'yes quite' or 'surely' or 'I see' …." Dittmann and Llewellyn (1967, 1968) used the term "listener response."

The term used in this paper was suggested by Yngve (1970: 568), who discussed the "back channel, over which the person who has the turn receives short messages such as 'yes' and 'uh-huh' without relinquishing the turn."

SPEAKER-STATE SIGNAL   The speaker-state signal is defined as the display of at least one of a set of four discrete cues.

1.   *Shift Away in Head Direction*   Turning of the head from pointing directly toward the *vis-à-vis* to an "away" position. This cue is the exact opposite of the within-turn cue (Number 1).

2.   *Initiation of a Gesticulation*   Beginning a gesticulation as defined above. The distinction of gesticulation from self- and object-adapters was maintained. Adapters were excluded from the definition of this cue.

3.   *Audible Inhalation*   A sharp, audible intake of breath. Even when an inhalation was visually observable on the videotape, it had additionally to be audible in a distinct and unambiguous manner.

4.   *Paralinguistic Overloudness*   The transcription of at least one degree of overloud intensity (Trager 1958) for the speech syllables in question. Transcriptions of paralinguistic overhigh pitch were not considered to be elements of this cue.

RESULTS

The turn-system signals and rules were designed as an initial account of some of the conventions used by participants in face-to-face dyadic conversations. It is reasonable to expect that these conventions would introduce clear-cut regularities in some of the actions of these participants, thereby aiding them in the solution of certain problems of coordination in conversations, such as the avoidance of excessive simultaneous turns.

It follows that the turn system should be capable of accounting for a significant number of instances of smooth exchange of speaking turns, simultaneous turns, and other relevant turn phenomena. The data analyses presented in this section are relevant to the evaluation of the turn system's descriptive adequacy for the transcribed conversations.

Unit of Analysis

In order to subdivide the interviews for purposes of analysis, a unit was chosen which in size lay between the phonemic clause and the speaking turn. Each cue display and each instance of smooth exchange of turns or of simultaneous turns occurring in the transcriptions was located with respect to these units. As with the signals in the turn system, the unit was defined in terms of the display of at least one of a number of behaviors in syntax, intonation, paralanguage, and body motion.

Specifically, boundaries of the units were defined as being: (a) at the ends of phonemic clauses, which (b) additionally were marked by the display of one or more of the turn cues described above and/or by the display of one or more of the following cues:

1. *Unfilled Pause*   An appreciable unfilled (silent) pause following the phonemic clause.

2. *Head Direction*   Turning of the speaker's head toward the auditor. This cue is identical to the within-turn cue described above.

3. *Paralinguistic Pitch and/or Loudness*   A drop in paralinguistic pitch and/or loudness in conjunction with a phonemic clause, either across the entire clause, or across its final syllable or syllables.

4. *Foot Flexion*   (For participant A (client) only.) A relaxation of the foot from a marked dorsal flexion. Throughout the conversation this participant's legs were stretched out in front of her and were crossed at the ankle. From time to time one or both feet would be flexed dorsally, such that they assumed a nearly perpendicular angle to the floor. Their returning to their original position, as the result of relaxing the flexion, was the cue.

As may be seen in Table 1, there were a total of 885 of these units in the two interviews subjected to analysis.

The definition of this unit, a necessary procedural antecedent to analysis, was formulated in a predominantly intuitive manner at an early stage in the research. The unit will be replaced by a more analytically derived unit, when such a replacement is possible. Further studies are underway, directed towards that end.

Turn and Gesticulation Signals

The research issue for the speaker's turn and gesticulation signals was the extent of their success in accounting for instances of smooth exchanges of the speaking turn, simultaneous talking, and auditor's attempts to take the speaking turn. Under the turn-system rules, the occurrence of simultaneous turns should be associated primarily with the auditor's claiming the turn when the turn signal is not being displayed by the speaker (that is, no turn cues displayed at that moment). The speaker's display of the gesticulation signal should sharply reduce the auditor's claiming the turn in response to yielding cues.

Table 1. Auditor turn claims and resulting simultaneous turns as a function of number of speaker turn cues displayed and the display of the gesticulation signal

Speaker turn cue display		Auditor turn claim			Simultaneous turns resulting from auditor claim		
(A)		(B)	(C)		(D)	(E)	
N conjointly displayed	Frequency of display	N	P^a	SD^c	N	P^b	SD^c
		No gesticulation signal displayed					
0	52	5	0.10	0.04	5	1.00	0.00
1	123	12	0.10	0.03	2	0.17	0.11
2	146	25	0.17	0.03	2	0.08	0.05
3	89	29	0.33	0.05	2	0.07	0.05
4	47	15	0.32	0.07	0	0.00	0.00
5	9	4	0.44	0.17	0	0.00	0.00
6	2	1	0.50	0.35	0	0.00	0.00
Σ	468	91			11		
		Gesticulation signal displayed					
0	56	7	0.13	0.04	7	1.00	0.00
1	109	0	0.00	0.00			
2	138	0	0.00	0.00			
3	105	2	0.02	0.01	1	0.50	0.35
4	6	0	0.00	0.00			
5	3	0	0.00	0.00			
Σ	417	9			8		

[a]   Column B/column A.
[b]   Column D/column B.
[c]   Standard error of the proportion ($\sqrt{PQ/N}$).

Table 1 presents the data, summed over the two transcribed conversations, on which the analyses of these and related phenomena were based. Percentages of auditor turn claims in response to a given number of cues were obtained by dividing the number of claims by the number of displays of those cues. Percentages of simultaneous turns were calculated by dividing the number of simultaneous turns by the number of auditor claims.

TURN SIGNAL   Inspection of Table 1 indicates that the cues, signals, and rules for the proposed turn system were capable of accounting for every smooth exchange of the speaking turn in our corpus. That is, every smooth exchange of the turn followed an auditor turn claim in response to a speaker turn signal.

Every auditor turn claim when no speaker turn signal was being displayed resulted in the state of simultaneous turns. That is, there was at least a momentary dispute over the turn whenever the auditor claimed the turn in the absence of a speaker turn signal. (For purposes of data analysis, simultaneous turns were considered to have occurred when a perceptible overlap of both participant's speech resulted from an auditor turn claim.)

The statistical relationship between the display of a turn signal (or its absence), and the occurrence of simultaneous turns resulting from a turn claim by the auditor may be obtained by applying chi-square to Table 2, a 2×2 contingency table derived from Table 1. The resulting $X^2 = 52.31$, corrected for continuity; $df = 1$. When $df = 1$, a X^2 of 10.83 has an associated probability of 0.001.

Table 2.   Smooth exchange of the speaking turn and simultaneous turns resulting from auditor's claiming the turn when the speaker turn signal is displayed and when it is not ($N = 100$).

	Smooth exchange of turn	Simultaneous turns
Turn signal not displayed	0	12
Turn signal displayed	81	7

It was observed that, when no gesticulation was being displayed, a strong positive relationship existed between (a) the number of turn cues displayed by the speaker and (b) the probability of a turn claim by the auditor. The correlations between these two variables was 0.96, $df = 4$. (This correlation included the data points represented by the display of 0 through 5 turn cues. The point for 6 cues was omitted from the analysis because it was represented by only two displays, thereby permitting only an unreliable estimate of the point.) This correlation included all turn claims by the auditor, both those resulting in smooth exchanges of turns, and those resulting in simultaneous turns. The data points for this phenomenon and their associated regression line are shown in the left half of Figure 2.

When turn claims resulting in simultaneous turns were removed from the analysis, so that only instances of the proper operation of the turn system were considered, the correlation between number of turn cues displayed and percéntage of auditor turn-claiming response to that display was 0.987.

ALTERNATIVE TREATMENTS OF TURN CUES   With regard to the conjoint display of cues to form signals, questions may be raised concerning (a) the possibility that certain conjoint displays may carry special significance as signals and (b) the possibility that certain cues should be weighted more heavily than others in the signaling process. These questions were carefully perused in the data analysis.

With regard to the display of cues, it is true that there is variation among the cues in their relative frequency of display. This appears to be in part a matter of personal style among individuals. However, there does not appear to be a similar favoring of certain specific conjoint displays, apart from the favoring of certain cues. This was verified by estimating the frequency of each specific conjoint display on the basis of the combined frequencies of its constituent cues. This basis of estimation was found to provide a close approximation of the obtained frequencies of the respective conjoint displays.

With regard to the special weighting of cues to account for auditor response, it may suffice to reiterate that the results on auditor response were obtained by simply adding the number of cues in any given conjoint display, without regard to the specific cues which made up the display, each cue being given the weight of one. No single cue was present in every conjoint display responded to. While there are many different rules available for combining a given number of stimuli, either discrete or continuous, the combination rule applied to this system was the simplest possible one.

GESTICULATION SIGNAL   The results on auditor turn claims were sharply different when the speaker was displaying a gesticulation signal along with his turn cues. Data on auditor claims in the presence of a gesticulation signal are presented in the lower half of Table 1 and in the right half of Figure 2. With the exception of the display of zero turn cues by the

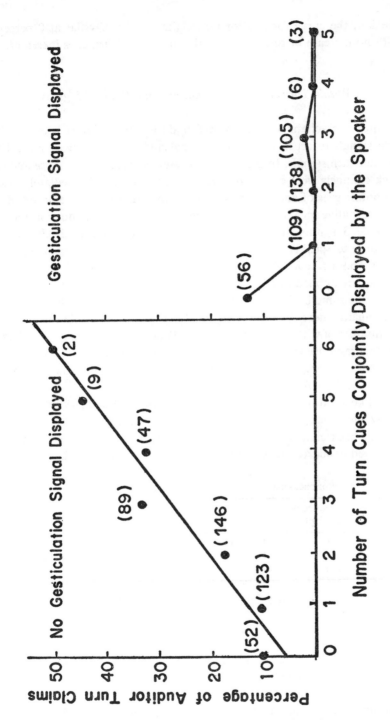

Figure 2. Auditor's turn claims in response to the display of speaker turn cues and gesticulation signal (Ns shown in parentheses)

speaker, the curve for auditor turn claims is virtually flat at 0 percent, with no increase of turn claims as the number of turn cues increases.

Speaker Within-Turn Signals and Auditor Back-Channel Signals

Auditor back-channel signals were found to be related to speaker within-turn signals in much the same way that auditor claims were related to speaker turn signals. In the analyses presented below, only those auditor back channels were considered which occurred at, or immediately after, the boundaries of analytic units. Also, those units which were followed by the alternative speaker action — claiming the turn — were not considered.

Table 3 summarizes the data and results on auditor back-channel response to speaker within-turn cues. Of the auditor back channels analyzed, 86.9 percent followed the display of a speaker within-turn signal. Chi-square applied to a 2×2 contingency table for these data, constructed on the same basis as that shown in Table 2, yielded a value of 27.73, once again where $df = 1$, and $p(0.001) = 10.83$. The correlation between the number of within-turn cues displayed and percentage of auditor back-channel response was 0.988. It should be remembered that this correlation was based on only three data points, although there were a large number of observations for each point.

Unlike auditor turn claims, auditor back-channel signals were unaffected by the speaker's display of the gesticulation signal. Considering all auditor back channels occurring in the transcriptions, 52.5 percent were displayed concurrently with the speaker gesticulation signal.

Table 3. Auditor back-channel response following speaker's display of within-turn cues

N cues displayed	Frequency of display	N	P	Percent of back channels following cues display	X^2	Correlation
0	285	14	0.049			
1	326	44	0.134	86.9	27.73	0.988
2	174	49	0.281			

Speaker-State Signal

It was proposed that the speaker-state signal was used, among other things, to differentiate turn beginnings from auditor back-channel signals. Rates of display of the speaker-state signal with turn beginnings and with auditor back channels are shown in Table 4, along with related statistics.

Table 4. Display of speaker-state signal in conjunction with turn beginnings and with auditor back channels

Signal	Turn beginnings			Back channels			X^{2a}
	N	Frequency of signal display	P	N	Frequency of signal display	P	
	Conversation 2: exploratory analysis						
Head shift and gesticulation	22	21	0.95	85	12	0.14	50.46
Full signal	22	21	0.95	85	16	0.19	42.04
	Conversation 1: validation						
Head shift and gesticulation	59	39	0.66	32	1	0.03	30.89
Full signal	59	44	0.75	32	3	0.09	32.76
Total	81	65	0.80	117	19	0.16	

[a] $df = 1; p(0.001) = 10.83$

In contrast to the other signals discussed above, the speaker-state signal was formulated on the basis of analyzing the transcription of Conversation 2 and then applying this formulation to Conversation 1 as a partial validation. Data from each conversation are presented separately in Table 4. For purposes of analysis a speaker-state cue was considered to be displayed when it was transcribed as occurring within an area extending from one unit of analysis prior to the initiation of a turn beginning or of an auditor back channel through to the first substantive word of that turn beginning or back channel. "Substantive" was taken merely to exclude phrases such as "well, uh," which are sometimes found at the beginnings of turns, as well as at other points in speech. Because turn beginnings must be vocalized, only vocalized auditor back channels were included in the analysis. Instances of simultaneous turns were not included in the analysis, because it was desired to consider only those instances of turn beginnings in which the turn system was apparently operating in its proper manner.

Taken as a whole, the speaker-state signal appears to mark a high proportion of turn beginnings, and to be displayed infrequently with auditor back channels. The chi-squares applied to the operation of the full signal in each of the two conversations yielded values comparable to those reported above for other signals in the turn system. The two-cue subset which includes the body motion cues — head shifting and gesticulation — appears to operate almost as effectively as the full, four-cue set.

The relatively positive exploratory findings on the two paralinguistic cues — overloudness and inhalation — were not replicated in the validation conversation. Data on these cues were included in this report because (a) they were significantly active in the exploratory analysis; (b) unknown circumstances in the validation conversation may have decreased the rate of their use; (c) the inhalation cue perfectly discriminated turn beginnings from back channels in both conversations — its increased use might have greatly increased its statistical significance; (d) the overloudness cue finds some support in the related findings of Meltzer, Morris, and Hayes (1971); and (e) these paralinguistic cues might be found to be more effective in other conversations, such as those in which gesticulations are used less extensively than in the two transcribed conversations. Thus, their inclusion in this report may be of some use to other investigators.

Unlike findings for the speaker turn and within-turn cues, no special effects on the response of the *vis-à-vis* have been observed for the conjoint display of two or more speaker-state cues.

DISCUSSION

The results presented above suggest that there are highly structured aspects of dyadic, face-to-face interaction. This structure provides the participants with the means by which to coordinate their respective actions with regard to speaking turns and other phenomena.

In dealing with strong regularities in interaction behaviors introduced by social conventions, it might be said that the object of research is a "grammar of interaction." However, because of the strong linguistic connotation of "grammar" it might be simpler and less potentially confusing simply to speak of social conventions applying to interactions.

Organization of the Signals in the Turn System

Several aspects of the composition and organization of signals within the turn system have already been emphasized: (a) cues for these signals were sought in a wide variety of interaction behaviors, (b) the signals and their constituent cues were treated as discrete entities, and (c) the display of a single cue was considered sufficient to constitute a display of its respective signal. Three other aspects of the formulation and analysis of these signals have particular relevance to the underlying organization of the system.

(It will be recalled that the organization of all signals, in terms of their respective cues, was handled in an identical manner, with the gesticulation signal representing a limiting case in that it was composed of a single cue.)

DESCRIPTION OF CUES   The cues were described in terms of general properties of behaviors. In the speaker turn signal, for example, it was not a specific intonation pattern that served as a cue but simply any deviation from the 2 2/ pattern; not a specific gesticulation but rather cessation of any gesture or relaxation of a tensed hand position; not a specific paralinguistic pattern but a drop from the preceding pattern in pitch and/or loudness; and so on. In this manner the cues were able to encompass a wide variety of individual communicational styles, while still functioning as clearly discriminable, discrete events.

WEIGHTING OF CUES   In analyzing the effects of the display of clusters of cues for any given signal, each cue in the cluster was simply assigned the weight of one and these weights were added to obtain the sum for that display. Considering the strength of the relationship between (a) sums for each display and (b) the probability of an appropriate auditor response found for both the speaker turn and the speaker within-turn signals, it seems unlikely that an alternative weighting procedure would yield superior results for these data.

One implication of this weighting procedure is that no special cueing preference is accorded to cues occurring in one of the behavior areas (paralanguage, body motion, and language) over cues occurring in the others. There appears to be more democracy in the operation of these signals than might be expected from the discussions often found in the literature. For example, we do not find within these signals behaviors in body motion serving to modify or to qualify behaviors in syntax or in content.

An identical weighting procedure appeared to be operating in a somewhat different aspect of face-to-face interaction: the unprogrammed communication of an experimenter's expectations to his subject (Duncan and Rosenthal 1968; Duncan, Rosenberg, and Finkelstein 1969). In this case the proposed cues were in intonation and paralanguage.

DISTINCTIVE CUE CLUSTERS   In consideration of the distinctive feature analysis model for language (Jakobson, Fant, and Halle 1952), a concerted data analysis was directed toward the possibility that the signals were composed of unique combinations of cues, as contrasted to being composed of indiscriminate aggregates of cues (including any single cue). This effort, described above in the RESULTS section, failed to produce positive results. No unique combination of cues and no single cue indispensible to the clue clusters could be found in displays prior to auditor responses. In general, the process of summing over equally-weighted cues contrasts sharply with the distinctive-feature analysis model and represents a considerably simpler principle of organization.

In view of the considerations discussed in this section, it would appear that the organization of the turn system varies in certain important respects from that of the language used by the interactants: American English.

Units of Interaction

Discussion to this point has centered on the organization of the signals displayed by a single participant. Jointly considering the respective actions of both participants leads directly to the issue of the organization of interaction, the ultimate goal of this research.

As the turn system is presently formulated, a speaker has a means by which he can segment his utterances on two hierarchical levels. The lower level is segmented by the within-turn signal; and the higher level is segmented by the turn signal. There appears to be a range of appropriate auditor responses to each of these speaker signals. To the within-turn signal, the auditor may appropriately respond with either silence or a back channel. To a turn signal unaccompanied by a gesticulation signal, he may appropriately respond with silence, a back channel, or a speaker-state signal, thereby claiming the turn. To a turn signal accompanied by a gesticulation signal, the auditor may appropriately respond with either silence or a back channel.

Data presented above on auditor's turn-claiming responses to speaker's turn signals clearly indicated that a turn-signal display did not automatically result in an auditor claim of the turn. At best, the probability of such a claim appears to be about 0.50. Comparable data were presented for auditor back-channel responses to speaker within-turn signals. Thus, it appears that the auditor retains considerable discretion over both the type and placement of his responses.

These findings, taken together, suggest the operation of two distinct, but interlocking, types of units: (a) units within individual messages, marked by the speaker and (b) units of interaction.

Units within individual messages are marked by only one interactant. In this sense they are comparable to traditional linguistic units on a given level. In the case of the turn-system, the units differ from traditional linguistic units, of course, in that the turn-system units use behaviors from paralanguage and body motion as markers.

Units of interaction cannot be marked by only one participant. These units must be marked by the appropriate, coordinated action of both participants (in the case of dyads).

Interaction units on a hierarchical level immediately below that of turns appear to be marked by a three-stage, sequential process: (a) the speaker displays a within-turn or a turn signal; (b) the auditor responds in the back channel; and (c) the speaker continues with his turn.

Interaction units on the level of the turn require a similar three-stage, sequential process: (a) the speaker displays a turn signal; (b) the auditor shifts to the speaker state, displaying a speaker-state signal; and (c) the previous speaker shifts to the auditor state, relinquishing his turn.

At each stage of these action sequences (after the original signal display by the speaker), each participant ratifies, as it were, the actions of the other. Following the initial signal display by the speaker, each participant has several real options available to him. Each of these options has important implications for the immediately ensuing course of the interaction. Distinctive patterns of option choice by each participant over the course of the interaction may have important implications for the character of that interaction.

Interaction units, created through the coordinated action of both participants in a dyadic interaction, appear to have the potential of constituting a basic building block in the structure of interaction.

Research Method

Developing appropriate methodological concepts and techniques was a central problem at the onset of this research. In time, an approach was evolved that drew variously from linguistics, psychology, and systems theory. The fine-grained transcriptions of behaviors in language, paralanguage, and body motion, and the initial emphasis on discrete units and hierarchical structure were derived from linguistics, as expanded by the work of McQuown, Bateson, Hockett, Birdwhistell, and others in "The natural history of an interview" (McQuown 1971). The use of discrete functions to represent the relations between discrete units was suggested in systems theory (Klir 1969). Finally, statistical techniques typically used in psychology were applied in evaluating the proposed signals and rules.

In general, for dyadic interactions it does not appear difficult to formulate criteria in terms of which a proposed convention can be evaluated statistically. For the turn system, criteria were derived directly from hypothesized regularities introduced by the convention in question into the behavior of participants. These regularities are reflected in nonrandom distributions (a) in specific behaviors of the *vis-à-vis* and (b) in resulting interaction states.

However, in applying statistical methods to conventional phenomena, it seems reasonable to expect significance levels considerably higher than those typically encountered in psychological research, assuming that the convention in question is operating effectively in the interaction. Research results that are just at, for example, the 0.001 level of significance might well be interpreted as indicating that the convention has not yet been adequately described or that, in the contexts from which the data were gathered, the convention in question was not reliably applicable.

Further Research on Interaction Structure

The initial stage of this research, before the turn signals had been formulated, was necessarily laborious, in that fine-grained transcriptions were required for as wide a variety of behaviors as possible. Further research may proceed at a more rapid pace, as hypotheses are formed regarding the behavioral composition of the signals. In Scheflen's (1966: 277) words, the signals then become "RECOGNIZABLE AT A GLANCE AND RECORDABLE WITH A STROKE" (original emphasis). Work is currently under way to transcribe the turn-system signals (and certain other, interesting behaviors) in a series of further videotaped dyadic conversations, with the aim of validating and potentially extending the findings reported here.

The findings reported above were directed at documenting the operation of signals that serve to mark various phenomena in conversations. There is no claim, however, that the lists of cues described as comprising the signals are necessarily complete. Other undetected cues may be present in the conversations studied, as well as in other conversations in the culture of the interactants. These possibilities will be considered in further research, both on the initial two conversations and on new transcriptions.

Research is continuing on the notion of interaction units as structural elements of conversations. The distribution of a number of different phenomena with regard to interaction units is being examined.

Initial analyses suggest that the speaker-state signal, beyond marking the beginnings of turns, may also be used throughout the speaking turn to mark the beginnings of within-turn units. If this suggestion proves correct, means will have been established whereby speakers may mark both the beginning and the ending of units. This possibility is being pursued.

The question arises concerning the auditor's initiation of interaction units. He might do this, either through a back channel in the absence of a speaker within-turn or turn signal or through a speaker-state signal in the absence of a speaker turn signal. (Auditor initiatives of this sort may account for some of the speaker-state signals found in association with auditor back channels.) Attention is being paid to the interactional consequences of such auditor initiatives. Table 1 indicates, however, that an auditor initiation of a turn in the absence of a speaker turn signal leads invariably (in our data) to simultaneous turns.

REFERENCES

BERNSTEIN, B.
  1962 Social class, linguistic codes, and grammatical elements. *Language and Speech* 5:221–240.
CRYSTAL, D.
  1969 *Prosodic systems and intonation in English.* Cambridge: Cambridge University Press.
CRYSTAL, D., R. QUIRK
  1964 *Systems of prosodic and paralinguistic features in English.* The Hague: Mouton.
DITTMANN, A. T., L. G. LLEWELLYN
  1967 The phonemic clause as a unit of speech decoding. *Journal of Personality and Social Psychology* 6:341–349.
  1968 Relationship between vocalizations and head nods as listener responses. *Journal of Personality and Social Psychology* 9:79–84.
DUNCAN, S. D., JR.
  1972 Some signals and rules for taking speaking turns in conversations. *Journal of Personality and Social Psychology* 23:283–292.
  1973 Toward a grammar for dyadic conversations. *Semiotica* 9:29–46.
DUNCAN, S. D., JR., M. J. ROSENBERG, J. FINKELSTEIN
  1969 The paralanguage of experimenter bias. *Sociometry* 32:207–219.
DUNCAN, S. D., JR., R. ROSENTHAL
  1968 Vocal emphasis in experimenters' instruction reading as unintended determinant of subjects' responses. *Language and Speech* 11:20–26.
EKMAN, P., W. V. FRIESEN
  1969 The repertoire of nonverbal behavior: categories, origins, usage, and coding. *Semiotica* 1:49–98.
FRIES, C. C.
  1952 *The structure of English.* New York: Harcourt, Brace.
GOFFMAN, E.
  1963 *Behavior in public places.* New York: Free Press.
  1967 *Interaction ritual.* Garden City: Anchor.
HYMES, D.
  1967 "The anthropology of communication," in *Human communication theory.* Edited by F. E. X. Dance. New York: Holt, Rinehart and Winston.

JAFFE, J., S. FELDSTEIN
  1970   *Rhythms of dialogue.* New York: Academic.
JAKOBSON, R.
  1964   "Discussion of 'Factors and forms of aphasia' by A. R. Luria," in
         Ciba foundation symposium on disorders of language. Edited by A. V. S.
         de Reuck, and M. O'Connor. Boston: Little, Brown.
JAKOBSON, R., C. G. M. FANT, M. HALLE
  1952   *Preliminaries to speech analysis: the distinctive features and their
         correlates.* Cambridge: MIT Press.
KENDON, A.
  1967   Some functions of gaze-direction in social interaction. *Acta Psycho-
         logica* 26:22–63.
KLIR, G. J.
  1969   *An approach to general systems theory.* New York: Van Nostrand
         Reinhold.
LEIGHTON, L. A., G. E. STOLLACK, R. L. FERGUSON
  1971   Patterns of communication in normal and clinic families. *Journal of
         Consulting and Clinical Psychology* 36:252–256.
MC QUOWN, N. A., *editor*
  1971   "The natural history of an interview." Microfilm Collection of
         Manuscripts on Cultural Anthropology, Fifteenth Series, The Univer-
         sity of Chicago Joseph Regenstein Library, Department of Photo-
         duplication. Chicago.
MELTZER, L., W. N. MORRIS, D. P. HAYES
  1971   Interruption outcomes and vocal amplitude: explorations in social
         psychophysics. *Journal of Personality and Social Psychology* 18:392–
         402.
MILLER, G. A.
  1963   Review of J. H. Greenberg (editor), *Universals of language. Con-
         temporary Psychology* 8:417–418.
ROSENFELD, H. M.
  1966   Instrumental affiliative functions of facial and gestural expressions.
         Journal of Personality and Social Psychology 4:65–72.
SCHEFLEN, A. E.
  1966   "Natural history method in psychotherapy: communicational
         research," in *Methods of research in psychotherapy.* Edited by L. A.
         Gottschalk and A. H. Auerbach. New York: Appleton-Century-
         Crofts.
  1968   Human communication: behavioral programs and their integration
         in interaction. *Behavioral Science* 13:44–55.
SCHEGLOFF, E. A.
  1968   Sequencing in conversational openings. *American Anthropologist* 70:
         1075–1095.
SULLIVAN, H. S.
  1947   *Conceptions of modern psychiatry.* New York: Norton.
TRAGER, G. L.
  1958   Paralanguage: a first approximation. *Studies in Linguistics* 13:1–12.

TRAGER, G. L., H. L. SMITH, JR.

1957 *An outline of English structure*. Washington, D.C.: American Council of Learned Societies.

VON CRANACH, M.

1971 "The role of orienting behavior in human interaction," in *The use of space by animals and men*. Edited by A. H. Esser. New York: Plenum.

YNGVE, V. H.

1970 "On getting a word in edgewise," in *Papers from the sixth regional meeting of the Chicago Linguistic Society*. Chicago: Chicago Linguistic Society.

Human Linguistics and Face-to-Face Interaction

VICTOR H. YNGVE

The small but growing group of people working on the phenomena of face-to-face interaction is confronted with a critical lack of an adequate theoretical framework. Research is impeded because we lack the understanding and insight that a satisfactory theory would give and the guidance it would provide for observational and experimental programs. Lacking an appropriate theoretical structure, we find it difficult to state results and more difficult to relate them with one another. I think I can assume a consensus both for the intrinsic interest and importance of the phenomena studied, and the desperate need for an appropriate framework. The situation has reached the proportions of a crisis.

Ten or fifteen years ago I lived through a similar confrontation. The lack of adequate theory was seriously impeding the development of mechanical translation. The computer was not giving us any trouble, the problem was that we had no adequate theory of translation on which to build workable translating programs. In the early days we had pinned our hopes on linguistics. The expectation seemed reasonable that structural linguistics could provide us with relevant theory, but we encountered serious difficulties. Later we became enthusiastic about the promise of transformational-generative grammar, but we were soon disillusioned and disappointed again, for that framework did not provide what we needed either.

Today, a similar disappointment and disillusionment is sweeping through linguistics itself. The realization is growing that the transformational-generative framework is also inadequate for the very discipline for which it was designed. We are thus faced with a crisis in linguistics as well. It is interesting to note the similarities between these three crisis situations. I believe that the similarities are not just coincidental: the three crises are related, and in fact are merely three aspects of the same common crisis.

THE SCOPE OF THE TASK

Those working in the field of face-to-face interaction probably realize more clearly than others the broad range of phenomena that seem to be interconnected and need to be related to one another by some appropriate theoretical structure or framework for examining the organization of social interaction from cultural, social, and psychological perspectives through discussions of the interrelationships between speech and gesture, facial expressions, and posture and spacing.

Starting with an interest in face-to-face interaction we have been led to consider a number of diverse disciplines and a great breadth of relevant observational phenomena. In seeking an integrated framework we can start first by surveying the scope of observational phenomena that seem to be interrelated in spite of the diversity of the disciplines and theoretical frameworks through which these observations have traditionally been approached. Then, after taking this observational inventory, we can turn and consider the task of finding an integrated framework capable of embracing that full range of phenomena.

To aid in thinking about the problem it is convenient to conceive of a single observationally defined discipline that encompasses the full range of phenomena. I have been calling this field BROAD LINGUISTICS. After defining the scope of broad linguistics we will then want to search for a proper theoretical framework for it. Those who are concerned with the observations of broad linguistics will be called linguists, in the broad sense, whether they have been recruited into this field from traditional linguistics, anthropology, sociology, psychiatry, or wherever else.

First of all, broad linguistics includes the types of observations typically made by traditional linguists when studying particular languages: such data as texts, recordings, and informant responses, together with distinctions of same or different, acceptable or not acceptable, paraphrase relations, rough translational equivalences, notes on typical situations of use, and so on. These materials have traditionally gone into the production of grammars and lexicons of different languages, comparative studies, and the like. Broad linguistics also includes the materials used by historical linguists, and the observations of dialectologists on the geographical and social distribution of various linguistic items.

On the border with sociology, data on the correlation of linguistic and social variables are of interest, particularly in relation to social class, role, and relative status. There is an interest in bilingualism and the phenomena of languages in contact, and in data on pidgins and creoles and how they change with time. Broad linguistics, of course, includes considerations of how people enter conversations, maintain them, and adjourn them. It is concerned with the variables of space and distance as studied in proxemics. It does not ignore gestures and postural variables as studied in kinesics, and it includes paralinguistic phenomena.

Broad linguistics includes the linguistic data obtained by the anthropologist in his field work. This involves considerations of kinship terminology, folk taxonomy, special ritual use of language, how language and communication serve the various functions of the society, and many other related considerations. Linguists are concerned with the instrumental use of language in accomplishing certain tasks, and attention is given to the situations of use of language and how they affect communicative behavior.

On the border with psychology, broad linguistics is concerned with the results of psychological studies directed toward the capacities and limitations of speaker and hearer, since they may be very relevant to an understanding of certain basic questions. There is interest in data on the relations of language to psychological variables in perception, conceptualization, and problem solving. Linguists want to be able to handle data on language acquisition by the child as well as by the adult.

Linguists also study data related to stylistics, poetics, and the artistic use of language in general. In short, the field of broad linguistics is very broad indeed, but it is fairly clear what the scope of it is in terms of the concerns of the investigators in a number of related fields.

It is difficult to characterize broad linguistics in any more precise way than as the range of interests of a particular diverse group of investigators, yet broad linguistics does include within its scope the phenomena that seem to present themselves naturally as being somehow interconnected and inviting explanation and unification by means of a proper theory. Such is the nature of broad linguistics; it is an observationally defined discipline in search of an appropriate theoretical structure.

THE INADEQUACY OF A LINGUISTIC APPROACH

It is perhaps obvious that no presently existing discipline offers an appropriate theoretical structure capable of covering broad linguistics. Instead, we have a number of diverse disciplines, each covering some part of that observational scope, and each being unable to cover the rest. The reason for this seems to be that each discipline has its central thrust directed somewhat outside the general area of broad linguistics, or else its central thrust is too narrowly conceived to cover more than a limited portion of the area of broad linguistics. We could show this by going through the various disciplines one by one but will limit ourselves to a discussion of the current discipline of linguistics. Linguistics today enjoys the reputation of having the most comprehensive and systematic unifying structure in the general area, a structure that many have turned to for guidance. But it is easy to see that linguistics, as presently conceived, is completely inadequate for our purposes.

Linguistics is usually defined as the scientific study of language. Language is defined as the relation between sound and meaning. This relation is expressed in terms of grammar and lexicon, which lay out the rules of the language, and implicitly or explicitly specify what expressions belong in the language and what expressions fall outside it. In linguistics, grammar and lexicon play the role of a unifying theory that serves to relate the phenomena to one another and explain them.

Although this view of the conceptual structure of linguistics is almost universally accepted today, it is not new. It is a traditional conceptual structure carried down almost unchanged in its most basic elements from the Greek thought of 300 to 150 B.C. It was developed in that era by the Stoic philosophers and by the Alexandrian literary scholars. For the Stoics, it served as an integral part of a theory of knowledge. The Alexandrians were interested in preserving a great literary heritage in the face of evident language change and dialectal variation in Greek. The combined grammatical tradition that grew up was preserved and elaborated by the later Greeks and the Romans, and it reaches us today through an unbroken line. This conceptual structure was very relevant to the interests of the Greeks, but today it is largely irrelevant to the needs of broad linguistics, as we shall presently see.

Nevertheless, there has been a tendency to turn to linguistics for guidance in theory construction, for the system of rules found there seems eminently suited, with perhaps some modification, to our task.

But such attempts are doomed to failure if they are deemed to be anything more than exploratory attempts to organize some limited area of data, for the basic concepts are inappropriate.

Furthermore, linguistics, even within its own house, does not enjoy an enviable position, for there has been continual revision of theory over the last 2,000 years within the general limits of the traditional framework, and the current transformational-generative theory has been admitted by many of its main advocates to be in great trouble (Dingwall 1971).

THE UBIQUITY OF TRADITIONAL LINGUISTIC CONCEPTS

Even if we do not consciously follow the lead of the grammatical tradition in our search for a unifying framework, we are apt to fall prey to its basic conceptual structure. This is because our everyday language incorporates this conceptual structure in the very structure of its vocabulary. It is very difficult to think about much of the phenomena of broad linguistics without thinking in terms of traditional grammatical concepts. This can cause great difficulty if these concepts are in fact inadequate or irrelevant, as I believe they are.

First of all, let us examine the word LANGUAGE. The Greeks distinguished between Greek and barbarian (foreign) languages, and for Greek, they distinguished between Good Greek and corrupt or deviant Greek, filled with foreignisms and errors. Their object of study was Good Greek, and they defined this in terms of the literary traditions of earlier centuries. They were little interested in the languages of the uncultured (non-Greek) peoples, and little interested in informal discourse or conversation. Their concept of language, therefore, was normative and prescriptive in its emphasis on Good Greek, and it carried an implication of uniformity. Indeed, the observed linguistic diversity was rejected and condemned as being incorrect or uncultured. In spite of the efforts of recent generations of linguists, the normative and prescriptive implications have not disappeared, and the implication of uniformity is as universally evident as is the observational evidence against it: no two people speak the same. The Greeks discussed facial expressions and gestures in rhetoric but treated only the formal style of the orator. This tradition and the tradition of gestures in the theater were not unified with grammatical thought. Their concept of language did not include nonverbal components, but only what was expressed in alphabetic writing. These several serious limitations remain today in our concept of what a language is.

But there is more. In the very influential Stoic philosophical tradition, language was treated as a part of dialectic, the study of arguments true and false, the part of philosophy that investigated how we know the truth and how we express it. Long before Saussure, the Stoic theory of the sign distinguished the signifier, the signified, and the referent. Under the signifier, they treated sound in terms of the grammatical levels of voice, diction, and speech. Under the signified, they treated meaning in terms of the logical levels of the proposition, notion, presentation, perception, and sensation, by means of which we come to know the truth.

Language is still considered a relation between sound and meaning in spite of the fact that this static view, adapted to a theory of knowledge, offers no concepts appropriate to much of the study of conversation. If we are not careful, our theories will be similarly limited to propositional speech and the expression of meanings that are little nuggets of knowledge. Much of conversation falls outside these narrow bounds — for example, greeting behavior. The concept of language as a relation between sound and meaning survives in spite of the fact that philosophers have long ago abandoned the Stoic theory of knowledge; and in linguistics, only the treatment of the signifier has survived. Grammar has developed for 2,000 years with no explicit connection to a theory of knowledge. Linguists think they know what sound is: it can be observed; but for 2,000 years they have lacked a theory of meaning. Language as a relation between sound and meaning stands with only one leg on the solid ground of an observable phenomenon. Yet even such an astute linguist as Chomsky would like to assume that both legs stand solidly (1970:52). Such is the strength of the grammatical tradition, and a traditional but indefensible notion of meaning survives to haunt us in our everyday language.

Next, notice the popular conception of the communicative act. We have what might be called the transportation metaphor. Words are considered as vehicles that carry our meanings or convey our thoughts from one mind to another. We send a message as we would send a messenger, and we understand the burden of the message. This whole way of speaking can befog the mind and lead us into the traditional pitfalls. Not only is the concept of meaning that is involved here very misleading; we tend to forget that it is not by words alone that we communicate.

There are many illustrations of the confusions that this whole traditional conceptual apparatus has led us into. Let me mention just one. Much of the literature since Charles Darwin on facial "expressions" has operated under the assumption that there was a repertory of expressions, each conveying a particular emotional meaning. Typical experimental designs would consist of listing various emotions that were thought to be involved, such as pleasure, hate, fright, anger, and so on, and then asking a subject to express these emotions by means of facial expressions, which would be photographed. Then the procedure was to see if other subjects could correctly identify the emotions expressed. The several confusions embedded in this experimental paradigm are perhaps obvious.

THE QUESTION OF AN APPROPRIATE GOAL

If there is no appropriate unifying framework for the observational concerns of broad linguistics, and if traditional linguistics cannot be looked on except with distrust as a source of concepts and methods, what are we to do? There seems to be a need for a reassessment of the various traditionally defined disciplines that relate to portions of the phenomena studied in broad linguistics. Is it possible to build a theoretical framework capable of covering all of the concerns of broad linguistics in a unified way? If so, how would a discipline so constituted relate to existing disciplines?

In seeking an adequate framework, it is appropriate that we start with a consideration of what would be the unifying goal of such a discipline. The traditional goal of linguistics, which we have rejected, is to achieve a scientific understanding of language. Each of the other relevant disciplines has a traditional goal, and none is adequate for the whole of broad linguistics. It would seem difficult to constitute a discipline by somehow combining these diverse goals. It would be better if we could find a single goal with the desired coverage.

I should like to suggest that our goal be TO ACHIEVE A SCIENTIFIC UNDERSTANDING OF HOW PEOPLE COMMUNICATE. Such a goal, I believe, does have the coverage appropriate to the scope of broad linguistics.

It is the nature of a goal that it directs our choice of paths in trying to reach it. It is therefore important to consider carefully the exact wording of the goal. We would do well to avoid the use of terms that appear to prejudge the approach or limit the means for finding the answer. As an example of the danger, a previous wording of a goal to cover the scope of broad linguistics (Yngve 1969) was to achieve a scientific understanding of how people use language to communicate. Despite expressed intentions to the contrary, this formulation has the same problem that the current goal of linguistics has (to achieve a scientific understanding of language). The use of the term "language" appears to presume part of the answer in that it implies close ties to the grammatical tradition. As another example, the organization of behavior in face-to-face interaction is inadequate as a goal for several reasons. In the first place, it prejudges the task by focusing on the organization of BEHAVIOR, and may mean to some a behavioristic approach. Secondly, the restriction to face-to-face interaction may be too constraining — for example, it might be conceived as ruling out an interest in interactions by telephone, as well as written interaction. These might well be considered as derivative, but we would not want to rule out their consideration by the wording of our goal. Another inappropriate suggestion would be to achieve a scientific understanding of communication. This would bring the presumption that there is some abstract entity called communication that is appropriate as an object of study, but then we would be left with the task of defining communication, and this could lead to confusions as great as with the presumption of an abstract entity called language.

Our chosen wording, "to achieve a scientific understanding of how people communicate," does not seem to suffer from any of these defects. There should be no problem with the phrase "achieve a scientific understanding," for a limitation to a scientific approach seems appropriate. The term "people" can be taken in its ordinary meaning in English. Its use merely carries the reasonable presumption that there are people. The only possible problem is with the verb "communicate"; we did have a problem before with "communication." But, whereas the nominalization is vague, even ambiguous, presuming some kind of entity or abstraction, the verb does not share this problem. The only presumption is that people communicate. But, again, taking the ordinary meaning of the word, we know from observation that people do communicate. This statement of the goal thus simply points to an interesting observable phenomenon, that people communicate, and proposes to achieve a scientific understanding of it. The scope of this goal should be approximately, if not exactly, the same as the observational scope of broad linguistics.

I have called the discipline answering to this goal HUMAN LINGUISTICS. This is to eliminate any confusion with the traditional linguistics of language but at the same time to recognize that the interests of linguists today probably come closer to this goal than the interests of any other current sizable group of scholars, and, furthermore, linguistics has probably already given us more insights into this area than any other discipline.

THE BASIC CONCEPTS OF HUMAN LINGUISTICS

It is a great advantage of our new goal that we can start with people. An appropriate scientific concept of people for the purposes of human linguistics should not be difficult to formulate, for people are objects that are given in advance and that can be considered from different viewpoints: there are several other sciences that study people. Since a person is a real physical object that can be known from points of view other than human linguistics, the concept of person does not suffer from the difficulties associated with the concept of language or the concept of communication.

Of course, we are not interested in studying every aspect of people, but only those aspects that are related to how they communicate. It is thus appropriate that we set up as our first concept in human linguistics an abstraction that includes just those properties of people that are of interest. We define the COMMUNICATING INDIVIDUAL as an abstraction in linguistics that includes just those properties of the person that are required to account for his communicative behavior. In defining the communicating individual in terms of properties of interest in human linguistics, we simply exclude from consideration that which is irrelevant while at the same time maintaining the flexibility required to accommodate new observations about people that can be related to their communicative behavior.

The communicating individual, as thus defined, becomes the central concept in human linguistics and represents its major object of study. This being the case, it is clear from the very beginning that human linguistics is a part of psychology. The relationship of the traditional linguistics of language to psychology has been far from clear and has caused no end of confusion in the literature.

Communication is a group or social phenomenon, and it would seem that we would need in human linguistics at least one concept related to groups of individuals. But what kind of a concept should this be? One such concept that has been used extensively in linguistics is the concept of the speech-community. This concept is usually defined in such a way that the members of a speech-community are those people who speak the same language. The concept has given much trouble and has been discussed extensively in the literature. For our purposes it is inadequate because it is related to a concept of language which we have rejected as a basic concept in human linguistics.

We have defined the communicating individual on the basis of observable phenomena — that there are people and that they communicate. For setting up a concept of groups of individuals in human linguistics, we look again to observable phenomena for guidance. We observe that there are many people in the world but that no two are exactly alike in their communicative behavior. Yet we do observe groups within which the individuals can easily communicate with each other. We must somehow take into account both the similarity and the diversity of individuals. With a focus on people instead of on language, we are in a much better position to do this. Being free of the tyranny of the concept of language, we no longer have any reason to conceive of an individual as a language-speaker. We are then not led to an unrealistic assumption of homogeneous communities of language-speakers. We can define our groups in ways that properly reflect the facts of communication.

An individual obviously belongs to many different groups at the same time. We can accommodate the observed diversity of communicative behavior by taking these different groups into account and thus solve a number of problems that concepts of speech-community have raised. We define a COLINGUAL COMMUNITY as a group of individuals who can communicate with each other in certain ways characteristic of the group. An individual is normally a member of many different and partly overlapping colingual communities. Each colingual community is characterized by one or more linguistic features or items that serve to define the community and to set it apart from the others. The concept of colingual community is not related to the totality of communicative potentialities of the individual but only to those that are characteristic of that community and serve to distinguish it from other colingual communities.

When individuals engage in communicative activity, they will be expected to make use of linguistic features belonging to several of the colingual communities to which they both belong. Thus, a member of a profession would belong to a colingual community distinguished by certain communicative forms such as vocabulary items. When he communicates with other members of this community, he may make use of these forms. But he will also make use of linguistic features characteristic of other colingual communities. These will, of course, include larger communities with a geographic base, as well as smaller or overlapping ones related to such special interests as hobbies, sports, religion, fraternal organizations — and even to intimate family groups.

Colingual communities are thus defined in terms of people and their observable behavioral properties related to communication. It would seem that all of the phenomena previously associated with the similarities and differences of languages, dialects, jargons, technical languages, and the like can be analyzed, described, and understood in terms of colingual communities and the communicative features used to define the communities and to identify individuals as members of them.

We have defined the communicating individual as an abstraction in linguistics that includes just those properties of the person that are required to account for his communicative behavior. We may call these properties LINGUISTIC PROPERTIES and note that by definition they account for all the properties of the communicating individual, these being a subset of the properties of the person. An investigation of linguistic properties will be a major concern of human linguistics, since the communicating individual is its central concept.

There are various ways in which linguistic properties may be classified. One way is to divide them into INNATE PROPERTIES and ACQUIRED PROPERTIES. This method of classification runs into the well-known problem that a mature individual is a product of both heredity and environment, and for any given observable property there may be both hereditary and environmental contributing factors. For example, the characteristics of the voice of an opera singer could probably be traced to both genetic factors and training, and it may be impossible to separate these two essential components in the observed singing voice. Nevertheless, the classification into innate properties and acquired properties does have some merit since their methods of study are somewhat different. For studying innate properties we have, for example, methods worked out in genetics, and for studying acquired properties we have, for example, methods worked out in developmental and educational psychology.

It would seem far off the mark to approach the innate properties of the communicating individual through linguistic universals. Grammar is not a property of a person but a construct of the grammarian that purports to show the relation between sound and meaning given by some language. The idea of universal grammar as including just what is common to the grammars of all languages is an interesting abstraction in the linguistics of language, but to represent this as being an innate property of the individual characteristic of the species is to make a category mistake of the most glaring kind.

Care must also be exercised, when studying the innate properties of the individual, not to assume that just because an observed property is thought to be universal (that is, possessed by all individuals), it is therefore shown to be innate. It is quite possible that there are universal communicative requirements that would be realized in all communicating individuals through acquired properties. For example, one might expect all individuals to have a means of communicating assent or dissent, or for selectively addressing another individual in a group. Such properties might well be universal, yet acquired.

Another way of classifying linguistic properties is according to their apparent function in communication. A full understanding of the communicative function of various linguistic properties will, of course, have to await the results of a considerable amount of research. We can, however, suggest a tripartite classification that is based on some initial observational evidence. Linguistic properties can be classified as BASIC PROPERTIES, which represent the physical properties that the individual uses in communication; COLINGUAL PROPERTIES, which represent those properties by virtue of which the individual is a member of various colingual communities; and SITUATIONAL PROPERTIES, which represent the individual's changing internal accommodation to the communicative situation.

The BASIC PROPERTIES of the communicating individual are probably largely innate, but there may be a non-negligible acquired component. They represent the physical mechanism, the basic equipment, that the individual uses in communicating. Examples include the so-called organs of speech, the equipment for hearing, arms and hands to gesture with, facial features, and a nervous system and brain. In human linguistics we consider these basic properties from the point of view of their communicative function. Included among the basic properties are a large permanent memory and a small temporary memory capable of holding about seven items (Yngve 1960). It is not the task of human linguistics to discover the physiological mechanisms of nerve conduction, but eventually all the basic linguistic properties may be understood also at a lower biological level in terms of anatomy and physiology, and then ultimately understood by scientific reduction in terms of biochemistry and physics. This possibility of reduction to levels of explanation in the biological and physical sciences is one of the advantages of human linguistics over the linguistics of language. Reductions of this sort strengthen both the higher level science and the lower level science.

The COLINGUAL PROPERTIES of the communicating individual are those acquired linguistic properties by virtue of which the individual is a member of various colingual communities. Such properties are the basis for generalizations about communicative behavior because they represent aspects of communicative behavior characteristic of groups of individuals. Thus, we have a wider observational base than the single individual for the study of colingual properties, yet they are properties of the single individual. The colingual properties include a knowledge of the communicative relevance of various roles that are recognized in certain colingual communities, and how to act and react appropriately according to these roles. They are those acquired properties by which the individual knows what to do or say or what to understand in various communicative situations. Thus, under the colingual properties of the individual we understand much of what would be covered under language, or under various cultural or social concepts, but from a quite different point of view that allows us to have an integrated framework.

The SITUATIONAL PROPERTIES of the communicating individual are those acquired and changing properties by which he accommodates to the changing communicatively relevant situations in which he finds himself. Of course, the external physical environment may have communicative relevance, but it is more appropriate to take this into account only through information residing in the individual about the external physical environment. The superiority of this view can be easily shown: when the individual has a misapprehension of what the situation really is, it is his misapprehension and not the reality of the environment that controls or governs his communicative behavior. Under situational properties we include not only a knowledge of the physical situation, objects and persons in the vicinity, their names, roles, characteristics, and so on, but also more abstract situational factors such as the topic of conversation, knowledge of common experiences, attitudes, wishes, hopes and aspirations, knowledge of events — current and historical — and many other pieces of knowledge that have communicative relevance. Both colingual and situational properties, though acquired and perhaps temporary, have their basis in real biochemical differences in the individual, and at the psychological level, an individual who knows something of communicative relevance is demonstrably different from a person who does not, or who knows something different.

The basic, colingual, and situational properties of the communicating individual are exhaustive, and together they can completely account for the communicative behavior of the individual. The basic properties cover the mainly inherited mechanisms operative in the individual for communication; the colingual properties cover the knowledge that the individual has of what to do or understand in various communicative situations; and the situational properties provide the individual with a knowledge of the operative situations. Human linguistics can thus proceed with the study and elaboration of four structures: the structures of the basic, colingual, and situational properties, and the structure of their interrelation. These are structures of real physical properties of the individual considered from their communicative function. Since we are studying in human linguistics an aspect of physical reality, we can ask meaningful questions that can be approached through observational and experimental methods.

AN EXAMPLE

Perhaps a concrete example would help to clarify these basic concepts. Suppose I meet my friend John on the street, invite him to my house for the evening, and he accepts. Much is known about interactions such as this from the work of a number of perceptive observers. How would this bit of face-to-face behavior be approached from the point of view of human linguistics?

As I walk along the street, I am aware of a figure approaching and set my course so as to avoid a collision. Now the behavior involved in foot navigation and the avoidance of obstacles shades into non-communicative behavior. But the fact that I am a person who passes on the right is a colingual property. But I can adapt in cities where they pass on the left, so my knowledge of which is currently appropriate is a situational property. I note that he has also moved so as to pass on the right. Thus, I am aware of being in an impending right-passing situation, and my situational properties change. I become a person who is about to execute right-passing behavior, and if the on-coming person should change his course I may be caught off-guard.

I also know I am in a neighborhood where I may meet a friend — a situational property — and I know how to handle head position and direction of gaze up to the point of recognition — a colingual property. When recognition takes place, the situation has changed and I behave appropriately. I will do this even in the case of mistaken recognition, until I realize my mistake. The situational properties now are that I recognize my friend, I remember that his name is John, and I have available certain relevant information about our relationship. It is also a situational property that I choose to stop and speak with him rather than execute the minimal appropriate greeting and pass on.

I know how to do this: how to indicate that I wish him to stop, how to engage him in conversation, and he knows how to react appropriately to my behavioral cues. These are colingual properties. I know how to ask him over for the evening. I know that to do this I must be in conversation with him and must have the conversational turn. I do all this, and the situation has changed. He becomes a person who is in conversation with his friend, has just been asked over to the friend's house for the evening, and now has the conversational turn. These are his relevant situational properties, together with other situational properties that will determine whether he accepts or not.

He knows what the options are as part of his colingual properties. He decides to accept and knows how to do that. He does so. He is now a different person. His situational properties have changed again. He is a person who has been invited over for the evening and has accepted. I can predict with some degree of certainty that he will show up on my doorstep. And I am a different person, too. My situational properties are different. I now expect him to show up.

MUCH REMAINS TO BE DONE

Needless to say we are very far from a complete understanding of the structure of the communicating individual in terms of his basic, colingual, and situational properties, and in this brief discussion I have not been able to treat fully what is already known. Many questions have been raised that can be decided only by observation and experiment, and much needs to be done to work out the details of these structures.

It would seem premature at this point to try to specify more exactly the abstract or formal nature of these properties of the individual: we do not yet have enough observational evidence. There is a danger in the premature adoption of a formalism: we may get overly committed to an inadequate framework that would constrain further research. Witness the problems that the grammatical tradition has caused in the study of communicative phenomena.

Nevertheless, there are indications that some kind of a state theory of the individual would be appropriate (Yngve 1969). There are many formal state theories available, but I feel we do not yet have enough observational evidence to choose among them. I have several pieces of research that tend to make me favor a state theory of the individual. The first is the work done on the depth hypothesis (Yngve 1960). Although this work was strongly influenced by concepts from the linguistics of language, with its emphasis on the sentence, it did succeed in relating a basic and undoubtedly innate property of the individual, that of a limited temporary memory, to observed syntactic structures in language and to language change. Whatever success this work has can be traced in large part to the type of state theory postulated for the individual as a producer of sentences. The astute reader will be able to recognize in that model the precursors of the basic, colingual, and situational properties of human linguistics. The other relevant pieces of research are more recent. One (Yngve 1970) reported work on conversational turn and was entirely motivated by considerations of a state theory. The other reports further work on the relation of temporary memory to conversational behavior (Yngve 1973). It has opened up a line of observation and experiment that may be crucial in deciding on the appropriate, more detailed structure of human linguistics.

REFERENCES

DINGWALL, W. O.
  1971   *A survey of linguistic science.* College Park: Linguistics Program, University of Maryland.
CHOMSKY, A. N.
  1970   "Deep structure, surface structure, and semantic interpretation," in *Studies in general and oriental linguistics, presented to Shiro Hattori on the occasion of his sixtieth birthday.* Edited by R. Jakobson, et al. Tokyo: TEC Company.
YNGVE, V. H.
  1960   A model and an hypothesis for language structure. *Proceedings of the American Philosophical Society* 104:444–66.
  1969   "On achieving agreement in linguistics," in *Papers from the fifth regional meeting, Chicago Linguistic Society.* Edited by R. I. Binnick, et al. Chicago: Department of Linguistics, University of Chicago.
  1970   "On getting a word in edgewise," in *Papers from the sixth regional meeting, Chicago Linguistic Society.* Edited by M. A. Campbell, et al. Chicago: Department of Linguistics, University of Chicago.
  1973   "I forget what I was going to say," in *Papers from the ninth regional meeting, Chicago Linguistic Society.* Edited by C. Corum, et al. Chicago: Chicago Linguistic Society.
  f.c.   *An introduction to human linguistics.*

Interactions and the Control
of Behavior

GLEN McBRIDE

The messages of this paper are simple ones. Animals interact with each other, in courtship, fights, allogrooming, allofeeding or care-giving. In each interaction, the behavioral unit is not two separate animals making behavior towards each other but the whole single interaction, in which the behavior of both must be treated together, as each responds to the other at all times. Yet once two animals initiate a first interaction, they start immediately to sort out appropriate and inappropriate responses in each other. This sorting out, or a summary of it, is carried forward into their next encounter with another of the same type — male, female, intruder — or with the same animal, and becomes a part of the context for future behavior, a controller of behavior.

The experience carried forward may organize perceptions, attention, the types of interactions expected, and the times and places of the interactions or meetings with individuals. The term "relationship" expresses the construct we use to describe this mutual residue of the interactive behavior. Yet there is little precision about the way we use this word. Other behavior, such as sleep or rest, or movement, does not have this effect of generating relationships, though other interactions (actonic) with objects such as places, nests, watering points, and investigations do.

Relationships arising from face-to-face interactions seem to be a feature of most animals, and it is the resulting organization of the animals in space and time, and their perceptions of each other as they monitor the activities of those around them, that fashion a number of individuals into a society. Moreover, it seems equally clear that animals are able to exert controls over ongoing streams of interactive behavior, shaping them into specific experiences which will be appropriate to the future contexts; that is, they "know" the effect of every move in a face-to-face interaction on the relationship that will emerge from the behavior.

If relationship formation is a general property of face-to-face inter-actions in any species of animal, what then may be said about the human conversational interaction? To answer this, it is necessary to trace something of the evolution of the human communicative system, for this history seems to show how the ancient mechanisms for building relationships may have been modified to serve human needs, based on more complex communicative behavior.

I have suggested that speech began with the linking of a social en-gagement with the acting out of an event, perhaps a hunting scene, in mime, by means of a play metasignal (McBride 1968, i.p.). The mes-sage carried in the mime may have been an event that happened to the actor earlier in the day, at a distant place, so that, in one step, the space and time barriers were broken, and a typical human communica-tion occurred. The step was huge, yet only involved a new combination of existing behavior. But this was not language.

Mime requires no agreement on the units of meaning. Over time, mime gave way to signs, and later to the use of sounds. The step to signs does require agreement on units, and so sign languages were probably the first true languages. The steps to signs and sounds were probably not discrete ones, and indeed we still regularly use signs, and occasionally mime, when words fail. Throughout the whole process, there was always a double interaction, and this is still true of either signing or spoken interactions. The new message codes were used with-in the context of the primary or social interaction, which remained in the ancient animal form, dealing only with issues of the type "between you and me, here and now."

The modern conversation is carried out in words, occasionally re-verting to signs or even mime to supplement meaning. But the primary interaction has now become completely integrated with the flow of language. There is but one communicative system in man, though the two components may normally be recognized in all conversations. The primary interaction is carried out in visible behavior, spacing, orienta-tion, eye contact, in touch, or in the paralinguistic component of the flow of sound. Yet there is much interchange between the two; for ex-ample, it is possible to supplement and modify the content of the speech by the use of nonverbal signals. Similarly, it is possible to turn into words the expression of the relationship, such as "I love you," or the requirements of the primary interactions, as "pay attention." This in-timate complementarity of the two interactions is the product of the last two or more million years of human evolution, for language evolved in conversations!

The study of language has eclipsed that of the other components of our communicative system to such an extent that the primary interaction is still virtually unknown. I shall return to the discussion of speech and its organization from time to time, where it is necessary to dissect out the components of the conversational interaction.

What seems most important now is to ask questions about the manner in which the conversation is turned into the social relationship. I shall argue that, throughout a conversation, the verbal component is arranged in such a way as to stimulate nonverbal responses which contribute to the primary interaction. These are then decoded automatically by the observer and summarized automatically. In other words, the summary system, already highly evolved in our primate ancestors, was carried forward into man, perhaps with some changes which summarize verbal behavior, but basically still operating through nonverbal behavior in the formation of human social relationships. And thus the features of the words which will contribute to the future relationship are first converted into the nods, frowns, or movements of affect which may then be summarized automatically. Thus the form of the summary is more likely to be in relationship terms than in the conceptual content of the conversation, i.e. in terms of "he's a stimulating person," rather than "the stories he told me were stimulating." Further, because the summary system affects future behavior, the longer into the future the memory is examined, the more likely is the relationship summary to appear.

Already I have discussed a variety of behavioral phenomena. It seems useful now to pause, to ask questions about the nature of behavioral phenomena, and how they differ from and are related to psychological and physiological phenomena, that is, to specify the universe of discourse.

In another context, we could be discussing magnets and magnetism. Should we choose to study magnetism, then we need not concern ourselves with how magnetic fields are generated, for we may examine the properties of fields provided only that we have some magnets. The magnet becomes a black box. If on the other hand, we are interested in magnets, then fields and their properties become irrelevant, provided that we have some device that detects their presence. Now we may concentrate on the processes by which magnetic fields are generated.

It seems to me that when we are talking about behavioral phenomena, we have similar problems and may choose to discuss behavior and its organization, or the generative processes — the mechanisms, and how they operate. These are two logical types of phenomena, quite different from each other. I suggest that it is a reasonable generalization that most human ethologists are concerned with behavioral phenomena, and that most psychologists concentrate more on mechanisms, sensory, perceptual, learning, and motivating. Physiologists interested in behavior attend also to mechanisms, trying to relate the mechanisms found by psychologists to the functioning of the neural and endocrine systems.

Within either of these areas of study, one may erect clear universes of discourse, each complementary to the others. Whatever is known of the structure and functioning of the system within one universe of discourse must be compatible with what one knows of the others and even may be used to make predictions about another type of system for study. Within each, one may erect a hierarchy, defining levels, with function organizing the units within any level, and complementarity providing the basis for the grouping of units at any one level into a unit at the next level.

Within the human conversational interaction, there appear to be two sensible universes of discourse: that concerned with the speech itself, emphasizing its semantic content, and that concerned with the behavioral organization of the primary interaction. It is the organization of behavioral phenomena that is central to this essay. Yet it is also necessary to examine the mechanisms by which behavior is generated.

I am assuming that the generative processes producing behavior are essentially similar for all behavior, be it a fight or courtship, a display or a speech. All appear to be produced with a hierarchical organization, all involve almost infinite variety, whether this be in the verbal composition of a conversation or in the movement sequences of a cockfight. I think it is possible to see what these generative processes do. To produce a well-formed sentence, a sequence of words is produced in an arrangement that will complete semantic and syntactic goals, conceptual and complementary, respectively. Each of the component words, phrases, or clauses has specified relationships with each other's parts, and ordering is arranged so that completion, which involves complementarity, is achieved while maintaining the structural relationships between the parts. The sentence constitutes one functional segment of information.

It seems that, in the evolution of behavior, functional activities were not achieved by single movements, and sequences of movements were needed. The generative mechanisms that evolved dealt with activities that could be divided up into a sequence of functional steps or operations, rather in the way that an operations researcher may divide up a complex productive task into separate human roles, and these again into smaller sequences of operations. At any level of the division, the significance and function of any subsidiary operation depend only on its meshing with the other divisions of the task. The sentence is the best known example, where clauses are the first division and are themselves built up of smaller units, defined in their relationships to each other, as subject, verb, predicate, and so on.

If the generative processes look complex when considering a completed sentence, they become more so when we look at their operation in interactive sequences. Here a sentence which started off as a statement. may change its goal from concept to argument in response to an eyebrow raised in doubt, or may trail off into a question should it meet a negating head shake. Alternately, a segment already generated may suddenly appear to give offense to the listener, making it inconsistent with the relationship existing between the interactants; here the speaker may draw the new goal of conciliation or apology from the primary interaction, so modifying the semantic goal of the speech.

There are many ways that goals may change in interactive behavior, and this seems true of the behavior of most species. In any fight, a blow may change to a parry; the eager courting male, passing on from stage to stage, may be halted many times by reluctant responses from the female — witness the many false starts of a mammalian male to a not-quite-estrous female! And so it is that generative processes are considerably more complex in interactive situations, yielding fewer completed sentences but more satisfying and effective interaction!

In a generative process, the term goal can be defined only in terms of an end point, the finish of an operational unit. At these terminating points, multiple goals may become apparent, each different in type and involved in different universes of discourse. In speech, the conventional goals are conceptual, each contributing to the flow of ideas. Yet there are also different syntactic goals, and within the primary interaction, there may be another type of goal of a sentence, that of acknowledgment — by a nod of understanding.

The flow of speech involves a steady stream of such terminating points, at any of which contributions may occur within the primary interaction. Sometimes the nods may be drawn from the listener by "don't you?" or "didn't it?" or a hundred equivalents. Moreover we often say something aimed to directly elicit some increased arousal and special response within the primary interaction. Jokes, insults, or teasing are among many verbal transformations into the primary interaction.

This feature of interchange between the message and the primary interactions seems to be important in the understanding of face-to-face interactions and the relationships that emerge from them. Clearly, there is a large variety of behavior that may appear in the primary interaction as a result of speech. Some examples illustrate this.

Nods of understanding are probably the most common primary signal, deriving directly from the semantic component. Jokes generally elicit smiles or laughs, compliments may lead to preening motions, teasing can evoke laughter, anger, or tears, or statements of helplessness may yield complementary supportive or protective expressions.

The physical appearance of a person may facilitate or hinder social intercourse, handsomeness or ugliness contributing to the ease of establishing close rapport within the primary interaction — here usually quite irrelevantly. Equally irrelevant may be the effect of a physical disability, which causes many people to increase their spacing, affecting rapport.

There are also historical features of people that may be interpreted as part of the primary interaction; these include loudness of voice, a tendency to make too much or too little eye contact, or to stand too close or too distant in the interaction. All of these behaviors contribute to the primary interaction but are not appropriately a part of the interactive sequence. Nevertheless they may certainly affect the future behavior between the interactants.

There is another whole segment of the primary interaction, related directly to speech, that is probably concerned with the process of encoding and decoding. It seems to operate as an automatic marking and grouping system for both semantic and syntactic units of speech. The studies of Kendon (1972) have helped to clarify its operation.

He analyzed the structure of speech into a hierarchy of units which he called phrases, locutions, locution groups, and locution clusters. He found that during the passage of any of these units, a speaker tended to hold some part of his body in a constant posture, so that the changes in posture of that part also marked the change in the speech unit. He found also that the larger the speech unit, the larger and more central was the part of the body that marked its passage. The phrases were grouped by the pitch of the speaker's voice. Other markers included the beginning and end of locutions by specific movements of the head.

The picture of the primary interaction is, then, one of close interdependence with speech. Yet this component has its own conventions, format, behavioral tools, and controls, as befits the social event in which speech occurs. Thus there is a greeting and farewell, usually some acknowledgment or expression of the relationship, an expression of involvement throughout, and a variety of behavior, which is often highly synchronized between the interactants. An outsider looking in could learn much about the interactants. Yet as Goffman (1971) has pointed out, a conversation is largely protected from intruding observation from without, and this buffering is an integral part of the social event. Without it, new constraints would hamper interactive behavior, and the intruder would become a part of the social event, however inappropriate.

The complexity of the primary interaction as we know it will certainly be increased by the confirmation of the findings of Clynes (1969). He has shown that a wide range of seemingly irrelevant movements, perhaps any movement, may express the moods of affect that he calls "sentic states." Moreover, the character, or essentic form given to movements by affect appears to be highly consistent (for the same sentic state) between people, even when they come from quite different cultures. While he has made no studies which look specifically at the communication of sentic information by essentic form, such regularity as he finds is characteristic of a communication system.

The primary interaction has the essential property of face-to-face communication in any species: "between you and me, here and now." Bound within these time and space barriers, two interactants adjust their behavior to each other throughout the interaction. Yet each brings to the interaction a unique set of interactive experiences gathered throughout life, and then the particular context and performance of the interaction will bring some additional specificity to the mutual experience. From this unique experience, the adjustments the participants have made to each other will be carried forward into their next meeting, if they have a second interaction of the same type. This next meeting, then, has a history that is part of its context, and the behavior observed would not be fully intelligible without some knowledge of the history.

Though the interaction is unique, all of the experience used by both parties to adjust to each other gave some course to the interaction. There was an outcome, mutually designed, which may in turn become one step along an interactive progression, along which the participants may travel until some stable and mutually acceptable relationship is reached. The goal of the interaction is not to make a complete relationship but merely to take an adequate step along the path. Just as the suitability of the interactive behavior for making that adequate step is "known" by the interactants, so also is the appropriateness of the step along the progression, toward the final goal of friendship or bond, or enmity relationship.

The recognition of final and intermediate goals, and the appropriateness of each step, small or large, toward these goals must be present. There can be no navigation without a destination! From where do these destinations derive, and how does the guidance and transport system work?

Within any species, there is a great variety of social behavior, displays in each modality, and responses to these behaviors, along with appropriate releasing situations and controls that regulate their use. Using these tools, animals build such relationships as are appropriate to their species. Each relationship has special properties, of adjustments to each other, and of divisions of labor between the two, seen in their different responses to each context.

The relationships are major controllers of the behavior of the pair. Their mutual adjustment eliminates their need to sense all of the behavior emitted by each other, leaving only the need to monitor the stream to detect deviations from the set of habituated expectations. Each relationship becomes a "channel" built by experience into the structure of their attention. All social information passes along these channels to maintain, change, and operate the society. The relationship structure is the structure of the society, built into the attention structure of all individuals. Yet there is also design, for the different relationships within any group must complement each other before the group becomes a unit that will function effectively, contributing to the preservation of the species.

It is clear that all of the design in any society must lie within the organization of the individuals of any species, males, females, juveniles, or infants. All was built by interactive behavior, using behavioral tools especially shaped by evolutionary processes. These are in the processes that generate behavior, the sensory processes that perceive and code it and summarize it, and those monitoring systems that assess its appropriateness.

Every relationship has a form, fashioned along with the behavioral tools that shape it through evolution. But there is also variability, and ontogenetic experience may modify this form. The form is also in part specific, reflecting the unique character of its history. But for man, there is also another control operating on his interactive behavior at every stage. For man has not one society, but many. Within each culture, different forms of relationships complement each other in different ways to achieve stable systems.

There is a large variety of functional relationships in man, particularly because one of man's greatest specializations is the ability to make special functional groups, with specified functional relationships within them. Different relationships demand different intermediate goals, and different interactive processes with different homeostatic adjustments during face-to-face interactions. Whether or not this variety in social relationships is real is not clear. Certainly it is clear that there is an enormous variety of functions with special interactions carried out within the social context. But how much variety is there in the social contexts for such operations?

This raises another complexity in human relationships, which I have avoided; one which is not present in any other animal. I have emphasized the summary system of affect that generates social relationships from the primary interactions in face-to-face interactions, drawing from the speech only through the primary interaction. Yet what is said, the concepts, arguments, and imagery also contribute to human interactions, as presumably do the functional interactions, usually of an actonic type. It is not my intention to avoid these; they are simply different stories.

REFERENCES

CLYNES, M.
  1969 "Toward a theory of man: precision of essentic form in living communication," in *Information processing in the nervous system.* Edited by N. Leibovic and J. C. Eccles, 177–206. Springer-Verlag.
GOFFMAN, E.
  1971 *Relations in public.* New York: Basic Books.
KENDON, A.
  1972 "Some relationships between body motion and speech," in *Studies in dyadic communication.* Edited by A. Seigman and L. B. Pope, Elmford, New York: Pergamon Press.
MC BRIDE, G.
  1968 On the evolution of human language. *Social Science Information* 7:81–85.
  i.p. Miming, signing, and speech. *Current Anthropology.*

Proxemic Research: A Check on the Validity of Its Techniques

ROBERT F. FORSTON

INTRODUCTION AND PROBLEM

Over a decade ago Edward T. Hall (1963, 1966) coined the term PROXEMICS and argued for the necessity of a systematic observational and recording technique. The importance of such a system has been substantiated by its multidisciplinary use in fields such as anthropology, speech communication, psychology, and sociology. During the past decade, the number of empirical studies on personal space behavior has mushroomed. Each of these hinges on the validity of the methodology for determining the distance between the interactants. If a methodology lacks sufficient validity or reliability, the results of the entire investigation are questionable.

The techniques for determining distance between two people can be classified into three general methodologies: measurement, estimation and projection. Willis (1966) and Horowitz (Horowitz 1965; Horowitz, et al. 1964) actually measured nose-to-nose distance in the presence of the subjects. Rosenfeld (1965) used a method of marking the bottom tips of chair legs with chalk. Forston and Larson (1968) took still photographs and interpolated personal space between the subjects from picture measurements of objects in the pictures of known length. Batchelor and Goethals (1972) assumed that the chairs remained stationary and that the subjects sat up straight; then, after the subjects had completed their task, the researcher measured the distance from the center of one chair to the center of another chair.

Regarding estimation techniques, several studies – Watson and Graves (1966), Baxter (1970), Aiello and Jones (1971), and Forston and Ericson

This research was supported by a Drake University Summer Research Stipend.

(1973) – have estimated spatial distances through the use of trained observers who were present during the experiment. Jones (1971) also used trained judges for estimating distances, but the judges made their determinations from slide pictures. Sommer (1961, 1962) and Albert and Dabbs (1970) employed a technique of calculating distances by placing chairs at various predetermined distances and having observers note the movement of furniture and different angles of posture.

Projective techniques, the third method of determining preferences of spatial relationships, were involved in several other studies. Little (1965), Guardo (1966), and Dosey and Meisels (1969) had subjects make placements of cardboard stick figures or of silhouette figures in relation to someone else. Horowitz (1965) and Pedersen (1971) both used forms where the subjects either drew pictures or drew circles indicating distance preference. Mehrabian (1968a and 1968b) developed a technique where a subject would react to an imaginary person in a variety of communication situations rather than to another person.

If one is in a position to make actual measurements of the distance between subjects, the question of validity of the measurement methodology is unimportant. Too many times, however, researchers find it necessary to determine personal space without the knowledge of the interactants so as not to influence or possibly contaminate the behavior of the interactants.

To date, none of the various techniques for calculating personal space has been evaluated in the literature. The primary purpose of this study was to test both the validity and the reliability of ten measurement and estimation techniques for determining distance (projective techniques will not be covered in this paper).[1] A secondary purpose was to help pin-point those methodologies for determining distances which were found to be the most accurate and reliable.

PROCEDURES

Thirty still photographs were initially taken of two interactants sitting in chairs at various distances, angles, and depths from one another. The actual nose-to-nose distances were measured by the researcher before the positions were changed for the next picture. This actual nose-to-nose measurement provided the researcher with known distances against which he could check the accuracy of the estimation and measurement techniques employed in previous studies. Slide pictures were also made from the still prints. Pictures 1 through 10 were used exclusively for training purposes

[1]   I believe the validity of projective techniques for determining personal space preferences is complex enough that they should be the subject of a separate study.

while Pictures 11 through 30 were used for checking the accuracy of the methods under investigation.

For the measurement technique, six conditions were investigated, using the process of interpolating personal space from picture measurements of objects of known length. The six measurement conditions consisted of three known reference objects using both prints and slides (projected on a wall). For the estimation technique, four conditions were used in comparing the accuracy of looking at a picture to estimate the nose-to-nose distance: both trained and untrained judges made estimations from prints or from slides.

MEASUREMENT TECHNIQUES

In performing the task for the accuracy of measurement techniques, three assistants were provided with a ruler with a sixty-unit-per-inch scale and with the actual distances of three natural reference objects included in each picture (the width of a door, the width of a small blackboard, and the length of a horizontal rung of a chair). The assistants were not told the actual nose-to-nose distances between the subjects in the pictures. Each assistant independently calculated the personal space from the twenty prints and twenty slides by an interpolation process; the assistant measured the picture distance of the reference object of known length and then calculated the unknown nose-to-nose distance.

The validity of personal space measurement techniques using printed photographs and slide photographs was examined with the t-test of means. Table 1 reports the accuracy and mean deviation of the measurement process using printed and slide photographs.

Table 1. Measurement technique: accuracy and mean deviation from actual distance using prints and slides

Reference objects	Prints		Slides	
	Mean deviation (Inches)	Accuracy (percent)	Mean deviation (inches)	Accuracy (percent)
Door	5.8	80.1	4.0	85.3
Chair	3.7	88.0	10.2	71.4
Blackboard	4.1	86.1	3.2	91.0
Combined	4.5	84.7	5.8	82.6

For the measurement technique using prints, the known length of the rung of a chair was slightly more accurate than that of the blackboard, but the difference in accuracy was not significantly different (t=0.42). The width of the door as a reference object was least accurate. The t-test of means revealed the following significant differences in accuracy: between the chair and the door as reference objects — P <.05 (t=1.79), and between the blackboard and the door — P=.10 (t=1.32).

Although the chair proved to be an excellent reference for prints, it was least accurate for slides. The blackboard and the door as known lengths were best for the interpolation process for slides. The mean difference between blackboard and chair data was significant at P <.025 (t=2.1), and the mean difference between the door and chair data was significant at P<.05 (t=1.88). The differences between prints and slides were statistically significant for the doors (.10>P> .05) and for the chairs (.05> P >.01); but not for the blackboards.

ESTIMATION TECHNIQUES

For the accuracy of the estimation techniques, untrained and trained judges were asked to estimate independently the nose-to-nose distance between two people from printed photographs and from slide pictures projected on a screen. The judges were never asked to estimate the distances from the same numbered picture for both the print and the slide. The untrained judges were randomly picked university students.

The training session for the trained judges involved the following. A pool of twenty university students was shown ten slides at thirty-second intervals. During the intervals, each student independently made his estimate of the personal space. For the first five slides, the pool was informed of the actual nose-to-nose distances after each picture was shown in order to help the potential judges to improve their performance. For the remaining five slides, the actual distances were not revealed. This researcher examined the estimates of the last five slides and chose the

Table 2. Estimation technique: accuracy and mean deviation from actual distance using prints and slides

Type of judge	Prints		Slides	
	Mean deviation (inches)	Accuracy (percent)	Mean deviation (inches)	Accuracy (percent)
Untrained	8.7	71.2	9.0	62.2
Best-trained	2.7	92.2	4.3	77.1

three individuals who came closest to guessing the actual nose-to-nose measurement to be the trained judges. Hence, although the entire pool would be qualified as trained judges, this study used only the best judges from a pool of trained judges.

The validity of the spatial distances as determined by estimation techniques using printed and slide pictures was investigated with the t-test of means. Table 2 describes the accuracy and mean deviation of the estimation process using printed and slide pictures.

The best-trained judges were clearly more accurate in their estimation of spatial distances both from prints and slides. The t-test of mean differences between trained and untrained judges revealed statistically significant differences as follows: prints at P < .001 (t=3.65) and slides at P = .025 (t=2.12).

DISCUSSION

For a comparison of the reliability and accuracy, Table 3 displays the rank order accuracy of the ten methods of determining personal distance from the most to the least accurate methods. Table 3 also shows the corresponding intermeasurement or interjudge reliability.

Table 3.   Rank order accuracy and reliability of various methods of determining personal space

Description of technique	Accuracy (percent)	Inter-agreement reliability (percent)
E/prints/BT judges	92.2	75.7
M/slides/blackboard	91.0	97.8
M/prints/chair	88.0	96.7
M/prints/blackboard	86.1	96.4
M/slides/door	85.3	95.6
M/prints/door	80.1	94.5
E/slides/BT judges	77.1	86.7
M/slides/chair	71.4	92.7
E/prints/UT judges	71.2	69.2
E/slides/UT judges	62.2	57.1

E = estimation, M = measurement, UT = untrained, BT = best-trained.

Although the use of the best-trained judges to estimate distances from prints (92.2 percent) was slightly more accurate than the measurement technique of using slides with the blackboard as a reference (91.0 percent), the 97.8 percent reliability among those calculating the measurements was substantially higher for the latter technique as compared with the 75.7 percent reliability among the best-trained judges.

The use of estimation techniques to estimate distances will probably be risky for those investigating spatial relationships. Unless the researcher is able to select the BEST from a pool of trained judges, he may reduce the validity of his study by employing a method of determining distances which is neither highly valid nor reliable. The measurement techniques with known reference objects of sufficient length which show clearly defined edges on slides or prints proved to be quite a satisfactory method.

The mean reliability for the six measurement techniques was 95.6 percent with a narrow range of only 5.1 percent, while the mean reliability for the four estimation techniques was 72.2 percent with a wide range of 29 percent. The agreement among the best of the trained judges (81.2 percent) was considerably better than the agreement among untrained judges (63.2 percent).

REFERENCES

AIELLO, JOHN R., STANLEY E. JONES
  1971   Field study of the proxemic behavior of young school children in three subcultural groups. *Journal of Personality and Social Psychology* 19: 351–356.
ALBERT, STUART, JAMES M. DABBS, JR.
  1970   Physical distance and persuasion. *Journal of Personality and Social Psychology* 15:265–270.
BATCHELOR, JAMES P., GEORGE R. GOETHALS
  1972   Spatial arrangements in freely formed groups. *Sociometry* 35:270–279.
BAXTER, JAMES C.
  1970   Interpersonal spacing in natural settings. *Sociometry* 33:444–456.
DOSEY, MICHAEL A., MURRAY MEISELS
  1969   Personal space and self-protection. *Journal of Personality and Social Psychology* 11:93–97.
FORSTON, ROBERT F., JON L. ERICSON
  1973   Black-white nonverbal communication: personal space analysis. *Iowa State Journal of Research* 48:1–6.
FORSTON, ROBERT F., CHARLES U. LARSON
  1968   The dynamics of space: an experimental study in proxemic behavior among Latin Americans and North Americans. *Journal of Communication* 18:109–116.
GUARDO, C. J.
  1966   "Self-concept and personal space in children." Unpublished doctoral dissertation, University of Denver. (Ann Arbor, Michigan: University Microfilms.)

HALL, EDWARD T.
1963 A system for the notation of proxemic behavior. *American Anthropologist* 65:1003–1026.
1966 *The hidden dimension*. Garden City, New York: Doubleday.

HOROWITZ, MARDI J.
1965 Human spatial behavior. *American Journal of Psychotherapy* 19:20–28.

HOROWITZ, MARDI J., D. F. DUFF, L. O. STRATTON
1964 Body-buffer zone. *Archives of General Psychiatry* 11:651–656.

JONES, STANLEY E.
1971 A comparative proxemics analysis of dyadic interaction in selected subcultures of New York City. *Journal of Social Psychology* 84:35–44.

LITTLE, KENNETH B.
1965 Personal space. *Journal of Experimental Social Psychology* 1:237–247.

MEHRABIAN, ALBERT
1968a Inference of attitudes from the posture, orientation, and distance of a communicator. *Journal of Consulting and Clinical Psychology* 32:296–308.
1968b Relationship of attitude to seated posture, orientation, and distance. *Journal of Personality and Social Psychology* 10:26–30.

PEDERSEN, DARHL M.
1971 "Some personality correlates of personal space and the effects of two treatments on personal space." Paper presented at the Child Development and Family Relationships Colloquium, Brigham Young University, April 30.

ROSENFELD, HOWARD M.
1965 Effect of an approval-seeking induction of interpersonal proximity. *Psychological Reports* 17:120–122.

SOMMER, ROBERT
1961 Leadership and group geography. *Sociometry* 24:99–110.
1962 The distance for comfortable conversation: a further study. *Sociometry* 25:111–116.

WATSON, O. MICHAEL, THEODORE D. GRAVES
1966 Quantitative research in proxemic behavior. *American Anthropologist* 68:971–985.

WILLIS, FRANK N., JR.
1966 Initial speaking distance a function of the speaker's relationship. *Psychonomic Science* 5:221–222.

A Photographic Method for the Recording and Evaluation of Cross-Cultural Proxemic Interaction Patterns

SHAWN E. SCHERER

Several field studies in the area of human ecology have been directed in recent years at the investigation of proxemic behavior patterns. The stimulus for much of this research has been E. T. Hall's speculations on intercultural conversation interaction distances, as outlined in his book, *The hidden dimension*. Specifically, Hall has noted that peoples of different cultures not only speak different languages but inhabit DIFFERENT SENSORY WORLDS (Hall 1966:2). As a result, normal everyday conversation distances differ among culture groups. This, Hall suggests, often creates uncomfortable situations when individuals of different cultures attempt to interact socially.

Attempts to evaluate Hall's contention have, as yet, met with little success. While some studies find wide differences in spatial behavior among culture groups (e.g. Aiello and Jones 1971; Watson and Graves 1966), others find only slight variations (Willis 1966) or none at all (Forston and Larson 1968). The failure to show consistent findings is likely due in part to the lack of sophisticated techniques for monitoring and evaluating proxemic interaction data. Past studies have relied almost entirely on eyeball techniques, often obtrusive in nature, for recording human interaction distances (Aiello and Jones 1971; Hall 1955), with very little attention being paid to the use of photographic recordings. Undoubtedly, one reason for the present paucity of photographic studies is the difficulty in obtaining good photographs of dyadic groupings in the

I am indebted to Oded J. Frenkel, Anthony N. Doob, and Abraham Ross for many helpful ideas which have been incorporated in the present technique. I am grateful to Oded J. Frenkel, Elaine J. Scherer, and Lynne R. Saltzman for their assistance during experimentation stages and in the preparation of this manuscript.

horizontal plane, free from obstructions by other persons in the immediate vicinity, and yet still remaining unobtrusive.

Another problem seems to be the inadequacy of present photogrammetric methods in determining physical distance between interacting members, which takes into account the subject's angle of orientation. Since orientation has been shown to be a salient variable in evaluating individual distance (Aiello and Jones 1971; Scherer and Schiff 1973), any appropriate observational technique must necessarily take angle of orientation into consideration.

Still another problem plaguing present proxemic behavior recording methods is the lack of stringent sets of criteria and uniform procedures for obtaining reliable data. Few studies, for instance, have attempted to ensure for randomization in the selection of subjects from their samples. The incongruity among past studies could well be due to this problem alone.

Because of existing inadequacies in proxemic recording and evaluation methods, I undertook to develop a methodology that would overcome those problems just mentioned. Three pilot studies allowed for extensive experimentation with an assortment of photographic recording and data scoring techniques. The photographic procedure that is outlined below was found to be the most precise and also the most reliable method tested. This method has subsequently been utilized, with considerable success, in two independent cross-subcultural studies of proxemic behavior of black and white primary schoolchildren observed in school playground settings (Scherer i.p.). For explanatory purposes, sections on data collection and acceptance criteria for negatives are described with reference to these recent investigations.

DATA COLLECTION

A tripod-mounted camera with a 300-millimeter telephoto lens was erected at a predetermined position in a park adjacent to the schoolyard. The location was distant enough from the play area to be relatively inconspicuous to the great majority of students.[1] Precautions were taken to ensure that only those children not aware of the observers would be included. This was accomplished by angling the camera so that the closest subjects that could be photographed were at least one hundred feet (thirty meters) away.

---

[1] Our studies have shown that only those subjects standing within twenty-five yards of the observation point appear to show any interest in the camera and observers.

Only dyads meeting the following criteria were selected. Subjects must (1) be relatively stationary; (2) be engaged in verbal interaction — i.e. at least one of the subjects must be observed to be moving his lips; and (3) have no physical objects or individuals obstructing their freedom of movement.

For data collection, one observer acted as photographer, the other as recorder. At the onset of a play period, the photographer began scanning the schoolyard with the camera from left to right. The recorder then called out the required dyad to scan for[2] (chosen from a prepared list of random orderings). When the photographer found a dyad (meeting the criteria outlined earlier) he stopped scanning and called out, "Now." This signaled the recorder to begin clocking a predetermined time interval, taken from a prepared list of random time periods covering from 0.5 to 3.0 seconds, in one-half-second intervals.[3] Once this period had elapsed, the recorder signaled the photographer by saying, "Now," at which time the photographer immediately clicked the camera shutter mechanism. The photographer then described the sex, approximate age, position in the yard (separated into three quadrants), and distance from the observation point. Filming proceeded in this fashion until the play period ended. During any data collection session only the recorder knew the random order of conditions[4] and the random time intervals.

If one uses the data collection procedure just described, there is no possibility for SYSTEMATIC bias to enter because human error is avoided at each stage of monitoring through both the utilization of a stringent randomization procedure and photographic recordings.

Acceptance Criteria for Negatives

Only those negatives that fulfilled the following criteria were included in the photogrammetric analysis:
1. no physical obstruction of movement evident;
2. clear silhouette of complete dyad, including all bodily parts;

---

[2] In studies referred to here, dyads were either black or white primary schoolchildren.
[3] These time intervals are determined prior to the data collection stage and will probably vary as a function of the age and culture of interactants. In the studies referred to, fifty independent observations of break-up time for black and white dyads indicated that mean break-up time was 1.8 seconds for blacks, 1.6 seconds for whites, with individual values ranging from 0.1 to 4.0 seconds. The actual range to be utilized should be determined with reference to the variance obtained.
[4] Conditions were either black or white dyadic groupings.

3. both feet, including toe and heel points of each interactant, in clear view;
4. relatively little apparent movement; and
5. both faces clearly shown.

PHOTOGRAMMETRY

A measure of the true separation, D_t, between two interactants can be obtained from a photographic image of the pair if exact distances to each member of the pair are known. In order for the observer to remain as unobtrusive as possible, and because interactants to be observed are generally spread over a fairly wide area, the determination of exact distances is considered to be undesirable and impractical. Instead, proxemic distance scores can be obtained by using the ratio D_t/H as a measure of proximity, where D_t is a measure of average separation between members of a dyad, and H is their average height on the photographic image. This ratio is independent of the average distance of the dyad from the camera. It is, however, not independent of the orientation of the dyad to the camera. A method for taking the orientation into account is described below. Note that the ratio D_t/H is an unbiased measure of any differences between members of any two culture groups, provided that members of one group are not markedly different in average height from the other. This assumption seems justified.[5]

The procedure for determining the ratio D_t/H is a follows. Using the thirty-five-millimeter frames of the (negative) film, the image of a pair is projected onto the bed of an enlarger, and curves and lines are carefully drawn. Figure 1 depicts one example. The curves T_1G_1 and T_2G_2, designated here as "skewer" lines, are drawn to represent imaginary curves in a vertical plane (or nearly vertical plane) which are centrally located within the body of each subject, extending from the tip of his head to a point between his feet. In drawing these curves, the positions of the arms need not be taken into account. In practice, it is found that there is little doubt as to where a skewer curve should be drawn, regardless of the orientation of a subject to the camera. The curve is localized by the tip of the head and the neck and is drawn just ventral to the spine and parallel to it through the trunk. It tends to come nearer the leg on which most of the weight of the subject is resting.

---

[5]   If we assumed the average height of members of one culture group to be greater even by two inches, this would only introduce a bias of about 5 percent into the ratio D_t/H.

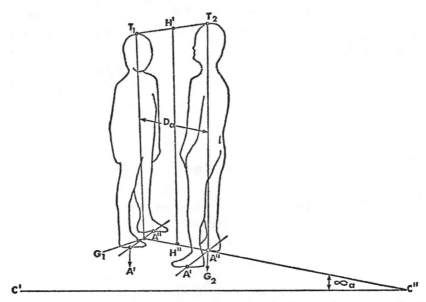

Figure 1. Geometrical parameters for determining the distance between a pair of subjects and their orientation to the camera

The points G_1 and G_2 are the intersections of the skewer curves with a line joining the midpoints (A' and A'') of the arches of the feet. G_1 and G_2 mark the intersections of the skewer curves with the ground. The angle α which the line G_1G_2 subtends from a horizontal line C'C'' gives the orientation of the pair of subjects with respect to the camera. D_a is the apparent average distance between the skewer curves, measured parallel to G_1G_2. When the two skewer curves are very nearly parallel, then D_a may be taken simply as the distance between them. Otherwise, D_a is calculated by dividing the area $T_1T_2G_2G_1$ by the average height of the subjects (H'H'').

The apparent separation D_a has to be corrected for the true angle of orientation α_t of the line C'C''. C'C'' is at right angles to the line of sight of the camera.[6]

The true separation D_t is given by D_a/Cosine α_t. The angle α_t can be determined approximately from the apparent angle α_a (as measured from the projected images such as that depicted in Figure 1) by the relation

---

[6]   This can be ensured by orienting the camera so that a vertical edge of its frame, as seen through the viewfinder, is parallel to a vertical line (e.g. the edge of an apartment building) in the field of view and remains in this orientation as the camera is swung from one side of the observational field to the other.

$$\tan \alpha_t = \frac{R_d}{R_h} \tan \alpha_a$$

where R_d is the approximate distance (to the nearest fifty feet) from the camera to the subjects and R_h is the height of the camera above the ground. R_h should be fixed and not altered throughout the data collection stage. R_d is free to vary and should be estimated for each photographic shot by reference to objects of known distances in the field of view.

COMMENTS

Although reference has been made to dyadic groupings only, this observational and photogrammetric procedure can be used to study proxemic behavior patterns of groups of any reasonable size, provided that clear images can be obtained of all of the interactants of interest. For researchers intent on studying more diverse patterns of human spatial behavior, the technique can also easily be extended to the use of moving pictures. However, both eight- and sixteen-millimeter films require a considerably greater initial expenditure for both film and developing than does print film.

In addition to the habitual problem of human error discussed earlier, the present method also overcomes those difficulties inherent to observational rating techniques commonly used. Because large numbers of individuals are to be observed in most proxemic investigations, experimenters in the past have been forced to make use of many different observers in each setting, and thus outcomes have been subject to the alternative explanation of differential observation styles. This, in turn, requires experimenters to run extensive reliability checks, creating unnecessary additional time and financial expense.

One common problem plaguing past studies seems to be the issue of exactly when the observer should make his distance judgment. Most investigators at present direct their observers to make their estimates at the first instant in time when they can "ascertain that at least one of the interactants is verbalizing to the other" (Aiello and Jones 1971:353). Despite such explicit instructions, it is nevertheless still possible that different observers tend to record their judgments at different temporal stages (i.e. one observer may wait considerably longer to confirm that two subjects are communicating), and that proxemic behavior is a function of the temporal stage of the conversation. These problems are also overcome by using the present technique.

REFERENCES

AIELLO, JOHN R., STANLEY E. JONES
  1971 Field study of the proxemic behavior of young school children in three subcultural groups. *Journal of Personality and Social Psychology* 19:351–356.

FORSTON, ROBERT F., CHARLES U. LARSON
  1968 The dynamics of space. *Journal of Communication* 18:109–116.

HALL, EDWARD T.
  1955 The anthropology of manners. *Scientific American* 162:85–90.
  1966 *The hidden dimension.* Garden City, New York: Doubleday.

SCHERER, SHAWN E.
  i.p. Proxemic behavior of primary school children as a function of their socioeconomic class and subculture. *Journal of Personality and Social Psychology.*

SCHERER, SHAWN E., MYRA R. SCHIFF
  1973 Perceived intimacy, physical distance and eye contact. *Perceptual and Motor Skills* 36:835–841.

WATSON, O. MICHAEL, THEODORE D. GRAVES
  1966 Quantitative research in proxemic behavior. *American Anthropologist* 68:971–985.

WILLIS, FRANK N., JR.
  1966 Initial speaking distance as a function of the speakers' relationship. *Psychonomic Science* 5:221–222.

Linguistic and Kinesic Correlates in Code Switching

WALBURGA VON RAFFLER ENGEL

Linguists are gradually returning to join anthropologists and psychologists in the common attempt to analyze the communicative behavior of man.

My research follows within the traditional lines of Boas and Sapir on the relationship between language and culture, both as a social phenomenon and how this relationship affects man's image of himself and his view of the world.

Because of the scarcity of funds my surveys are limited to a small number of subjects, of both sexes, children and adults.

The focus of the research is on minority-majority interaction, minority being understood in respect to the dominant culture or language. The minority group may or may not be numerically inferior. Thus in Montreal, for example, the status of French as a minority language is rapidly passing to that of a majority language due to changes in political power and attitudes. In Montreal the majority of the population has always spoken French and no drastic change has occurred to alter that pattern during the last decades.

The relationship of language and culture is based on a variety of factors and their multiple interactions. The only thing we know for sure is that this relationship is in no way a one-to-one correspondence. Co-occurrence obtains in many instances but a matching relationship seems to result only from cumulative effects. My work in language acquisition leads me to believe that language and culture are two distinct aspects of the psychological and the sociological makeup of man and his behavior. There is a reciprocal influence between language and culture.

The original issue focused on by Boas comprised language, culture, and race. The present-day concept of ethnicity would add a fourth dimension. To investigate the relationship between language, culture, ethnicity, and race, I am in the process of conducting a survey among French-Canadians, but for the moment I have to limit my discussion to language and culture. My conclusions will be adjusted when the new data are in and a fuller picture emerges.

I have tried to approach the relationship of language and culture with some empirical research. The results point to the separation of language and culture and to some aspects of language behavior being more influenced by culture than others. The impact of language on culture, which loomed large in some previous research of mine, in these instances was minimal.

I have chosen the conversational mode. Among linguists it is more common to study monologues. The dialogue is infinitely more frequent in natural language and should provide us with some insight on what language is and how it relates to culture.

Before the speech act can be analyzed, several specific instances of the latter must be described with full coverage of all the factors that go into it, inclusive of the linguistic aspects but not exclusive of any (or all) others.

Language can certainly be analyzed as a self contained system. Such an analysis, however, does not explain the speech act. To understand the latter, one cannot isolate the verbal aspect from the situation and the context in which the language was produced (Gumperz and Hymes 1964). The situation is frequently accidental while the context is usually purposive.

In our final analysis, the major difficulty consists in correlating the linguistic and the kinesic factors and we have as yet no secure guidelines for accomplishing this. Before we can extrapolate the universals of human communicative behavior, it seems to me that we should view each speech act within the culture, the social system, the situational and contextual setting, the personalities (age, sex, and other), and the interpersonal relationship in which it happens.

It does not seem to me that we are yet ready for a comprehensive theory to be tested against further occurrences. We are probably still largely in the stage of data collecting, if not of pilot studies.

In several sub-areas of the speech act we already have some workable theories and it may not be too long before we will be able to formulate an all-inclusive theory. By theory I mean a loose and open-ended theory, essentially a working hypothesis that is constantly checked against the new data and improved as work progresses all the while the heuristics are being refined.

In the speech act taken as a whole, as happens in the meaning of the sentence compared to the words that make up a sentence, the total of all the features which make up the communicative event does not equal their sum. The totality of its features modifies each speech act and adds to it the multiple relationships of the subfeatures among themselves. The subfeatures can act as single entities and also as entities formed by certain groupings of the latter.

These relationships are extremely complex. Just as social dialects differ in the developmental sequence of language acquisition and the subsequent frequency of certain linguistic patterns (von Raffler Engel 1964; Parisi, et al. 1971), it is likely that differences in the system of kinesics influence the development and frequency of occurrence of certain gestures. It is not impossible that those differences have implications for the process of verbalization.

Besides the more observable overt features mentioned earlier in this paper, a description of the speech act must report the meaning of its message. As a firm believer in a complicated, but nevertheless workable, relationship of co-occurrence between form and meaning, I am convinced that different surface structures correspond to different thought processes (von Raffler Engel 1972a). It is likely that the generative concept of "competence" will eventually turn out to be a myth like the Freudian symptom substitution (Baer 1971).

In comparing the communicative behavior of groups of different languages and/or cultures, the researcher can take the behavior of one group as the basic one, either because he assumes that this is standard for the language or culture in question or because he has decided upon certain universals. Rather than matching the other group against the group which he has selected as standard or measuring it against some universal concept of speech behavior, a researcher could consider both groups on an equal footing and proceed by abstracting some common concept from the behavior of the two groups.

I attempted this latter approach in an analysis prepared with the cooperation of a student of mine (von Raffler Engel and Sigelman 1971). We analyzed a series of freely told stories which I had previously collected from black and white fourth graders. Among others, we isolated the concept of "bringing a character to life." The white children achieved this goal by giving each character a personal name while the black children let their characters speak in dialogue. In the same vein, we looked for the presence or absence of a formal beginning of each story. Seventy-six percent of the black children and 42 percent of the white children started their stories with "Once upon a time." We then refined our analysis and found that a full 75 percent of the white children used the word "once" in some way or another in their introductory remarks. The difference between black and white children with respect to story beginnings was therefore minimal.

The two studies in verbal and kinetic code switching on which I am reporting in this paper followed these same lines of evaluation. Essentially, my procedure is based on an adaptation of Hockett's concept of deep structure (Hockett 1958).

It is difficult to formulate Hockett's concept with great precision. For the time being, such formalization is pointless as our knowledge of deep structure in language is still limited. Our knowledge of deep structure in kinesics is even less extensive. The relationship between language and kinesics, in a certain sense, has been investigated more on the level of structural relationship than on the surface level.

When we know so little about the verbal and kinetic interaction within one language and one culture, it may appear premature to start working on bilingual and bidialectal situations. On the other hand, the researcher can readily identify and isolate the variable of language or dialect change. It is sometimes less easy to document the moment of switching within some of the other variables, such as, for example, would be change of subject domain.

The basic problems in language or dialect switching may tentatively be listed as follows:
1.   Does code switching in the language necessarily accompany kinesic code switching, and *vice versa*?
2.   Is kinesic code switching synchronous, or are there delays? If so, which modality precedes the other?
3.   Are (1) and (2) universal or are there linguistic and cultural differences? If so, are these differences inherent in the system of the kinesics or of the language? Are these differences due to cultural, social, attitudinal, or interpersonal factors?
4.   How do kinetic interferences correlate with linguistic interferences?
5.   Can kinetic and linguistic interferences be traced to the same causes?
6.   How does the development of language and kinesics correlate? Leaving second language acquisition completely out of the picture, are there differences between the dominant and the secondary language and/or culture in bilinguals?

7. Is it possible to have dominance in one linguistic code and at the same time in the kinetic code that usually belongs to the secondary language?

8. Is it possible to have linguistic interference without kinetic interference, or *vice versa*?

9. Are there kinetic pidgins that accompany full languages, or *vice versa*? Under such conditions, will the pidgins creolize or revert to the full system that is generally associated with the accompanying language or kinesics, as the case may be?

10. Is the subject and person division of linguistic bilingualism equally valid for kinetic bilingualism? In any case, does the same division apply to both language and gesture within the individual?

11. Are there societal kinetic systems comparable to the well documented societal bilingual languages?

12. In a bilingual community, can one group keep its language and its kinesics, while the other group keeps its language but has fully adopted the other kinetic system?

I surveyed two situations. One was bidialectal, involving black and white speakers of American English (von Raffler Engel 1972b, 1972c). The other was bilingual (von Raffler Engel 1972d, 1972e).

The bidialectal survey was carried out in a welfare office of the central South. Videotape equipment was installed in the room where the social worker interviews her clients as well as in the adjacent waiting room.

After several days of recording without the subjects being aware of it, I evaluated the resulting videotapes and prepared the log. To start the analysis, I isolated one welfare client whose picture and voice came through clearly in both interview and waiting rooms. I then had photographic prints made from selected frames of the video to match the corresponding sections of the audio tape. The latter were transferred to a tape recorder and from there transcribed on strips of paper to be attached to each photograph.

The examination of the photographs with their matching discourse transcripts, comparing the facial expression and the speech patterns of the subjects on videotape in the formal interview situation and in the unstructured waiting room setting, revealed the following:

1.a. In the waiting room, speech tempo in both substandard English and black English was faster (more syllables per second) and the phonation ratio was lower (longer pauses between utterances). The facial expression was more varied and proxemics was closer.

b. During the interview, speech tempo was slower and phonation ratio higher. This greater regularity of verbal expression was accompanied by a more composed face.

2.a.   When changing register, the adult black subjects appeared first to adjust their total composure and speak only after that. This was essentially the same for adult whites except that their paralinguistic behavior, as well as their dialect, did not differ so extensively with change of communicative situation.

As I had expected from my previous informal observations of the lower classes in the South, the greatest divergence between blacks and whites was manifest in the unstructured situation.

b.   Of considerable sociolinguistic interest is the fact that the younger generation among black adults — and among these the females in particular — showed much less kinetic variation in code-switching than older blacks.

The bilingual situation involved the comparison of the communicative behavior of Francophone and Anglophone children in the first two elementary grades at the demonstration school of the University of Ottawa Child Study Center.

A videotape recording device was installed in the testing room, a small spot reserved for us in each school. The microphone was firmly taped to the table around which the children were to be seated because children tend to play with such devices. Two small chairs were placed on each side of the table facing each other diagonally for best channeling their voices into the speaker. The television camera and earphones for silent audio monitoring were placed in an adjacent spot, out of the children's sight.

I then entered the testing room with one child to tell him a story he was to retell to another child with whom he was also to comment on the story. This procedure was adopted because, without a firm seating arrangement and a definite commitment to talk about a pre-established subject matter, children of grade school age will not necessarily talk to each other. They play, fight, or inspect the room, moving all around. If the tester asks the children to speak without structuring their theme, they may stare at each other or burst out in giggles, not knowing what to say.

I narrated an identical story to all children, in French and English respectively. Upon completion of the story, I left the room. The child to whom the story was to be retold entered the room to take my chair. The same procedure was repeated for each new set of children. I alternated the combination of children by Francophone-to-Anglophone and Anglophone-to-Francophone groupings.

The evaluation of the videotapes showed that:

1.a.   French children signal their readiness for a friendly chat by leaning forward toward each other, while English children convey the same message by leaning back on the chair and extending their feet in a relaxed manner.

b.   Francophone children underscore what they say with paralinguistic (Bolinger 1968) gestures on the word level. They do this particularly with qualifiers, adjectives, and adverbs.

Anglophone children act out whole situations. They employ what could be termed discourse paralinguistics.

The difference in paralinguistic behavior between the two ethnic groups is striking; the gestures of Francophones are strictly language-related while Anglophone children act out a theme which they also describe verbally at the same time. Their gestures are discourse-related rather than word related.

2.a.   When Francophone children speak either French or English to Anglophones they tend to modify their customary kinesics. They lean forward, but only slightly, and they make far less frequent use of para-linguistic gestures. When they do employ these gestures, they expand their hands less vividly.

b.   When Anglophone children speak English to Francophones, their kinesics do not differ from when they speak to Anglophones.

When speaking French either to another Anglophone — as would be the case in practicing for their school work — or to a Francophone, these children make an effort at copying some kinetic features of the Francophone population. The features copied appear at random but are consistently exaggerated.

I have not observed this behavior in adult Anglophones. The latter generally keep their kinesics identical whether they are speaking French or English. This is more likely due to a difference in the social attitude of the present generation than to a difference inherent in the two age groups.

3.a.   To conclude, bilingual Canadian children seem to have one full kinetic system and two languages. But the two ethnic groups differ radically.

b.   In code switching, the Anglophone children maintain their own customary kinetic system, but sometimes intersperse it with exaggerated Francophone kinesics. Over-correctness is particularly evident when the children are not completely fluent in the French language.

The Francophone children do not correlate kinesics with language code switching. They correlate kinesics with ethnic group switching.

When speaking either French or English with an Anglophone, they will employ a reduced version of their own customary kinesics. When speaking English to Francophones (this instance is more frequent than outsiders would presume), they seem more relaxed when not altering their native kinesics. My data are only scanty and this issue is still in a working stage.

The sociolinguistic implications of the different cuts of relationship between language and culture among Canada's two ethnic groups are profound and merit further investigation.

In the two studies on which I have briefly reported above, it is apparent that "units of communication" (von Raffler Engel 1972b) involving both speech and body motion can be clearly isolated and that the duration of each such unit exceeds that of the spoken message. Thus, the spoken message forms the inner core of the communication unit. Code switching involves both language and kinesics; but the two modalities are not treated in parallel fashion.

The black minority in the United States mastered two languages and two kinetic systems. The Francophone population in Canada has two languages and two types of their own kinesics, the full system and a reduced version of the same.

In both instances, the majority essentially employs only one form of kinesics. Condon (1964) and Kendon (1972) have observed that an interactional synchrony obtains in the rhythm of speech and body movements between two partners in conversation. From the behavior of the subjects it appears that the minority generally adjusts to the rhythm of the majority when interlocutory contact is established.

Kinesics seems more closely associated with culture than with language. This was most clearly evidenced by motion pictures taken by a student of mine in an independent project designed by her to supplement the videotapes in the black and white comparison (French 1973). The work shows that in an experimental situation, children speaking black English demonstrate a somewhat more highly coded system of kinesic expression. Their kinesic messages were decoded more successfully by other children speaking black English, bidialectical black undergraduates and adults, and adult and undergraduate standard English speakers than were messages encoded by standard English speakers of the same age. A complete switch of the two modalities of language and kinesics appears indicative of extreme caution by the minority.

My studies support the division of gestures proposed by Condon (1964) into speech-preparatory and speech-accompanying movements. They also support Kendon (1972) who suggests that these speech-preparatory movements serve to regulate the interchange between interlocutors and that these speech-preparatory movements differ according to the function of the following speech unit in relation to the others in the discourse. Speech-preparatory positioning varied markedly in in-group and out-group situations. In conclusion, my observation of covert videotaping gave evidence for kinesic use in dialect speakers. A change in kinetic style appeared as an integral part of register switching in response to change in social situation. Such changes in register occurred only after the shift in kinesic behaviors. Culture preceded language.

What I have so far reported is incomplete, but hopefully suggests the need for further research in the triple relationship of language, kinesics, and culture. In the realm of culture certain aspects of behavior are due to ethnic differences while others are due to social stratification. The combination of these two forces is not uniform and varies greatly depending on the country in which they occur. In addition, all age groups do not react in the same manner, and men and women may be affected in different ways. More research is needed to explore the ways in which complexities of culture patterns interact with various patterns of language and nonverbal behavior.

REFERENCES

BAER, DONALD M.
    1971   Let's take another look at punishment. *Psychology Today* (October): 34.
BOLINGER, DWIGHT D.
    1968   *Aspects of language.* New York: Harcourt, Brace and World.
CONDON, W. S.
    1964   "Process in communication." Unpublished manuscript, Western Psychiatric Institute and Clinic, Pittsburgh, Pennsylvania.
FRENCH, PATRICE L.
    1973   "White bias in black language studies." Paper presented at the ninth meeting of the Southeastern Conference on Linguistics, Charlotte, West Virginia.
GUMPERZ, JOHN J.
    1971   *Language in social groups.* Essays selected by Anwar S. Dil. Stanford: Stanford University Press.
GUMPERZ, JOHN J., DELL HYMES, *editors*
    1964   The ethnography of communication. *American Anthropologist* 66: 137–153.
HOCKETT, CHARLES F.
    1958   *A course in modern linguistics.* New York: Macmillan.

KENDON, ADAM
1972   "Some relationships between body motion and communication," in *Studies in dyadic communication*. Edited by F. Seigman, 177–210. Elmsford, New York: Pergamon Press.

PARISI, DOMENICO, PAOLA BARBERI, VALERIA SAVONA PIZZINO
1971   *Ruolo della madre nello sviluppo cognitivo del bambino; Differenze di classe sociale*. Rome, Italy: Consiglo Nazionale delle Ricorche, Istituto di Psicologia.

VON RAFFLER ENGEL, WALBURGA
1964   *Il prelinguaggio infantile*. Brescia, Paideia.
1972a Some phono-stylistic features of black English. *Phonetica* 25(1):53–64.
1972b "Language in context: situationally conditioned style change in black speakers," in *Proceedings of the Eleventh International Congress of Linguists, University of Bologna*.
1972c "Sociolinguistic research techniques: some new developments," in *Readings in applied educational sociolinguistics*. Edited by Glen Gilbert. (Selected papers from the Workshop on Research Problems in Areal Linguistics, University of Texas at El Paso.)
1972d *Linguistique appliquée et apprentissage des langues: la place de la psychologie*. Proceedings of the Troisième Colloque Canadien de Linguistique Appliquée. University of Quebec, Montreal.
1972e "The use of videotape in dialectology." Paper presented at the International Conference on Methods in Dialectology, University of Prince-Edward-Island.

VON RAFFLER ENGEL, WALBURGA, CAROL K. SIGELMAN
1971   Rhythm, narration, description in the speech of black and white school children. *Language Sciences* 18:9–14.

Towards an Operational Definition of Self-Awareness

GORDON G. GALLUP, JR.

The purpose of this paper is two-fold. First an attempt will be made to review the literature on the psychological properties of mirrors as determined by research on a variety of species, and then to show how such surfaces may provide a means by which an objective assessment of self-awareness can be accomplished.

Since most organisms rarely look at sources of direct light, for perceptual purposes most light can be characterized as reflected light. Mirrors can be distinguished from ordinary reflecting surfaces by the fact that they reflect almost as much light as they receive. Moreover depending on their surface characteristics, mirrors can provide fairly accurate or wildly distorted visual reproductions of other reflecting surfaces.

While there are a few naturally occurring mirrors, such as the surface of calm water under conditions of appropriate incident light, for most organisms it is reasonable to assume that this is an atypical or at least infrequent type of reflected light. However, with the advent of fabricated mirrors, this has become a common visual experience for man. Written records show that men have been contriving mirror-like surfaces for purposes of self-inspection for well over 3,000 years (Swallow 1937). The ancient Chinese, who were the first to use artificial mirrors, believed that supernatural powers emanated from mirrors and they were used to diagnose and even treat many physical ailments and diseases. Currently one still finds much of the modern literature laced with subtle, recurring, and sometimes superstitious references to the mystical properties of mirrors.

In recent times mirrors have had many applications in the behavioral sciences, ranging from such things as learning to cope with reversed visual cues in mirror drawing tasks, to the use of the one-way or half-silvered mirror as a device for obscuring the observer in clinical and social experimentation, and they continue to be used in a variety of settings. The principal concern of this study will be with what is called mirror-image stimulation (MIS), which refers specifically to situations in which an organism, human or otherwise, is confronted with its own reflection in a mirror.

SOCIAL STIMULUS PROPERTIES

Since much of the earlier work on the psychological properties of mirrors has been reviewed elsewhere (Gallup 1968), only a brief overview will be presented here.

In front of a mirror an observer is in the rather peculiar position of being able to modify and control certain aspects of his visual environment without coming into direct physical contact with it; i.e. manipulating the reflected image of one's self in the mirror. Since the behavior of an animal can, and frequently does, serve as a source of stimulation for the responses of another, this ability to effect changes at a distance is true of many types of social behavior and can be thought of as one of its distinguishing characteristics.

Indeed, for many animals with adequate visual sensitivity MIS does seem to function in the capacity of a social stimulus, despite the fact that the reflection only mimics the behavior of the observer. Many organisms, when confronted with their own reflection in a mirror for the first time, respond as if in the presence of another animal of the same species, and mirrors have been used to simulate a variety of social situations in animal research (e.g. Simpson 1968; Yerkes and Yerkes 1929). For example, aggressive displays are readily obtained using MIS with fish (Lissman 1932), birds (Ritter and Benson 1934), sea lions (Schusterman, Gentry, and Schmook 1966), and primates (Schmidt 1878).

There is even a report that chaffinches and hedge sparrows will occasionally fight with their reflected images in stationary automobile hubcaps, sometimes to the point of physical exhaustion (Smythe 1962). Other evidence that the image is initially interpreted as another organism comes from the finding that isolated pigeons will not normally lay eggs unless given the opportunity to see other pigeons or, as the previous example might suggest, view their own reflection in a mirror (Matthews 1939). Lott and Brody (1966) observed a similar effect of MIS on ovulation in ring doves.

A well-established finding in social psychology is that organisms behave differently in the presence of other organisms than they do in isolation. An example of such an effect is social facilitation, which refers to a behavioral enhancement due to the mere presence of others. For instance, it is known that chickens will eat appreciably more food in the presence of other chickens than they will in isolation. As evidence for the idea that a mirror may carry the same psychological significance as another organism, this same enhancement effect has been obtained on the feeding behavior of chicks by substituting a mirror for the presence of a companion (Tolman 1965). Exposure to mirrors even causes the adult males of certain strains of squirrel monkeys to show pronounced penile erections (MacLean 1964), which might appear to be a case of extreme narcissism, but is not, because this is a typical aggressive gesture to the presence of another male.

As further support for the proposition that the reflection is initially interpreted as representing another individual, many animals, including human infants (e.g. Dixon 1957), frequently try to look behind mirrors when presented with a reflection of themselves.

In summary, many responses to mirrors could be characterized as other-directed behaviors since the subject acts as if it were viewing another animal. In all instances of other-directed responsiveness the reflection operates as the referent for, or object of, the behavior. In view of their profound social stimulus properties mirrors are ideally suited as a laboratory technique for studying visually induced and visually guided social responses because they eliminate the presence of confounding cues in other modalities. To study the degree to which social activities are solely dependent on visual cues would otherwise require cumbersome and elaborate controls. On the other hand, human behavior in the presence of mirrors is typically self-directed in the sense that the self becomes the referent, and the reflection is used to respond to or inspect personal features. Humans, unlike many animals, seem capable of realizing the dualism implicit in a mirror surface and show the ability to identify and recognize correctly their own reflections.

AN UNFAMILIAR OTHER

In addition to its social stimulus properties, for an inexperienced organism MIS ought to also simulate the presence of a new or unfamiliar companion. That is, when an animal views itself in a mirror for the first time it should be confronting the image of an animal it has never seen before, and one would therefore expect to find responses typical of those emitted in the presence of a stranger. In support of this expectation consider the case of the pigtailed macaque (*Macaca nemestrina*). Anyone familiar with adult male pigtailed monkeys knows that they show a distinctive social gesture during courtship or in the presence of another unfamiliar male which consists of crouching and protruding the lips while retracting the scalp. By presenting a caged pigtailed monkey with a small pocket mirror you can readily elicit immediate and intense gesturing, whereas responsiveness in a well-established colony typically occurs at a rather low and infrequent level.

The behavior of domestic chickens (*Gallus gallus*) provides another good illustration of the fact that the mirror image is perceived as not only another animal, but an unfamiliar one. Domestic fowl are notorious for establishing stable dominance hierarchies or peck orders. The initial formation of the hierarchy and attainment of status positions within the flock is based on overt aggression, but once complete, individual rank is maintained largely through threat postures and appeasement signals. On the other hand, presenting a dominant or alpha chicken from a well-established flock with a mirror elicits considerable hostility accompanied by attempts to attack the reflection, whereas aggression in the original group is minimal. Thus, when confronted with a mirror the chicken appears to make an attempt to establish status lines with this "new" bird.

MOTIVATIONAL PROPERTIES OF MIRRORS

Another well-established characteristic of MIS is that it carries incentive value for many animals. One of the most frequent demonstrations of this effect has been to show that brief access to the mirror will serve as a reward for learning to make new responses which are instrumental in the production of such stimulation. Reward or reinforcing-like effects of MIS have been reported in Siamese fighting fish (Thompson 1963), paradise fish (Melvin and Anson 1970), fighting cocks (Thompson 1964), squirrel monkeys (MacLean 1964), pigtailed monkeys (Gallup 1966), and rhesus monkeys (Gallup and McClure 1971).

Figure 1, for instance, depicts data gathered (Gallup, Montevecchi, and Swanson 1972) on baby chicks which were required individually to run down a narrow six-foot runway in order to obtain thirty seconds of exposure to themselves in a small mirror. As shown in Figure 1, the birds receiving brief access to their reflection were running about four times faster by the sixth trial than control chicks not receiving the mirror reward. This indicates that MIS can be a potent visual incentive for young chicks.

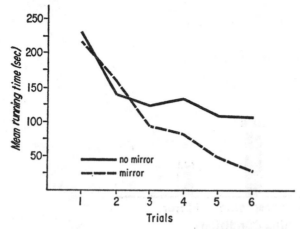

Figure 1. Mean running time in a straight alley for chicks receiving either thirty seconds of MIS in the goal box or no mirror exposure as a function of trials (Gallup, Montevecchi, and Swanson 1972)

SUPERNORMAL STIMULUS EFFECTS

Not only will animals learn to make novel responses to seeing themselves in a mirror, but there is recent evidence that a mirror may be more effective than a live companion for eliciting and sustaining certain classes of motivated behavior. In other words, in some species MIS seems to be what the ethologists call a SUPERNORMAL STIMULUS, or a contrived stimulus situation which is more effective than the natural stimulus for eliciting a particular pattern of behavior.

As an illustration of the possible supernormal stimulus properties of MIS, Baenninger, Bergman, and Baenninger (1969), using male Siamese fighting fish, found that a mirror was more effective than visual access to another live male for eliciting the elaborate aggressive display characteristic of this species. Similarly, adolescent chickens show aggressive behavior to their own reflection at rates that are four to five times higher than they are to other, like-sexed, unfamiliar chickens (Gallup, Montevecchi, and Swanson 1972). In much younger three-week-old chicks, which are momentarily separated from their brooder mates, MIS is better than a live companion for reducing distress vocalizations (see Figure 2).

The tendency for mirrors to elicit exaggerated social responses may also extend to certain species of primates. In an unpublished study (by M. K. McClure and myself) using six adult male patas monkeys (*Erythrocebus patas*), which show a peculiar aggressive gesture consisting of what appears to be a deceptively harmless yawn, a higher inci-

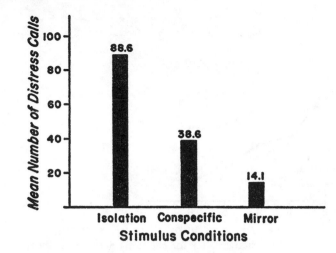

Figure 2.   Mean number of distress calls as a function of the conditions in effect during a three-minute period of separation from brooder mates (Gallup, Montevecchi, and Swanson 1972)

dence of threats directed to a mirror was found as compared to threats toward another unfamiliar male, and yawning reactions to the mirror did not habituate nearly as fast over a five-day period as they did to the other male.

PREFERENCE FOR MIRRORS

Related to the notion of supernormal stimulation is an increasing number of reports which show that when given a choice between viewing their own reflection in a mirror or looking at another conspecific, some animals seem to prefer MIS in the sense that they spend more time in association with the reflection. Baenninger (1966), for example, found that when given a continuous choice between MIS and visual access to another male, Siamese fighting fish spent up to three times more time orienting in front of their own image.

More recently, Gallup and Hess (1971) found a similar effect of MIS in goldfish (*Carassius auratus*). Using ten goldfish in an underwater alley, provided with a continuous choice between viewing a mirror or another conspecific behind plexiglas, a significant preference for MIS was obtained. Figure 3 shows that much like Siamese fighting fish the goldfish spent about three times more time in association with the reflection. Recently, Ternes, Jemail, and Laborde (1972) report finding that mirrors produce a more potent social facilitation effect on the extinction performance of goldfish than does the presence of a live companion.

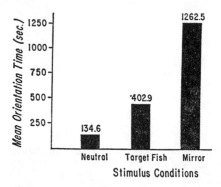

Figure 3. Time spent in the vicinity of the three different stimulus conditions averaged over three ten-minute recording sessions (Gallup and Hess 1971)

Using birds, Gallup and Capper (1970) found evidence of a preference for mirrors in weaver finches (*Passer domesticus domesticus*) and domestic parakeets (*Melopsittacus undulatus*). The birds were tested in a square plywood box containing four small perches, one on each wall. Each perch was associated with a different visual incentive: on one wall hanging immediately in front of the perch was a mirror, in front of the opposite perch was a comparably dimensioned window through which the bird could view a like-sexed conspecific contained in a small wire cage, and the remaining two perches provided access to food and water or a blank piece of cardboard attached to the wall. Each perch was designed so that the weight of a small bird would activate a switch and start an electric clock, thereby providing an estimate of the amount of

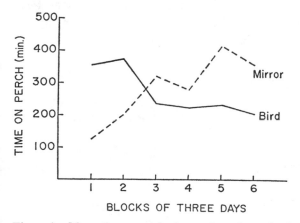

Figure 4. Mean time spent in front of a mirror (broken line) and in front of a target bird (solid line) by two adult finches as a function of blocks of three days (Gallup and Capper 1970)

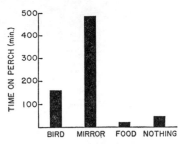

Figure 5.   Mean times spent in front of four stimulus conditions by adult parakeets averaged over five days (Gallup and Capper 1970)

time a bird spent in association with the different stimuli.

Starting with two adult male finches, each bird was left alone in the box for eighteen consecutive days. Recording was carried out during daylight hours for approximately twelve and one-half hours each day, and to obviate the possible influence of extra-apparatus cues the test box was rotated ninety degrees every other day. Figure 4 shows the average time spent by both birds on the mirror perch and the perch which provided visual access to another finch as a function of days. Although there was an initial preference for the other bird, after the ninth day of testing both subjects were spending significantly more time in association with their own reflections.

As a check on the generality of these findings, two female and three male parakeets were tested sequentially in the same apparatus for five days each. Figure 5 shows the results for the parakeets averaged over days, and reveals a highly reliable preference for the mirror perch. Figure 6 depicts the average amount of time spent per day by all birds on the two perches, providing social stimulation over the five-day test period. In concert with the finch findings, it is interesting to note that

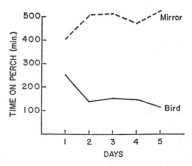

Figure 6.   Mean time spent in front of a mirror (broken line) and in front of a target bird (solid line) by parakeets as a function of days (Gallup and Capper 1970)

the mirror preference potentiates over days, with birds initially spending about one and one-half times more time in the mirror perch and four and one-half times more time by the fifth day. On the sixth day, as a control for possible perch or position preferences related to extraneous intrabox cues, the mirror was transferred to the perch previously associated with cardboard and remained in that position for an additional three days. In spite of the change, all subjects still preferred the mirror and spent most of their time on the new perch.

Although it appeared that a clear demonstration of a mirror preference in birds had been achieved, the testing situation might have been confounded. Since the target animal was confined in a cage the preference could simply have been based on the greater attractive potential of a noncaged companion. So finally, as an additional control procedure, small metal bars were placed across the surface of the mirror in a pattern similar to that used in the construction of the target bird cage. Then, in an attempt to assess preferences for the "caged" image, two additional parakeets were tested for three days with no bars, followed by two days with bars. The introduction of bars over the mirror surface produced virtually no effect on perch time, with both birds still spending four times more time in front of the mirror.

Unlike finches and parakeets, in domestic chickens and turkeys a preference for mirrors may be dependent on early social experiences. Schulman and Anderson (1972) found that group-reared fowl preferred orienting toward other conspecifics, while those raised in the presence of a mirror preferred mirror-image stimulation. On the other hand, chicks and turkeys raised in social isolation showed no consistent preference for either mirrors or conspecifics. One interpretive problem with the Schulman and Anderson study, however, was that the testing situation required subjects to choose between seeing their own image versus looking at TWO conspecifics behind glass. Due to the unequal levels of social stimulation associated with the visual alternatives, an equally tenable interpretation of their findings might be that the rearing conditions simply influenced a preference for viewing multiple companions, and the data may not, therefore, reflect on the attractive potential of a mirror.

More recently, in an attempt to determine whether primates might show a preference for mirrors, Gallup and McClure (1971) conducted a study using differentially reared rhesus monkeys (*Macaca mulatta*). The apparatus consisted of two cages mounted end to end. One cage was designated the experimental cage and the other the target cage. Both ends of the experimental cage were fitted with plywood partitions, and built into each partition was a guillotine door. A nylon rope was attached to each door and was threaded through a series of pulleys, so that the end of each rope, which was tied to a metal ring, hung down into the respective ends of the experimental cage. Pulling one rope enabled the subject to look at another monkey in the target cage, while pulling the opposite rope gave him access to his reflected image in a mirror. Microswitches attached to the guillotine door runners, and wired to clocks and counters, provided measures of the number and duration of responses to the two visual incentives.

Fourteen preadolescent rhesus monkeys were employed as subjects. Six animals were feral (i.e. born in the wild) and eight were laboratory-born and reared in social isolation on artificial surrogate mothers. Each monkey was placed in the experimental cage by itself for two hours every day for five consecutive days, and was provided with a target monkey in the adjoining cage which had been subject to a rearing history comparable to its own. Figure 7 shows the average amount of time spent viewing the target animal and the mirror by feral monkeys as a function of days. It is interesting to note that unlike goldfish and parakeets, the wild-born rhesus show a clear and consistent preference for viewing another monkey. Figure 8 shows the same comparison for laboratory-reared isolates who, contrary to their feral counterparts, exhibit a reversed preference and spend more time viewing the mirror. Unfortunately, data gathered on isolate monkeys represent responses for only three of the subjects, since the other five animals never pulled either rope.

As a check on the apparent preference for MIS shown by some of the isolate animals, both guillotine doors were permanently raised to eliminate the instrumental component and the same eight animals were

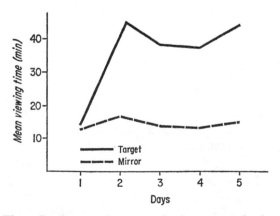

Figure 7.   Average time spent viewing target animal and mirror by feral monkeys for a two-hour session each day (Gallup and McClure 1971)

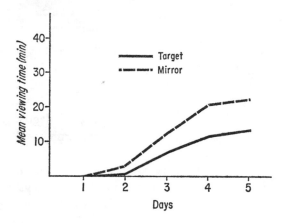

Figure 8.   Average time spent viewing target and mirror by surrogate-reared monkeys for five two-hour sessions (Gallup and McClure 1971)

re-tested two months later. The test consisted of placing a monkey into this free-choice situation for one hour, during which time its behavior was monitored from another room through a one-way wide angle lens. Data were gathered by time-sampling their behavior once every sixty seconds for the first and last fifteen minutes of each hour. Records were made on whether the monkey was viewing the mirror or the target animal, as well as the nature of the interaction with the stimulus. Data obtained using this procedure are presented in Figure 9. As can be seen the isolate rhesus monkeys were all found to view the mirror more frequently than the target animal while engaged in both passive looking and active interaction with the stimulus alternatives.

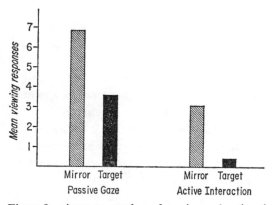

Figure 9.   Average number of passive and active time-sampled viewing responses made to mirror and target animal by surrogate-reared monkeys (Gallup and Mc-Clure 1971)

AN INTERPRETATION

At this point at least two questions arise. First, why do feral monkeys show a preference for viewing a live companion while fish and birds prefer mirrors, and second, why do rhesus monkeys reared in isolation make visual choices which are the opposite of those shown by animals born in the wild? The answers to both questions may relate to the degree to which the social behavior of different species depends on learning and early socialization.

In rhesus monkeys, for example, a large proportion of their social behavior is acquired as a result of early experiences with other monkeys, as evidenced by the devastating effect of early social isolation on adult behavior (e.g. Harlow and Harlow 1962). Thus, for a normal rhesus monkey MIS would probably represent a highly atypical kind of social stimulation, since the image in the mirror never responds independently of the observer and as a consequence never initiates a social gesture, nor does it ever reciprocate.

On the other hand, the social behavior of fish and birds may be so rigidly preprogrammed and inflexible that reciprocal stimulation arising from a conspecific may be needed to progress through the interdependent chain of events inherent in a normal social episode, so as to reach an end point. In other words, the fish or bird may perseverate in front of its own reflection by way of trying to approximate a more natural exchange of social stimulation. In the absence of being able to achieve a normal outcome, which would be required to exit from the loop and terminate the encounter, the subject remains bound to the situation. Thus, the preference for MIS in fish and birds may be more apparent than real and could represent the effect of short-circuiting the natural sequence of reciprocal events imposed by genetic instructions.

Perhaps isolate rhesus monkeys, on the other hand, really do prefer watching their own reflections in mirrors. Pratt and Sackett (1967), for example, have shown that rhesus monkeys subjected to varying degrees of early social deprivation spent more time viewing comparably reared, but unfamiliar, conspecifics than others with different rearing histories. Since like-reared companions were used as target animals in the Gallup and McClure (1971) study it would appear that its own image in a mirror has more attention value for a social isolate than visual access to a comparably deprived peer. One way of conceptualizing these data is in terms of varying degrees of predictability in intraspecific encounters. The behavior of a live companion is usually never completely predictable, but, if confronted with a conspecific with a rearing history similar to its own, predictability ought to improve. In the case of MIS it would have to be perfect.

Because the image never initiates a social encounter, the enhanced predictability, and implicit element of control over the behavior or the image, may provide the isolate animal with a greater degree of initial security in a new social encounter. Also it may be that an isolate is less capable of responding to the initiative of another monkey, whereas in front of a mirror its own behavior is the sole determiner of the ingredients of any social episode. What could be more compatible with the atypical and aberrant behavior of a socially deprived rhesus monkey than a reflection of that behavior in a mirror?

SELF-RECOGNITION IN PRIMATES

Another point about mirrors, and probably the most obvious one for humans, is that MIS represents a potential source of information about the self. Mirrors are unique in that they enable visually capable organisms to see themselves as they are seen by other animals. In front of a mirror an animal is literally an audience to its own behavior. However, for most animals, confrontation with themselves in mirrors represents a form of social stimulation rather than a means of self-inspection. In this sense MIS might be characterized as an instance of self-sensation rather than self-perception. Although ostensibly stimulated by an image of itself (self-sensation) the animal responds as if in the presence of another organism.

To the extent that there exists some kind of underlying continuity between animals and man with regard to most basic biological and psychological processes, the absence of self-directed behavior in animals might appear discrepant from many findings in other areas. Interestingly, however, this pervasive other-directed orientation to mirrors shown by animals has also been reported for humans who are inexperienced with mirror surfaces, suggesting that self-recognition of one's reflection may be an acquired or learned phenomenon. For example, although there is a lack of consensus on this question, the best current estimate is that children initially respond to the image as though it were another child and do not learn to recognize their reflections until about twenty months of age (Amsterdam 1972).

Similarly, people born with congenital visual defects, which are eventually corrected, not only misinterpret their own reflections as representing other people, but tend initially to respond to the mirror space as though it were real: e.g. reaching for reflected objects in the mirror (von Senden 1960). There are also reports of mentally retarded children, ranging up to nineteen years of age, who seem totally incapable of learning to interpret mirrored information correctly, and persist in showing other-directed responses even after prolonged exposure to mirrors (e.g. Shentoub, Soulairac, and Rustin 1954).

Finally, it is known that certain mental patients with serious psychotic disorders cease to be capable of recognizing themselves in mirrors or photographs and often show signs of other-directed behavior in the presence of their own reflections (Faure 1956; Wittreich 1959).

In view of the preceding examples it would seem reasonable to conclude that the ability to recognize one's own reflection depends in part on learning, and the opportunity for such learning should in part be related to the amount of mirror exposure. Moreover, most of us are undoubtably given explicit verbal instructions by our parents and others with regard to the identity of the reflection.

A major difference between the natural environment of humans and animals is in terms of frequency with which we see ourselves in mirrors. Naturally occurring sources of MIS are probably only occasionally encountered by most organisms, whereas the human milieu tends to be permeated with such surfaces. The question arises, therefore, as to whether an animal could learn to recognize its reflection if given sufficiently prolonged confrontation with a mirror.

In an attempt to test this conjecture (Gallup 1970), two male and two female wild-born, group-reared preadolescent chimpanzees (*Pan troglodytes*) were each given individual exposure to a full-length mirror for eight hours per day over a period of ten consecutive days. To insure enforced self-confrontation with the reflection during the ten-day period each chimp was kept by itself with the mirror positioned in front of a small empty cage in an otherwise empty room. Observations were made by watching the chimp's reflection in the mirror through a small hole in the wall of an immediately adjacent room, and data were gathered by time-sampling the subject's behavior every thirty seconds for fifteen minutes each morning and afternoon. Two observers recorded data and periodically compared results as a reliability check.

Figure 10 portrays the average incidence of time-sampled social responses or other-directed behaviors given to the mirror image over the ten-day period. Only behaviors typically made in the presence of other chimpanzees were scored as social, such as bobbing, vocalizing, threatening, etc. In all instances of social behavior the reflection was judged to have been the referent for the behavior. As can be seen, other-directed

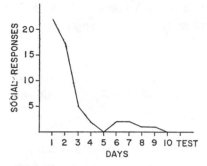

Figure 10.   Number of time-sampled social responses directed to the mirror image over days (Gallup 1970)

tendencies were initially quite strong but waned rapidly and became almost nonexistent after the third day of mirror exposure.

Figure 11 depicts the development of what appeared to be self-directed responses to the reflection. In all instances of what were identified as self-directed behavior, the self (body, face, arms, hands, etc.) was the referent via the reflection. Under conditions of self-directed responding the mirror was used by the chimpanzee to gain visual and, as a result, precise manipulatory access to what would otherwise be inaccessible information about the self. Examples of behaviors scored as self-directed were attempts to groom parts of the body while watching the results and guiding the fingers in the mirror, picking bits of food from between the teeth, visually guided manipulation of anal-genital areas, identifying and then picking extraneous material from the nose with the aid of the mirror, manipulating food wads with the lips while inspecting the reflection, blowing bubbles, and making faces with the help of mirror feedback.

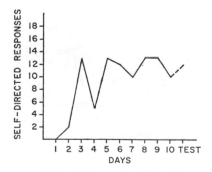

Figure 11.   Total number of time-sampled responses directed toward the self through the mirror reflection over days (Gallup 1970)

The following description represents a few selected examples of the development of self-directed responding taken from notes kept on "Marge," one of the females (Number 1825):

Day 3.   Marge used the mirror to play with and inspect the bottom of her feet; she also looked at herself upside down in the mirror while suspended by her feet from the top of the cage.

Day 4.   She was seen using the reflection to manipulate a metal clip which was situated on the outside of the cage and could not be seen without the mirror.

Day 5.   Marge used the reflection to groom and remove fecal material from the underside of her left forearm. She was also observed to stuff celery leaves up her nose using the mirror for purposes of visually guiding the stems into each nostril, and then began playing with the protruding stems while watching the reflection and batting at the leaves with fingers. Later the same day she was seen vigorously splashing water in her water pan while watching the results in the mirror. At the end of the day when an experimenter entered the room she watched him indirectly in the mirror and occasionally glanced back as if to confirm what she saw in the reflection.

Day 6.   She watched herself eat in the mirror, and continued to spend considerable time watching the reflection during feeding periods on subsequent days. (Increased visual attention to the image during feeding was evidenced by all four animals). She also looked at herself upside down in the mirror again and began slapping her face while inspecting the reflection.

Day 7.   Marge used the mirror for the first time to manipulate her genital area, which had begun to show signs of pubertal swelling. (After the original incidence of visually guided genital manipulation this behavior was seen repeatedly in both females in subsequent sessions.)

Day 8.   She was seen to curiously manipulate a chewed banana peel for a long time with her lips while intently watching the reflections.

Day 9.   She actively inspected her mouth, lips, and teeth using her fingers to apparently make these structures more accessible in the mirror.

Post-test. Two days after the completion of testing the mirror was moved to within a few inches of the front of the cage and while viewing the reflection Marge identified a piece of white mucus in the corner of her right eye and then, using an index finger to remove it, ate the material.

It is important to note that self-directed responding seemed to supplant the social orientation to the mirror on about Day 3 (see Figures 10 and 11), which would be expected, since MIS would have to effectively lose its social stimulus overtones in order for self-recognition to occur. More importantly, the emergence of self-directed responding would suggest that the chimpanzee has correctly determined the identity of the reflection.

Figure 12 shows the average amount of time chimps spent viewing their own reflections averaged over the two fifteen-minute recording sessions each day. These data show that prior to having realized the significance of the reflection the animals show considerable interest in the mirror, but at about the time self-directed responses begin to appear, viewing time decreases and continues to remain at a relatively low level on subsequent days.

Even though these data were impressive, particularly those relating to self-directed responding, it was felt that other investigators might not be particularly convinced by the seemingly subjective interpretations of self-directed responsiveness in the presence of a mirror.

In an attempt to objectify these impressions a more rigorous procedure was instituted as a further test of self-recognition. Following the tenth day of mirror exposure, each chimp was completely anesthetized with a one-milligram-per-kilogram dosage of phencyclidine hydrochloride (Sernylan). The mirror was then removed from the room and

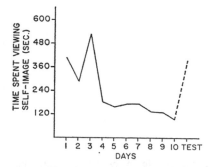

Figure 12. Average amount of time, during two fifteen-minute sessions, spent viewing the reflected image in the mirror over days (Gallup 1970)

the chimpanzee was lifted out of the cage. While the animal was unconscious, marks were applied to the uppermost portion of an eyebrow ridge and the top half of the opposite ear with a cotton swab dipped in a bright red alcohol-soluble dye (Rhodamine B base). After the marks were dry, the chimp was placed back into the small testing cage without the mirror and allowed to recover from the anesthesia.

It is important to realize that there were two special properties of this procedure. First, the chimpanzees would have no way of knowing they had been marked since the procedure was accomplished while they were unconscious, and the dye was selected because of its complete lack of tactile and olfactory properties, once dry. Second, the marks were carefully placed at predetermined points so that it would be impossible for them to be seen without the mirror after the subject recovered from anesthesia.

Following complete recovery, all subjects were fed and watered and then directly observed without the mirror for a thirty-minute pretest to determine the number of times any marked portion of skin was touched "spontaneously." After the pretest, the mirror was then reintroduced into the room for the first time since the marking procedure as a test of self-recognition, and each chimp's behavior was monitored in the presence of the mirror for an additional thirty minutes. Figure 13 shows the number of mark-directed responses (attempts to touch a marked area) made prior to mirror exposure and following the re-introduction of the mirror.

As can be seen, the number of mark-directed responses went up dramatically in the presence of the mirror, with a total of over twenty-five times more responses being shown when the reflection was made available for self-inspection. In terms of a chimpanzee's perception of its

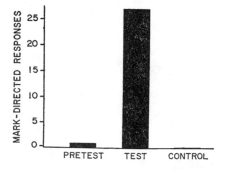

Figure 13.   Number of mark-directed responses made by experimental animals before being exposed to a mirror and by experimental and control animals during the test of self-recognition (Gallup 1970)

own facial features, it may be significant to note that of the mark-directed responses that occurred, over twice (2.36) as many visually guided responses were made to the eyebrows as compared to the marked ears. Occasionally a mark-directed response was also followed by direct visual inspection of the fingers which had been used to touch marked areas. In another case there were olfactory as well as visual attempts to inspect a finger which had made contact with a dyed spot.

Although seemingly unimportant, these instances of visual and olfactory inspection of the fingers are critically related to an interpretation of the data based on self-recognition. Given the demonstration of self-directed responding and even mark-directed behavior, the skeptic could still argue that these observations do not necessarily show that the subjects recognized themselves. However, if the reflection was still being interpreted as another animal there would be no reason for the chimps to smell or look at their own fingers on the test of self-recognition because these would not have been the fingers that made actual contact with the red spots. Only if the animals had correctly identified the dyed area in the mirror as pertaining to themselves, and not another chimpanzee, would there be a reason to inspect their OWN fingers.

Not only did the incidence of mark-directed behaviors increase with exposure to the mirror, but there was also a profound increment in the amount of time animals spent watching the reflection (see Figure 12). Visual access to themselves after having been marked with red dye produced over a threefold enhancement in average viewing time, which suggests that there was something about being able to inspect these spots which increased their visual attention to themselves in the mirror. Also, as Figure 10 reveals, other-directed responsiveness on the test day was completely absent, showing that the effect of the marking procedure was not to cause the subjects to revert to responding as though the reflection were another chimpanzee.

Although it seemed obvious on the basis of these data that the animals had learned to recognize their own reflections, it could still be argued that mark-directed responses might somehow have been an artifact or residual effect of anesthesia. To circumvent this objection a further check on the source of these reactions was instituted. One additional preadolescent male and female chimpanzee were anesthetized and marked with dye. Both animals were feral and neither had ever received prior exposure to mirrors. When given access to the mirror for the first time, the red dye was completely ignored and there were no mark-directed behaviors whatsoever (see Figure 13). Instances of self-directed response to the reflection were likewise absent. As was the case for the other chimps on the first day of MIS, their predominant orientation to the mirror throughout the test was unmistakably social, indicating that self-recognition must have been learned by the previous animals sometime during the eighty hours of mirror exposure antedating the test.

To investigate this capacity in other primates, four adult, wild-born, stumptail macaques (*Macaca arctoides*) and two adult male rhesus monkeys were given twelve hours of mirror exposure for fourteen consecutive days under conditions comparable to those employed with chimpanzees. Following the fourteenth day of mirror self-confrontation, the monkeys were anesthetized and marked with red dye. On the test of self-recognition all animals failed to show signs of self-directed behavior or self-directed responding and continued to maintain a distinct social orientation to the reflection. Moreover, informal observations of the monkeys during the fourteen-day period of mirror exposure indicated that all subjects persisted in showing more or less unabated other-directed responsiveness to the reflection.

Although these data could mean that monkeys do not have the capacity for self-recognition, it might be argued that the monkeys were simply not given enough time to learn to recognize themselves, even though they received over twice as much total mirror exposure (168 hours) before being tested. Also, both the stumptailed and rhesus monkeys were adults, and therefore not developmentally equivalent to the chimps who had just begun to show signs of sexual development.

To circumvent these latter two objections, three male and one female preadolescent cynomolgous monkeys (*Macaca fascicularis*) were given twenty-one consecutive days of mirror exposure, twelve hours each day, for a total of 252 hours, or over three times more time in front of the mirror over the twenty one days, and no mark-directed responses were seen on the tests of self-recognition. Thus, chimpanzees were the only mirror over the twenty one day, and no mark-directed responses were seen on the tests of self-recognition. Thus, chimpanzees were the only ones capable of extracting this more abstract information from mirrors.

Following the initial report of self-recognition in chimps and negative findings with monkeys, there have been at least two additional attempts to demonstrate self-recognition in primates. In concert with our results M. Bertrand (personal communication) failed to find evidence of self-recognition in macaques and, perhaps more importantly, K. H. Pribram and his students (personal communication) were unable to demonstrate this capacity in gibbons, which are classified as apes rather than monkeys. To date, man and chimpanzee are the only species which have been found capable of recognizing themselves in mirrors. It is unfortunate that so far orangutans and gorillas have not been systematically tested for self-recognition, since it could contribute greatly to our knowledge of great ape mentality and might help to clarify our own taxonomic relationship to chimpanzees.

One of the most striking aspects of these findings is the apparent inability of monkeys to recognize themselves in mirrors. Although macaques can learn to use mirrors to manipulate objects (Brown, McDowell, and Robinson 1965; Tinklepaugh 1928) they do not seem capable of learning to integrate features of their own reflection sufficiently so that they can use mirrors to respond to themselves. When looking at an experimenter or a piece of food in the mirror they seem quite capable of recognizing the inherent dualism as it pertains to objects other than themselves, and after adequate experience do respond appropriately by turning away from the mirror to gain direct access to the object of reflection; but for some curious reason they fail to interpret correctly their own reflected image. Since other investigators (for a good review of the literature see Rumbaugh 1970) using more traditional behavioral tasks, such as learning set, have found only slight quantitative differences in learning and problem-solving performance between monkeys and chimpanzees, perhaps the deficiency is unrelated to learning *per se*.

Given the fact that there are no very profound or qualitative differences in learning ability between macaques and chimpanzees, maybe the deficit is due to the absence of an integrated self-concept in monkeys. Since the identity of the observer and the mirror image are one and the same, without a rudimentary identity of its own it would seem difficult, if not impossible, for an observer of a mirror to infer correctly the identity of the reflection. Thus, the deficiency may be much more cognitive than mechanistic.

The fact that chimpanzees appear rather unique in their ability to recognize themselves in mirrors would also seem to mesh quite nicely with other recent findings on chimpanzee mentality, such as the demonstration of intermodal equivalence of stimuli by Davenport and Rogers (1970), and the claims for language acquisition in chimps (e.g. Gardner and Gardner 1969; Premack 1971). It is important to point out, however, that since systematic attempts have not been made with monkeys, a claim CANNOT be made for the notion that language acquisition is a unique feature of human and chimpanzee mentality.

It remains a remote possibility that the demonstrations of language learning in chimps may be more a reflection of the expertise, patience and skill of the human trainers than of an intrinsic, higher mental process in the chimpanzee. Anytime an organism must be subjected to a complex training regime in order to demonstrate a particular effect, there is always the danger that the outcome may be more a function of the experimenter's capabilities than those of the subject. As is often the case, the real significance of any behavioral phenomenon may only come to light when viewed from a broad comparative perspective. The demonstration of language capability in chimpanzees will contribute very little to our understanding of the evolutionary relationship between man and other nonhuman primates until such time as the species limits of this phenomenon are established. As it stands, language in the chimpanzee may or may not have anything to do with biological or phylogenetic boundaries of learning.

SELF-RECOGNITION AS A CRITERION FOR SELF-AWARENESS

To the extent that self-recognition implies the existence of a self-concept, the data on chimpanzees would seem to qualify as one of the first experimental demonstrations of a self-concept in a nonhuman form. As already indicated, the ability to discern correctly the identity of the reflection would seem to necessitate an already established identity on the part of the organism making that inference. Indeed, these findings would seem to imply that man may not be the only creature who is aware of himself, and contrary to popular and contemporary dogma, humans may not have what heretofore has been assumed to be a monopoly on the self-concept.

Moreover, to the extent that consciousness refers to the ability to reflect on or be aware of one's own existence then these data might also be construed as evidence for consciousness in chimpanzees. Contrary to the claims of some (e.g. van Lawick-Goodall 1972), the fact that a chimp that has learned sign language can make symbolic gestures seemingly referring to himself, in the presence of MIS, does not necessarily implicate an unequivocal concept of self, but rather may simply represent an operant or instrumental response maintained by reinforcement, much like the behavior of a rat pressing a bar for food, and need not be accompanied by a state of explicit self-awareness. Labeling the reflection may be quite different from self-recognition (see following section on Self-Recognition in Man).

More recently, data have been obtained (Gallup et al. 1971) which give reason to suspect that the capacity for self-recognition in chimpanzees may be influenced by certain kinds of early experience. To the extent that one would require an already integrated concept of self before he could learn to recognize himself in a mirror, it seemed reasonable to suppose that the development of self-awareness could be influenced by early experience, and that it, too, might be an acquired phenomenon.

One of the early proponents of this view was Cooley (1912), who theorized that an individual's concept of self could arise only out of social interaction with others. For Cooley the self-concept was seen as an interpersonal phenomenon in the sense that the way other people react to an individual constitutes the primary source of information a person has about himself. Similarly, Mead (1934) held that it was the immediate social environment which prompted an individual to become aware of himself as a separate and distinct entity. In order for the self to emerge as an object of conscious inspection, from Mead's point of view, it requires the opportunity to examine one's self from another's point of view.

If, by chance, the speculations of Cooley and Mead bear on the development of self-awareness, it was reasoned that chimpanzees reared in social isolation might not have the necessary information to achieve self-awareness and acquire an identity, and therefore might be expected to show an inability to recognize their own reflections. In an attempt to assess the effects of early social deprivation, six additional preadolescent chimps were selected for testing. Two females and one male were born in the wild, and in captivity were usually kept in group cages containing at least one other companion. The remaining three chimps, also two females and one male, were born in captivity, separated from their mothers shortly after birth, and reared in individual cages which prevented physical contact with other animals and minimized visual contact.

The experimental procedure was the same as that employed in the original 1970 study. All animals were given eight hours of mirror exposure each day, followed on the tenth day by the test of self-recognition. In concert with the previous findings, social responsiveness to the mirror was initially quite high for feral chimps but disappeared after two to four days. Isolate chimpanzees, however, failed to show any of the typical other-directed responses to the reflection throughout the experiment; this should not be surprising since they had never been subject to normal social encounters.

The average amount of time the animals spent viewing themselves in the mirror during the thirty-minute recording session each day is presented in Figure 14. Very much like the animals in the initial study, feral chimps showed a gradual decline in the amount of time spent viewing the reflection, while isolates showed significantly higher and

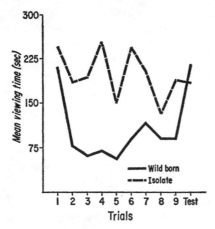

Figure 14. Average time during ten thirty-minute sessions spent viewing their reflections in the mirror by wild-born and isolate chimpanzees (Gallup et al. 1971)

more stable levels of visual attention to the image over days. The accentuated interest in the mirror exhibited by deprived chimpanzees seems strikingly reminiscent of the preference for MIS shown by isolate rhesus monkeys (Gallup and McClure 1971), and could be taken to mean that isolate chimps resemble similarly reared rhesus monkeys more than they do feral monkeys. Curiously, there are also data which indicate that prolonged mirror gazing, often accompanied by an apparent loss of self-recognition, may be symptomatic of impending schizophrenia in man (Abély 1930; Delmas 1929; Ostancow 1934).

Figure 15 depicts the number of mark-directed responses made to dyed portions of the skin following recovery from anesthetization. In accord with the prediction from Cooley's theory, the feral chimps showed 13.5 times more mark-directed responses on the test for self-recognition than did the isolates. Moreover, the number of mark-directed responses made by isolate animals on the test was equivalent to the number shown by the ferals on the pretest, implying that the isolates were unable to infer correctly the identity of the mirror image (despite the fact that they spent more time watching their reflections).

It is also important to note that the wild-born chimps, much like previous animals, showed a substantial increase in viewing time (see Figure 14) when they saw themselves in the marked condition. However, as further evidence of their inability to determine the significance of the reflection the isolate chimps showed virtually no change in viewing time as a result of being allowed to see themselves after having been marked with red dye.

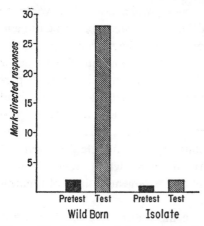

Figure 15.   Number of times any marked portion of the skin was touched during a thirty-minute pretest without the mirror and a thirty-minute test by wild-born and isolate chimpanzees (Gallup et al. 1971)

As added evidence for the notion that the formation of a self-concept may be critically tied to early social experiences (Hill et al. 1970), two of three additional young isolation-reared chimpanzees were given twelve weeks of "remedial" social experience by housing the pair together in the same cage at eighteen months of age which, according to Cooley and Mead, should provide for conditions conducive to the emergence of some kind of personal identity. In accord with the prediction, the two chimps given a three-month opportunity to interact did show some signs of being able to recognize their reflections when tested following ten days of mirror exposure, whereas the chimp that remained in isolation failed to show evidence of self-recognition.

There are, however, at least two other, perhaps more parsimonious interpretations of the data obtained using differentially reared chimpanzees. It might be argued, for example, that the inability of isolate chimps to interpret correctly mirrored information about themselves could be indicative of a learning deficit engendered by early and prolonged maternal and peer deprivation.

On the other hand, Harlow, Schlitz, and Harlow (1968) contend that apparent deficiencies in learning ability evidenced by socially isolated primates may in fact be due to heightened levels of emotionality early in the testing regime. For instance, they report that with sufficient adaptation to the testing situation isolate rhesus monkeys do just as well as their feral counterparts on a variety of tasks. In this regard it is significant that none of the isolate chimpanzees showed enhanced emotionality after the first few days of mirror exposure, which was what would be expected since the only appreciable difference between experimental and ordinary housing conditions was the presence of the mirror.

Alternatively, it could be argued that since the isolate chimps never had the opportunity to become familiar with other chimpanzees, perhaps they failed to "speculate" about the curious behavior of the animal depicted in the mirror, who never initiates a social encounter nor reciprocates. Therefore, they may never entertain any hypotheses concerning the significance of the reflection. Although this second interpretation will account for the data, and cannot be ruled out, we tend to favor the idea that the absence of self-recognition is due to a general lack of identity or self-awareness.

The Cooley-Mead interpretation is a more attractive one because it encompasses much more data. Why, for example, should some psychotic patients begin spending excessive amounts of time watching themselves in mirrors and show a progressive inability to recognize their reflections; because they have lost interest in speculating about the identity of the reflection, or because of the loss of personal identity? Indeed, to the extent that viewing time is indicative of the attractive potential of MIS, isolate rhesus monkeys, isolate chimpanzees, and schizophrenic humans have NOT lost interest in the reflection because in all instances they spend inordinate amounts of time looking at mirrors.

As pointed out by Gallup, McClure, Hill, and Bundy (1971) the Cooley-Mead conceptual scheme can be used to account for a number of other curious findings with chimpanzees. Rogers and Davenport (1969), for example, report that the sexual behavior of chimpanzees reared in complete social isolation is less impaired than that of chimps given human maternal care. If the interpersonal nature of self-concept formation holds, then this finding should come as no surprise since the chimpanzee reared by humans would be expected to show a self-concept based on the reflected appraisals of another species which, in turn, could conceivably distort its own species identity.

As support for this interpretation Hayes and Nissen (1971) describe the case of a home-raised chimpanzee named Viki who, when given the task of sorting photographs into an animal and human pile, placed her own picture in the human stack.

Certainly all of this is highly speculative and the answers must await further experimentation. On the other hand, questions often have to be asked before answers can be obtained. Contentment with the wrong answers, or no answers, would seem to be much more dangerous than the risk entailed in asking a question. Perhaps the reason an attempt to operationalize and come to grips with self-awareness has been so long in coming results from a reluctance to even consider the questions.

To return to the question of self-recognition in chimpanzees, a number of additional studies remain to be done. For example, it might be interesting to devise techniques for accelerating the development of self-recognition. One obvious possibility would be to expose simultaneously two familiar cage-mates to the same mirror. Presumably each chimp would be able to recognize the reflection of its partner, and therefore would have considerably more preliminary information with regard to the identity of the "other" unfamiliar animal in the mirror. It would also be interesting to know what effect various drugs and/or neurological "insults" might have on a chimp who has learned to recognize his reflection (see section on Latent Social Stimulus Properties).

SELF-RECOGNITION IN MAN

It may sound ridiculous, but to date better quantitative evidence of self-recognition exists for chimpanzees than for man. Most attempts to assess self-recognition in humans have taken the form of trying to determine when infants learn to identify themselves in mirrors. Unfortunately the vast majority of these studies, particularly the earlier ones, are based on subjective impressions and lack rigorous control procedures.

While almost all investigators agree that prior to the attainment of self-recognition most children treat the image as another child or "playmate," there is very little agreement as to the average age at which children learn to recognize themselves in mirrors. The lack of consensus is not because too few studies have been attempted, but rather seems to have been due to an inability to devise an unconfounded and objective technique. Preyer (1893), for example, was satisfied that his son could recognize his own reflection at fourteen months because he showed evidence of recognizing his mother's image at about that time, a finding which might reflect on an ability not unlike that of a macaque who has learned to recognize objects other than himself in a mirror. Dixon (1957) was content to infer self-recognition anytime a child was observed to look at both his mirror reflection and a corresponding body part, which occurred between six and twelve months of age in a sample of five subjects. Stone and Church (1968) contend that most children recognize themselves in mirrors at around ten months of age.

Darwin (1877) felt that his own boy recognized himself at nine months because when called by name the child would turn to the mirror and say "ah." However, since children are often held in front of mirrors with parents repeatedly calling out their names this could merely mean that the child has learned to associate a name with the reflection, and not that he has acquired explicit self-awareness. Simply labeling the reflection may be quite different from an accurate awareness as to the source and identity of the image, and therefore cannot be used as conclusive evidence for self-recognition. On the other hand, Gesell and Thompson (1934), on the basis of a study of over 500 children, questioned that any self-recognition occurs in early childhood up to fifty-six weeks of age, and Shirley (1933) was also skeptical of early recognition based on her observations of children between forty and fifty weeks.

The only semi-convincing study with humans is a recent one by Amsterdam (1972), in which the assessment of mirror self-recognition was accomplished by marking children with a spot of rouge placed on the side of the nose, and then a few minutes later noting whether the nose was touched when subjects were exposed to a mirror. Using this technique she reports the emergence of self-recognition at between twenty and twenty-four months of age in about 65 percent of her subjects. Unfortunately the procedure employed by Amsterdam may have provided the child with considerable confounding information about the presence of the marks prior to the test of self-recognition.

Of the various human facial features, the sides of the nose are unique in that they are the most readily available to visual inspection without a mirror, and thus mark-directed responses might not be indicative of self-recognition. Rhesus monkeys, for example, are notorious for the efficient removal of paint and dye which has been applied to various body parts for identification purposes, but as previously noted they fail to respond to mirrored cues concerning otherwise visually inaccessible marks on their eyebrows and ears.

Moreover, since the rouge was applied a few minutes before mirror self-confrontation, while the child was fully awake, there is also the very real possibility that subjects may have been responding to tactual cues associated with the marking procedure and not to the reflection of those spots in the mirror. Finally, apparently no provisions were made in the Amsterdam study to monitor and record the number of mark-directed responses made prior to the test of self-recognition. Thus, while it may be introspectively and intuitively obvious that humans recognize themselves in mirrors, a clear and unequivocal experimental demonstration of this capacity has yet to be recorded.

LATENT SOCIAL STIMULUS PROPERTIES

Although most humans eventually do learn to recognize themselves in mirrors there are reasons to suspect that MIS may never completely lose its original, and perhaps more fundamental, social stimulus qualities (Gallup 1971). As already stated, people with serious mental disorders have been known to revert to an other-directed orientation in the presence of their own reflection and commonly show signs of a progressive inability to recognize themselves in mirrors.

Many people have had the rather startling experience of suddenly seeing themselves in an unexpected mirror surface, and responding as if confronted by a stranger (e.g. Wolff 1943). Similarly, the ingestion of certain chemical agents, such as alcohol and marijuana, has caused some people to report a feeling of strangeness and detachment or unfamiliarity with themselves in mirrors (e.g. Kraus 1949). Also there are anecdotal reports of gradual fragmentation or satiation of self-recognition after prolonged inspection of one's own mirror image, and people often find themselves temporarily unable to identify the reflection.

As previously stated, it is well known that performance is often affected by the presence of other organisms, as in the case of chickens who eat more in the presence of other chickens. In humans, Wicklund and Duval (1971) recently found a striking social facilitation effect on the performance of college students tested alone while facing a mirror, as compared to students without mirror-image stimulation. Mark P. Behar, a graduate student working in my laboratory, has been able to replicate this effect of mirror facilitation in an unpublished study by having college students press a simple hand-operated counter in the presence or absence of their own reflection. The average number of counter presses in a five-minute period was significantly higher when subjects were required to respond in front of a mirror, with a mean of 1,089 responses in the MIS condition as compared to 923 without the mirror. Thus, even for normal, self-recognizing adults a mirror image may still carry psychological significance comparable to the presence of another person.

REFERENCES

ABÉLY, P.
    1930   Le signe du miroir dans les psychoses et plus spécialement dans la démence précoce. *Annales Médico-Psychologiques* 88:28–36.

AMSTERDAM, B.
1972   Mirror self-image reactions before age two. *Developmental Psychobiology* 5:297–305.

BAENNINGER, R.
1966   Waning of aggressive motivation in *Betta splendens*. *Psychonomic Science* 4:241–242.

BAENNINGER, L., M. BERGMAN, R. BAENNINGER
1969   Aggressive motivation in *Betta splendens:* replication and extension. *Psychonomic Science* 16:260–261.

BROWN, W. L., A. A. MC DOWELL, E. M. ROBINSON
1965   Discrimination learning of mirrored cues by rhesus monkeys. *Journal of Genetic Psychology* 106:123–128.

COOLEY, C. H.
1912   *Human nature and the social order*. New York: Charles Scribner's Sons.

DARWIN, C. R.
1877   A biographical sketch of an infant. *Mind* 2:285–294.

DAVENPORT, R. K., C. M. ROGERS
1970   Intermodal equivalence of stimuli in apes. *Science* 168:279–280.

DELMAS, F. A.
1929   Le signe du miroir dans la démence précoce. *Annales Médico-Psychologiques* 87:227–233.

DIXON, J. C.
1957   Development of self-recognition. *Journal of Genetic Psychology* 91:251–256.

FAURE, H.
1956   L'investissement délirant de l'image de soi. *Évolution Psychiatrique* 3:545–577.

GALLUP, G. G., JR.
1966   Mirror-image reinforcement in monkeys. *Psychonomic Science* 5:39–40.
1968   Mirror-image stimulation. *Psychological Bulletin* 70:782–793.
1970   Chimpanzees: self-recognition. *Science* 167:86–87.
1971   Minds and mirrors. *New Society* 18(477):975–977.

GALLUP, G. G., JR., S. A. CAPPER
1970   Preference for mirror-image stimulation in finches (*Passer domesticus domesticus*) and parakeets (*Melopsittacus undulatus*). *Animal Behavior* 18:621–624.

GALLUP, G. G. JR., J. Y. HESS
1971   Preference for mirror-image stimulation in goldfish (*Carassius auratus*). *Psychonomic Science* 23:63–64.

GALLUP, G. G., JR., M. K. MC CLURE
1971   Preference for mirror-image stimulation in differentially reared rhesus monkeys. *Journal of Comparative and Physiological Psychology* 75:403–407.

GALLUP, G. G., JR., M. K. MC CLURE, S. D. HILL, R. A. BUNDY
1971   Capacity for self-recognition in differentially reared chimpanzees. *The Psychological Record* 21:69–74.

GALLUP, G. G., JR., W. A. MONTEVECCHI, E. T. SWANSON
1972   Motivational properties of mirror-image stimulation in the domestic chicken. *The Psychological Record* 22:193–199.

GARDNER, R. A., B. T. GARDNER
1969   Teaching sign language to a chimpanzee. *Science* 165:664–672.

GESELL, A., H. THOMPSON
1934   *Infant behavior: its genesis and growth.* New York: McGraw-Hill.

HARLOW, H. F., M. K. HARLOW
1962   The effect of rearing conditions on behavior. *Bulletin of the Menninger Clinic* 26:213–224.

HARLOW, H. F., K. S. SCHLITZ, M. K. HARLOW
1968   Effects of social isolation on the learning performance of rhesus monkeys. *Proceedings of the Second International Congress in Primatology, Atlanta, Georgia,* volume one. New York and Basel: Karger.

HAYES, K. J., C. H. NISSEN
1971   "Higher mental functions in a home-raised chimpanzee," in *Behavior of nonhuman primates,* volume three. Edited by A. M. Schrier and F. Stollnitz. New York: Academic Press.

HILL, S. D., R. A. BUNDY, G. G. GALLUP, JR., M. K. MC CLURE
1970   Responsiveness of young nursery-reared chimpanzees to mirrors. *Proceedings of the Louisiana Academy of Sciences* 33:77–82.

KRAUS, G.
1949   Over de psychopathologie en de psychologie van de waarneming van het eigen spiegelbeeld. *Nederlandsch Tijdschrift voor Psychologie en haar Grensgebieden* 4:1–37.

LISSMANN, H. W.
1932   Die Umwelt des Kampffisches (*Betta splendens* Regan). *Zeitschrift für Vergleichende Physiologie* 18:62–111.

LOTT, D. F., P. N. BRODY
1966   Support of ovulation in the ring dove by auditory and visual stimuli. *Journal of Comparative and Physiological Psychology* 62:311–313.

MAC LEAN, P. D.
1964   Mirror display in the squirrel monkey. *Science* 146:950–952.

MATTHEWS, L. H.
1939   Visual stimulation and ovulation in pigeons. *Proceedings of the Royal Society of London* 126:557–560.

MEAD, G. H.
1934   *Mind, self and society.* Chicago: University of Chicago Press.

MELVIN, K. B., J. E. ANSON
1970   Image-induced aggressive display: reinforcement in the paradise fish. *The Psychological Record* 20:225–228.

OSTANCOW, P.
1934   Le signe du miroir dans la démence précoce. *Annales Médico-Psychologiques* 92:787–790.

PRATT, C. L., G. P. SACKETT
1967   Selection of social partners as a function of peer contact during rearing. *Science* 155:1133–1135.

PREMACK, D.
  1971   "On the assessment of language competence in the chimpanzee," in *Behavior of nonhuman primates,* volume four. Edited by A. M. Schrier and F. Stollnitz. New York: Academic Press.

PREYER, W.
  1893   *Mind of the child,* volume two: *Development of the intellect.* New York: Appleton.

RITTER, W. E., S. B. BENSON
  1934   "Is the poor bird demented?" Another case of "shadow boxing." *Auk* 51:169–179.

ROGERS, C. M., R. K. DAVENPORT
  1969   Effects of restricted rearing on sexual behavior in chimpanzees. *Developmental Psychology* 1:200–204.

RUMBAUGH, D. M.
  1970   "Learning skills of anthropoids," in *Primate behavior,* volume one. Edited by L. A. Rosenblum. New York: Academic Press.

SCHMIDT, M.
  1878   Beobachtungen am Orang-Utan. *Zoologischen Garten* 19:230–232.

SCHULMAN, A. H., J. N. ANDERSON
  1972   "The effects of early rearing conditions upon the preferences for mirror-image stimulation in domestic chicks." Paper presented at the meeting of the Southeastern Psychological Association, Atlanta.

SCHUSTERMAN, R. J., R. GENTRY, J. SCHMOOK
  1966   Underwater vocalization by sea lions: social and mirror stimuli. *Science* 154:540–542.

SHENTOUB, S. A., A. SOULAIRAC, E. RUSTIN
  1954   Comportement de l'enfant arriéré devant le miroir. *Enfance* 7: 333–340.

SHIRLEY, M. M.
  1933   *The first two years,* volume two: *Intellectual development.* Minneapolis: University of Minnesota Press.

SIMPSON, M. J. A.
  1968   The display of the Siamese fighting fish, *Betta splendens. Animal Behaviour Monographs* 1:1–73.

SMYTHE, R. H.
  1962   *Animal habits: the things animals do.* Springfield, Illinois: Charles C. Thomas.

STONE, L. J., J. CHURCH
  1968   *Childhood and adolescence* (second edition). New York: Random House.

SWALLOW, R. W.
  1937   Ancient Chinese bronze mirrors. Peking: Henri Vetch.

TERNES, J. W., J. A. JEMAIL, J. E. LABORDE
  1972   "Social facilitation of extinction in goldfish." Paper presented at the meeting of the Psychonomic Society, St. Louis.

THOMPSON, T. I.
  1963   Visual reinforcement in Siamese fighting fish. *Science* 141:55–57.

1967   Visual reinforcement in fighting cocks. *Journal of the Experimental Analysis of Behavior* 7:45–49.

TINKLEPAUGH, O. L.
1928   An experimental study of representative factors in monkeys. *Journal of Comparative Psychology* 8:197–236.
1971   Opinion change and performance facilitation as a result of objective self-awareness. *Journal of Experimental Social Psychology* 7:319–342.

TOLMAN, C. W.
1965   Feeding behaviour of domestic chicks in the presence of their own mirror images. (Abstract.) *Canadian Psychologist* 6:227.

VAN LAWICK-GOODALL, J.
1972   *In the shadow of man.* Boston: Houghton Mifflin.

VON SENDEN, M.
1960   *Space and sight: the perception of space and shape in the congenitally blind before and after operation.* Glencoe: Free Press.

WICKLUND, R. A., S. DUVAL

WITTREICH, W.
1959   Visual perception and personality. *Scientific American* 200:56–60.

WOLFF, W.
1943   *The expression of personality.* New York: Harper.

YERKES, R. M., A. W. YERKES
1929   *The great apes: a study of anthropoid life.* New Haven: Yale University Press.

Communicative Styles in Two Cultures: Japan and the United States

DEAN C. BARNLUND

Man and society are antecedent and consequent of each other: every person is both a creator of society and its most obvious creation. Individual acts are framed within cultural imperatives, but cultures derive their imperatives from the acts of individuals.

Perhaps for this reason there are essentially two modes of inquiry that have been used in the study of cultures. One of these views society as an integrated totality and emphasizes the interlocking premises and values which it manifests. It proceeds by seeking to determine the philosophical assumptions, political structures, ideological premises, and world view of the culture. The other treats society as the patterns of actual behaviors that people manifest in their day-to-day encounters with each other. It proceeds by seeking to discover the dialectic that governs the conduct of ordinary affairs. The risk in the former is of reifying abstractions that do not actually regulate behavior; the risk in the latter is of becoming lost in a multiplicity of irrelevant detail. Yet, when sensitively employed, both methods should wind their way back to the same reality. Individual acts are no more than social beliefs particularized, and cultural premises no more than a multitude of individual acts generalized.

Here the effort is to contribute to a better understanding of two highly industrialized societies which differ in a multitude of significant ways, by focusing upon the most commonplace of ordinary acts — the messages by which men express their own inner experience and bind

This research was supported in large part by a Visiting Scientist's grant from the Japan Society for the Promotion of Science. A full report of the investigation will be published in Japanese early in 1973 by Simul Press, Tokyo, Japan.

themselves to the community of other men. Three specific aims guided the study: to develop a theoretical framework for exploring cultural differences in the communicative styles of Japanese and Americans; to gather data on the actual content and conduct of face-to-face encounters in both cultures; to speculate on the personal and social significance of any differences in communicative patterns.

UNIVERSE OF DISCOURSE

Every culture creates for its members a "universe of discourse," a way in which men can interpret their experience and convey it to one another. Without some common system of codifying sensations, life would become meaningless, and all efforts to cooperate would be doomed to failure. This "universe of discourse," the most precious of cultural legacies, is transmitted to each generation, in part consciously and in part unconsciously. Parent and teacher give explicit instruction in it by praising and criticizing certain ways of thinking, of speaking, of gesturing, and of responding to the messages of others. But often the more significant aspects of any communicative style are conveyed implicitly, not by edict or lesson but through modeling behavior. The child is surrounded by others who through the mere consistency of their actions display what is regarded as "sensible" behavior. Since the grammar of any culture is so often assimilated unconsciously, one's own cultural assumptions and distinctive modes of address are difficult to recognize.

It is when men nurtured in sharply differing societies meet that such cultural norms interfere with their ability to comprehend each other. Occasionally the interpersonal crises that accompany intercultural encounters are sufficiently dramatic, or the communicants sufficiently sensitive, to permit recognition of the source of trouble. Where there are patience and constructive intention, these misunderstandings may be explored and clarified. But more often the outsider, without knowing it, leaves behind him a trail of confusion, anxiety, mistrust, and hatred of which he is totally unaware. Neither communicant recognizes that his difficulty is buried in the rhetoric of his own society. Each sees himself as acting in ways that are thoroughly sensible, honest, and considerate. And — given the rules governing his own universe of discourse — each is. Unfortunately there are few cultural universals, and the degree of overlap is always less than adequate. The symbolic universe each occupies is governed by codes that are unconsciously acquired and automatically employed. Yet as long as men remain blind to the sources of their meanings, they are imprisoned within them. Cultural frames of reference are no less confining because they are symbolic and cannot be seen or touched.

PUBLIC AND PRIVATE SELF IN JAPAN

The object of this study was to probe the rules of discourse in two cultures by examining in detail the communicative styles of Japanese and Americans. Earlier research led to the postulation of a basic difference between Japanese and Americans with regard to the extent to which the self is exposed in everyday encounters. It was hypothesized that the Japanese prefer an interpersonal style in which the self made accessible to others, that is, the "public self," is relatively small, while the proportion of the self that is not revealed, the "private self," is relatively large. This has been diagrammatically represented in Figure 1.

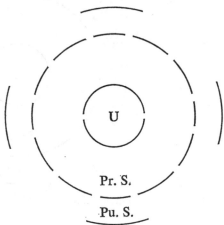

Figure 1.   Japanese public and private self

At the center of the personality stand those nearly inaccessible assumptions and drives that comprise the "Unconscious." Surrounded by nearly impenetrable walls, this part of the personality is rarely exposed to communication, except in the most intimate human relationships or under professional treatment. The next area, identified as the "Private Self," marks off aspects of the person that are potentially communicable but are not often or not usually shared with others. It consists of different material for each person — past experiences, feelings about the self, latent fears or needs — that he knows and can reveal if he chooses. But this material is not ordinarily shared unless the inner need is great or unless there is considerable trust in the other person. Then these matters may become the focus of conversation. The outer area, the "Public Self," identifies those aspects of personal experience that are readily available and easily shared with others. Again the content of the public self differs with each person. It may consist of facts about one's work, personal tastes, family activities, or opinions about public issues. Information of this type is often volunteered, or willingly supplied, in reply to questions from others. Along with small talk, it comprises the most common resource for conducting conversation.

The plus and minus signs that appear in the interpersonal model (Figure 2) merely indicate that encounters within a culture may produce agreements or disagreements. But within the confines of a shared

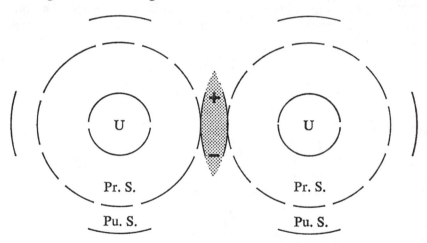

Figure 2.   Japanese interpersonal communication

communicative style, the meaning of a gesture, or a word, or an inflection is more likely to be shared even if the conclusion to which it points is not. In this sense people of the same culture often do not misunderstand each other, they disagree. Conflicts may be readily recognized and may be resolved by employing a common symbolic code for exploring the grounds for disagreement.

If a dominant orientation among Japanese is to permit only a relatively small proportion of inner experience to be made accessible to others, then some of the following predictions should characterize their communication with each other:

A.   THE JAPANESE SHOULD INTERACT MORE SELECTIVELY AND WITH FEWER PERSONS. Interaction with acquaintances is safer because they will know and respect limits of self-revelation. The risk of unexpected self-exposure is reduced by limited contact with strangers whose communicative styles may be unpredictable.

B.   THE JAPANESE SHOULD PREFER REGULATED OVER SPONTANEOUS FORMS OF COMMUNICATION. The greater the degree of formality that surrounds interpersonal encounters, the smaller the chance of exceeding conventional limits on personal revelation.

C.   THE JAPANESE SHOULD, ACROSS A VARIETY OF TOPICS, COMMUNICATE VERBALLY ON A MORE SUPERFICIAL LEVEL. Outer events will be seen as more suitable material for conversation than inner realities; private feelings and thoughts will be avoided where possible.

D.   THE JAPANESE SHOULD SHOW A RELUCTANCE FOR PHYSICAL AS WELL AS VERBAL INTIMACY. Since all physical contacts are self-revealing, often more so than words, it might be expected that touching behavior and reinforcing actions might be less used. Reducing the number of channels through which information is carried reduces the likelihood of self-exposure.

E.   THE JAPANESE SHOULD RESORT TO DEFENSIVE REACTIONS SOONER AND IN A GREATER NUMBER OF TOPICAL AREAS. The more of the self that is guarded the more one is vulnerable to exposure. Defensive modes tend to be consistent with prevailing interpersonal orientations, hence passive-withdrawal will be preferred to active-aggression in the face of threat.

F.   THE JAPANESE, BECAUSE THEY EXPLORE INNER REACTIONS LESS OFTEN AND AT MORE SUPERFICIAL LEVELS, MAY BE LESS KNOWN TO THEMSELVES. Less communication of self may reduce the frequency and intensity of interpersonal conflict; but if disclosure to others is a major means of exposure to self, the Japanese may develop less self insight and have less accurate self perceptions.

PUBLIC AND PRIVATE SELF IN THE UNITED STATES

The same variables, the public self and the private self, may be used to describe the distinguishing features of American interpersonal behavior (Figures 3 and 4). It is postulated that Americans prefer a communicative style, in which the self made accessible to others is

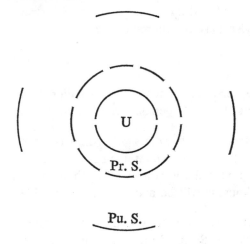

Figure 3.   American public and private self

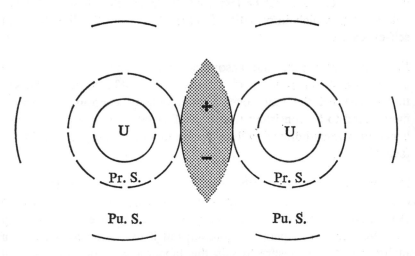

Figure 4.   American interpersonal communication

relatively larger, and the proportion that remains concealed is relatively smaller. If this assumption is correct, what specific communicative behaviors should be manifest when Americans interact?

A.   AMERICANS SHOULD COMMUNICATE WITH A LARGER NUMBER OF PERSONS AND LESS SELECTIVELY. They may be less discriminating about whom they talk to because there is less to be hidden, and they may be more consistent in what they talk about with a broader range of people.

B.   AMERICANS SHOULD PREFER MORE SPONTANEOUS FORMS OF COM-MUNICATION. Ritualized interactions, where conversation conforms to restrictive norms and rules, should occupy a smaller proportion of their social experience and, because it interferes with fuller expression, be less attractive to them.

C.   AMERICANS SHOULD COMMUNICATE ON A DEEPER AND MORE PER-SONAL LEVEL ACROSS A VARIETY OF TOPICS. Personal opinions and private feelings may be more highly valued as contributions to conversation than are impersonal remarks.

D.   AMERICANS SHOULD SEEK PHYSICAL AS WELL AS VERBAL INTIMACY. Because they seek fuller expression of the self, they may utilize more channels of communication and engage in a greater frequency of physical contact.

E.   AMERICANS SHOULD, SINCE THREAT IS PROPORTIONAL TO THE EXTENT OF SELF-CONCEALMENT, BE DEFENSIVE WITH FEWER PERSONS AND IN FEWER TOPICAL AREAS. When threatened they should favor active-aggressive over passive-withdrawal techniques as forms of defense since the former gives greater opportunity for self-expression.

F.   BECAUSE THEY EXPOSE THEIR INNER EXPERIENCES MORE FREQUENTLY AND TO A WIDER VARIETY OF PERSONS AMERICANS SHOULD BE MORE FULLY KNOWN TO THEMSELVES. Greater communication of the self should provoke a higher incidence and higher intensity of interpersonal conflict but should also contribute to a deeper knowledge of the self.

What is postulated, thus, is a difference not of kind but of degree between the psychic structure and communicative behavior of Japanese and Americans, a difference that is significant rather than trivial. This difference, reflecting cultural norms and values, causes members of these two cultures to talk differently, about different topics, in different ways, to different people, with different consequences.

INTERCULTURAL COMMUNICATION

It might be useful before proceeding to speculate on some possible sources of tension or confusion that may arise in cross-cultural communication. The precise nature of such difficulties between Japanese and Americans should become clearer and more specific as our data unfold.

As the models suggest (Figures 5 and 6), such intercultural encoun-

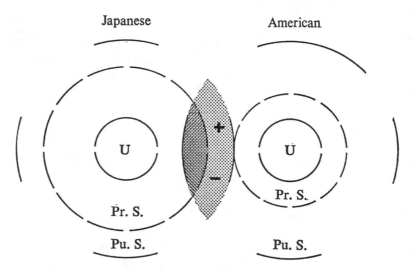

Figure 5. Intercultural communication: American style

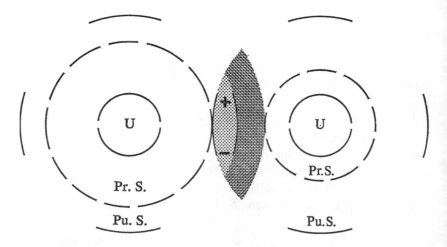

Figure 6. Intercultural communication: Japanese style

ters involve not only the normal sorts of agreement and disagreement that are probable in any conversation, but these are now compounded and aggravated by differences in communicative style as well. Each party seeks to define the relationship according to his own rhetorical tradition; each attempts to focus on topics and meanings appropriate to his own culture; each tries to prescribe a different form and script for their engagement.

In the first instance (Figure 5), the American conversational norms prevail, either because of the insistence of the American or the reluctance of the Japanese to resist them; in the second instance (Figure 6), the Japanese norms prevail, again either because of the greater influence of the Japanese or the reluctance of the American to oppose them. In most instances there is a somewhat awkward, fluctuating compromise made between interpersonal styles.

Where the Japanese may be frightened at the prospect of being communicatively invaded, the American is annoyed at the prospect of never getting beyond formalities. The Japanese is annoyed with Americans for their "flippant" attitude toward formalities, their "insensitivity" to status distinctions, their "prying" questions, their "unnatural" physical intimacy, their "hasty" decisions. In Japan these are the meanings ordinarily attached to such behaviors.

The American, talking to a Japanese associate, similarly is baffled by rituals that seem "endless," by conversations that seem "pointless," by silences that "waste" time, by humor that seems "childish," by delays that are "inexcusable," by remarks that are "evasive," and by the "distant and cold" demeanor of his foreign counterpart. What seems clear to one is patently unclear to the other. And what seems clear may actually be misunderstood.

Each society must maintain some boundary between meaning and nonsense. It does so by distinguishing between signals — cues to which the society attaches meaning — and noises — cues which the culture ignores or treats as devoid of significance. The dividing line is invisible, symbolic rather than real. When the agreement concerning the boundary between signals and noises breaks down or is breached, as it regularly is when members of different cultures interact, useful symbols dissolve into gibberish. Lacking any way of calibrating the two cultural codes, of establishing some correspondence of meaning, the members of different social systems may simply suspend efforts to reach each other. Every attempt at meaningful interaction only seems to drive them farther apart. In their confusion, they surrender to indifference or to hostility. The identification of such potentially disruptive and

alienating differences in communicative styles might alert communicants from these two cultures to possible sources of misunderstanding
and might suggest ways of mitigating the antagonisms they generate.

THE INVESTIGATION OF COMMUNICATIVE STYLES

The research was conducted between 1968 and 1972 with the bulk
of the investigative work completed in the latter year. The subjects
questioned about their communicative behavior were Japanese and
American college students between the ages of eighteen and twenty-
four. All but one of the samples consisted of 240 subjects equally
divided between the two cultures and equally divided between males
and females.

A college sample, of course, is not representative of the entire
population of either country. But no limited sample would be completely satisfactory in this respect. And the college sample has certain
advantages. First, the young are an important segment of society and
may be more sensitive to its operation than their parents. Second, if
the shape of the future is to be found, it must be sought among those
who will shortly determine it. Finally, if there is likelihood of greater
cultural communication between East and West, especially among the
younger generation, data secured from college students will minimize
rather than exaggerate any cultural differences that may be found.
Thus, any conclusions drawn from these data should reflect a conservative rather than an extreme bias.

A number of instruments were used to gather information concern-
ning the communicative behavior of Japanese and Americans. The
following sections of this report summarize findings obtained from a
Role Description Checklist, a Self-Disclosure Scale, a Nonverbal Inventory, and a Defensive Strategy Scale. The data reveal to whom
Japanese and Americans talk, what they talk about, how much of
themselves they share, what kind of physical contact they maintain
with significant others, and how they defend themselves in threatening
social situations.

PROFILES OF TWO CULTURES

The first question is a broad, macroscopic one: What are the GENERAL
features of Japanese and American communication? In what respects

are members of the two cultures alike? In what respects do they differ? And are the differences sufficient to warrant a detailed examination of the specific content and form of interaction?

A Role Description Checklist, developed originally for use in classes in interpersonal communication, provided a list of adjectives for describing the communicative attributes of people. Japanese equivalents for all the items on the scale were selected, and four additional terms, commonly used by Japanese to describe interpersonal behavior, were added. The forms were completed by Japanese and American college students who were able to speak both languages and who had opportunity for observation of the opposite culture as well as their own.[1]

The profiles obtained for each culture were highly consistent, no matter whether they originated within or outside the culture. The Japanese were seen and saw themselves as "reserved," "formal," "cautious," and "evasive." While the Japanese also added such high priority terms as "silent," "serious," and "dependent," the Americans dropped "silent" and added "cooperative." Americans were seen and saw themselves as "frank," "self-assertive," "spontaneous," "informal," and "talkative." Where Japanese respondents placed "humorous" among the high frequency adjectives, Americans substituted "impulsive."

In general, the profiles conform closely to predictions made from the theoretical models: Japanese appear to prefer more formal and regulated encounters, tend to be reserved and cautious in expressing themselves, prefer to be evasive or silent rather than open and frank. This picture is consistent with a highly contained self that is controlled or cautiously expressed, and a larger private self that is hidden or unknown. The Americans appear to be more self-expressive and self-assertive, to prefer more informal encounters, to be more spontaneous and talkative, to be more open and frank about their experience. The single adjective chosen most frequently to describe each culture, by nearly every subject in both samples, was "reserved" for Japanese and "self-assertive" for Americans.

A comparison of the composite profiles of these two cultures provides an impression of extreme contrast, even of contradiction. The qualities most frequently attributed to the Japanese — "reserved,"

[1] The Role Description Checklist, since it required opportunity to observe nationals of the opposite culture, consisted of 122 Japanese and 42 American students enrolled at International Christian University in Japan. Students sampled were able to communicate in both languages and had opportunity for daily face-to-face interaction with members of the other culture.

"formal," "evasive," "cautious," "silent," "serious," and "dependent" — are attributes on which Americans score zero or only slightly above zero. The qualities most frequently assigned to Americans — "self-assertive," "frank," "informal," "spontaneous," "talkative," "humorous," "independent," and "relaxed" — are those on which Japanese score close to zero.

A review of the extensive literature on both cultures by critical observers tends to validate these attributes. In the writings of Benedict (1946), Doi (1962), Halloran (1969), Moloney (1954), Maraini (1965), Nakamura (1964), Nakane (1970), and many others, one finds descriptions that are highly compatible with the terms above and that tend to validate them. It would appear, thus, that although all human beings enter the world with roughly the same sensory and nervous potentialities, each culture rapidly undertakes to cultivate a particular syndrome of interpersonal attributes. By adulthood, and usually long before, its members display sufficient distinctiveness in their interpersonal relationships to permit them to be culturally classified. Few highly industrialized cultures, however, will demonstrate such wide differences in communicative style as those that have been suggested here. And the contrast is sufficient to encourage examination of the actual mechanics of interaction within these two social systems.

VERBAL SELF DISCLOSURE: TOPICS, TARGETS, LEVELS

Perhaps there are no more basic questions to ask of a person or a culture than these: To whom does one speak or not speak? About what does one talk or not talk? How completely is inner experience shared or avoided? Answering these questions should provide some insight into the structure of human relationships and the norms governing interpersonal communication in Japan and the United States.

A Self-Disclosure Scale, developed by Jourard and Lasakow (1958), permits measurement of these three critical variables. Each respondent is asked to indicate his level of disclosure of thoughts and feelings on a variety of topics, with a series of significant other people in his life. The tests were administered, as were all tests used in this study, anonymously, and subjects were given unlimited time to finish.

The findings reveal that what people prefer to talk about appears to be surprisingly similar in the two cultures. The Japanese most prefer to discuss matters of interest and taste followed by opinions about public issues and attitudes toward work. The Americans order these slightly differently but the same three general topics are the most discussed in this culture too. Both cultures appear to talk least about financial matters, aspects of personality, and attitudes toward the body and sex. Males and females in neither society show any significant differences in their topical priorities.

The most thoroughly discussed of the specific questions within these broad categories are those relating to tastes in food, music, reading, television, and film, attitudes toward race, and male and female relations. The least popular specific questions are clearly those dealing with sexual adequacy, facts about sexual behavior, and feelings about appearance or personality. Thus, the evidence is overwhelming in support of similar cultural orientations among Japanese and Americans, regarding what they prefer to talk about and what they prefer to avoid talking about.

If conversational topics can be ranked according to attractiveness, is it not likely also that a hierarchy of persons exists with whom to talk? One might expect that all potential communicative partners are not equally attractive, or that they might vary in attractiveness according to the subject under discussion.

Although all potential associates score substantially higher with Americans, both cultures and both sexes appear to favor communicating with friends most, then with parents, and least with unknown or untrusted persons. Although the overall figures give a slight advantage to male over female friends, each sex appears to prefer somewhat talking with friends of the same sex rather than the opposite sex. This preference is somewhat higher among Japanese than among Americans.

With regard to parents, however, there is a sharp difference between the cultures. Mothers score proportionately higher than fathers in Japan; Japanese women rank mothers second only to friends of the same sex. As one Japanese respondent spontaneously explained, "She is my friend." Fathers, however, score significantly lower and appear to be only slightly more attractive conversational partners than are unknown and untrusted persons. In contrast, American respondents see mothers and fathers as almost equally attractive communicative partners.

Both cultures appear to regard talking with unknown people and untrusted acquaintances as unattractive, but both Japanese and Americans prefer talking to a stranger than to an untrusted aquaintance.

Choice of partner and choice of topic would not seem to be independent of each other. It might be expected that people would seek specific persons with whom to discuss certain topics. But the data from this investigation raise doubts about that conclusion. Instead, target person rankings tend to be consistent, that is, the attractiveness of a particular partner does not appear to vary but is generalized across topics. Thus, in spite of cultural differences in attitudes toward mothers and fathers, there appears again to be a striking similarity between the cultures with regard both to what is talked about and to whom communication is directed.

The most critical aspect of verbal behavior, however, is the depth of personal expression encouraged in verbal encounters. The scoring of the Self-Disclosure Scale provides a precise estimate of this level for each topic and with each partner. A score of 0.0 indicates that respondents have "told nothing about this aspect of myself," a score of 1.0 indicates that they have talked "in general terms about this aspect of myself," and a score of 2.0 indicates that they have "talked in full and complete detail about this aspect of myself."

The results indicate that the average level of self-disclosure across all topics and all target persons for the Japanese is 0.75 and for Americans is 1.12. A more representative index of personal accessibility may be obtained by omitting scores based on conversation with strangers and untrusted acquaintances. When these two categories of target persons are omitted, the average level of disclosure to trusted acquaintances (mother, father, male friend, and female friend) rises to 1.00 for the Japanese and to 1.44 for Americans. A slight sex difference appears in both samples but of such size as to be negligible.

Thus, interpersonal distance is substantially greater among Japanese than among Americans. And this holds true whether communicative partners include or exclude unknown and untrusted persons. On the whole, Japanese express themselves only in "general terms" with their closest associates. For Americans the comparable statistic lies midway between talking in "general terms" and in "full and complete detail." For them, approximately half of reported interpersonal communication with intimates appears to involve a relatively full exposure of the inner self.

It is when one examines individual questionnaires that the full impact of these results can be seen. Depersonalized averages tend to obscure the extremes and blunt the human significance of these figures. There are more than a few — especially among the Japanese sample — who, on nearly all topics and with nearly all persons, report they have told the person "nothing about themselves." As one data processor remarked while scoring the questionnaires, "Do these people ever reveal anything of themselves to anyone? Are they known to any other human being at all?"

The averages for each topical area provide a similar picture of cultural contrast (Figures 7 and 8). On all topics American respondents show a consistently higher level of self revelation. Their disclosure on the LEAST attractive conversational topic surpasses the level of disclosure of Japanese respondents on all but the MOST attractive topic. That is, Americans share as much of themselves with regard to physical and sexual adequacy as Japanese do with regard to their taste in food, music, reading, and television programs. There is also evidence of "communicative blanks." Though most subjects talk with some intimacy to some people on some topics, there are areas of private experience that are sometimes blotted out altogether. Some may avoid talking about illnesses or debts while others avoid conversations touching upon race relations or work difficulties.

The same pattern emerges from an analysis of disclosure to various communicative partners. The Japanese talk only in the most general terms even with their parents and closest friends. The average level of disclosure for Americans with all target persons, including even strangers and untrusted persons, exceeds the level of verbal disclosure of Japanese in even their most intimate relationships.

The most provocative single figure relates to verbal involvement with fathers. Although fathers tend to rank as relatively unattractive communicative partners in many cultures, this result is dramatically true of the Japanese sample but doubtful with regard to the American one. Americans apparently disclose their private thoughts and feelings as much to strangers as do Japanese to their own fathers. The data provide strong support for Benedict's (1946) characterization of Japanese fathers as "depersonalized objects" and Doi's (1962, 1972) description of Japan as a "fatherless society."

Conversation may be seen as an activity sustained by two or more persons who use their experience as a resource on which to build a human relationship. The quality of that relationship depends on their capacity to sustain a superficial or deep linkage with each other. This exploration of verbal habits suggests there is both universality and distinctiveness in the character of verbal interaction in these two cultures. In both, a similar set of priorities exists with regard to topical appropriateness. In both, there is a similar hierarchy of communicative partners. But here the similarity ends. Each culture encourages a different level of personal disclosure in interpersonal encounters. Japanese and Americans differ significantly with regard to the degree

TOPIC		Stranger	Father	Mother	Same Sex Friend	Opposite Sex Friend	Untrusted Acquaintance
Opinions	1. Religion						
	2. Communism						
	3. Integration						
	4. Sex Standards						
	5. Social Standards						
Taste & Interests	1. Food						
	2. Music						
	3. Reading						
	4. TV & Movies						
	5. Parties						
Work (Studies)	1. Handicaps						
	2. Assets						
	3. Ambitions						
	4. Career Choice						
	5. Associates						
Money	1. Income						
	2. Debts						
	3. Savings						
	4. Needs						
	5. Budget						
Personality	1. Handicaps						
	2. Self Control						
	3. Sex Life						
	4. Guilt/Shame						
	5. Pride						
Body	1. Facial Feelings						
	2. Ideal Appearance						
	3. Body Adequacy						
	4. Illnesses						
	5. Sexual Adequacy						

TARGET

0 – 50 / 51 – 100 / 101 – 150 / 151 – 200 / 201 – 250

Figure 7. Summary of topic, target, and level of disclosure: Japan

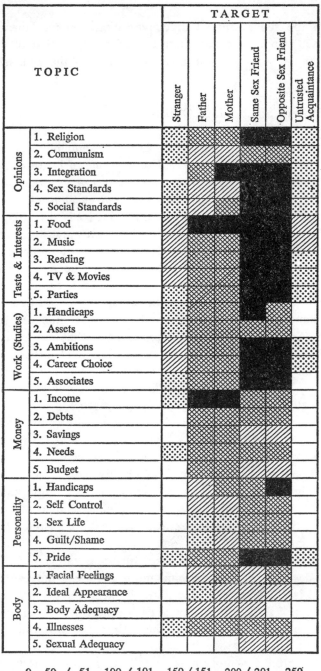

0 – 50 / 51 – 100 / 101 – 150 / 151 – 200 / 201 – 250

Figure 8. Summary of topic, target, and level of disclosure: United States

to which the self is shared in conversation: among Japanese, the "public self" appears to constitute a smaller proportion of the total self and among Americans, a larger proportion of the total self.

NONVERBAL SELF DISCLOSURE

For every human being the earliest form of communication with the world is through touch. It may well remain one of his primary means of expression and of linkage with other persons. A vast range of meaning can be conveyed through physical contact alone. The ultimate hostile act is, of course, a physical one. But so is the ultimate intimacy. Fighting and sexual intercourse represent only the extremes on a scale of expressiveness that includes an infinity of subtle feelings.

The amount of physical contact appears to be a sensitive barometer of interpersonal distance. Enemies rarely approach each other closely, and any contact is limited to destructive acts. Strangers, too, usually stand at some distance, avoiding all but ritualized forms of touching. Among acquaintances there is somewhat greater ease and spontaneity, while close friends are often visually identifiable because of their unusual physical responsiveness to each other. The more comfortable people are with each other the more one expects them to communicate by physical as well as verbal means.

Toward so potent a form of self-disclosure, cultures naturally adopt radically different attitudes. A substantial number of the most critical norms in every culture focuses on whom one can touch, when one can touch, and what one can touch. No matter how expressive a child is physically, he is soon trained to control these impulses. Casual observation alone would lead to the suspicion that people raised in Japan and the United States are exposed to different rules regarding physical contact.

The object of this research was to substitute hard fact for impressionistic description, to determine more precisely the character of nonverbal interaction in Japan and the United States. How frequently do members of these cultures touch each other? Whom do they touch or avoid touching? What areas of the body are involved in such contacts?

The Nonverbal Inventory used to collect data on patterns of interpersonal contact was adapted from Jourard's Body Accessibility Questionnaire (1966). Each person is asked to examine diagrams which reproduce front and rear views of the human body which are sectioned off into twenty-four numbered areas. Each respondent is asked to indicate whether he has "touched" or "been touched" by his father, mother, same sex friend, or opposite sex friend. By revealing areas of contact and avoidance and by indicating persons with whom the respondent has or avoids contact, the results provide profiles of physical accessibility within cultures.

There is evidence that both cultures sharply differentiate between areas of permitted and proscribed contact. There is also agreement on what specific parts of the body belong in each category. The regions of highest physical contact in both cultures include the hand, shoulder, forehead, back of neck, back of head, and forearm. Areas of avoidance include the front pelvic region, rear pelvic region, rear thigh, and leg.

In both cultures the same hierarchy of persons is involved in non-verbal contact: Japanese and Americans report their highest contact with opposite sex friend, next with mothers, next with same sex friends, and finally with fathers. However, there are some differences within this broad grouping. Where Japanese treat opposite sex friends as only somewhat more eligible than mothers or same sex friends, Americans treat opposite sex friends as considerably more attractive; where Americans treat fathers with nearly the same degree of physical intimacy they manifest with same sex friends, Japanese interact dramatically less with fathers than with other target persons. There is also remarkable consistency between "touching" and "being touched." In both Japan and the United States initiating and receiving physical contact co-varies: a higher or lower frequency of touching is accompanied by a higher or lower frequency of being touched. Males in both cultures report slightly more "touching" contact with the opposite sex, while females report a somewhat higher incidence of "being touched."

Although distinctions in nonverbal expressiveness WITHIN the cultures reveal considerable similarity between Japanese and Americans, there is a dramatic contrast between the cultures with regard to the extent of physical communication reported (Figures 9 and 10). In nearly every category the amount of physical contact reported by Americans is twice that reported by Japanese. Although Americans indicate slightly less than double the bodily contact with their mothers, they show more than triple the amount with their fathers as do Japanese. Physical contact is reported more than twice as often by Americans with the opposite sex as well.

Again reference to individual cases imparts some sense of the significance of these findings. The most striking instances are found among

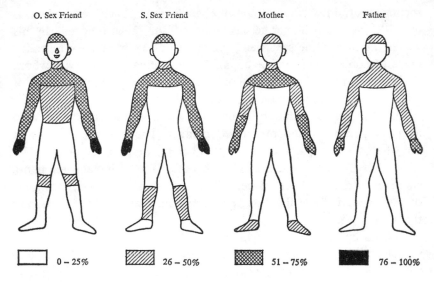

Figure 9. Physical contact: Japan

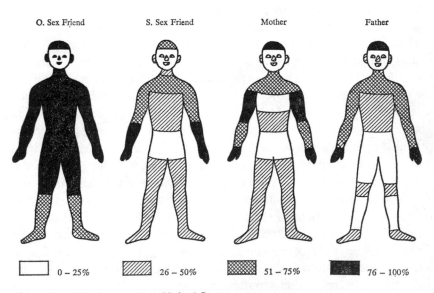

Figure 10. Physical contact: United States

the Japanese. Among the 120 persons who comprised the Japanese sample are several dozens who report very limited physical contact with any acquaintance of any kind. Among these there are a number who report no physical contact whatsoever after the age of fourteen, either with one parent or with same or opposite sex friend. Several reported they could never remember any contact with their fathers, and there are a few cases of almost total isolation even from peers. Among Americans there are no instances of this sort. All had physical contact with one or both parents and friends of one or both sexes. There were cases of relative isolation but none approaching the extremes found among Japanese. With Americans, the extreme was in the opposite direction: Most students reported physical contact with an opposite sex friend in all areas of the body, and many indicated contact in at least two-thirds of the areas with the same sex friend and with mother and/or father.

There is strong evidence here of cultures differentially enforcing norms that regulate physical communication in interpersonal relationships. Americans appear to be more physically accessible and more physically expressive to mothers, fathers, same sex friends, and opposite sex friends. The widest discrepancy exists with regard to fathers; Japanese report only a third as much touching behavior with them as do Americans. Apparently, the intense physical intimacy that characterizes infancy in both cultures takes a different course in later childhood, and by adulthood results in wide cultural differences with regard to the communication of self through physical contact.

Two quite opposite interpretations might be made of this contrast: perhaps the atrophying of this channel of communication is evidence of "growing up," of passing through no more than an infantile stage on the way to communicative maturity through words; or it may represent the curtailing of an indispensable channel that limits the capacity for empathy and intimacy. At any rate the picture of nonverbal communication obtained lends further support for the hypothesized differences in communicative style. Physically, as well as verbally, the Japanese appear to disclose less of themselves, manifesting a more limited "public self," while Americans appear to disclose more of themselves, manifesting a more extensive "public self."

DEFENSE AGAINST DISCLOSURE OF SELF

In the face of messages that challenge or threaten their private view of the world of or themselves, one might expect Japanese and Americans to favor different defensive tactics. For the Japanese it is hypothesized that the dominant communicative strategy should be one of "passive withdrawal," that though there may be variety in the content and form of their reaction, the latent psychological theme will be to avoid further exposure of their views, reduce involvement with others, and attempt to withdraw from further interaction. Americans, in the face of disturbing messages, should be predisposed to different defensive reactions. Here the underlying communicative strategy should be one of "active aggression," in which threat will be met by increasing involvement, further elaboration of beliefs, and aggressive reply to those who challenge core beliefs.

A Defensive Strategy Scale was developed that would differentiate between levels of threat, specify a wide range of possible sources of threat, and provide a spectrum of different types of defensive response. The instrument provides for reactions to low and high levels of interpersonal threat and identifies target persons who are older and younger, superior and subordinate, same and opposite sex, admired and not admired, mother and father, closest same and opposite sex friend, and stranger. The defensive messages include fourteen frequently reported reactions to threat: (1) remain silent, (2) act as if I didn't hear, (3) show nonverbally I preferred not to answer, (4) hint verbally I preferred not to answer, (5) laugh, (6) change the subject, (7) reply in abstract or ambiguous language, (8) ask others what they think, (9) say I did not want to discuss it, (10) try to talk my way out of the situation, (11) answer the remark directly, even though uncomfortable, (12) defend myself by explanation and argument, (13) use humor or sarcasm to put him in his place, and (14) tell him to mind his own business. Respondents were urged not to speculate about what they might do but to report what they had actually done in such encounters in the past.

The scale makes it possible to distinguish broadly between "passive" and "active" forms of interpersonal defense. Although the reactions that fall in the middle of the spectrum might be subject to alternative interpretations, the five that fall at either extreme would appear to be readily identified as passive or active. In the former, the person handles his anxiety by reducing involvement, disguising his reaction, or avoiding further participation. In the latter, he expresses himself more fully, extends and elaborates his position, risks deeper involvement, and may even counterattack those who threaten him.

When considerations of sex, traits of the target person, and intensity are set aside, the Japanese show considerable variety and less contrast among their defensive reactions than do Americans. They most frequently prefer to "say I did not want to discuss it," "hint verbally I preferred not to answer," and "remain silent." They rarely report "tell him to mind his own business," "use humor or sarcasm to put him in his place," or "defend myself by explanation and argument." With one exception the most favored replies are of the "passive" type, and without exception the least favored are "active." And this holds true generally for both low and high levels of threat.

A quite different pattern characterizes the reactions of Americans to the same circumstances. Here there is a sharp contrast in the defensive techniques they favor and reject. They prefer responding to threatening communications by using active forms such as "answer the remark directly, even though uncomfortable," "defend myself by explanation and argument," and "use humor and sarcasm to put him in his place." They least choose to "ask others what they think," "laugh," and "change the subject." The preference for active reaction to threat is striking with all five highest choices falling at the active end of the scale. Again the level of threat introduces no substantial difference in the response pattern.

Are there differences in the way males and females respond to threatening interpersonal situations? One would expect so. But the results do not indicate any substantial difference. Partly this is due to cultural differences overriding sexual ones. Americans distinguish so sharply between preferred and avoided defensive techniques that their scores overwhelm the less dramatic differences among the Japanese. But the expectation of large sex differences may be incorrect; to be born Japanese or American appears to be far more influential in determining communicative style than being born male or female.

Nor is there much evidence of adaptation to the source of threatening remarks. There is some tendency in that direction, especially among Japanese, but it is not a strong one. Japanese tend to favor different defenses for older and superior persons in contrast to younger and subordinate ones. They differentiate slightly between those they respect and do not respect. But essentially the same defenses are reported with mothers and fathers and with opposite and same sex friends. There is striking consistency in defensive communication among Americans. The same defensive tactics are employed with everyone, regardless of status, sex, power, or relationship.

There are, of course, individual differences. Some persons rely almost exclusively upon two or three kinds of defensive messages. In the case of the Japanese, it was often a preference for remaining silent, laughing, replying ambiguously, or preferring to talk about something else. Among Americans there were those who relied heavily upon sarcasm, talked their way out of the situation, or defended themselves by argument. Yet others reported using nearly every form of defense under some social circumstance. Some respondents differentiated little between low and high levels of threat, but others chose from an almost entirely different repertoire of messages, depending on the intensity of anxiety.

Cultural factors would appear to complicate the interpretation of the findings on defensive behavior. There are cultural differences in the concept of threat and particularly in the meaning of evasion. The American cannot understand why his Japanese associate gives such puzzling answers to such simple questions; the Japanese cannot understand how his American associate can give such glib answers to such puzzling questions.

It would appear, too, that the Japanese are among the most diligent of peoples in preventing the occurrence of embarrassing or threatening confrontations. Formalizing human relationships is a way of neutralizing differences and intercepting conflicts that might prove disturbing. Preserving harmony appears to be a cardinal virtue within Japanese society (Embree 1939; Halloran 1969; Maraini 1965). Americans, largely as a consequence of a fuller expression of inner reactions, are more likely to be exposed to threatening encounters. In short, one culture may cope with interpersonal anxiety by carefully managing conversations so that threatening situations rarely occur. The other may cultivate skill in coping with such situations because they seem inevitable or even desirable.

Finally there are linguistic and stylistic differences in speech that complicate the analysis of defensive behavior. The restricted use and availability of personal pronouns in Japanese may reduce the degree of personal involvement. The lack of number and gender, along with restrictions in tense, may make for less precise identification of referents. Greater verbal ambiguity, of course, cuts two ways communicatively: it makes assertion more dangerous because one cannot know the precise meaning assigned a remark by the receiver, and it makes every reply partly defensive by obscuring the intended meaning it contains.

Habits of language usage also may contribute to the reduction of interpersonal friction in Japan. The ubiquitous use of "ne" and "yo" may have the effect of softening or blunting the abrasive edge of bold assertions. The high frequency with which "ka" appears in conversation, transforming declarative statements into questions, may also change the temper of discussion. Conversation proceeds not by negation or contradiction as in the West, but by affirmation where the speaker seeks continual confirmation and approval from the listener. Talk becomes a means of seeking areas of consensus rather than a process of identifying differences.

Yet there remains substantial evidence of a cultural difference in defensive behavior. Regardless of the social circumstances, Americans prefer to defend themselves actively, exploring and developing the rationale for positions they have taken. When pushed, they may resort to still more aggressive forms that utilize humor, sarcasm, or denunciation. Among Japanese the reactions are more varied, but defenses tend to be more passive, permit withdrawal, and allow greater concealment. Rejected defensive modes in both cultures provide an even clearer picture. Japanese tend to avoid active and aggressive tactics in meeting threat, while Americans consistently avoid passive forms of defense. Where the Japanese may ritualize encounters to avoid the triggering of threat, Americans may find such situations an inevitable consequence of their greater expressiveness.

REFLECTIONS

At the outset, a proposition was formulated to guide inquiry into the communicative behavior of Japanese and Americans. This proposition was that the proportion of inner experience that was shared with others, the public self, and that was not shared, the private self, differ in these two nations. The first hypothesis derived from this was that the Japanese would prefer to converse with fewer people and with greater selectivity, while Americans would interact more widely and with less discrimination. This was not tested directly but there is indirect support of it in the findings. Americans, it was found, communicate at deeper levels both verbally and nonverbally with all their associates than do Japanese.

The second hypothesis was that Japanese should prefer more regulated and Americans more spontaneous forms of communication. Here, too, the evidence is indirect, but the cultural profiles suggest that such is the case. Japanese described themselves and are described as "formal," "reserved," "cautious," and "evasive," while the most common adjectives attributed to Americans are "frank," "self assertive," "informal," and "talkative." It would be difficult to identify profiles that would be more compatible with preferences for regulated or for spontaneous conversation.

With regard to level of verbal disclosure the cultures differ sharply.

Japanese rarely talk in more than "general terms" on any topic to any person, while Americans disclose on all topics and to all persons at significantly deeper levels, often approaching full and complete disclosure. The cultures differ sharply, too, on the extent to which they encourage or discourage physical expressiveness. Touching behavior is reported nearly twice as often in all categories and with all persons by Americans as by Japanese. It would appear that where one culture severely limits physical communication, the other encourages it as a legitimate form of interaction.

When interpersonal threat occurs, it appears that both cultures respond by employing forms of defense that are consistent with their prevailing communicative style. Japanese prefer to reduce involvement, to withdraw from interaction, and to withhold further disclosure of self. Americans, consistent with their more expressive style, prefer defenses that permit continued involvement and further disclosure. Thus, there is strong if not conclusive evidence of cultural divergence in coping with anxiety-arousing conversations. Practical limitations prevented any exploration of the hypothesis that these cultural differences would tend to limit the degree and accuracy of self-knowledge among Japanese and permit wider and more accurate self-knowledge among Americans.

Having come this far in identifying cultural styles, what are the further implications of these findings? In what way do such communicative patterns frustrate or enlarge human potentials? In what way do these styles promote more or less accurate communication? Toward what social pathologies do they tend when carried to extremes? Although extremely hazardous and unavoidably controversial, it is relevant to probe such questions.

What are the psychic consequences of the personality structures each culture imposes? Will the Japanese, expressing inner meanings less often and less deeply, become less known to themselves and to each other? If thoughts and feelings are continually inhibited is there risk of driving them irretrievably into the unconscious? Conversely, will repeated opportunities for fuller expression contribute to greater self-knowledge? In short, is expression of the self essential to growth of the self? Or does confining areas of expression limit psychic development?

In infancy, of course, there is no private or public self, there is only an undivided self. Whatever is experienced is announced. Yet every culture cultivates some distance, some formality, and some dishonesty in human affairs; by adulthood an inner split is accomplished and the self is compartimentalized. This division, necessary or not, is bought at a price. It takes considerable psychic energy to monitor reactions continuously, carefully segregating what must be concealed from what can be shared. This inner guardedness makes it difficult for men to experience events deeply and makes them suspicious of their own reactions. They must continually guard their own lives, sensitively forecasting reactions to each word or gesture, censoring those that may be disapproved. The result is not only to alienate men from each other but from themselves as well.

There is reason to believe that restrictions on expression may limit psychic development. A self appears to develop best through experience, the wider and deeper the better. But experiences do not acquire meaning except through symbolic transformations, and this may best be stimulated through attempts to share it with others. Some forms of mental retardation appear to result from living in environments that discourage self-expression. Gifted people — artists, poets, scientists — seem to experience both inner and outer worlds most abundantly, and this may be linked to more frequent and fuller self-expression.

Studies of human interaction from casual encounters to therapeutic ones seem to reinforce this view. Goffman (1961: p. 41) notes that "there seems to be no agent more effective than another person in bringing a world for oneself alive, or by a glance, a gesture, or a remark, shriveling up the reality in which one is lodged." It appears to be the challenge of deep verbal involvement with another person that also aids therapeutic recovery. Takeo Doi, one of Japan's leading psychiatrists, has commented on the extent to which his patients seem to possess "no self."

Yet many spokesmen of Eastern cultures would dispute this emphasis on self-expression. They would argue that men arrive at a more sensitive, more complete, and more individualistic experience of the world and of themselves through contemplation and introspection. Is silence any less effective a route into the interior of man than speech? Can externalizing every thought and feeling diminish rather than extend the dimensions of the self?

Or perhaps the two views are reconcilable: one valuing private reflection and one valuing a full sharing of inner reactions. Both seem essential and may combine in the communicatively mature person. Here there is a capacity for private reflection that is neither a defensive retreat nor a repression of response and a capacity for self-expression that is neither an aggressive confrontation nor a compulsive drive for attention.

Next, how do these communicative styles complicate or facilitate interpersonal understanding? If the cultures of the world could be placed along a disclosure gradient, neither Japan nor the United States might occupy the extreme ends, but there would be a wide gap separating them. There is evidence both of greater superficiality of contact and of greater interpersonal isolation in one culture compared to the other. How does this affect the quality of communication?

Even when men earnestly and honestly seek to understand each other, there are immense obstacles to this achievement. Each occupies a world of his own and brings to every conversation different assumptions, backgrounds, and motives. No two people perceive alike even within a single culture. And the words they employ to bridge this experiential divide are vague and diffuse in meaning. But these intrinsic difficulties are compounded when conversational partners do not even permit themselves to be known. Each presents, in part at least, a facade; what is felt is not expressed, what is believed is not reported. The messages are no longer clues to meaning but are consciously manipulated to camouflage meaning. If communication is difficult when people express themselves authentically, imagine the complications when they do not even attempt this. Concealment of self does not merely prevent understanding, it encourages misunderstanding. Even if one succeeds in grasping what has been said, it may be only a contrived public self that he understands, not the real or private self.

Yet differences in cultural styles may have still another communicative consequence. To share an experience involves not only encoding or symbolizing that experience but the decoding or the comprehension of such symbolization. The effect of encouraging such traits as "talkativeness" and "self assertion" among Americans may be the cultivation of a highly self-oriented and sensitive transmitter of meaning, while the effect of encouraging such traits as "caution" and "reserve" among Japanese may be the cultivation of a highly other-oriented and sensitive receiver of meaning. A kind of communicative specialization occurs, so that what one society does well, namely listening, the other society may do poorly; and what the other society does well, namely speaking, the former society may do less effectively.

Speculations concerning the larger social consequences of these cultural differences are the most hazardous of all. The Japanese appear to place the highest value on preserving the harmony of the group, on meeting role expectations. There is greater respect for silent introspection, less for public eloquence. Words are somewhat suspect, and the expression of feelings, particularly negative ones, is avoided. Relations appear to be more superficial and more governed by social convention. Among Americans the highest value lies in preservation of individual integrity. Conforming is a form of psychic suicide. Strength comes from the capacity to stand alone or even against the group. Actualizing oneself is the primary aim. There is less respect for private reflection and more for public eloquence. The ability to express oneself in a compelling way is highly prized.

Each of these communicative styles appears to carry its own destructive potential. The denial of selfhood, or abdication of it in favor of social harmony, can dangerously encourage conformity. A submissive self is prerequisite to a dominated self; authoritarian control might appear the ultimate destiny of a self-denying culture. Yet the opposite consequence may contain equal risk. Where priority is always granted the individual, where self-expressive acts are unrestrained by considerations of others, the outcome is not alienation from self, but from others. A society of private individuals, each preoccupied with his own self-expression, reduces to no society at all.

CONCLUSION

The "universe of discourse" in Japan and the United States — the form and content of daily interaction — appears to differ in significant respects. What people talk about and to whom they talk, what parts of the body they touch and whom they touch, seem consistent from one culture to another. But the depth of verbal disclosure and the degree of physical intimacy that is cultivated differ sharply. Patterns for coping with threatening social encounters also take different forms. Through all these symbolic activities, verbal and nonverbal, there appears a recurrent theme: individuals in one culture are encouraged to share less of their personal experience with significant other people, while individuals in the other culture are encouraged to communicate a larger portion of their private thoughts and feeling. Such differences in modes of communication carry with them serious psychic, interpersonal, and social consequences for both the individuals and the cultures.

REFERENCES

BENEDICT, R.
1946   *The chrysanthemum and the sword.* Boston: Houghton Mifflin.
DOI, L. T.
1962   "Amae: a key concept for understanding Japanese personality structure," in *Japanese culture: its development and characteristics.* Edited by R. J. Smith and R. K. Beardsley. Chicago: Aldine.
1972   Remarks to Japan Society for the Promotion of Science Seminar, Tokyo, Japan.
EMBREE, J.
1939   *Suye Mura: a Japanese village.* Chicago: University of Chicago Press.
GOFFMAN, E.
1961   *Encounters: two studies in the sociology of interaction.* Indianapolis: Bobbs-Merrill.
HALLORAN, R.
1969   *Japan: images and realities.* Tokyo: Tuttle.
JOURARD, S.
1966   An exploratory study of body-accessibility. *British Journal of Social and Clinical Psychology.* 5:221–231.
JOURARD, S., P. LASAKOW
1958   Some factors in self-disclosure. *Journal of Abnormal and Social Psychology* 56:91–98.
MOLONEY, J.
1954   *Understanding the Japanese mind.* New York: Philosophical Library.
MARAINI, F.
1965   *Meeting with Japan.* New York: Viking Press.
NAKAMURA, H.
1964   *Ways of thinking of Eastern peoples.* Honolulu: East-West Press.
NAKANE, C.
1970   *Japanese society.* Berkeley: University of California Press.
WAGATSUMA, H.
1969   Major trends in social psychology in Japan. *American Behavioral Scientist* 12:36–45.

The Social Function of Experiences of Altered Perception

CRAIG JACKSON CALHOUN

The object of this study is the experience of altered perception, an intrinsically individual event. The focal point from which it is viewed is society. Social scientists are not always the first to be explicit with definitions and frequently look down upon those who don't understand precisely what they mean. This problem, a characteristic of what Kuhn calls the "pre-paradigmatic" stage of a science (Kuhn 1970) forces scholars to spend a great deal of their time working out definitions. Perhaps since definitions not only affect our communication but shape the very substance of our thought the effort may be seen as worthwhile. As scientists we attempt to surmount any phenomenological notion of the subjective constitution of the world; we should continue our effort, not delude ourselves into thinking we have succeeded.[1] Such battles are never won, only pushed further.

It will be noted that the definitions I offer overlap each other in that all are a part of the same scheme and that scheme is being demonstrated at the same time. No rigorous attempt is made to define the terms outside their relationship to one another.

Social function is considered to be the way individual acts, entities, and experiences determine and are determined by the interpersonal context, both immediate and infinite, in which they take place. The immediate context refers to real, live actors in their responses, the infinite is the net-

---

[1] Of course, it is the subjective constitution of the world which this paper postulates, and to a large extent, it is that with which it deals. The author wishes to recognize a considerable otherwise uncited debt to several phenomenological philosophers. In particular, Husserl, a bit corrupted in my thinking by shared emphasis on Kierkegaard, Heidegger and Merleau-Ponty, has influenced this paper. In fact, I am occasionally convinced that he must have said it all somewhere and I have only missed the passage. Consider, for example, this passage from *Ideas:*

work of interrelations and continuities which exists beyond individual lives and actions. Social function, for the purposes of this paper, refers to the tie between the individual unit and the larger system. Thus, kinship, seen as an analytic system, does not have social function but is social function. Particular kinship acts have social functions. Any particular individual's internalizations of kinship systems have social functions. Those concepts (externalizations) which help the scholar or native tie together the diversities of experience and observation are plasma holding the individual unit within them. The observer delimits the notion of unity, thus being able to treat a single structure at different times as a concept (fabric of smaller units) and as a percept (immediate whole, gestalt). We must be cautious in our classifications, and avoid assuming an intrinsic and exclusive unity at one level.

Something of the relationship between social and individual functions should be noted as well. The way in which something functions within the life of the individual is not, as such, a social fact.[2] It may be, however, depending on certain other conditions. For example a psychological function, such as an emotional release from strictures, may be seen as a social need.[3] Thus whatever fills this individual need has a social function as well. Individual acts are always social in effect. Even the choice of an

---

... the nullifying of the world means, correlatively, just this, that in every stream of experience (the full stream, both ways endless, of the experiences of an Ego) certain ordered empirical connexions, and accordingly also systems of theorizing reason which take their bearing from these, would be excluded. But this does not involve the exclusion of other experiences and experiential systems. Thus no real thing, none that consciously presents and manifests itself through appearances, is necessary for the Being of consciousness (in the widest sense of the stream of experience) (Husserl 1931: 137).

The doctrine of intentionality, that to be conscious OF something is an act of the Ego which constitutes the thing the Ego is conscious of, a starting point for much of Gestalt psychology, is also an implicit postulate of the argument of this paper. The world is essentially structured by the individual, and he may learn his structures from society, and they may be changed in various ways.

[2] Durkheim remains the most prominent discussant of social fact. He suggests in *The rules of sociological method* that the social is that which is not completely contained in the individual act. There is an important dichotomy in his work among things which meet this rather ambiguous criterion. There are those which are abstractions of particular events, i.e. language, and those which are particular in time and space, i.e. mob action. Thus one distinguishes collective organization and collective patterns of perception and categorization from collective behavior. We are concerned here principally with the former.

[3] This is how Freud, for example, viewed the situation and attempted, in *Totem and taboo*, to account for rituals which allowed extremes of illicit (otherwise) behavior. An element of this seems quite plausibly the case, although certainly it is an insufficient account of ritual in its particular forms.

individual to opt out of society by committing suicide or defining himself as psychotic is social in as much as it is a choice having both a social rate and a particular interpersonal history (effect and determination). The choice need not involve immediate action with other people to be a social choice. What the individual does always has a social function since he is always a potential social actor. What he is, or what happens to him, has only a social function in so far as it is expressed in behavior, and/or the result of the behavior of other persons. While this may include nearly all possible situations, it will be noted to include only certain analytic aspects of them.

In a way, experience and perception are two sides of the same coin. Perception is an externalized image of an event or scene; experience is its internalizing relation. Perception is what our bodies tell us we have sensed; experience is the system into which we fit the perception. Perception is non-temporal, the act of an instant;[4] experience is completely temporal, the changing of one moment into the next, dependent on the past, determining the future, but without a break, having the individual life as its continuity. Perception is a sensory act of definition, with a beginning — contact with a stimulus — and an end — termination of contact. For both perception and experience the individual is the crucial factor. It is the single organism that perceives and experiences.

For perception, we need not distinguish between humans and other animals. Human experience, however, includes consciousness. As inclusive of consciousness, it includes the process of CONCEPTION of ideas. Experience is not limited to consciousness, of course. It is the whole of the connection between the individual and his life; it is mediated by its own history, and by perception.

Just as perception, at its level, may perceive different external realities, so experience, at a higher level, may experience different internal processes — recollection and expectation as well as perception. These three vary, of course, about a temporal focus. Further differentiation may be noted by considering the mode of thought as well as the temporal representation. We may recollect, for example, in original perceptions, in conceptions, or in abstract theoretical structures. On some level perceptions remain intact; they may also fade, fuse, and change with time. Each recol-

---

[4] Put well by Durkheim: "Sensual representations are in a perpetual flux; they come after each other like the waves of a river, and even during the time that they last, they do not remain the same thing. Each of them is an integral part of the precise instant when it takes place. We are never sure of again finding a perception such as we experienced it the first time; for if the thing perceived has not changed, it is we who are no longer the same" (Durkheim 1915: 481).

lection is a distinct psychic act which involves a new perception, conception, etc. whether or not it is identical with the old.

When we speak of experiences of altered perception, then, we speak of experiences in the "now" in which perception follows different patterns from other, more statistically modal, "nows" [everyday life][5] and in which this differentiation is not random, but specifically altered. Such experiences are always intense and climactic, as a move from everyday structures must be. Whether or not the cause is also climactic does not matter in predicting that the event will be overwhelming. It is the dramatic effect which dissembling everyday structures has which gives the experience of altered perception its cruciality. Where everyday operations for dealing with data are suspended, what happens to the data becomes extraordinarily important. In the absence of the usual categorizations for perceptions, the mind must deal with them in terms of a range of alternate structures which are not necessarily available to more casual adoption. Whether these are supplied by society, or created *ad hoc* by the individual, or systematized by other orders, they exercise a telling influence on the individual and through him on society.

We can show four rather simple categories of experiences of altered perception: (1) Individual experience. This refers to such individual deviations as a "nervous breakdown." The criteria are that the experience not be shared and that the individual be alone while he experiences it. (2) Individual experience within a group having different individual experiences. In this instance, while the experience itself is not shared, there is interaction with other people who, though they may not be seeing the same things, are also seeing things as different from their usual manifestations. An example would be a group of individuals "tripping" together in a non-structured situation on different psychotropic drugs. (3) Shared experience with a group not present. Here the individual's perception is altered in the same way as other persons' are or have been. For example, all individuals undergoing strict Freudian psychoanalysis experience certain similar alterations of experience such as the transference neurosis. Another example would be the use of popular books in counter-culture drug experiences. Works such as *The psychedelic experience*, a manual based on the *Tibetan book of the dead* and created by Timothy Leary, Richard Alpert (Baba Ramdass), and Ralph Metzger, determine to a large

---

[5]   The phrase "everyday life" is used instead of the more formal "normative" because of the implication normative carries for approved, socially sanctioned behavior. Behavior during ritualized experiences of altered perception may very well be normative in this sense; it is proper under the circumstances. It is not, however, usual in everyday life.

extent the nature of experiences of altered perception for a very large, noninteracting population. (4) Experience shared within a present group. Here the persons have qualitatively similar alterations of perception and are present and experiencing them together. The *communitas* experiences described by Victor Turner (1969, in particular) often seem to fall into this category, including religious experiences within such a group as the members of a pilgrimage, the experiences of some participants in rites of passage, and the experiences of members of encounter groups or other therapeutic collectives.[6]

The classification criterion shared-individual is very rough, and is included to point up what the author thinks are crucial differences between experiences where the particulars of alteration are shared, and those where only the fact of alteration is held in common. Where particulars are shared the experience itself is much more likely to produce commonalities in future behavior and/or experience.

It is our intention to examine the social function of experiences of altered perception more closely than by simply setting up categories. Each and every part of such an experience, each constituent unit, is likely to have very specific referents as well as very particular effects. In addition, of course, the larger units, at each level of the componential structure up to the whole of the experience, have causes for and effects of their particular structures. The structures and particulars experienced in this high intensity are likely to be traceable in their determination of later organizations of data and behavior corresponding to their specificity. For example, rolling a "joint" of marijuana in paper bearing the picture of an American flag is a clear signatory act of disrespect, but one which reaffirms the symbolic importance of the flag although placing it in a different context from most American ideology. It is the context which determines the import of the symbolic gesture. A more diffuse gesture such as drawing a pentangle requires all the more complex integration into a structure to place it in an important position socially, and to identify the import.

An experience of altered perception may support or attack either particular points or an entire structure. Indeed, such experiences may constitute some of the strongest supports or most devastating attacks possible on a social order. Two variables are involved in determining the effect

---

[6] *Communitas* is a rather unclear term in Turner. It can usually be taken to mean an intense experience of oneness, human-ness, commonality amongst fellows. The unity of all is a general feature. There are exceptions to this description in Turner's examples, however. In addition, the question remains as to whether *communitas*/liminality are necessarily temporary (as I would suggest) or whether they may be perpetual, as in Turner's example of the early Franciscans. We may hope that a clearer definition of this most useful concept will be worked out soon.

of experiences of altered perception in a social situation. Experiences may be more or less ritualized, and more or less provided for in the social order. The interplay of these two variables provides the mechanism for these experiences' contribution to the maintenance or change of the social order.

As it tends toward ritualization, the experience builds in its participants an internal perception of the ritualizing order. Durkheim, considering this to be the central feature of the religious cult, comments:

The cult is not simply a system of signs by which the faith is outwardly translated; it is a collection of the means by which this is created and recreated periodically. Whether it consists in material acts or mental operations, it is always this which is efficacious ...

We have seen that this reality, which mythologies have represented under so many different forms, but which is the universal and eternal objective cause of these sensations *sui generis* out of which religious experience is made, is society (Durkheim 1915: 464, 465).

Society, the external ritualizing order, is seen as creating the religious cult. Yet, equally, society is a development out of religion for Durkheim:

In summing up, then, it may be said that nearly all the great social institutions have been born in religion. Now in order that these principal aspects of the collective life may have commenced by being only varied aspects of the religious life, it is obviously necessary that the religious life be the eminent form and, as it were, the concentrated expression of the whole collective life. If religion has given birth to all that is essential in society, it is because the idea of society is the soul of religion (Durkheim 1915: 466).

In as much, then, as experiences of altered perception may be analogous to what Durkheim treats as religious experiences (an amount limited, for one thing, by the amount to which they are ritualized) they constitute symbolic representations of the social order. Where not analogous, that is, where the experiences are not ritualized reflections of the social order, they act as attacks upon it. Where highly ritualized by the social order they support it. In either event, the experience of altered perception is highly determinant of behavior toward the ritualizing and any other orders.

Ritualized experiences of altered perception need not represent society as it is usually viewed in order to be supports (they would hardly qualify as ALTERED were that a requirement). As Victor Turner, among others, has shown, reversal of the social order in a ritual situation can often be correctly interpreted as affirmation of that order.

Cognitively, nothing underlines regularity so well as absurdity or paradox. Emotionally, nothing satisfies as much as extravagant or temporarily permitted illicit behavior. Rituals of status reversal accommodate both aspects. By making the low high, and the high low, they reaffirm the hierarchical principle. By making the low mimic (often to the point of caricature) the behavior of the high, and by restraining the initiatives of the proud, they underline the reasonableness of everyday culturally predictable behavior between the various estates of society (Turner 1969: 176).

The ritualizing order, however, need not be the dominant order of the society in which the experience takes place. If it is not, then the experience is likely to act as an agent of social change, construct an internal model of a new order and be an occasion for transition. For example, religious conversion experiences, or psychedelic experiences ordered around many valuational systems are often highly ritualized, yet they are not creating the image of, say, modern American society, or of its ideology. They are converting a portion of the populace more or less away from that system, and thus changing the society. Certainly society is not the only possible order and persons in societies have different perceptions, but without dealing with the whole complex question of what constitutes society, we may suggest that in such experiences central values are at issue and all experiences not involving a social order are challenges to it as it requires an element of centrality. The orders in question need not be social at all. In psychoanalysis, the individual patient through the experiences of altered perception is changed in his internal order primarily, rather than in his view of the order of society (though quite likely that as well).

If experiences of altered perception are provided for by the social order they are not necessarily reaffirmations of the status quo. They may be used to deal with change, to construct a transition which saves the identity of the group and/or the society. Barbara Myerhoff has reported that members of a Huichol Indian pilgrimage identify themselves as "the ancesstors, the first Huichol." They then perform a number of rituals in which the deer and the maize (representative of successive hunting and agrarian phases of Huichol culture) are parts of a triad with the mediating figure peyote and are represented as being "one thing." Thus changing social order and life style are kept from changing the identification "Huichol." The modern participants are still one with their ancestors, the Huichol are still one people (Myerhoff 1973).[7]

When experiences of altered perception are provided for in the social order, then there is less likelihood (obviously) that the occurrence of such

---

[7] A bit of an apology is due both Myerhoff and the Huichol for this extremely oversimplified account of a major and complex ritual. Interested readers are referred to her excellent forthcoming discussion entitled *The peyote hunt*. I owe a debt to both Professor Myerhoff and to Riv-Ellen Prell-Foldes, as many of the ideas expressed here were developed in their early stages in joint discussions and the products of those must be considered communal property.

experiences will be a threat. To be a threat, the experience must then be contradictory to the social order in its specifics. In other situations, where experiences of altered perception are forbidden, or considered not to exist for healthy individuals (say, much of America where they would be regarded as evidence of insanity) any such experience is an attack on the social order. If there were any universal drive for certain kinds of experiences (as Turner seems to regard implicitly to be the case for *communitas*) or if release in this form is a human need, then societies which do not allow for experiences of altered perception have a precarious existence. The non-ritualized experience of altered perception tends to be always destructive, leading as it does towards (or from) chaos rather than order. It is, however, less likely to occur where society has a perceivable (internalizeable) order, and where this order allows for cathartic emotional experience, particularly where that experience is so ritualized as to be a support for that order.

REFERENCES

DURKHEIM, EMILE
  1915   *The elementary forms of the religious life*. Translated by J. W. Swain (first edition Paris 1912). New York: Free Press.
  1938   *The rules of sociological method*. Translated by G. E. G. Catlin (first edition Paris 1895). New York: Free Press.
FREUD, SIGMUND
  1952   *Totem and taboo*. Collected works, volume seven. London: Hogarth Press.
HUSSERL, EDMUND
  1931   *Ideas*. Translated by W. R. B. Gibson. New York: Collier Books.
KUHN, THOMAS S.
  1970   *The structure of scientific revolutions*. Chicago: The University of Chicago Press.
MYERHOFF, BARBARA G.
  1973   *The peyote hunt*. Cornell: Cornell University Press.
TURNER, VICTOR W.
  1969   *The ritual process: structure and antistructure*. Chicago: Aldine.

PART THREE

The Individual as a Crucial Locus of Culture

JOHN L. FISCHER

Let us begin with a definition of culture as persistent, socially transmitted and shared information. This definition covers the kinds of things that most anthropologists talk about under the label of "culture" and it is simple enough to be workable.

Information can be coded in various ways. The prime locus of cultural information is in the brains of members of the society who participate in the culture. However, in order to be transmitted from one member to another the information in the brain of a transmitter must be recoded from time to time and made manifest in overt behavior. For instance, a language must be made manifest in the words of actual speech for children to learn it from their seniors. Moreover, cultural information is sometimes further recoded from overt behavior in various more or less permanent material forms. Thus speech may be recoded into written form or on magnetic tape or plastic discs from which it may eventually be reconstituted into audible sound and transmitted to a human listener or reader after a delay.

Some shared information is too ephemeral to be regarded as cultural in the strict sense. The specific information that individual A in family X went to the store and bought a list of groceries may be known to other members of the family at the time and thus constitute "shared information," but this is not the sort of information which persists for long. In a year or less the specific trip to the store is likely to be completely forgotten. Thus we limit culture to socially shared information which is persistent for years or preferably generations, and we may measure culturality along this dimension of persistence or extent in time.

An item of information which an individual possesses by himself is not to be regarded as cultural in the strict sense. It may become cultural if he communicates it to a fellow group member and thus shares it. The most clearly cultural item, other things being equal, is one which is shared by all appropriate members of a society or lasting social group. A private word which a child invents and uses mostly within his family is only marginally cultural. The phonemes and semantic concepts which are combined into the word are shared as a general rule and therefore are cultural, but the unique total combination which constitutes the word is idiosyncratic. A second dimension of the culturality of an item of information is, therefore, the extent to which the item is shared within the society of the bearers. This dimension may be termed social distribution.

Some cultural items, e.g. basic vocabulary, common recipes and items of diet or other basic subsistence technology, are shared among all normal adults of a society. These score at the top end of the scale of social distribution. These items constitute the core of a culture and are a special object of study of cultural anthropologists. But we may also wish to regard some items of information known mainly to specialists as high on the scale of social distribution if they are shared by all appropriate specialists, e.g. the basic technical vocabulary, materials, and tools of electricians. By definition, specialists must always be fewer in number than the total population of the society. Yet their shared information has generally been regarded as equally cultural with the core of the culture. By using the criterion of proportional sharing among the group of specialists rather than in the entire society we may acknowledge the full culturality of some of the information of specialists.

Incidentally, it is evident that in small, relatively homogenous societies the total store of cultural information for the whole society is relatively small because of the lack of many kinds of specialists. At the same time it seems likely that the total store of cultural information per capita is more or less comparable to that for individuals in large, complex, literate societies. This implies that the proportion of the cultural core (as defined above) to cultural specialities is larger for members of homogenous societies than for large, differentiated societies. At the same time, a certain minimum cultural core is probably necessary for a large society to persist and retain its unity. The effect of long-range cultural evolution therefore would be to expand cultural specialities, partly at the expense of the cultural core but much more by simply multiplying the number of kinds of specialists and by increasing the population of the society to provide enough personnel and clientele for the various specialist roles.

In any case, however, with the increase in number and variety of specialists it is clear that the fraction of the total culture of the society mastered by any one individual must decrease. The fraction mastered by a member of a large modern society is quite small. This poses a problem for the cultural anthropologist hoping to study modern societies unless he is willing to concentrate on the cultural core.

We may also look at the mastery of culture in terms of the individual life span. The newborn infant has no culture in the strict sense, although the culturally influenced behavior of his mother (diet, exercise, drugs, etc.) will have already influenced his physical development in the womb. Specialists dispute the nature and amount of early post-natal learning, including cultural learning. At any rate it is clear that infants lack an active mastery of even the cultural core, although they begin to acquire it rapidly along with the attainment of grammatical speech. In early childhood learning seems quite labile, including the acquisition of the cultural core: new information is easily learned but it is also rapidly forgotten or ignored if the child is removed from the setting where it is useful. This is the age when a child can get a working knowledge of a new language and culture within a few months and shame his less adaptable parents.

One issue in the study of enculturation (the acquisition of culture by the individual) is the extent to which typical early experiences prepare the child for later mastery of a much more extensive culture core and perhaps many cultural specialities as well. Such investigators as Freud and Piaget have emphasized the importance of early experience, but others, often using the perspective of experimental animal psychology, have postulated that the learning of each cultural item is relatively distinct and independent. To be sure, even this school has recognized the development of "learning sets," where much experience in handling a certain type of information leads to quicker and more effective learning of further examples of the same general type.

As the child approaches adolescence, he also approaches mastery of the cultural core and at the same time his cultural information becomes more firmly established or overlearned. If he is exposed to a new culture at this point adjustment is still possible but slower. After full adulthood adjustment to a new culture is perhaps generally "grafted on," so to speak, to a childhood culture. The exact nature of the relationships between childhood and adult cultures for individuals who have shifted societies deserves further investigation and has important implications, both practically and theoretically.

Presumably all other animal species have much less culture than humans (in the sense of persistent, socially shared information). Nevertheless it is easy to demonstrate that individuals of many mammal species, including subhuman primates, have a wealth of individually learned non-cultural information about their territory, kinds of food, predators and parasites, etc. The acquisition of this information is largely guided in each species by its innate sensory capacities and its drives or instincts, in the broad sense. This acquisition is cumulative for the individual, in the sense that the earlier experiences of the animal influence its reactions (including further learning) to later experiences.

When people refer to "nature" in contrast to "culture" they are usually referring to information, including behavior patterns, acquired separately by the individual animal in accord with its senses and drives and experience, as contrasted with information transmitted by other members of the society. Of course, in a broad sense culture is a special part of nature and it would be more accurate to speak of "culture versus the rest of nature" or "most of nature versus the cultural part of nature." "Culture versus nature" should be understood as a convenient abbreviation for something like these expressions.

In other species of animals much of the "natural" information acquired by individuals of the same species living in the same area is closely similar, not because of any elaborate social communication but because of the basic similarity for different individuals of their sensory capacities, drives, and experience of a common environment. In humans there is considerable overlap between cultural and natural information, in that human cultures take into account many things which the individual could learn by himself if he were raised, say, by gorilla foster parents. Thus, for instance, all cultures have a concept of the sun and a word for it in their language. Nevertheless, the individual's knowledge of the sun is derived in an important part from his direct experience of it. He often notices the warmth and light and position of the sun even when there is no one around to talk to about it. When he himself talks about the sun to others he is often commenting on an immediate direct natural stimulus (e.g. "The sun is hot today"), not on socially transmitted cultural accretions to the concept of the sun (e.g. "Thanks be to the Sun, our Father"). In this sense, all cultures contain a core of natural information around which there clusters more complex, often arbitrary or elaborately derived, socially transmitted information.

Some of this natural information in culture concerns universal human experiences, but there can also be much individually specialized natural information (non-cultural) where a man has unique experiences which he does not need or wish to communicate to others. For instance, some small tropical islands have a wide variety of marine environments and some fishermen may become specialists in exploiting one or another of these. While the fisherman learns some basic vocabulary and techniques of fishing from his elders, he may acquire much additional knowledge by personal observation while fishing. Much of this knowledge may never be verbalized: familiar conformations of the reef, species of fish which are recognized but for which there are no local names, etc.

While the human species is everywhere crucially cultural, in that people depend for their birth and existence on culture-bearing societies, it seems likely that in the sense just discussed, there is something to the old idea that some societies, and within a particular society some individuals, are closer to nature than others. A society is closer to nature if a relatively large part of its culture is simply a socially transmitted reflection of direct observations and reactions to the unmodified non-human environment.

An individual is closer to nature if a relatively large part of his knowledge of the world is acquired directly from his personal experience of the unmodified non-human environment. Probably the average amount of information, cultural and natural, per capita is very close in all societies and is dependent on the innate capacity of the human nervous system, but the proportion of natural information is probably greater, and the proportion of cultural information correspondingly smaller, among members of small, non-literate societies with simple subsistence technologies. At the same time, the difference between relatively natural and relatively cultural societies should not be exaggerated. Where good reports exist for nature-oriented societies before destruction by civilization (e.g. a group such as the Aranda of Central Australia) it appears that the members greatly valued leisure time (i.e. time not directly devoted to subsistence activities) which they spent in creating and maintaining culture in the forms of dancing, personal ornament, ceremonies, mythology, regulation of marriage, etc.

In discussing the individual as a crucial locus of culture we must consider why a child should acquire culture to start with. Some earlier investigators, influenced by experimental psychology and the example of formal education in modern society, have emphasized the role of older people in applying reward and punishment, intentionally or not, to mold the child's behavior to an ideal pattern. In an extreme version of this view, a culture can contain almost anything which the elders have happened to decide on, perhaps by a process of working out the logically possible variations of the pre-existing culture, a process they may have learned from their elders. It is admitted that culture must contain sufficient practical information to be consistent with the survival of enough members of the society to reproduce the next generation, but it is assumed that a wide variety of cultures are sufficient for this purpose, as is evidenced by ethnographic reports.

Actual observation of enculturation in non-Western societies has often revealed very little application of reward and punishment applied to children, except to keep the children quiet and out of the way when the adults do not want to be bothered. Children in many societies can and do learn to walk, talk, eat, and do many other things with little help or encouragement from parents and caretakers. In some societies, in fact, busy caretakers even try, with only partial and temporary success, to discourage walking, talking, and other activities which make the child more trouble to care for.

An alternate view of enculturation emphasizes the function of culture in satisfying various individual needs. Bronislaw Malinowski is a well-known advocate of this view. In this view the child is naturally interested in mastering his environment, human and natural, and he actively seeks out information which he can use to achieve his goals, whether or not anyone wants to teach it to him. This view may be reconciled with a more sophisticated learning theory which recognizes that in real life, as contrasted with the psychological laboratory, there are many more rewards and punishments from a variety of sources than those controlled by the experimenter, parent, or other authority figure. One of these rewards, incidentally, appears to be simply an optimum variety and quantity of sensory stimulation; in short, the satisfaction of curiosity.

Noam Chomsky's postulation of an innate universal grammar in human children is also consistent with the view of culture — in this case language — as intrinsically rewarding and actively investigated by the child, with or without adult instruction or sanction.

If culture is functional for the individual and if individuals everywhere have similar basic needs, why should different societies have different cultures and how can cultural differences be explained? One answer to this is historical: particular items of culture solving particular human problems often have originated only once in history at a particular place and have not yet had time to spread everywhere. Thus the fire plow was found recently in areas which did not have matches, but once matches became available the fire plow was dropped as a means of making fire.

Another answer is environmental: many items of culture depend on the availability of certain natural resources. Thus metal tools were absent from the oceanic islands of the Pacific until brought in from outside areas by trade, since these islands lacked suitable metal ores.

However, it must be recognized that any item of culture can acquire a double function for the individual: a specific objective function and an identifying social function. The objective function is often regarded as the primary function, e.g. the main purpose of growing a certain staple crop is to satisfy hunger. At the same time, eating this food may also identify the individual as being a proper member of his society in contrast with some other nearby society which uses a different staple food. In other words, sometimes either kind of food could be produced with equal effectiveness by either society if the members wished, but the societies limit themselves each to a different kind of food as a sort of badge of identity and unity. If the two societies become politically united on fairly equal terms and fused through intermarriage this distinction can be expected to disappear quickly, although a new set of cultural badges of identity would then have to be developed for the new, larger society in contrast to other neighbors. To some extent, any item of culture probably has at least a little identifying function for the bearer. If he uses it he identifies himself to himself and others as a member of some society or social group: "We men of tribe X do this;" "we old people of village Y do this;" etc.

The identifying function of culture is at times a source of both stability and innovation. Where two neighboring societies might rationally adopt items of culture from each other they may refuse to do so on the grounds that this would compromise their identity. Where two neighboring societies share certain items of culture at one period, increased competition between them may result in the selective abandonment by one or the other of shared items in order to emphasize the boundary between the societies by additional marks of difference.

The social identifying function probably provides a very important motive for children to learn culture. In the other higher primates some sort of social hierarchy is present in which junior animals not only defer but pay close attention to and imitate the actions of senior animals. It is this attentiveness which holds the group together physically and permits the sharing of important information about the food supply and predators. The imitation of older animals is at times without reference to any clear specific reward, as when a captive chimpanzee scribbles with a pen in imitation of his keeper. Similarly with human children, the motive of identifying with an admired adult or senior peer may be often the principal force behind the acquisition of culture from him.

To the extent that a society is divided into conflicting groups, each group will have its own store of cultural items which serve as badges of group identity. If one group is in a stronger position than another or if individuals pass from a weaker to a stronger group (e.g. age grades, socioeconomic classes) conscious efforts may be made by the leaders of the stronger group to make the members of the weaker group abandon their earlier badges of identity and adopt new ones. Thus an infant who at one point is encouraged to drink milk from a bottle is later encouraged to use a cup if he does not do this on his own initiative. Probably these situations of shift of identity within a society and of intrasocietal group conflict are among the most common where rewards and punishments in the learning of culture are regularly applied by authority figures.

Anthropologists often assume that the transmission of culture from one generation to the next is pretty much automatic. There is some justice in this assumption since striking examples of the continuity of cultural items for millennia can sometimes be cited. In any society there are always some deviant individuals with respect to a number of important cultural items (neurotics, criminals), but cultural stability could be consistent with a number of culturally mutant individuals in each generation, just as the genetic stability of a biological population is consistent with a certain number of recurring genetic mutations which are regularly selected out.

Resistance to some items of the culture of one's society, however, is not limited to obvious deviants but is to some degree characteristic of every individual in a society. For the individual, each item of culturally prescribed behavior has its costs and rewards, the reward being generally greater than the cost, but the cost sometimes coming quite close to the reward. Transmission of an item between generations may well be automatic as long as there is a consistent balance in favor of rewards for the individuals, but for some items a relatively slight increase in psychic cost may be enough to cause individuals to reject them, while others are much more firmly established. In predicting cultural change the reward/cost balance of cultural items for the average individual becomes important. It is also important in trying to understand the acquisition of culture by the young: items where the reward is obvious and the cost low are presumably acquired more rapidly than those for which the cost more nearly balances the reward.

A variety of techniques is useful for investigating the relationships of individuals to their culture. Ethnographic interviewing may be directed at establishing individual membership in special groups within the society, and establishing the various recognized roles which the individual enacts during his life time. The ethnographer would want to learn which groups and roles are or tend to be mutually exclusive and which are compatible in the same individual. Much of this information could be obtained in a few extended individual life histories.

The investigation of individual attitudes toward the culture is also a major issue. These attitudes may appear clearly in some autobiographical interviews but they may be more easily obtained for many individuals by more specialized techniques.

The anthropological investigation of expressive culture — religion, magic, mythology, games and other kinds of recreation — with special attention to participant preference and reaction is one guide to individual reaction to other aspects of the culture which are represented symbolically in expressive culture; e.g. attitudes toward family practices may be represented indirectly inl rituals dealing with family crises and in mythology in which family relations are represented. Many informants are more willing to discuss culturally stereotyped rites and myths with the ethnographer than they are to discuss personal family problems, although the rites and myths may represent in somewhat disguised form typical family practices and problems, and the informant may use them to talk indirectly and non-specifically about his own personal problems.

Anthropologists interested in individual/culture relationships have used projective tests, such as the Rorschach ink blot test, the Thematic Apperception Test (TAT, in which respondents are asked to invent stories about pictures of ambiguous social situations), etc. The psychologists who developed these tests were mostly interested in investigating personality differences among individuals sharing a more or less homogenous background of modern Western culture and have developed interpretations of responses in terms of this background. When these tests are administered in societies with greatly different cultures, responses are generally given which are culturally distinctive and would be given only by abnormal individuals, if at all, in Western culture. From an anthropological point of view, these differences are expectable, but it has proved difficult to interpret the specific results as plausibly as clinical psychologists do in our own society. Most anthroplogists who have worked with these methods feel that for their purposes those tests which are somewhat more structured (e.g. the TAT) provide more useful material than those which are extremely ambiguous (e.g. the Rorschach).

In theory, a psychoanalytic-type interview in which informants would be encouraged to make free associations and say whatever came to mind would provide excellent data for studying the relation of individuals to their culture. In practice, very few ethnographers are trained to conduct such interviews and even the few who have received such training have not found it possible to make much direct use of it, probably in part because of the difficulty of establishing suitable rapport with informants across the sociocultural gap, and in part because of the difficulty of motivating informants to produce apparent nonsense.

Something analogous to free association data may be possible to obtain from informants in some societies by questioning them about dreams and daily activities without attempting to interpret them at length to the informants. In many societies people pay little attention to everyday dreams but informants can often be stimulated and trained to remember and recount recent dreams with a little show of interest by the ethnographer. One way of initiating such a study is to begin by using a dream questionnaire in which the informant is asked if he has ever dreamed of the items or events in a prepared list. With this sort of stimulus, informants who initially disclaim remembering their dreams can often come up with past dreams which made a special impression of them, and proceed from there to more recent dreams.

Perhaps the most useful type of data which anthropologists could gather on individual/culture relationships would be running accounts of current activities for several weeks for a small sample of informants, accompanied by questions on the cultural background of these activities and the reasons for the individual's decisions and his emotional reactions where these are not immediately apparent to the ethnographer. A current activities interview of this sort is likely to produce a lot of trivia and to miss most major life crises at the time of their occurrence, but it has the advantage of providing more information on what really happens in the lives of people as distinct from what is said to happen after the cultural editing, exaggeration and suppression of detail which are applied to more important events retold from distant memory and presented in life history interviews.

Both the life history and current activities interviews are valuable in their own way, of course. In fact, the most promising strategy to develop a deep understanding of the individual/culture relationship would be to select several individuals and apply all the methods discussed above: life history, current activities interview, projective tests, dreams, individual use of expressive culture. The closest published approach to this ideal may still be Cora Du Bois' *People of Alor* (1960, Harvard University Press). With further analysis of her work in the light of later theoretical developments, it should be possible for an ethnographer already familiar with the local language and culture to make a great contribution to the understanding of the relationship of individuals to their culture in small non-literate societies. In view of the increased rate of economic development and the expansion of world trade leading to cultural homogenization it is desirable to do this soon.

Biographical Notes

DEAN C. BARNLUND (1920–   ) received his B.S. and M.S. degrees from the University of Wisconsin, his Ph.D. from Northwestern University. Most of his academic career has been spent at Northwestern University and San Francisco State University. His interests focus on communication theory, interpersonal and intercultural communication, verbal interaction analysis, and the ecology of communication. His research papers have appeared in a variety of academic journals in the behavioral sciences; his books include *The dynamics of discussion* (1960), *Interpersonal communication: survey and studies* (1968), *Nihonjin no hyogen kozo* (1973), and *Public and private self in Japan and the United States* (1974).

JUDITH K. BROWN (1930–   ) received her Ed.D. from the Harvard Graduate School of Education in 1962. Her dissertation was a cross-cultural study of female initiation rites. She holds a Certificate in Child Development from the Institute of Education of the University of London (1955), where she studied on a Fulbright Grant. As a Fellow of the Radcliffe Institute (1967–1969), she engaged in research on the role of women in subsistence activities. Her publications deal with female initiation rites, the relationship of these rites to the economic role of women, the division of labor by sex, and the relationship of the economic role of women to socialization. Since 1969, she has been an Assistant Professor of Anthropology at Oakland University.

MARGARET BULLOWA (1909–   ) was born in New York City. She earned an A.B. from Barnard College, an M.S. in Public Health from

Columbia University, and an M.D. from New York University. She is now retired from the practice of psychiatry. Her interest in failure of communication, especially in the language sphere, led to initiating research, at first directed to language acquisition. Studies were based on weekly longitudinal recording of infant vocalization and behavior from birth to thirty months in the infants' own homes. Pilot work was started in 1959 and a research project was begun at the Massachusetts Mental Health Center in 1960 and continued in the Speech Communication Group at the Massachusetts Institute of Technology since 1965. A number of linguists and social scientists have collaborated in the studies from time to time. As the thinking and writing about the data appeared to be converging with the work of ethnologists working on issues of child development, she is spending a year (August 1974–August 1975) in the laboratory of N. Blurton Jones at the Institute of Child Health of the University of London.

CRAIG J. CALHOUN (1952–) is currently at St. Anthony's College, Oxford University. He was previously at the Department of Social Anthropology in the University of Manchester on a post-graduate research studentship, and was a member of the staff of the Bureau of Applied Social Research and the Department of Sociology in Columbia University. He has also been Research Associate in the Horace Mann-Lincoln Institute at Teachers College, Columbia, and was educated primarily at the University of Southern California and Columbia and Manchester Universities. His publications include "Continuity and change: the significance of time in the organization of experience" and "General status; specific role."

STARKEY DUNCAN, JR. (1935–) received his Ph.D. degree in psychology at the University of Chicago and is now Associate Professor on the Committee on Cognition and Communication there. His primary research interests are in the organization of language, paralanguage, and body-motion behaviors in face-to-face interaction, and in the behavioral regularities deriving from individual differences within that organization.

GERALD M. ERCHAK (1945–) was born in New Jersey. He received his B.A. from Ohio State University in 1967, his A.M. from Harvard in 1970, and is currently completing his work for a Ph.D. from Harvard. He is interested primarily in problems of cross-cultural education and is an Instructor in Anthropology at the State University of New York College at Geneseo, New York.

JAMES L. FIDELHOLTZ (1941–) received his S.B. in Mathematics (1963) and his Ph.D. in Linguistics (1968) from M.I.T. He has been in the linguistics program at the University of Maryland since 1969. His major interests include Micmac and English phonology, and generative phonological theory. He is editor of the *Conference on American Indian Languages Clearinghouse Newsletter*. Recent publications are on mathematical linguistics, language teaching, English orthography, and Micmac verb morphology. Recent research is in semantic organization of the lexicon, English vowel reduction, and a Micmac lexicon.

JOHN L. FISCHER (1923–) is Professor of Anthropology and Chairman of the Department at Tulane University, New Orleans. He received the degrees of B.A. (1946), M.A. (1949), and Ph.D. in Social Anthropology (1955) from Harvard. He has conducted field research in Micronesia, a New England village, and a Japanese city, studying folklore, child rearing, and language. His most recent field research concerns the oral poetry of Ponape, Caroline Islands.

ROBERT F. FORSTON (1940–) was educated in psychology and communications at the University of Minnesota. Now Chairman of the Speech Communication Department at Drake University, Des Moines, Iowa, he is author of *Public speaking as dialogue, Visit into the jury room*, and several articles on communication.

GORDON G. GALLUP, JR. (1941–) is Professor of Psychology at Tulane University. He received his Ph.D. from Washington State University in 1968. His research interests include cognitive capacities in primates, learning, ethology, comparative psychology, and behavior genetics. Currently his work concerns tonic immobility ("animal hypnosis") and its relation to various kinds of human psychopathology.

ESTHER NEWCOMB GOODY (1932–) was born in the United States and took a B.A. in Sociology from Antioch College (Ohio) in 1954. An interest in personality and culture took her to England to study with Meyer Fortes at Cambridge, and from there to fieldwork in northern Ghana in 1956–1957. Since taking a Ph.D. in Social Anthropology in 1961 she has been teaching at Cambridge, and has been a Fellow of New Hall since 1966. Research interests in the relationship between domestic roles and social structure have led to a general study of the Gonja (*Contexts of kinship*, 1973) and several articles. Later focused field studies have concerned traditional fostering by kin (1964, 1965) and informal education (1974) in Ghana, and conjugal and parental roles among West Africans in London (1971).

ANEES A. HADDAD (1931–   ) was born near Beirut, Lebanon. For twelve years he was the Executive Director, Middle East Region, of the International Commission for the Prevention of Alcoholism and Drug Addiction. He received his B.A. from Middle East College, Beirut, in 1957; his M.A. from Loma Linda University, California, in 1968; and his Ph.D. from the University of Southern California, Los Angeles, in 1971. Residing in the United States since 1966, he is now Professor of Sociology and Coordinator of the Middle Eastern Studies Program at Loma Linda University, Loma Linda, California. He has authored numerous studies on family solidarity and mental health and has published widely in both Arabic and English. His special interests include the fields of multi-generational family interaction, socialization, age-stratification and gerontology, medical sociology, and social psychology. He is very active in professional and honor societies, and in 1973 he was elected Outstanding Educator of America.

JOHN A. HOSTETLER is Professor of Sociology and Anthropology at Temple University in Philadelphia, Pennsylvania. He has conducted fieldwork in rural communities in the United States and Canada, and as a Fulbright Scholar studied the origins of Anabaptist communitarians in Central and Eastern Europe. His interests lie in cultural anthropology, the socialization practices of cultural groups, and communitarian movements. He is the author of *Amish society* (1963, revised 1968), *Hutterite society* (1974), and other ethnographic field studies.

KEIKO IKEDA (1949–   ) was born in Kobe. She studied Sociology and Social Psychology at Kobe College where she received her B.A., continued her studies at Kyoto University, Osaka University, and Kōnan University. In 1974, she moved to Tokyo after her marriage. Now she is working with the members of National Council for Privacy Safeguard & Against Integrated Personal Data System (NCAPD).

ALLAN R. KESSLER (1941–   ) is on the research staff of the Center for International Studies and the Research Laboratory of Electronics at the Massachusetts Institute of Technology. He received his S.B. in 1964 and his Ph.D. in 1972 from M.I.T. in Political Science. His present research is in the area of computer-based information management systems and their application to longitudinal records of human behavior.

GEORGE KURIAN did his undergraduate work at Madras University, India, and received his Doctor's degree from the State University of Utrecht, Netherlands. He has taught in Osmania University, India; Victoria University, Wellington, New Zealand; and since 1966 has been with the Department of Sociology, University of Calgary, Alberta, Canada. His books *The Indian family in transition: a case study of Kerala Syrian Christians* (1961) and *Family in India: a regional view* (1974) are published by Mouton Publishers. He has published many articles on family studies and is the Founder Editor of the *Journal of Comparative Family Studies*.

BELA C. MADAY is an anthropologist with the National Institute of Mental Health in Rockville, Md., and Adjunct Professor of Anthropology at The American University in Washington, D.C. Born in 1912, he was educated at the University of Budapest and received his doctorate in 1937. He has had a long and distinguished teaching career. His research interests are East European peasant cultures, especially Hungarian folk culture, culture change, acculturation, and the interface between anthropology and psychiatry. He has edited or co-authored 4 books and 58 articles in Hungarian, and 22 books and 14 articles in English. He is editor of the *Hungarian Studies Newsletter* and was President of the Anthropological Society of Washington (1973–1974).

GLENORCHY MCBRIDE (1925–) is Reader in Ethology in the Animal Behavior Unit, Psychology Department, University of Queensland, Brisbane, Australia. He graduated in Agricultural Science (Adelaide) specializing in Genetics for his Master's (Queensland) and Ph.D. (Edinburgh) degrees. Most of his experimental and observational research has been on the behavior of chickens, both domestic and feral. Theoretical studies have examined societal structures in animals, the relationships between animals and their environments, both husbandry and physical environments, and the structure of the communicative systems in animals and man, including the evolution of the human communicative interaction. He has been a Fellow at the Center for Advanced Studies in the Behavioral Sciences at Palo Alto, California, and a Professor of Man-Environment Relationships at Pennsylvania State University.

DAVID W. PLATH (1930–) is Professor of Anthropology and Asian Studies at the University of Illinois in Urbana-Champaign. He holds M.A. and Ph.D. degrees from Harvard and has been on the Illinois faculty since 1966. His current research deals with topics in aging and human development. Previous publications include: *The after hours* (1964), *Sensei and his people* (1969), *Aware of utopia* (1971), and numerous essays on modern Japanese society and culture.

MARGARET SANFORD (1912–). Educated at the Catholic University of America, she is now Assistant Professor of Anthropology at Longwood College in Virginia. She has made field studies of the Kiowa Apache and the Black Carib of Belize, and has published some of the results of her work.

SHAWN E. SCHERER (1948–) studied at York University and the University of Toronto and is now a clinician with the Addiction Research Foundation, Toronto. He is the author of several papers on proxemics and drug use.

SUSAN SEYMOUR (1940–) studied anthropology at Stanford University (B.A., 1962) and Harvard University (Ph.D., 1971). Her dissertation was based on two years of field research in Bhubaneswar, Orissa, India, where she made a comparative study of family organization and child-rearing practices. Her publications to date have dealt with these materials. She has taught anthropology at Whittier College (1970–1973), the University of Southern California (1973–1974), and is currently at Pitzer College, Claremont. Her special areas of interest are urban anthropology and psychological anthropology.

ELEANOR WENKART SMOLLETT (1937–) is Associate Professor of Anthropology at the University of Regina (Saskatchewan, Canada) where she has taught since 1968. She received her B.A. from Brandeis University and her Ph.D. from Columbia University (1969) with a dissertation on "Occupational change in an urban fringe village in Mysore, India." Her principal research interests have been (1) education and society, especially with regard to social class, and (2) social change in rural communities. Most recently, she has been engaged in field research on social change in a village in Bulgaria.

CAROL B. STACK (1940–   ) is a Professor of Anthropology at Boston University. Before joining the Boston University faculty in 1972 she taught Anthropology at the University of Illinois. In 1974 she was a Visiting Professor at the University of California, Berkeley. She received her B.A. from U.C. Berkeley in Philosophy and a Ph.D. in Anthropology from the University of Illinois (1972). Her special interests include family and social change in the U.S., and she has done research in Afro-American and Irish-American communities in American cities. Long interested in ethnicity in American life, she recently wrote a book on black family life and culture in a Midwestern city, *All our kin: strategies for survival in a black community* (1974, Harper and Row), and is currently doing research on the urban Irish.

LORAND B. SZALAY (1921–   ) has studied modern languages in Budapest and received his Ph.D. in psychology (minor in anthropology) from the University of Vienna (1961). Director of research projects on communication and psychocultural analysis at The American Institutes for Research, Washington, D.C., he is senior author of a book on the Associative Group Analysis method as well as author of communication lexica and articles focusing on perceptions and attitudes and their inferential assessment. Recent publications include: "Measurement of psychocultural distance: a comparison of American blacks and whites," "Analysis of subjective culture," and "Ideology: its meaning and measurement."

WALBURGA VON RAFFLER ENGEL (1920–   ) was born in Munich, Germany. She studied Classical Languages and Archaeology at the University of Turin and at the Italian Institute of Archaeology (Doctor of Letters, University of Turin) and General Linguistics at Indiana University in the United States (Ph.D.). She has held appointments at various universities in Europe and the United States and held a visiting professorship in Canada. Since 1965, she has taught at Vanderbilt University where she is presently Chairman of the Committee on Linguistics of the Nashville University Center, a joint program in Linguistics among Vanderbilt University, Fisk University, Peabody College, and Scarritt College. Her special interests include language acquisition (she is Secretary of the International Child Language Association); nonverbal behavior (Chairman, Anniversary Film Committee, Linguistic Society of America); bilingualism, especially with American and Canadian immigrant languages; and sociolinguistics (her most recent book presents a critical survey of language developments for the socially disadvantaged).

THOMAS R. WILLIAMS (1928–   ) was educated at the University of Arizona (M.A., 1956) and Syracuse University (Ph.D., 1956) and is now a Professor of Anthropology at Ohio State University. He has authored papers and books with a focus on North American Indian and Borneo ethnography and topics in psychological anthropology, including cultural transmission and the cultural structuring of personality, with particular attention to the process of socialization. He is the author of *The Dusun: a North Borneo society* (1965); *Field methods in the study of culture* (1967); *A Borneo childhood: enculturation in Dusun society* (1969); and *Introduction to socialization: human culture transmitted* (1972).

VICTOR H. YNGVE (1920–   ) was educated in Physics at Antioch College (B.S., 1943) and the University of Chicago (M.S.; Ph.D., 1953). He then spent twelve years at the Massachusetts Institute of Technology, and is currently a Professor at the University of Chicago in the Departments of Linguistics and Behavioral Sciences, and the Graduate Library School. He has worked on the design of computers and programming languages, on the mechanical translation of languages, and on the syntax of English and German. His current interests embrace the relation between linguistics and psychology, the effect of memory limitations on language structure and language change, and the general question of how people communicate.

Index of Names

Index of Subjects